Thanks for the Memory

UNFORGETTABLE CHARACTERS IN AIR WARFARE 1939–45

Laddie Lucas

GRUB STREET • LONDON

This book was originally published in hardback in 1989
by Stanley Paul and Co. Ltd.

This edition was first published by Grub Street in 1998

A catalogue record of this book is available from the British Library

ISBN 1 898697 85 X

Printed and bound in Great Britain by Biddles Ltd, Guildford and King's Lynn
With thanks to Frank Smith

EDITOR'S NOTE

The portrayals in this book were originally penned in 1998. Wherever
possible they have been left as written but when necessary and applicable,
small changes and updates have been made without in any way altering
the integrity of the text.

PUBLISHER'S NOTE

After making the changes for this edition, and whilst the book was in
production, Laddie Lucas sadly died. He was a remarkable man and this
book is dedicated to him.

CONTENTS

PART THREE

1 The Commanders

2 'Far Beyond the Normal Call...'

List of Illustrations

Leonard Cheshire VC, OM; Freddie de Pelleport and Bernard Duperier with 242 squadron; Adolf Walter and Gunther Rall; Raoul Daddo-Langlois and Laddie Lucas; Gianni Caracciolo; South African quartet; Bert Rademan; A.B. Woodhall; Sid Seid; Rhodesian trinity; Don Jandrell; Ben Drew and Bill Kemp; Sadaaki Akamatsu; Sir Arthur Harris; Sir Hugh Pughe Lloyd; Sir Keith Park; Ralph Cochrane; Werner Molders and Adolf Galland; Hans-Joachim Marseille and Eduard Neumann; Sir Harry Broadhurst; Sir Basil Embry; John Dundas; Sir Hugh Dundas; the Douglas-Hamiltons; Sir Richard Atcherley; Victor Beamish; Ludwig Franzisket; Kaj Birksted and Rolf Berg; Hannes Faure; Gus Walker; Brian Kingcome; Al Deere; Tiny Nel; Duncan Smith; Derek Walker; Lou Greenburgh; Sir Douglas Bader; Helmut Lent, Heinze Wolfgang Schnaufer and Hans-Joachim Jabs; Bobby Bradshaw; Charles Pickard; Johnnie Johnson; Don Blakeslee; Guy Gibson VC; Adrian Warburton; Hughie Edwards; Leonard Trent VC; 'Sailor' Malan; David Foster; Roman Czerniawski; Bob Braham and 'Sticks' Gregory; HM King George VI.

PHOTOGRAPHIC ACKNOWLEDGEMENTS

The editor and publishers wish to thank the following for permission to reproduce photographs:
Hulton Picture Company, Imperial War Museum, D. Maree, The Polish Institute and Sikorski Museum, Popperfoto, Royal Air Force Museum and SADF Archives.

All other photographs are from private collections and are reproduced by courtesy of their owners.

ACKNOWLEDGEMENTS

I thank those of my old Service friends, comrades-at-arms, allies and former opponents who have contributed so notably to this collection, thereby bringing distinction to the record. In so doing, they have secured for later generations a picture of some of the splendid characters whose personalities enriched the terrible epoch through which we passed. Their contributions were voluntarily and selflessly offered.

I am also indebted to those who provided willing help with the translation of the foreign language texts, and their treatment . . . Jane Addison (whose typing contributed, additionally, to the work), Alexander Bell, Tony Liskutin, Colonel Giovanni Mocci, Italian Air Attaché in London, Charles Pretzlik and Henry Sakaida, in the United States.

I am grateful, too, to my wife, Jill, whose discerning literary eye is sharpened by her experience as a young girl in having lived, on and off, with her sister and brother-in-law, Thelma and Douglas Bader, at Duxford and Tangmere in the rough days of 1940 and 1941, when Douglas was leading squadrons and wings: her comments have aided the copy.

Finally, to my good friend Peter Atkins, lead navigator in the South African Air Force's famous 24 Squadron in the Western Desert, and, later, a fine journalist with South Africa's Argus Press in Johannesburg, I offer my humble salute. This collection was Peter's idea in the first place – a happy thought indeed, but one for which at times, with all the work it provoked, I would gladly have brained him . . .

BEFORE READING ON ...

Let us be clear what this book is.

It is a collection of first-hand personal studies of some of the unforgettable characters of the world's air forces during the Second World War... Unforgettable, not necessarily because they are famous (although some certainly are), but memorable because each, no matter how humble, has meant much to someone even, maybe, the difference between life and death.

The portrayals, which have been left untouched since they were first collected in the latter part of the nineteen-eighties, respect no frontiers. They were specially written by authors many (but not all) of whom were themselves numbered among the élite. In a sense, therefore, it is a dual collection – of most memorable characters on the one hand and authors of exceptional or unusual experience on the other.

Some have long since departed this life. In terms of aerial conflict it draws diverse and rare talent together under one roof. It is a united international effort. The air, for those who fought in it, was a great leveller. It provided a common denominator for friend and foe alike.

It is now well over half a century since the global fighting stopped... Partners and opponents can – and, thank God, do – sit down happily together and exchange old experiences and, with all the humour, a few downright lies.

An intense and very rough struggle is behind. Mostly – but not always – it was fought under Queensberry rules. That is why we are comfortably together again now. But while there's life the memories will remain. What better moment, then, to recall some of the players who adorned the world stage – before it is too late?

Laddie Lucas
South Kensington
London SW7
1998

FIRST OFF!

Putting Down the Marker

'Find a strong start and a good finish to a story and you can get away with murder in the middle.'

One wonders . . . Still, the advice was offered years ago by one of Fleet Street's longest-serving and most successful editors, a compulsive yet encouraging critic of a young reporter's copy.

He would have been hard put to quarrel on such grounds with the selection of the initial study of this collection – or with the judgement of the authors who made the subject their choice.

Leonard Cheshire
VC and OM
THE UNANSWERABLE DOUBLE

Air Chief Marshal Sir Christopher Foxley-Norris's own background fits him specially to portray the character which made Leonard Cheshire one of World War II's – and the 20th century's – exceptional men...

An intimate of Cheshire's for more than half a century . . . After Winchester and Trinity, Oxford, a Harmsworth Scholarship to the Middle Temple, and an intended career at the Bar frustrated by war . . . And what a war!

Lysanders in the Battle of France in 1940, followed at once by fighters in the Battle of Britain . . . Then, later, lethal anti-shipping strikes with Beaufighters around the enemy's western coasts . . . And, finally, five years after the beginning in France, Mosquitoes against naval and other maritime targets in the Skaggerak and Kattegat, and along Germany's north-western seaboard as Hitler's forces battled on to the end. Few who were in at the start of the fighting in World War II were still dishing it out at the finish . . .

It made a solid operational base for high command, and all the other peacetime appointments that have followed, not least the Chair of the Battle of Britain Fighter Pilots' Association. Allied to Sir Christopher's manifest ability to write, is a secure platform on which to rest this engaging picture of Geoffrey Leonard Cheshire, the only man ever to hold the Victoria Cross and the Order of Merit – the unanswerable double.

'The Most Memorable Character I Knew in the Air Force in World War II'

For me the above title is perhaps not strictly accurate, for I knew Leonard Cheshire in peace and war for well over fifty years. In 1936 we were undergraduates together at Oxford, whence he had arrived from Stowe. From neither of these institutions emerged any clear indication of his later extraordinary record of achievement. His Headmaster at Stowe wrote of him 'He is an excellent boy. As a scholar he is hard-working but not very gifted; but he has ambition.' This last word was to prove most significant.

At Oxford these ambitions were very much those of the young extrovert hedonist. He coveted high living but did not have the material means to secure it. Perhaps as an approach to attaining it, he sought and attracted publicity by various harmless but irresponsible escapades. At one stage, somewhat ironically in view of his eventual achievements, he avowedly modelled himself on Leslie Charteris's fictional hero 'The Saint', sleek hair, laconic speech, long cigarette holder, Alfa Romeo – the lot.

Leonard joined the University Air Squadron, but at first did no flying. It was at a party in my rooms that I introduced him to my flying instructor, Charles Whitworth. Leonard's reaction was typically casual and sardonic. 'Flying instructor, eh? I suppose you can fly?' The challenge had been laid down and both parties took it up eagerly. Leonard took to flying avidly. He proved to be a natural pilot, but at that stage lack of application prevented him from becoming an outstanding one.

He was one of the comparatively few who not only foresaw the imminence of World War II but did something about it, wishful thinking making ostriches of many of his contemporaries. In the summer of 1939 he received what was to be one of the last peace-time permanent commissions awarded by the RAF, and as war was declared we both reported to Hullavington for advanced training. But Leonard's adventurism was still alive as was shown when, still not fully trained, he applied unsuccessfully to fight in Finland when volunteers were called for. The training aircraft provided were Harts and Furies for half the course members, the sedate twin-engined Anson for the rest. Leonard drew the Anson, but if he was disappointed he showed no sign of it. Indeed, when on graduation the majority of us opted for fighters or Army Co-operation, Leonard chose bombers. When I asked him, 'What are you up to this time?' he replied, 'It's pretty obvious isn't it? There's lots of you, there's only one of me. They'll hear about me.' And they did. Within a year he had won the DSO, the first of three, and thoroughly deserved it.

During the long winter of 1940–41 Cheshire and his crew gained much operational experience; he also acquired considerable scepticism about the prescribed tactics and heights for bombing, which seemed to him to guarantee both inaccuracy and vulnerability. However, in a raid on Cologne he was sticking to the briefed height of 8000 feet when a heavy shell smashed the nose of his Whitley, set it ablaze amidships and seriously wounded his wireless operator. In freezing cold, after many hours they eased the battered bomber home. Cheshire was genuinely indignant that only he and his wireless operator received decorations; unfortunately the award of his own DSO revived some of his old hunger for publicity. It was followed in March 1941 by a DFC.

Interdependence and trust were vital lessons that all operational aircrews had to learn and Cheshire took it further and established a uniquely strong bond of friendship and loyalty with his ground crew also; without it he realised that the dangers of operational flying would be markedly increased. Furthermore he developed a genuine affection for the men who serviced his aircraft, an affection which proved mutual at all levels of age and rank. His aircrew, too, acquired a strong faith in him despite his unorthodox tactics and apparent contempt for danger.

In April 1941 he was temporarily assigned to ferry aircraft from the United States, and fell once more under the spell and glamour of luxury and high living. He married Constance Binney, an actress and sophisticated socialite twenty years his senior, and contrary to general predictions, they both derived real if short-lived happiness from the marriage. On his return to operations he soon re-established his outstanding qualities as a bomber captain and pilot, now flying the Halifax, and continued to improvise and experiment with tactics, including one nearly disastrous attempt to approach the target with all engines feathered, when only the solid support of his crew saved him from finishing in a POW camp or a premature grave.

Before long photographic evidence began to disclose with embarrassing frequency the woeful inadequacy of our bomber attacks, emphasising still more the value of the few really expert captains and crews. The new Commander-in-Chief, Sir Arthur Harris, accepted, perhaps *faute de mieux*, the policy of area bombing. At that time Cheshire took over command of 76 Squadron, which he led with skill and dash, at the same time inspiring, training and briefing his crews and seeking to conserve them against the dreadful casualty rates by introducing safety and protective measures to their aircraft. He also remained convinced that precision bombing was not only a preferable but a practicable alternative to area bombing. At the end of another arduous tour he was awarded a second bar to his DSO; by now he had learnt to accept such awards without ostentation, as he did his appointment as the youngest Group Captain in Bomber Command, but before long he not only accepted but personally arranged his own demotion so that he could assume command of the incomparable 617 Squadron, the 'Dam Busters'.

He inherited an impressively strong and experienced team on the Squadron, in spite of sadly heavy past casualties. They had been through a lot together under Guy Gibson's command and formed a close-knit team, justifiably jealous of the Squadron's reputation, and it was perhaps surprising how readily they accepted the quietly spoken Cheshire both as comrade and as leader. Initially their early operations together, such as Operation Cross Bow against the V-weapon sites, had only limited success. Justifiably, it appears, Cheshire blamed inadequate target marking by the Pathfinder force. He determined on innovation. 617 must be trained to mark its own targets; to do so the marking must be from very low level, the markers being put down right on top of the target. This inevitably added to the risk from massed light anti-aircraft barrages, but Cheshire accepted this risk, in nearly every case personally, since he saw it as part of his job to do the Squadron's marking.

At first many of the targets successfully marked were industrial installations in the occupied countries, the squadron using its own heavy Lancasters for the purpose, but Cheshire had become convinced that the ideal aircraft was the fast, manoeuvrable Mosquito. By various approaches, some straight to higher command, some more roundabout, he managed to obtain two of the aircraft he needed. The results obtained against such targets as Munich, critical railway pinpoints and submarine pens pre-empted further debate.

In one further experiment he chose to mark his target from a single-engined long-range Mustang fighter, his first flight ever in the aircraft being on the afternoon immediately preceding the raid. On nearly all of his low-level missions his aircraft was riddled with gashes and holes, but he never received any personal injury; outwardly at least he never seemed to give it a thought. He has been described as fearless. I take leave to doubt this. No one with the intellect and imagination of Leonard Cheshire could have been without apprehension of the risks he faced and without a natural fear of them; what I believe he did manage was to put those fears behind him for the duration of each operation. I did meet a very few operational pilots who were genuinely without fear, but I am convinced that Leonard Cheshire felt his full share of fear but that he concealed and conquered it.

In August 1944 he was awarded the Victoria Cross, usually given for a single outstanding act of gallantry. Cheshire's citation mentioned rather his unparalleled record of a hundred missions against the most heavily defended targets. It has been said that his was one of the few VCs whose deserts nobody questioned. His own reaction, in such sharp contrast to earlier days, was one of genuine surprise and shyness. It may be said that when he had little to be proud of, he was conceited. When he had everything, he was modest. He remains so to this day.

Cheshire, together with Professor Penney, was chosen as the British witness of the dropping of the second American atom bomb, on Nagasaki, and it has been suggested that this experience instantly changed his whole life and outlook. This is not true. Indeed his immediate reaction was not humanitarian, rather he was enormously impressed by the scientific, industrial and military potentialities of nuclear energy. He reported to Prime Minister Attlee, 'If this demonstration shows anything, it is that we ourselves must participate in the nuclear future, including the possession of the necessary weapons.'

It has been supposed by some that by some instant and miraculous conversion, like Saul on the road to Damascus, he determined to devote his life to the welfare of humanity against whom he had helped to wreak such destruction. Again, this simply is not true. It was a much longer and more difficult process. For a while after leaving the RAF he sought various outlets for his nervous energy, his intelligence and his ambition; and to complicate matters his health was fallible and unreliable, including a severe bout of TB, a disease which struck many operational pilots. Among other schemes his interest in the welfare and training of ex-servicemen led him to an ambitious project for communal living and trade, which he christened VIP, acquiring for the purpose extensive premises, including some of the innumerable disused but fully equipped wartime airfields. The scheme proved idealistic, impracticable and financially disastrous. The eventual lone survivor of this failure was a large, rambling house in Hampshire called Le Court. Having no real use for it and no money to support it, he agreed to a local hospital's request to accept from it the care of an incurable cancer patient, to free a bed for someone who could respond to treatment. His name was Arthur Dykes.

Although Arthur arrived almost by chance and although Leonard had at the time no concept of a major mission or vocation for the care of the disabled or handicapped, history may regard Dykes as the first resident of a Cheshire Home. Today there are more than 250 Leonard Cheshire Homes in 47 countries, and many thousands of residents, whose sole qualification is that they are sufficiently handicapped, sometimes mentally but usually physically, to be unable to make their own way in society unaided. The Leonard Cheshire Foundation, through the very real personal inspiration and untiring dedication of Cheshire, in his lifetime, enables them to enjoy a fuller, freer and more competent life than would otherwise be possible.

The life of St Francis of Assisi could be divided into three distinct parts. As a youth he was not admirable, leading his fellows in noisy dissipation, a constant nuisance to the representatives of the law; as a young man he became a dashing and successful wartime leader of *condottieri*; in maturity his care for humanity and all life shone through and illuminated the medieval world. It has always surprised me that it seems to have occurred to no one to draw a parallel between his life and that of Leonard Cheshire.

Christopher Foxley-Norris,
Henley-on-Thames,
Oxfordshire

Leonard Cheshire
Squadron Commander
AN AMERICAN VIEW

No. 617 Squadron possessed some rare characters in Cheshire's time with the unit. Such a one was the American Major Hubert C. (Nick) Knilans, a dairy farmer from Delevan, Wisconsin. He was one of the 6000 selfless volunteers who, long before Pearl Harbor and the United States' entry into World War II, travelled north from the security of their homeland to join the Royal Canadian Air Force, and thence to Europe, to make Britain's cause theirs. When, later, Knilans transferred to the US Army Air Force, he still elected to fly with 617 and the Royal Air Force.

His run of 53 operational missions with Bomber Command won for him the award of an immediate DSO and the DFC – and, ultimately, a changed way of life. Overtaken 'by a dream, if you like' during a night attack on Berlin in November 1943, he decided there and then, amid the flak and the searchlights, to make a resolution. 'If I survive this trip tonight, and then the rest of the war,' he thought, 'I'll try to do some public work – good deeds versus destruction . . . Berlin told me where my destiny lay . . . '

Post-war, Knilans became a teacher until his retirement. He now recalls Cheshire's leadership of the Squadron and the spirit he injected into it.

Ten Lancasters were diving and swooping at near-ground level over the airfield at Woodhall Spa on the Lincolnshire coast. 617 were changing their home base from Coningsby. The Station Commander, Group Captain Philpott, was on top of the control tower frantically waving his arms in upward motions. Lancasters were hurtling towards him at 300 mph. On the other side of the control tower, Squadron Leader 'Ding-dong' Bell and I were moving our arms downwards to encourage the pilots to fly even lower. The 40 Packard-Merlins were putting out over 40,000 horsepower as they roared over the airfield.

We thought we saw one Lanc fly through the maintenance hangar and out the other end . . . either that or it was taxiing like bloody hell! We suspected the pilot to be Squadron Leader Mick Martin, an Australian with a penchant for low flying. He used to claim that, by returning at tree-top level in the dark from bombing a German city, he could avoid enemy fighters and flak. It must have worked because he retired as Air Marshal Sir Harold Martin, KCB, DSO & bar, DFC & two bars, AFC, now of greatly respected memory.

Helping him beat up the airfield that day were the crews of Flight Lieutenant David Shannon, another Australian, Flight Lieutenant Les Munro, from New Zealand, and Flight Lieutenant Joe McCarthy, a Brook-lyn-born, Coney Island lifeguard.

Leading these highly skilled pilots and their crews was Wingco Leonard Cheshire. At 25, he had stepped down from Group Captain to take over 617. I had already heard stories about his somewhat erratic behaviour . . . How, for instance, to win half a pint of beer, he had hitchhiked from Oxford to Paris with no money in his pocket.

When the Wingco began to lead us on raids against precision targets like the V-1 or Buzz-bomb sites, he quickly became dissatisfied with the results of the Pathfinders' marking. Mick Martin showed him how to dive-bomb a target with much greater accuracy. Doing it in a four-engined bomber in total darkness didn't seem to disturb either of them.

But the Wingco didn't just send us into combat with the enemy, he led us there. His own courage was so inspirational that crew-members not scheduled for an operation would actually go along for the ride with another crew. They just wanted to be with the Squadron and their beloved commander wherever he led them . . .

Some of his wilder plans, however, made some of his followers nervous – like when his brother had been shot down and was a prisoner in Germany. Wingco Cheshire had what he thought was another of his brilliant ideas. We were still at Coningsby at the time. He wanted to paint three Lancasters white with red crosses on wings and fuselage. He, Mick Martin and David Shannon, and their crews, would then fill their aircraft with food parcels and drop them on the POW camp, Stalag Luft III, on Christmas Day. The plan was to fly up near the Polish border by night and then return in daylight across the Baltic without any escorting fighters – at least not ours.

All the flight crew members – except Cheshire – were thankful when the trip was cancelled by higher authority.

Our Mess at Woodhall Spa was the Petwood Hotel, which still thrives today in a beautiful 40-acre setting. 617 didn't damage it too much during their frequent celebrations, but Wing Commander Cheshire was indirectly responsible for some of it. For some reason, he convinced himself, as D-Day and the invasion of the Continent approached, that German para-troopers would be landing on our airfield. In preparation for the assault, he gave us a choice of weapons – a revolver, Sten gun, rifle or hand grenade. It was a sad mistake which lasted about three days.

25

Some of us, I remember, were coming across the Petwood's back lawn after closing time in the 'local' when we all had to dive for cover behind trees, hedges and shrubs as bullets began flying about us. Flight Lieutenant Jack Buckley was firing his Sten gun from his second-storey window ostensibly over our heads. He was a wild Yorkshireman and David Shannon's rear gunner. He never hit any of us, although he claimed he 'did manage to put the wind up a few of the lads'.

Dinner plates, scattered about the lawn, made good targets for the guns crackling from the hotel windows. The young WAAF girls, working in the Petwood, were becoming highly agitated by the explosions and the rather raucous behaviour of the marksmen. But it was short-lived; we had soon to return our weapons.

Another quirky idea of the Wingco's was to put us through an escape exercise. He figured this would be good training for when we were shot down over enemy territory.

He took away our hats and money and put us all on a bus with the windows papered over. Then we were dropped off in threes some 20 miles from Woodhall Spa. Meanwhile he had notified the police and the Home Guard to nab any aircrew not wearing a hat. Anyone making it back to the Petwood would earn a free bottle of beer.

It became a bit hilarious as some aircrew were chased across fields, others stole bicycles, a few got lifts from lorry drivers and one punched out a constable. My flight engineer, Ken Ryall (later Wing Commander, DFC), and my Aussie rear gunner, Roy Learmouth, plus myself started off down a road. Then a friend from 9 Squadron picked us up and dropped us off at a pub in Boston. The sister barmaids, Twink and Rose Brudenell, let us charge the price of a few beers on the house.

We borrowed the bus fares and had almost made it home when the police stopped the bus. We promptly bolted. When I trudged in through the entrance to the Petwood, everything was dark and silent. I never did get my free beer.

Funny thing about courage . . . The Wingco kept his two Siamese cats with him at the Petwood. They would crouch side-by-side on the dimly lit upper hallway. Their eyes had a greenish glow, their tails twitched back and forth and they kept up a snarling whine all the while. We had some brave souls on the Squadron, but none of them would challenge those crazy cats. We all went down the back-stairs instead!

Leonard Cheshire had completed 100 combat missions by 5 July, 1944, when Air Vice-Marshal Cochrane, the head of 5 Group, told him to quit. It was after this that his Victoria Cross was awarded (*London Gazette* 8 September 1944), not for one courageous act, but for sustained bravery over those 100 trips.

Leonard and I remained friends for more than 50 years. I visited his Cheshire Homes in England, Jordan, Nigeria and India. He used his intellect, compassion and faith to fund and operate them. Several former 617 guys helped to run or raise finance for them. The disabled for whom they cater revered the Group Captain and loved him. They looked forward eagerly to his next visit.

It was an honour to have served under Leonard in 617 and a privilege to have been his friend...

Hubert (Nick) Knilans,
New Auburn,
Wisconsin

PART ONE

The Long Climb
1939-42

The characters who lit the way in the opening years of
the air war were a rugged and spirited lot. They needed
to be for, mostly, it was a question of fighting to get
back on to the level and then working up – with the
enemy making most of the running.

With the equipment which was available, and the
chances that were there, it was rough going. In such
conditions the leaders and the personalities – the
'characters' – quickly rose to the top. Some then stayed
there and, having made their mark, went on and on,
brushing fatigue and stress aside and remaining fresh.

Others, having had their 'crowded hour', left the
stage to their heirs and successors, content in the belief
that a job had been done. Much in the air in the opening
rounds of war was unknown and had to be learnt – the
hard way. To get to the point where, by half-time,
disaster had been averted and all was left to play for
demanded much of the early players.

They met the challenge, set the standards for courage
and endeavour and left it to others to follow suit.

Bill Lucy

COURAGEOUS CLOSURE

Dick Partridge (Major R. T. Partridge, Royal Marines (ret)) is in the record books on two counts... First, as the recipient in the Norwegian campaign of 1940 of the first DSO to be awarded in World War II, a signal distinction for a Royal Marines officer flying with the Fleet Air Arm. Second, as the pilot of a Blackburn Skua who was obliged to force land on a frozen lake near Aandalsnes after shooting down a marauding Heinkel 111 bomber. After the combat, he and the Luftwaffe pilot had a good-natured meeting in the snows of Norway before the German was taken prisoner.

Thirty-five years after the Skua sank when the ice melted, the aircraft was discovered in good shape at the bottom of the lake by a Norwegian sub-aqua group. It was subsequently raised successfully and is now in the Fleet Air Arm museum at Yeovilton.

When the story was eventually reported in the Press, Shopis, the Heinkel pilot, then living at Neukirchstockach, Brunnthal, in Germany, was put in touch with Partridge, who had himself been shot down later in Norway and taken prisoner. A happy reunion and enduring friendship followed.

I was at Eastleigh at the outbreak of hostilities and during some of the so-called 'phoney war'. Also there was a great friend of mine, Lieutenant Bill Lucy, a senior lieutenant in the Royal Navy. We were getting a lot of routine flying, mostly giving trainee air gunners rear-gun practice at drogue targets over the sea at Littlehampton.

The start of the Norwegian campaign in the spring and early summer of 1940 put a sudden end to our 'phoney war' and I parted company with

31

Bill to find myself first at Wick in northernmost Scotland and, then, at Hatston in the Orkneys.

It was at Hatston that Bill and I met up again, he as CO of 801 Squadron and myself as CO of 800. Both squadrons were equipped with the new fighter/dive-bomber, the Blackburn Skua.

Bill and I were great friends and had shared many happy days in *Glorious* in the Mediterranean in those halcyon pre-war days of 1937–38. He was a most competent pilot and not prone to 'split-arse' manoeuvres so often associated with fighter pilots! He was steady and reliable and his deck landings both by day and night were a joy to watch.

Up in the Orkneys in those early war days we were doing a lot of flying, mostly defensive patrols over the sea, out of sight of land, and lasting four to four and a half hours. Occasionally one came across a lone merchant ship being attacked by a Heinkel 111. We were usually able to chase it off, but due to lack of performance we were unable to catch it. It was rewarding, however, to return low to the ship to be greeted by the crew on deck wildly waving their thanks.

Bill seemed to be more successful than the rest of us and already was able to claim two He.111s shot down and another possible. I questioned him about his success and he explained that he always patrolled either at 12,000 feet or as high as the cloud base would allow, so that, hopefully, he would have a height advantage over any enemy aircraft and catch up with it in the ensuing dive. He then added quite casually that he never opened fire until he was just about to collide with the enemy's rear turret! This sounded a very hazardous form of attack to me and when I suggested to Bill that one day the rear gunner was going to get him first, he smiled, shrugged his shoulders and said he was sure it was the best way of 'blasting the buggers out of the sky'. Any suggestion of opening fire with a short burst at about 300 yards, closing in with short bursts until the final kill, cut no ice with Bill. Nor would he concede that the enemy rear gunner's aim and peace of mind might be affected by the sight of tracer coming towards him!

Today, 9 April, 1940, there was mist and low cloud swirling over the islands and there was no question of flying defensive patrols or of enemy attacks. I always welcomed these heaven-sent lulls when one could relax with a clear conscience, but not so Bill. He would be pacing the Operations Room, watching the reports coming in with one eye on the weather forecasts, praying for a clearance so that he could get 'at them' again.

Meanwhile, I was having a quiet and peaceful lunch when Bill burst in excitedly, saying, 'There's a German cruiser alongside in Bergen harbour and the Met men say the weather will be clearing shortly.'

I had a horrible feeling that Bill had in mind something I wouldn't approve of or like very much – and I wasn't far wrong. 'Let's take both Squadrons over and dive-bomb the cruiser at dawn tomorrow morning,' said Bill airily.

My quiet, peaceful lunch in ruins, I pointed out to Bill that in still air, Bergen was two hours' flying away and two hours back and that the Skua's endurance was only four hours and 20 minutes; a head wind, a forced diversion or a tangle with enemy fighters and we would never get back. Bill would have none of this and merely said that even if some of us had to ditch on the way back it would be worth it if the raid was successful.

Bill's daring and complete dedication to the prosecution of the war was infectious and there was no doubt that such a raid would have the invaluable advantage of surprise. I firmly closed my mind to what, and how many, casualties we might have and found myself agreeing that both squadrons would take off at 0500 hours the following morning, 10 April, in order to attack at dawn at Bergen.

The attack on the German cruiser *Königsberg* has been written about and recorded elsewhere. Suffice to say here that it was successful and that she was sunk with the loss of only one Skua. So Bill was right and I, with my craven misgivings, was wrong!

This triumph was not enough for Bill, and he organised long and hazardous reconnaissance flights over to Norway searching for further worthwhile targets. He revelled in those trips and I hated them; the longest I did lasted 4 hours 35 minutes – so much for the official endurance of 4 hours 20, but it was stretching things and I had only just enough fuel left to taxi in after landing. Menwhile, Bill's luck (or skill?) was holding and he had managed to pounce on another Heinkel 111.

A day or two later, on 25 May, Bill and I were parted. I was ordered to fly my Squadron on to the aircraft carrier *Ark Royal* for a trip to northern Norway to cover our withdrawal, which was then taking place.

Before taking off, I looked round for Bill to say good-bye and found him as usual in the 'Ops Room' champing to find some worthwhile target, the more hazardous and unexpected the better! That was the last time I saw him, as a few days later I was shot down in Norway and made a prisoner of war.

It was in the POW Camp, Dulag Luft, in Germany, a few weeks later, that a new incoming Fleet Air Arm prisoner gave me the news that Bill had been killed. He had been seen doing one of his attacks on an enemy aircraft and just as he was about to collide with the enemy's rear turret he had broken away in a steep dive with smoke pouring from his Skua – the rear gunner had got him first.

It was pretty miserable anyway as a new POW, and this sad news completed my gloom, especially as I learnt that Bill had been shot down before he knew that he had been awarded a very well-deserved DSO. I had lost a great and fearless friend. Had he survived I am certain he would have become one of the Fleet Air Arm's great wartime leaders.

'Whom the gods love die young', was said of yore . . .

Dick Partridge,
Fletching,
Uckfield,
East Sussex

Tom Cooper
PUTTING BACK THE FIBRE

It is perhaps significant that one who has sat in judgement over his fellow beings for a quarter of a century should pick for his subject a character whose example and leadership lifted the morale of a Coastal Command squadron when it was badly needed.

Sir George Waller, as a wartime flying officer in the Royal Air Force, completed an exacting tour flying anti-U-boat patrols far out into the Atlantic in the first years of war. It was unpleasant work. He saw there at first hand the insidious effect which even the slightest vestige of Lack of Moral Fibre (for such it was called in the Service) could have upon a squadron – and the need for its instant dispatch.

There was precious little LMF in the Royal Air Force in wartime, for every member of aircrew was a volunteer. None was drafted.

I was posted to 502 Squadron in September 1940 at a time when it was being re-equipped from Ansons, doing short anti-U-boat flights, to Whitleys equipped with the then latest anti-U-boat radar and extra petrol tanks in the bomb bays giving an endurance of 8–10 hours and flying both by day and by night. While the danger of suffering from enemy action was not great, the distances flown over the Atlantic were substantial, and since we flew at 1000 feet and since the Whitley could not maintain height if one engine failed, the task was much more arduous than had been the case with Ansons. Some of those whose flying had been virtually confined to the Irish Sea in daylight did not take to the Atlantic in the dark.

About a month after the re-equipment, Wing Commander Cooper was posted to the squadron as commanding officer. One of his tasks was to deal with the morale of the squadron and he made it his business to fly frequently. Shortly after his arrival three crews, including mine, were sent off on detachment to Wick for two months. On our return, the squadron had been moved from Aldergrove to Limavady, and we found a lack of enthusiasm among our fellow pilots. The work was important because, even if we did not spot a U-boat, and there was one in the neighbourhood, it would have to dive to escape detection. As a result its speed would be reduced to two or three knots and it would fail to get to the convoy to attack it, but the pilot of the Whitley would not know this. The three crews which had been on detachment had remained enthusiastic and we were struck by the lack of enthusiasm, the emphasis on difficulties and the private grumbles about the CO which appeared to prevail in the squadron.

One day a young officer, a stockbroker in peacetime, took off with his crew at 2 a.m. for a patrol taking 8 hours, so he should not have returned until about 10 a.m. Instead he returned almost immediately and landed at 3 a.m. Wing Commander Cooper, the CO, who lived nearby, heard the aircraft returning and got up and went down to the aerodrome to see the pilot and find out why he had returned. This young officer said that one engine was not running properly, whereupon the Wing Commander rebuked him, saying there was nothing wrong and that it was his imagination. The officer was very upset and angry, but of course could say no more.

At 10 o'clock that morning, however, the officer was summoned to the CO's office. There Wing Commander Cooper said that inspection showed there was something wrong with one engine and that he, the pilot, was quite right to return. The CO asked the officer to accept his apology for what he had said at 3 o'clock that morning and explained that he had jumped to the conclusion that there was nothing wrong because there were too many early returns on account of alleged engine trouble when inspection showed that there was nothing wrong at all.

The officer returned to the Mess, told the story and finished by saying 'If the Wing Commander can apologise to me, a pilot officer, that's good enough for me.' That incident was a turning point for the morale of the squadron, which over the next few weeks improved dramatically; so much so that three or four months later, when there was a rumour from Group headquarters that the CO was about to be posted elsewhere, there was almost a mutiny in the squadron.

I did not appreciate the real seriousness of the problem until two years after I left the squadron and was in a staff job at Coastal Command headquarters. We were asked for a Whitley pilot to go to another Command to help in converting pilots to Whitleys. The man who was sent had been in 502 squadron. Two or three days later, the telephone rang and Group Captain Cooper, now a station commander, was on the line. 'What do you mean by sending X to me?' 'He was a Whitley pilot', I replied. 'But you know,' he countered, 'that he it was who took off for a flight (i.e. an 8-hour flight towards mid-Atlantic) and never left the coast. He flew round and round Tory Island for seven hours and then returned to base.' Tory Island is only a few miles from the north-west coast of Ireland and this was a striking example of the sort of problem the CO had had to face.

Cooper was a regular officer and apart from being a general duties officer he was an engineering specialist. When war came he was determined to fly and not be an engineering officer; hence his appointment. He did not have a crew of his own in the squadron, but he so arranged things that he regularly flew on operations. The effect was that while some of his administrative duties may not have been performed as well as they might have been, the morale of the squadron became as high as it is possible to imagine. The risk of enemy action against the aircraft was remote, and the operational conditions, with members of the crew taking turns to keep watch on the radar, did not provide the excitement that rather more dangerous activities did. However, being 300–400 miles west of Ireland in the dark and/or stormy weather, looking for U-boats, did cause some to falter.

Tom Cooper, by his behaviour and example, strengthened the determination of the whole squadron. When he was posted at the end of the year, he left behind the loyal support of all who had flown in the squadron. He afterwards commanded a station where glider-towing operations were being carried out and, sadly, later in the war he was killed.

George Waller,
Kingsley Green,
Haslemere,
Surrey

Bill Luard
NAVAL INDEPENDENT

The relationship between a squadron, wing or station intelligence officer and the aircrews in the operational commands was founded upon trust and was often close. 'Spy', the sobriquet by which the 'IO' was frequently known, could be confidant and friend.

Lord Shackleton (Wing Commander E. A. A. Shackleton) had seen 'Intelligence' in most of its forms by the war's end, starting at the sharp end in the field, where he made a special mark with the crews, and finishing at the Air Ministry.

It was a prelude to Cabinet rank in post-war Labour governments and to senior appointments in commerce and industry, including the deputy chairmanship of the massive RTZ Corporation.

Commander Luard, OBE, RN, whom it was my good fortune to know as a colleague and close friend when I was stationed at RAF St Eval in 1941–43 was a special friend to the Royal Air Force and to Coastal Command. Through circumstances which I will briefly relate we had in Bill Luard the benefit of an absolutely first-class Naval officer as an unofficial liaison officer and adviser during a quite crucial part of the Battle of the Bay of Biscay.

Bill Luard had entered the Navy through Osborne and Dartmouth before World War I. He served in destroyers, torpedo boats and battleships. In 1916, having volunteered for submarines, he injured his hip following a jump down a conning tower in a 'C' boat and a year later was invalided out with TB in the left hip. This was followed by years of operations, 23 in all. Between the wars, he worked in various fishing boats, ranging from Hull trawlers to Cornish fishing craft and Breton tunnymen. It was this experience that was of such value during World War II.

On the outbreak of war, despite having a 100 per cent disability pension, he joined up, but was blown up in a minesweeper in 1940 by one of the first German acoustic mines, which caused him further severe injuries. However, he volunteered and was accepted to work with NID(c) – Naval

Secret Intelligence – where he was paid a flat £100 a year, but was later fully reinstated in the Navy.

Secret Naval Intelligence activities were then being developed from the Helford River in Cornwall, his old territory, and it was from there that he organised cross-channel operations using French fishing vessels, one of which I remember seeing anchored in the river. He played a crucial part in these operations, but by good fortune for the RAF he was stationed at St Eval, and it was there that he provided quite invaluable advice and experience to the aircrews who were hunting U-boats in the Bay of Biscay. He helped devise the reconnaissance patrols, escorts and searches.

Bill Luard did a great deal of flying himself and while this was supplementary to his official duties, it brought about a closer friendship and understanding between the two Services. It would be wrong to say the relations between the Navy and the RAF were bad, but they could be touchy. Not so with submariners, of whom, of course, Bill Luard was an historic member. His cheerful presence, limping around St Eval, made him a familiar and friendly Naval figure to many aircrews.

Meanwhile his relations with the Admiralty were not entirely easy, for he was much too much of an individualist to be told his job from Whitehall. On one occasion, when he was particularly incensed by a stupid instruction, he merely replied by signalling his resignation. With a 100 per cent disability pension there was nothing the Admiralty could do except give in – an apocryphal tale perhaps, but none the less it signified Bill's independent mind.

While continuing his secret intelligence activities he also helped in the area of Air Sea Rescue, producing with a friend the K-dinghy sailing gear, of which a great number were made. He simplified tidal stream data, which was of considerable value in working out search areas and establishing, after long experiments often undertaken in difficult circumstances, the drift rates of aircraft dinghies, his graphs being adopted officially by the Royal Air Force and the Fleet Air Arm.

He was also responsible for developing a submersible U-boat target on which I myself once did a practice bombing run many years after the war. He worked on this incessantly for the RAF and FAA improving details, supervising and finally giving the two Services a dual-purpose target with interchangeable full-scale schnorkel head. Quickly fitted, this enabled approach and depth-charge training to be carried out under realistic conditions.

The submersible targets were the most important of his inventions, which extended to a hinged and sectioned plywood aircraft boat for Whitleys (not put into production), outrigger canoes – successfully used in clandestine operations and designed to stow in submarines – and also a special chart plotter for use in the canoes. Small inventions included a new parallel rule, a navigrid and a tacking and windward indicator.

Perhaps his most notable achievement was his attempt to save the Breton Tunny Fleet, which is described vividly and effectively in *Secret Navies* by A. Cecil Hampshire, published by William Kimber. Much of the work involved leaflet-dropping by Coastal Command aircraft on French fishing boats – leaflets drafted by Bill Luard himself urging the fishermen to come to England. He also planned a combined operation with the Royal Navy, and I can still remember Bill being in the St Eval operations room continuously for three days while British destroyers sought to intercept French fishing boats. He was very annoyed, to put it mildly, when one of the destroyers got a tow line round its propellers!

After the war, he continued in the intelligence field, although he was re-invalided in 1948 when he returned to his beloved Cornwall. For his services he received the OBE and the *Croix de Guerre* and palm. A great and delightful character of real personal courage, and a devoted friend of the Royal Air Force.

Lord Shackleton,
London SW1

Freddie de Pelleport
THE PRICE OF FIVE MINUTES

Bernard Duperier fought through the Battle of France and, when it was over, made his way to England to operate with the Royal Air Force and continue the fight against Hitler's Third Reich. Once here, he fitted easily and quickly into 242, the Hurricane Squadron which, in 1941, was stationed at Manston in eastern Kent, no more than 10 minutes' flying time from the French coast.

The ability and experience he brought with him in those testing months were synonymous with advance and promotion. Squadron and then, later, wing leadership followed. Over 30 by the time he began to fly with the Royal Air Force, 'Skip' Duperier's maturity provided a leavening for the effervescent spirit which characterised those of his countrymen who formed the Free French squadrons, 340 and 341, as they battled for the day when their beloved France might again be free.

Judgement and discretion, when mixed with impulse and offence, were restraining qualities in the accomplished leader.

By the middle of 1941, the Royal Air Force had recouped the dreadful losses it had suffered in the Battle of Britain. Once again a squadron in Fighter Command could look to a complement of some 18 to 20 aircraft and upwards of some 20 operational pilots, but to husband the resources, the daily strength of the unit was maintained at 12 serviceable aircraft and a similar number of readily available pilots.

A front-line, day fighter squadron in those rough days was kept at varying states of readiness, dependent upon the degree of emergency which prevailed. The operations controller, who laid down the daily requirements, would normally have a section of two or four aircraft at 3 minutes (advance readiness) with the rest at 15, 30 or 60 minutes' call. This was known as the squadron's 'state'.

The pilots at advance readiness would have their kit in their aircraft and be standing by ready to take off instantly the order was received from

Ops. Information would then be passed to the section leader by RT* in the air.

Those in the squadron not required for readiness could ask for a day or half a day off. The request was seldom denied. The work-rate in the summer of 1941 was very high and a squadron commander would necessarily want to rotate his pilots on the daily 'state' to provide for rest and relaxation.

It was against this background that No. 242 Squadron, with its Hurricanes, was stationed at the forward airfield of Manston in East Kent, close by the North Foreland. From here the coast of France could easily be seen across the Straits on a clear day.

Also stationed temporarily at Manston, and detached from its East Anglian base, was a small strike force of Blenheims from 2 Group in Bomber Command. Its hazardous role was to attack in daylight enemy shipping passing through the Straits under cover of the French coast protected by very strong flak and, most of the time, by German Messerschmitt 109s. The attacks were pressed home at nought feet in the face of a lethal defence. The Blenheims' losses in those days were among the heaviest of the war, a flight of half a dozen aircraft often being turned round in as many days.

242's job was to draw off the convoys' gunfire by attacking the heavily armed flak ships which invariably accompanied them, and, at the same time, to cover the bombers against fighter attacks. It was a rugged role for which single-engine fighter aircraft were not primarily designed.

If the attacking force's losses were heavy so, too, were the enemy's losses in ships. Before long, the convoys moved by night, only to find themselves on the receiving end of the Navy's MTBs,† operating from Dover.

On 10 August, 1941, only four Hurricanes of 242 Squadron were on 3 minutes' stand-by at Manston, the remaining eight pilots, with François de Labouchère and myself among them, being held at 30 minutes' call. With our British comrades, we were lazing in the garden of our nearby Mess.

Then suddenly the Operations telephone rang. It was the controller calling us to instant readiness. An important convoy had been sighted making for Boulogne. Eight aircraft of 242 were at once to escort three Blenheims detailed to make the strike.

In little more than five minutes, the duty driver had rushed us in the pilots' van round to the Squadron's dispersal. The pilots of the four Hurricanes on advance readiness were airborne and about to set course. To our astonishment, the next four aircraft that we were supposed to fly were also rolling down the runway about to take off.

* Radio telephone.
† Motor Torpedo Boats.

A glance at the Squadron's 'state' and then the flight authorisation book confirmed that four pilots who happened to be down at dispersal, some of whom weren't even on that day's readiness, had jumped into our aircraft and were now getting airborne. One of them who certainly wasn't on that days's 'state' was Frederic de Pelleport, one of the Frenchmen in 242, a spirited and attractive officer, and a fine pilot, who was particularly well liked by his English comrades.

I might have guessed! Only a couple of days before I had found Freddie on his day off, down at the Squadron's dispersal. I had actually told him that morning that he could borrow my own car and take his girlfriend, Pamela, out for the day.

'What the hell are you doing here?' I asked. 'You aren't on readiness and I told you this morning that you could take my car for the day. What's happened? Have you and Pamela had a row or have you now pranged my car? Tell me.'

Pelleport's explanation didn't ring true. He had been with the Squadron for only a few weeks, but now I discovered that on virtually every one of his days off he had been hanging around the dispersal near the readiness aircraft, hoping that sometime there might be a scramble* and one of the pilots standing by might not be immediately available. It had happened. Freddie thought he could then jump into the missing pilot's aircraft and take off.

Now his scheming had paid off. With all his persuasive charm, he had encouraged three more of his comrades to join him, take off at once before the rest of the pilots arrived and follow the first section of Hurricanes. It would, he thought, save maybe five minutes.

Furious though we were, there was nothing that Labouchère and I could do about it except to await anxiously the gatecrashers' return. Then I would give them a piece of my mind!

There wasn't long to wait – and then what a sight it was! Only one of the three attacking Blenheims had returned and the survivor was heavily damaged and the crew badly wounded. Of the eight escorting Hurricanes which had taken off only seven were accounted for. Pelleport was missing.

After a series of hurried and untidy landings – always the sign of a squadron at odds after being heavily engaged – the story emerged. Our aircraft had been bounced by the convoy's fighter escort and one of the 109s, attacking unseen from behind cloud, had hit Freddie's aircraft, which was last seen spinning into the sea from some 400 or 500 feet. Freddie, it seemed, may well have been dead before he hit the water. . .

Freddie de Pelleport had done his service training with the French Air Force in 1939–40, but, despite all his protestations, he wasn't in time to take part in the Battle of France. After the Armistice he had crossed to

* Instant take-off for interception or other operation.

England to join General de Gaulle and serve with the Royal Air Force. He longed to engage the enemy, but he had had to wait many months before joining 242 and seeing the combat which, with every other Frenchman, he believed would contribute to the liberation of his beloved France.

But now, simply to try to save five minutes in a war that would last five years, his yearning had been cruelly satisfied. We could hardly believe it. We had had our losses – plenty of them – but somehow this one hit the hardest. Here was this exceptional young officer, with his privileged background and upbringing, his good looks and ready smile beneath a head of brown hair, his captivating ways and infectious spirit, suddenly taken from us after so short a time with the squadron. . .

That evening after dinner, we went, as we always did, to the little pub which was only a few hundred yards from our Mess. The beer flowed, we talked and we laughed, we spoke of everything – except our losses and the boys who were no longer with us. But the toughened and experienced young men who remained had not forgotten their departed comrades. They knew the extent of the sacrifice that had been made. . . And that it would be someone else's turn tomorrow.

Bernard Duperier,
Paris,
France

'Freddie'

SILLY BOY!

The day in 1941 when Dickie Murdoch (Squadron Leader Richard Murdoch), alias 'Stinker', went to work with the Intelligence Branch at Bomber Command headquarters, and later moved out to the stations, was certainly a turn-up for the Royal Air Force. Here was an actor of engaging talent, a star of musical comedy and revue who had already stamped his own personality upon West End productions in the Thirties.

Dickie, a product of Charterhouse and Pembroke, Cambridge, was the Almighty's gift to any Mess. And when, in the latter part of the war, he fetched up at the Air Ministry to work with Kenneth Horne, then a wing commander, in the Directorate of Administrative Plans, the radio show, Much-Binding-In-The-Marsh, was born.

Whitehall had never witnessed such a pair.

My own contribution to the RAF war effort was in a chairborne capacity. I was what was laughingly known as an Intelligence Officer and I certainly came across some memorable characters. For a time I was attached to a 2 Group Squadron in Norfolk and there appeared one character I shall never forget. Ralph Reader, famous for his Scouts' Gang Show in peacetime, was persuaded into uniform and rehearsed small companies who toured RAF stations giving performances.

In one of these troupes was a certain AC2 who was tremendously, what would now be known as gay. Let's call him Freddie. He specialised in female impersonation and his star turn was a semi-strip act. The dénouement consisted of suspending a tassel on each bosom and swinging these first clockwise and then anticlockwise and finally, simultaneously, in opposite directions. This was invariably a show-stopper. At one station the Gang were put in charge of a very pompous and officious Flight Lieutenant Adjutant who was obviously contemptuous of the whole outfit. He told them they were a disgrace to their uniforms – mincing about the stage, painting their faces – and should be actively helping the war effort, etc.,

45

etc. At the end of this tirade Freddie fixed the Adjutant with a withering glance and in sibilant tones just said 'Silly Boy'.

Another great character with whom I had pleasant dealings was one Wing-Commander Kenneth Horne. He had been with Balloon Command in the West Country and was second-in-command to a certain Wing-Commander Christian Stock. One day when Stock was on leave Kenneth had a telephone inquiry for him and answered, 'Sorry, Christian's away. Salute the Happy Horne.' At the end of the war I was at the Air Ministry, Whitehall, sharing an office with Kenneth and another unforgettable character, Squadron Leader Paul Bazeley. Kenneth was normally completely unflappable, but on one occasion a serious crisis cropped up, and even Kenneth was at his wit's end wondering how we could avoid a catastrophe. It was Paul Bazeley who saved the situation. 'I know,' he said. We hoped for salvation. 'What about – a quick game of shovers.' And out of the map cupboard came the shove-halfpenny board and we all felt much better.

Some Air Force stories went circulating round the theatres of war with progressive embellishment and 'certified' authorship. Seldom was it that we could nail down the true authorship and the actual place of derivation. Murdoch can help us with this one.

Near Swanton Morley – where I was stationed – was a fighter station called Horsham St Faith. This was under the command of the ever-popular Group Captain The Earl of Bandon, affectionately known as 'Paddy'. He was one of the really great RAF characters.

One day after playing squash and still in his shirt and shorts, he was lying on a sofa in the anteroom, reading a magazine, when in came an important-looking army officer with red tabs. We will assume his surname was Fortescue. Paddy took no notice and continued with his magazine. The man in khaki said, 'It's customary to stand up when a senior officer enters the room.' Paddy still continued reading – whereupon the soldier said, 'I'd have you know that I am Lieut.-Colonel Sir Charles Fortescue Bart.' Still without looking up Paddy said, 'And I am Group Captain Bandon, The Earl of, and that's got you beaten on both counts.'

Richard Murdoch,
Dorking,
Surrey

46

Zbigniev Wysierkierski
POLISH WHISKY

A man, looking back upon a successful career, can usually point to a period and say, 'That was the high spot, my best time, the spell when such qualities as I possess achieved, relatively, their greatest impact.'

The peak may come early, in the middle years or late. But once reached, it will seldom be attained again.

First-hand observers could well claim that for Sir Neil Wheeler, 'Nebby' to the Royal Air Force, the highest dividends were earned in the spring and summer of 1943. Then, in a space of a few rugged months, he turned a demoralised and ill-assorted Beaufighter strike wing, based at North Coates, in Lincolnshire, into a well-drilled, effective and immensely aggressive force whose results against enemy shipping across the southern North Sea confirmed the strength of his leadership.

The groundwork may well have been laid, years before, at Cranwell, and high office was to come much later; but the time with Coastal Command's Beaufighters in those middle war years must have been close to the summit of personal endeavour.

Just after the outbreak of the 1939–45 war I became a flight-commander in an Operational Training Unit equipped with Fairey Battles. In the early summer of 1940 we began to receive as trainees those Poles who managed to escape after the invasion of their country by Germany and the Soviet Union. Training them on British aircraft was not an easy job: we had no real evidence of their flying experience, and, if they were experienced pilots, they had become accustomed to a throttle which operated in the opposite direction to ours! With a strong instinct for self-preservation I chose to instruct in Polish and, as a consequence, I got to know my Poles quite well. Inevitably, in subsequent units, I seemed to attract the Polish aircrew.

In that same summer in 1940 I was posted to the Photographic Reconnaissance Unit, whose headquarters were at Heston, just west of

London. The Unit operated mainly from Heston, where we kept two flights, but we also had flights at St Eval, in Cornwall, and Wick, in the north-east of Scotland. In those days the main operational aircraft was the Spitfire, but it was occasionally supplemented, at low level, when there was cloud cover, by the Hudson and later the Blenheim.

The flights rotated between the three bases and, after a spell in a flight at St Eval, I took command of one of the flights at Heston in November 1940. There I found a most remarkable and memorable man, Flight Lieutenant Zbigniev Wysierkierski from Poland. Naturally he was always called 'Whisky' and it will make it easier if I refer to him henceforth by that name.

Whisky was of medium height but heavily built. His age was difficult to determine, but I knew he was some years older than me, and must have been around the 30 mark. He was clearly a very experienced pilot and a very good one who, as a pilot with the national Polish airline LOT, absolutely revelled in flying Spitfires – albeit on photographic reconnaissance. He was a superb navigator and, despite our limitations of no radio, no navigation aids and very unreliable forecast of high-level winds, an impeccable performer on PR sorties.

As a man he was cheerful, utterly fearless and justifiably confident of his own abilities as an aviator. He regarded natural problems, such as bad weather or engine failure, as negligible and was confident that, unless the enemy managed to intercept him, all would be well. To the astonishment of his RAF friends he used to wear the entire Irving suit – jacket and trousers – and, once inside it, he looked enormous and must have found the small Spitfire cockpit rather full of Whisky! Nonetheless, he said he would be warm and comfortable (we flew at anything up to 35,000 ft without cockpit heating) and that he would be able to perform all the better for it. He never wore a 'Mae West',* not even operating from Wick to Norway. He maintained that it would restrict his head movement and he would fail to see the aircraft that would shoot him down! I doubt, anyhow, that he would have found one big enough to fit over his Irving suit.

He always called me *Führer*, a title that I did not exactly relish during the war, and I was, in any case, the same rank if a little senior, but certainly much younger. He never questioned my orders and would do absolutely anything I wanted him to do. As a consequence I had to be careful to not ask too much of this great asset in my flight.

There were two important points about photographic reconnaissance. Firstly, whatever the risks, at least one knew that higher authority always wanted us to return – with the photographs they required. Secondly, one was able to get positive photographic evidence of a pilot's ability at the job. Most people concentrate on the risks of flying single-engined unarmed

* Life jacket.

aircraft deep into enemy territory; risks there certainly were, but the task itself was not easy. There was, for a start, the extreme cold (often in the region of −50°C) before cockpit heating was introduced in 1942. But navigation with maps often with a scale of 1:1,000,000 could be extremely difficult and, as I have said earlier, it was also very difficult for meteorologists to forecast high-altitude winds. Finally, the view from a Spitfire at high altitude was generally good, but was particularly poor in the area immediately under the aircraft. To pass directly over the target area required experience and fine judgement; as a consequence, it was not unusual for the camera not to have covered the target area. Despite all these problems, if the cloud cover of the target permitted, Whisky produced magnificent results. He was a most determined and highly professional operator, and certainly one of the best pilots we had.

The vast majority of the Poles that I came across were dedicated fighters, very strongly anti-German and determined to do everything to help the Allies, and in particular Britain and the RAF. I recall one unfortunate misunderstanding in late 1940. Because of the bombs on London and Heston, the pilots in PRU were billeted in an old house near the Thames, at Cookham. Most nights found us in the Bell & Dragon, a local pub with a very pleasant landlord. One night we were celebrating Whisky receiving a 'gong' – it could have been the DFC or the Polish Virtute Militari, both of which he was awarded – and we told the landlord the reason for the party. He immediately removed a large bunch of flowers from a vase and handed them to Whisky. He did not, and could not, understand that to Whisky his action was a deadly insult. It took us some time and energy to restrain Whisky. I was glad I was there because we were great friends and, as I have already said, Whisky had great respect for his flight commander.

It so happened that we did have another Pole in the flight to whom such a spontaneous gift would not have come as quite a surprise. He was not a success at PRU and fell so far short of Whisky's standards that he was an embarrassment, especially to Whisky, who inevitably felt ashamed of him.

In early January, 1941, my flight took its turn operating from Wick. It was a formidable task operating single-engined aircraft, with no cockpit heating, no seat-type dinghies and no radios, in the worst weather months of the year over the northern North Sea. It certainly sorted out the sheep from the goats and I had to ask for Whisky's countryman to be found some other job. He was posted to Jurby in the Isle of Man and I got permission to fly him there from Wick, but the weather was atrocious for days. Eventually, Whisky came to me and said that X must go and he, Whisky, would fly him to Jurby in a Blenheim whatever the weather.

Whisky hardly ever flew the Blenheims – we had two – but he was not to be put off, and set off in a snow storm. I had a good Blenheim navigator and asked him to put on his best performance for Whisky. On their return my navigator said that Whisky did virtually all the navigation, they were flying on instruments almost all the way and the only positive request he got was to look out of the nose to advise Whisky when he saw the sea on the descent! In fact, they broke cloud at a few hundred feet and very soon after arrived at the Isle of Man. Whisky was a superb navigator as well as being a first-class pilot.

Whisky left us soon after our return to the main base, which had changed to Benson from Heston at Christmas 1940. He went to the Atlantic Ferry Service, delivering aircraft from the United States. At the end of the war, he joined BOAC, and about that time I met him quite by chance in the foyer of the Mayfair Hotel. He told me that he had decided to stay in England and was endeavouring to get his wife out of Poland, but, alas, I have never seen or heard of him since. He remains somebody I can never forget – a most memorable character and a great aviator.

Neil Wheeler,
Cooksbridge,
Lewes,
Sussex

Adolf Walter
UNFORGETTABLE NCO

Generalleutnant Günther Rall started his operational service with the German Air Force in 1938 as a *leutnant*, aged 20. He was still 'in play' at the close of World War II in 1945, a major entitled to wear the Knights Cross with Oak Leaves and Swords. There have been few records like it in the history of air warfare.

Apart from spells in hospital, including one with a broken back when he was told he would never fly again, he served continuously with a combat unit (four years with JG 52, for a start). During this extraordinary run, he fought in the Battles of France and Britain in 1940, in the attack on Crete in 1941 and thereafter in the intense cold and heat of the Russian front until April 1944, when, in command, first, of JG 11 and then, in 1945, JG 300, with its lethal, long-nosed Fw.190s, he was back in business on the Western Front, battling it out daily with the B-17s, the P-47s and the P-51s of the United States' Eighth Air Force in the great daylight offensive against the Third Reich.

During this stretch, he destroyed 275 Allied aircraft (he had the advantage of plenty of game to shoot at and many seasons in which to do it), 269 of them against Russia and six of them over Western Europe and Germany. It was quite a bag.

Post-war, as a Lieutenant-General, Günther Rall rose to be Chief of the Air Staff of the new German Air Force and, eventually, his country's Military Representative at NATO headquarters in Brussels. You can't do much better than that.

It is perhaps typical that he should now pick a stalwart flight sergeant of the wartime Luftwaffe to be the subject of a notable contribution to this work.

He was not an ace nor was he a hero. Despite all his victories during the fierce fighting, such terms would have been anathema to him. But he was a man, reliable, responsible and loyal. He looked the part and he played his part. He could easily have been missed in a crowd, but never as an individual.

He was slim, not particularly tall, and his face was quite drawn; his eyes were kind and sometimes they smiled. He was quietly spoken and now and then his voice became rather hoarse. Every move that he made had a purpose which had been carefully calculated. Behind the extrovert man there lay an undemonstrative yet certain determination.

His fellow NCOs who, at the time, numbered about a third of the squadron, all willingly accepted his authority, although he was himself a reservist and his intended future lay not with the Service, but as an engineer with BMW...

Such is the picture I retain of *Oberfeldwebel* Adolf Walter...

Jagdgeschwader 52 was operating over French territory late in the afternoon of 18 May, 1940, eight days after the initial German breakthrough in the west. We were at some 20,000 feet near Metz escorting a Heinkel 111 which was on reconnaissance. Soon we spotted 12 specks above and behind our charge, apparently manoeuvring for an attack. In a flash they were all among us, the red, white and blue markings confirming their identity – 12 French-flown, P-36 Curtiss fighters, mixing it now with our ten Messerschmitt 109s. Here, at last, was the real thing – our first contact with the enemy!

The usual wild, hectic and exciting scramble ensued ... The split-second chances to score interspersed with the ever-tightening defensive turns, the blacking or the 'greying' out, the 'juddering' of the aircraft near the point of stall ... And then the luck which often went with this kind of instant combat, and there were three Curtiss fighters in front of us, blowing up and plummeting earthwards in flames.

After what seemed like an age of milling about, there followed the inevitable lack of orientation, with no one seeming to know where he was, where the sun was or where north, south, east and west were. Then it was all over and everything was quiet. The ending came just as suddenly as the fight had begun. Air combat was so often like this ...

Back at base, one aircraft was found to be missing. *Oberfeldwebel* Walter had not returned. The news tempered the excitement which we all felt at our success. Then, late in the evening, came a telephone call from afar. It was Adolf Walter. He had been forced to land, wheels up, between the lines. His aircraft had caught fire just as he had jumped out of the cockpit. As he did so, he had heard shouts of 'Take care, lie down and stay where you are.' But this did not deter him from crawling back behind our lines. Pale and shaken, he had then learnt that he had landed in a minefield! But his guardian angel had stayed with him. The squadron's relief was intense ...

Just over a year later, with Germany now at war with Russia, the squadron was stationed at Mamaia, in Romania, north of Constanza by the Black Sea. On 24 June, 1941, a patrolling section of our Me.109s reported seeing a strong force of Russian DB-3 bombers approaching Constanza, apparently heading for the oil refineries.

The alarm was at once given and the message passed to the squadron. We took off on a fast battle climb with Walter leading his section up to some 20,000 feet and working into a good position to attack. As he closed the gap with the attackers and opened fire, one bomber was seen to explode in front of him. But, with the Russian gunners resolutely defending their rear, Adolf was caught by return fire and forced to bale out.

As he floated down, he found that the ground (in fact, it was the sea) was covered with a thick mist and that the horizon was largely obscured. It was difficult for him to judge his height. However, when he thought he was about to land, he pressed the quick-release gear on his harness and let the parachute go. As it turned out, he was still 100 feet or so above the water. But, once again, his guardian angel was riding with him and soon a life-boat came to his rescue.

Walter had displaced his thorax in the fall and, after a spell in hospital, he became an operations officer for a while, there being no question of his immediate return to flying. But, as time went on, he became more and more impatient and restless to return to the squadron, and soon he was back, leading his section again on the various missions.

After Mamaia the unit was transferred to Russia and, one day, over the southern part of the front, the *Oberfeldwebel* led his section into battle against a huge Soviet formation which far outnumbered his own small force. He was seen to have shot down several aircraft, but he made light of it, brushing it aside and saying little of it. In the evenings, in any case, it was his custom to study his engineering books, for his mind, even then, was projected forward to the time when the war would be over and he could qualify and follow his chosen career.

In the meantime, he gave the squadron everything he had got, leading his section and never resting. But the strain of that long, hot Russian summer of 1941 began to tell; his face became drawn and thin and almost cadaverous, but his spirit and humour remained as buoyant as ever, serving as an example for the rest. It did the squadron good to see him always in the thick of the fighting behind the Russian lines.

Then one day in high summer, during some unusually heavy fighting over Russian territory, Walter's luck ran out. For once his guardian angel was not at his side and he did not return. No one saw or knew what happened to him. It was a sad and lonely end. . .

We felt his loss acutely, for he left a gap among his comrades that was never filled. He died as he had lived, quietly. But no one who had served with him would ever forget him. He left an indelible memory. . .

Such a man was *Oberfeldwebel* Adolf Walter, to whom the squadron owed so much.

Günther Rall,
Bad Reichenhall,
Germany

'Attie' Atkinson
'MAKES ME LOOK LIKE A BLOODY HERO'

Eric Chandler, a banker in the City of London for some four decades, was one of those wireless operator/air gunners in 2 Group of Bomber Command who, in 1940 and 1941, had only their Maker (and maybe their pilots) to thank for survival.

Based in those days either in East Anglia or, on detachment, in Malta, Chandler saw casualties of a magnitude which, over so protracted a period, had no parallel in any other airborne force at any time during the war. Low-level daylight operations in Blenheims against shipping and other heavily defended coastal and inland targets were murderous affairs. Squadrons were turned round in a month, sometimes less. Commanding officers came and went. Such was the mortality.

Chandler witnessed much of it – from the rear turret – and knew 2 Group's characters.

I first met the man face to face as I climbed down from my aircraft at Luqa in the evening of 20 June, 1941. All he said was, 'Don't leave anything in the aircraft otherwise it'll be missing in the morning.' He then hurried off to meet the next aircraft of 82 Squadron, no doubt to deliver the same message. He didn't show it, but he was a worried man. He said later, 'I was petrified.' He had reason to be.

Malta, at the time, was being bombed mostly three times a day. The morning and the dusk raids were the most regular. 'To guide our chaps coming in at last light,' he said, 'we laid out gooseneck flares as the air raid sirens began to wail. Then to my horror I saw a fellow running along and putting the flare path out, so I doubled back and began relighting the flares all over again.

'Our Blenheims were circling overhead, each waiting a chance to land. Then I turned round again and there was this fellow putting out the flares I had just relit. I soon put a stop to that as one of the aircraft overshot. Then I ran along one side of the flares again, relighting them, as Doc Monro attended to the other side. . .'

That was Malta in June 1941 as the siege built up. Wing Commander L. V. E. Atkinson was familiar with it. He had already taken six Blenheim crews out to the Island from England to see if it was feasible for 2 Group of Bomber Command to fly its squadrons out there, via Gibraltar, attack shipping bound for the Afrika Korps and then return, after a spell, to the UK for servicing. . .

Attie had become a lumberjack in Canada at the age of seventeen. He had had his first illicit drink there and met his first girlfriend. A toughened young man, he had returned to England on the compensation he had received after crushing the little finger of his left hand at work. Back home, he had changed the scene by getting a job as a probationary clerk at Church House, Westminster, meeting place of the English clergy and a kind of clerical club.

The Royal Air Force refused him entry at first because of a slight cast in his left eye; this, however, had righted itself by the time he was nineteen, so the Service took him on approval in 1936. He was given fifty hours' flying at Anstey, a field in Wiltshire, before being allowed to wear uniform and take the King's commission.

Attie then became an Acting Pilot Officer, 'on probation, under suspicion and in a state of alarm', as he put it. He flew Hawker Harts in his Service training and was then posted to 21 Squadron, which was being formed. Piloting a short-nosed Blenheim, he took part in the first attempted formation flight from the south of England to Scotland.

Over north-east England, drizzle turned to heavy rain and the visibility fell dangerously, and the leader elected to take the formation up through cloud. Nearly at the top of it, Attie found his blind-flying instruments and wireless had failed, so he spun off, coming down from some 10,000 feet. As he straightened out under the cloud base he saw a cathedral below. His time at Church House had taught him that there was only one cathedral in that part of north-east England and that was Durham. Relieved at his pinpoint, he made his way back to base at low level, using the valleys and avoiding the hills.

At noon on New Year's Eve 1940, his station commander, Wing Commander The Earl of Bandon, called him to his office. Visibility was again minimal. 'Could you take off in this weather?,' asked the CO. Attie, intending to be respectfully sarcastic, gave his instant reply. 'Nothing, sir, could be simpler.'

'Right, then,' retorted the Wing Commander, 'you're to fly to the island of Sylt off the north German coast, make a reconnaissance of these positions (pointing to them on a map) and return to Yorkshire – there's no fog there.'

With the aid of flares, Attie took off, completed his mission to the heavily defended island and set course back to Yorkshire. On the way home, he remembered he had invited his fiancée to the dance at his East Anglian base. What then to do? As he turned the options over, his WOP/AG* received a message. 'Return to own base, fog has cleared.' So Attie danced the night away. . .

'The real war,' as he called it, started for him on 10 May, 1940, with the enemy's breakthrough in the Low Countries. He was sent to bomb bridges to impede the German advance. In his first dive, he found he was aiming at the wrong bridge, broke away at low level and, flying through what he called 'muck, flak and corruption', he bombed his primary target in the fading light. Hit repeatedly by ground fire, he struggled back across the southern North Sea to his East Anglian base, there to make his first operational night landing.

Attie opened the campaign against what he termed 'fringe targets' on 31 March, 1941, with a successful operation. Two destroyers were found off the Frisian Islands. One was bombed from fifty feet, with hits scored on the ship's stern. She slewed round, listing heavily to port as a column of black smoke belched into the sky.

He then led the formation across the islands of the north Dutch coast. His report to Intelligence afterwards was typical. 'At Almeland, at about 1400 hours,' he said, 'we sighted what I suppose must have been an after-lunch parade. I alerted my gunner and we sprayed the lot of them. After this, we found a fellow on a gun emplacement, said "good afternoon" and went on our way.'

Attie quickly became dissatisfied with the tactics ordered by 2 Group's AOC, 'Black' Stevenson (Air Vice Marshal D. F. Stevenson) for the hazardous attacks on shipping. The AOC wanted the attacks made broad-side on, but Attie wouldn't have it. He said he wouldn't make beam attacks because (a) the enemy would see you coming miles off and (b) you would then feel the full blast of the ships' fire power. He reckoned that with a Blenheim's own almost total lack of fire power, success must depend upon surprise. This, he contended, could only be achieved in daylight by hugging the waves and attacking the target from astern.

He followed these tactics himself and instructed his crews to do likewise. His independence and outspoken attitude always managed to upset those in authority – not least because they knew that more often than not he was right!

Attie was eventually posted to a staff job at 2 Group headquarters for his operational 'rest', and there he found the portrait which Eric Kenning-ton, the artist, had painted of him. He examined this idealised creation closely. 'Makes me look like a bloody hero,' he said.

It had to be decided where the famous portrait should be hung. 'Better put it in my office instead of me,' he suggested. Attie disliked staff work and the bumph which went with it, and on what he called his 'days off',

* Wireless operator/air gunner.

57

he would at once speed back to his old squadron. His absences became more and more frequent and one day, after a search of 2 Group squadrons had failed to locate him, the civilian police were called in.

It was known that he had been drinking more heavily than usual – often the manifestation of long months of excessive operational stress followed by a period of bored inactivity. I believe it was this erratic behaviour which cost him a career in the Royal Air Force which could well have taken him to the top. He had the humour, ability, independence of mind and the intellect to get there. . .

It was known that he had been drinking more heavily than usual – often the manifestation of long months of excessive operational stress followed by a period of bored inactivity. However, it was a breakdown in his health which, to his great sadness, cost him his career in the RAF which otherwise might well have taken him to the top. He had the humour, ability, independence of mind and the intellect to get there...

It was not until some years after the war that I encountered Attie again as I was coming out of my office in Whitehall. He looked glum. He had been to see 'Them' (pointing in the direction of the Air Ministry). 'They' had told him that, as a result of a lung operation, his service must come to an end.

Soon afterwards, he began a new career in civil aviation eventually joining Freddie Laker as his operations officer. He offered me a trip any time I might be free. I never did quite manage it.

This most memorable character died of cancer in 1978 leaving his wife, Auriol, and three boys and a girl to carry the family torch.

Here was one of World War II's true aces. To fly with him was to feel that he and his Blenheim were as one. He was a man of great courage. Without it, he would never have survived two long tours in 2 Group, faced with the cataclysmic losses we endured in those first years of war. In one eleven-month period, 82 Squadron lost seven COs and I can count on the fingers of one hand the crews who survived with me during my time with the unit.

This was the environment in which Attie Atkinson made his indelible mark.

Eric F. Chandler,
Kenton,
Harrow,
Middlesex

Bob Bissett
THE CHARACTER AMONG MANY

When John Moutray travelled across Canada and the Atlantic to the United Kingdom in 1938 to join the Royal Air Force, he wanted above all to fly. He did not then have the educational background to opt for pilot training so he became a wireless operator. His subsequent 65 operational missions in Bomber Command, first as an NCO and later as a commissioned officer, brought distinction and reward and the right to be numbered among that exclusive circle of Canadians who, having enlisted in the Royal Air Force in peacetime, made good in the wartime Service.

When, eventually, Moutray opted for civilian life after the war, his ability as an artist (he draws and paints exquisite aeroplanes) pointed him towards printing and published work. In time, he rose to be Art Director of Canada's Evergreen Press. It has been quite a ride for the boy who left British Columbia as a teenager half a century ago and remembers the interim 'as if it was last week'.

How does one choose the most memorable character when there were so many? From a small cattle ranch in the mountains of western Canada to a world of complete change in the pre-war Royal Air Force, and the grand excitement of flying with new-found friends in biplanes and open cockpits . . . Characters emerged who have left an indelible mark.

It began for a young Canadian – inevitably – on the barrack square. There was the corporal inspecting the hair-cuts of a new batch of 'sprogs'.

'Am I 'urtin' yew?'

'No corporal!'

'Well, I should be. Oim standin' on yer 'air. Get an 'air cut!'

The expressions used by those drill instructors were not to be forgotten and were so well recorded by such cartoonists as David Langdon, Fougass, Brockbank and others.

I had been in the RAF for 11 weeks when I was caught puffing on a carefully hoarded, one-inch butt of a Woodbine. We were being marched from a class in a Nissen hut to another class in another Nissen hut 20 feet away! Charged with smoking in the Technical Section of RAF Station, Yatesbury, I was brought before a Flight Lieutenant who appeared not to hear the 'left right, left right, left right, prisoner and escort 'alt'. The resultant silence after the loud stamping of hobnailed boots on the wooden floor was supposed to accentuate the seriousness of the charge.

I stood between two guards minus my hat and waited for something to happen. The officer behind the desk was leafing through page after page of printed material. He finally looked up and spoke. 'Well, Moutray, I've been going over your Service record to date and as this is your first offence, against my better judgement I confine you to camp for a week. Dismiss!'

You see what I mean about marvellous characters. That officer was one of them, because he must have known we were confined anyway as we had to get used to wearing our new uniform before we were allowed out to chase girls and visit pubs and generally disgrace the Service. Anyway, this clot from the colonies did not fail to detect a faint smile on his face as I was marched out.

Time passed and this Aircraftman 2nd Class ended up on a bomber squadron, based in Yorkshire, flying Handley Page Heyfords, and lost a Vickers gas-operated machine gun over the Irish Sea. This loss was covered up by some marvellous characters in the Armament Section, who found enough spare parts to make another one!

I met some very fine young men and women and the 'characters' always stood out. I soon learnt not to let appearances cloud my judgement.

We went to war in Whitleys and 19-year-old 'schoolboys' matured very quickly. Some lost their hair and others turned prematurely grey. A sergeant pilot's word was law, the crew was made up of flight mechanics, armourers and other ground crew who became air gunners – we all had to look after our own equipment . . . We enjoyed low flying over the lovely Yorkshire countryside even though it was seldom sanctioned. When the chips were down and the adrenalin was flowing, it seemed as if the rest of the crew were fearless. They may have thought the same of me – but little did they know what went on behind my oxygen mask.

Later in the war, while filling in for the Squadron Adjutant as Duty Officer, I was checking incoming mail for the CO and came across a classic – a telegram from an air gunner. 'Sir, having a hell of a good time. Request a 48-hour extension.'

The CO laughed and said it was so honest and original and had such crust he deserved an extension, but he must report to him on his return.

'Keep an eye on this lad, Moutray, could be officer material!' That makes another 'character'.

Then again, one fine summer's evening, I was Duty Officer and walking round with the duty NCO and inspecting ground defences and their occupants – if any. We approached a sunken gun pit manned by a very new airman (his uniform was still fuzzy) who was equipped with a twin-mounted machine gun. At that moment a Halifax roared overhead at about 200 feet.

'Good evening,' I said.

'Good evening, sir.'

'I take it you are a ground gunner?'

'Yes, sir!'

'Take aircraft recognition?'

'Yes, sir!'

'What was that aircraft that just flew over?'

'Ee, I don't know, but it's a bloody biggun intit!'

An honest and open young character, backbone of the Service and all that. . . .

But the character of all characters for me was Bob Bissett, Flying Officer Robert Clare Bissett, my skipper on 51 Squadron in Yorkshire. I was wireless operator on his crew on Whitley V aircraft. We first flew on operations together on the night of 21 May, 1940, and in the following months, finishing on 25 August, 1940, we did another 25 trips. The last four all lasted over 8 hours 20 minutes and the final two – to Leipzig on 19 August and Berlin on 25 August – were of 10 hours 15 and 10 hours 20 respectively.

The comment in my log book after Leipzig was laconic, 'laid back' they'd call it today. 'Usual flak and searchlights.' After Berlin I went a little further. 'Same bods on duty at AA posts.'

I will never forget this fine man . . . Always so concerned for the welfare of his crew and ground crew . . . Always out at dispersal, whatever the weather, helping to do what had to be done – helping to load up bombs, etc., and generally ensuring that everything was shipshape. By his actions he caused everyone around him to be keen types. I was so fortunate in having such a man as my skipper.

When the time came to part, the RAF said that Bob was to go and be a flight commander in 405 Squadron in the newly formed Canadian 6 Group of Bomber Command in Yorkshire. I was to go to No. 22 OTU at Wellesbourne Mountford 'for a rest' as an instructor!

Squadron Leader Robert Bissett, pilot, No. 39778, with the DFC and bar and the Czech Military Cross, flew his first operation to the Ruhr in a Whitley of 102 Squadron from 4 Group in Yorkshire on 4 September, 1939, the day after the outbreak of war. He was killed in action, aged 28, flying a Wellington, on 30 November, 1941. It was his 39th trip.

61

I was saddened when I heard of his loss, for it was my loss, too. His name is on the War Memorial at Runnymede, Surrey, England. I go to look at it when I come to the Old Country . . . and remember.

John H. Moutray,
Langley,
British Columbia,
Canada

Flight Lieutenant Lyon
CRANWELL 'DRIVER'

Mike Henry (Flight Lieutenant F. M. Henry) shared with Eric
Chandler (see pages 55–8) the pleasure of being an air gunner sitting
in the rear turret of a 2 Group, Bomber Command, Blenheim in
1940 and 1941 during, debatably, World War II's most ruthless
carnage of aircrew. Both were decorated for their pleasure.

But there was a difference. Whereas Chandler had few pilots to
crew with, Henry flew with a variety, one or two being proficient and
able, the others . . . well . . . 'memorable'. He was allergic to them.

With his natural twinkle, amiable perversity and publicist's eye for
'a different angle', he sees the other side of the character story.
Twenty-odd post-war years producing Shell's in-house publications,
including the company's *Aviation News*, and writing his own *Air
Gunner* (G. T. Foulis, 1964), provide the base from which to present
it.

Memorable! The adjective could be applied to a multitude of events and
personalities . . . To the charm and humour of the Earl of Bandon ('The
Abandoned Earl, or 'Paddy' to his many admirers) . . . To the wartime
navigator friend, 'Twiggie' Branch, whose electric personality and sense of
humour fascinated all around him . . . Or to 'Bunny' Rogers, with whom
I flew, a tall Cornishman who served many years with the Royal Navy
before he decided to dice upstairs as navigator. He, too, tops my list. Dear
'Paddy' Maher, such a likeable man, whose size belied his skill as a pilot,
was another – the only one I knew with the AFM.* I flew with Paddy
many times; he even let me taxi a Blenheim I round the perimeter before
take-off, then permitted me some dual. I later operated with him on Boston
aircraft with 107 Squadron.

All of them have departed this world, as have so many of one's RAF
acquaintances.

However, 'memorable' can have other connotations – in my case a

* Air Force Medal.

sombre application, nonetheless memorable. It concerns the one and only flight, an operational sortie, I made with a pre-war Cranwell-trained pilot who held the rank of Flight Lieutenant in 1940. Despite his background and training he wasn't a natural Blenheim pilot. That marvellous aircraft could be handled only one way, and any deviation from laid-down procedures could prove fatal. In particular, landing at night demanded complete control; it was 'twitching' time for many a crew, and whoever coined 'only owls and idiots fly at night' might have had the Blenheim in mind.

At the stroke of midnight on 7/8 October, 1940, Flight Lieutenant Lyon at the controls and myself in the turret (don't remember the navigator's name), we took off from Wattisham in Blenheim IV L9310 of 110(H) Squadron, to make our way to, and discard our 'cargo' on, Boulogne – one of the Channel invasion ports. Mission accomplished we returned unblemished to base. Two and half hours after take-off we approached the airfield. Some distance from the gooseneck flarepath I noticed the angle of glide indicator showing RED. In the early-morning Suffolk haze I could only see the blurred passing of trees underneath our port wing (the landing light had been switched on).

Realising that his approach was at the wrong angle to the flarepath, the pilot opened up to go round again. We crossed the airfield boundary without hitting anything; my fingers and toes were crossed because I sensed that something nasty was pending. Nasty it turned out to be. Roaring across the airfield I prayed in 72-point bold italics that my driver would not retract the flaps until he had gained a useful piece of altitude. The landing lamp showed clearly how near the grass was to the belly of the aircraft. I wondered what was dead ahead – hangars? trees? Before either was reached to kill us all the port wing dropped; he was turning, but too low. The port wing hit the ground and only a few seconds after the initial shattering screech of tearing metal I was sitting with my feet in the turret cupola, which was on the ground. Any exit from the wreckage was blocked for me by the ladder across my back and I could see flames coming from the forward part of the fuselage. My immediate thought was that unless somebody hacked through the fuselage to get me out I would fry.

Looking round to my left I noticed a jagged hole in the fuselage. I put my head through it and pushed with my feet against the other side. Strength, lent by fear, was far more effective than a firkin of Guinness; with my shoulders protected by my Irving jacket and parachute harness, I fell out, almost on my head (that explains a lot of things), into the night air and into the glare of fire. I remember seeing the navigator, his face covered in blood, staggering about until the ambulance crew helped him away from the scene; the pilot also (how both of them survived is a miracle) came round the wreckage to be escorted to the Albion 'Blood Wagon' standing at the ready. The fire and ambulance crews were marvellous –

so quick at the scene and at their own risk they were among it all so efficiently.

The comparative silence of the flame-lit patch of aerodrome was suddenly rent by the noise of exploding oxygen bottles, the flash of Very cartridges and the frightening sound of ammunition popping off. I was helped into the ambulance and taken to sick quarters. The pilot and navigator were whisked away to a civilian hospital in Ipswich. I was visited by the CO and Duty Officer, who congratulated me on my escape. 'I gave you all up as dead when I saw the aircraft go in,' the Duty Officer added.

I told them exactly what had happened – after sipping a mug of very sweet tea and smoking a welcome cigarette. On reflection, I must have instinctively ducked before the aircraft hit the ground otherwise I would have been decapitated; I had a cut on the back of my head – might have been knocked unconscious; but would I have got out in time? I also gashed my right thigh – torn when squeezing through the jagged side of the fuselage.

I heard later that Flight Lieutenant Lyon was found dead in the middle of the airfield one night. Never sure whether he had been hit by a night-flying aircraft landing or taking off. I don't know whether he ever flew again after leaving hospital following our crash.

Four nights after the 'prang', I took off at 6.30 p.m. with Flying Officer 'Dolly' Arderne. Our target – Boulogne. We performed our duty and again returned unblemished, landing safely at 9.10 p.m. On every flight, for a long time after my crash, I had the escape hatch open just before landing; for a long time afterwards I could smell burning oil/petrol. Eventually I completely regained my confidence until the next non-Blenheim 'driver' came along (second of only two pilots who tried to exterminate themselves and me).

Mike Henry,
Walmer,
Deal,
Kent

John Magee
PILOT POET

Roderick I. A. Smith, the Canadian lawyer from Vancouver, was a 19-year-old pilot officer in the Royal Canadian Air Force when, in the late summer of 1941, he joined No. 412, the newly formed Canadian Spitfire Squadron, based at Digby, a Royal Air Force station some 10 miles south-east of the cathedral city of Lincoln in the east midlands of England. Mostly the Squadron spent its time at Wellingore, a satellite airfield beside an attractive Lincolnshire village lying four miles from the parent station.

Now and then 412 would make excursions southwards to 11 Group of Fighter Command, to Manston or West Malling in Kent, to take part in the offensive sweeps with the light bombers to targets in northern France.

It was, however, in the Battle of Malta, a year later, that Rod Smith made his mark as a flight commander with 126 Squadron. But with success came sorrow, for his brother, Jerrold, fighting alongside him on the Island in 1942, fell in action. The blow struck very hard. Everyone had taken to Jerry's easy, transatlantic ways and he and his brother were close.

Back on the Western Front, Rod Smith played out the war, first with his old Squadron, 412, and later, from 1944 until the end, as the twice-decorated CO of the RCAF's 401 Squadron in the drive through France and north-west Europe into Germany. He became a Wing Commander and it was upon this platform of a long operational war that a signally successful law practice in British Columbia was subsequently built. Recently, an interesting by-product has emerged from this distinguished Canadian life.

John Magee, the young poet whose *High Flight* (see page 69–70) has become in the last few years one of the most-quoted poems to arise from the literature of World War II (President Reagan paraphrased lines from it in his address at the service for the victims of the *Challenger* spacecraft disaster), was a fellow 19-year-old pilot officer with Rod Smith, also serving with 412 Squadron at Digby in the autumn of 1941.

The intellectual qualities of the two young officers provided a common denominator; the relationship, however, was to be cut tragically short with Magee's premature loss. Time enough, however, for a memorable impression to be formed.*

John Magee was introduced to me in the Mess at Digby; I still remember the occasion. He was tall and slender and had a small dark moustache – unusual in one so young. His expression was pleasing, his eyes in particular seemed to convey a fine spirit.

John loved squadron life. He was good-natured and usually full of humour. His companionship was attractive and he spoke with an accent which owed something to both England and New England. He was articulate and precocious – but always pleasantly so. He maintained high standards and was not indiscriminating.

As time passed we came to learn something of his unusual background. Although he was an American citizen, he had been born in Shanghai. His father had been an Episcopal missionary in China for many years; his mother was English. John had been educated in England – at Rugby, the well-known British public school – but he had returned to the United States in 1939, just before the outbreak of World War II. He had then spent a year at school in New England before coming up to Canada in the summer of 1940 to join the Royal Canadian Air Force. Earlier that year, his father had returned from China and had taken up an appointment with St John's Episcopal Church, on Lafayette Square, in Washington DC, where the family then lived.

John was a skilful pilot. His formation flying was tight and his practice dogfighting was tough. There were, however, times when he had curious lapses. There was the day when the wind was blowing strongly and he took off downwind at Digby towards the hangars at the very moment that the Duke of Kent was arriving to pay us a visit. He provided a memorable diversion by barely clearing the buildings.

Another time, he forgot to connect the tube to his aircraft's oxygen supply and passed out at 22,000 feet. He came to in a high-speed dive, just in time to pull out. Once also he let a wing drop on landing and caused it damage. He was so distraught at his mistake that he taxied into a parked aircraft, hitting one of its wing-tips with his own. His flight commander, Christopher Bushell, known as Kit, who was soon to become our CO, was not amused.

* Rod Smith has contributed first-hand impressions for Ivan Henson's extensively researched biography of the youthful poet, now in preparation – Ed.

But we all made errors from time to time and I'm quite sure that had John lived a few months longer, he would have made a fine fighter pilot.

I well remember one evening early in November 1941, when we were sitting around the bar of the Grange, a rambling old house which was our Mess at Wellingore, one of the pilots said that he had seen a sheep stuck in the edge of a pond about a mile away while he had been out walking during the afternoon.

'Come on,' said Kit Bushell, 'let's see if we can find it and try to get it out.' John Magee instantly responded, so we put on our fleece-lined flying jackets and started out. It was a black night and the fog was thickening, but we found the poor sheep, which bleated as we approached. As I was the tallest, I reached out over to it while Kit and John and one or two others hung on to the end of my flying jacket. I put my arms round the animal's chest while the others pulled hard. It gave a loud bleat as it came loose and we brought it up on to the bank. It must have been painful for it, but it loped stiffly away into the darkness and we could tell it was very happy. You could see how elated John was at our success, such was his acute sensitivity.

> The first show that John Magee took part in over enemy territory was an attack by the Blenheims on 8 November, 1941, on the loco-motive works at Lille in northern France. 412, operating from West Malling, were joined by two other Spitfire V squadrons and provided the cover as the bombers withdrew from the target area. The activity provoked a violent reaction from the Me.109s and the very new Focke-Wulf 190s from Adolf Galland's JG 26 in the Pas de Calais. 412 lost three aircraft including the CO's whose parachute was seen to stream. . .
>
> Magee, one of the few in the Squadron to fire his guns, somehow survived the baptism and landed by himself at Hawkinge, the nearest British base across the Straits, as Rod Smith recalls.

When we gathered at Wellingore the next day to give Hart Massey, the Squadron Intelligence Officer, our reports, John said that he had told a pilot at Hawkinge that he had fired his guns but had seen no damage. 'Oh,' said the fellow, 'put in a claim. You must put in a claim!' John was disgusted. When he finished his combat report, he read it aloud. It con-tained the line 'Foolishly I dived to the attack . . . ' We hid our smiles. John was quite naïve in some ways. As we left the room together, he stopped and turned to me at the doorway. 'Gee,' he said, 'I'd like to have a score!'

> A little over a month later, on 11 December, 412 were taking part in a wing exercise with another squadron from a nearby airfield. The

cloud base was at some 1500 feet and the top several thousand feet above. Before the squadron started to go up through the overcast, Rod Smith had to break away with an unserviceable aircraft and land. An hour or so later, the operations controller called to say a Spitfire had crashed between Wellingore and Cranwell, the RAF College which in wartime had become a Service Flying Training School equipped with twin-engine Airspeed Oxfords. The Spitfire had hit an Oxford, piloted by a student, as the Squadron was letting down fast through a hole in the clouds. Rod, another pilot and Hart Massey drove at once to the scene of the crash.

We walked across the field to within about 30 yards of the wreckage. It was John's Spitfire. We could not get closer as ammunition was exploding in the fire. Then we noticed a hole in the ground about 70 yards away. It contained the imprint of John's body about a foot deep in the soft soil. Nothing remained save a large pool of blood at the bottom of the hole. The wreckage of the Oxford was about half a mile to the east. The pilot had been killed and his body had also been removed. The three of us returned sadly to Wellingore.

John's funeral took place at Scopwick, a small village about a mile from Digby. I was a member of the burial party and I remember clearly that when the Air Force ensign covering the simple wooden coffin was removed, the brass plaque read

> 'P/O John Gillespie Magee, RCAF
> Died December 11, 1941
> Aged 19 years'

Afterwards, Jack Morrison, who had become 412's CO, wrote to John's father and mother. Three weeks or so later he received a reply. One line of it, I recall, ran 'Words can't tell you how much we miss John.' A copy of the poem 'High Flight' was enclosed. John had written it at his Operational Training Unit at Llandow, in South Wales, about ten days before he joined the Squadron. It was a complete surprise to us that he wrote poetry.

> Oh! I have slipped the surly bonds of earth
> And danced the skies on laughter-silvered wings;
> Sunward I've climbed, and joined the tumbling mirth
> Of sun-split clouds – and done a hundred things
> You have not dreamed of – wheeled and soared and swung
> High on the sunlit silence. Hov'ring there,
> I've chased the shouting wind along, and flung
> My eager craft through footless halls of air . . .
>
> Up, up the long delirious, burning blue,
> I've topped the windswept heights with easy grace

Where never lark, or even eagle flew –
And, while with silent, lifting mind I've trod
The high untrespassed sanctity of space
Put out my hand and touched the face of God.

Pilot Officer J. G. Magee, Jnr, 1941

Roderick Smith,
Vancouver,
British Columbia,
Canada

Alois Vašátko
THE GREAT AMOS

If a fellow Czech was to make the immortal Alois Vašátko the subject of a study then it is right that František Fajtl (Squadron Leader F. Fajtl) should be the one to do it. None had a closer, first-hand involvement or a more intimate witness of air events (or their principal actors) from the time of Czechoslovakia's subjugation under the Nazi jackboot until final victory; and none was to feel more acutely the remorseless repetition of history as the Soviet Union subsequently stamped its mastery over his homeland.

It is fortunate for posterity that there should have been available during these past five or six decades a Czech of Frankie Fajtl's experience, and ability and success as a writer, to record his impressions of these happenings (and the men associated with them) in all their tragic reality.

Alois Vašátko (Wing Commander A. Vašátko), known universally as Amos, the first leader of the Czechoslovak Wing in Fighter Command of the Royal Air Force, was killed in aerial combat on 23 June, 1942. When he died, he had destroyed 17 enemy aircraft and had probably accounted for another three. He had been decorated by his own countrymen as well as the French and the British.

I first met Amos in 1938, when we were serving together in the 2nd Air Regiment in Olomouc. He was then 30 and had graduated from the Military Academy as a lieutenant in the artillery seven years earlier. Later, he had transferred to the Air Force and trained as a pilot after first qualifying as an observer. We became close friends.

While he was a great believer in self-discipline and education, he did not at all frown upon the games players and those who enjoyed themselves; he was, in fact, an excellent tennis player. He had great self-confidence and a fantastic memory for detail. He had made a close study of military regulations, and when he encountered rules which he believed to be sense-less or unjustified, he was outspoken in his criticism of them and would not accept their validity.

71

At officers' conferences, he tended to overshadow his contemporaries with his intellect. He quickly became recognised as having the best mind among those with whom he served, and yet he was also the least well liked among them. He had been regarded as self-opinionated and obstinate ever since his time at the Military Academy. Although he graduated with the highest marks in the exams and the various tests, he was not awarded the equivalent of the Sword of Honour because he was often quite critical of the Staff if he thought this was justified. His attitude had caused his superiors to enter some caveats in his confidential report.

'Unusually ambitious, often dissatisfied with his lot, and unreasonably critical, he needs a firm hand on him. He has already been warned about his open criticism of conditions at the Academy. He is, however, energetic, smart and determined, and has all the intellect necessary to absorb the technicalities of advanced, modern equipment . . . '

The qualifications embraced in this report resulted in Amos finishing no higher than sixth in the Order of Merit table for his course.

There was an air of purpose about everything he did. He planned ahead. Thus it was that he used to worry about his periodical medical checks. He was concerned that his eyesight was somewhat suspect and that this might impede the realisation of his ambitions in the Service. It used to be said of him that he would copy out and then memorise the bottom lines of letters on the testing charts so that he might pass the eye tests without difficulty.

His obvious qualities as an officer ensured that Amos quickly became a flight commander in his unit. This at once gave him the chance to demonstrate his belief that every flight must adhere to a strict programme and purpose. This was reflected in his reaction to a rule which, in those days, required every pilot to complete four flights a month to qualify for flying pay, known then as 'existence' money.

In fact, these special allowances were quite substantial and were not to be lost. Often, in the case of the higher-ranking officers on the Staff, people would come along to the flying units asking to be allowed to do four five-minute flights and circuits before the month was out. But Amos wouldn't have this. He banned the practice in his flight because, he said, it interfered with his programme and schedule. He further issued instructions that all 'existence' flights would be undertaken in strict accordance with his routine training programme and that there would be no exceptions.

It was part of Amos's intellectual armour that he would never admit defeat or give in to adversity. I had a personal experience of this in May 1937, when he and I were flying from Olomouc to Košice, a matter of a few hundred kilometres, in a Zlin XII light communications aircraft.

We encountered three heavy thunderstorms on the way. If I had been captain of the aircraft, I would have turned back rather than risk such turbulence. We had no radio, only a compass and a map. But Amos was navigating, and the captain, and elected to try to go round the storms – the third compelled us to fly dangerously close to the Hungarian frontier, which we were forbidden to cross.

'Sir,' I ventured rather tentatively into the speaking tube, 'might it not be wiser for us to turn back?'

'Lieutenant,' he replied frostily, increasing my apprehension, 'stick to your course. We shall get through. These storms are only local.'

We pressed on through the darkened overcast amid flashes of lightning and considerable turbulence. As I was then flying on instruments, the elements were most distracting. However, when eventually we came out of this hell into clearer weather, Amos calmly gave me a correction to the course. 'In 10 minutes,' he added, 'we'll be there.' And so it proved.

Vašátko felt the German *Wehrmacht's* occupation of our homeland sharply. One day, when I went to his room, I found him deep in thought. There was a long pause before he acknowledged my presence. 'We must never surrender to all this,' he said, 'even although there are, sadly, so few of us . . .'

'But how, Amos,' I countered, 'are we going to do that?'

He pursed his lips as if rejecting the bitterness of the regime and the national humiliation it had brought. 'Each man for himself,' he said. 'But each of us must be governed by the conscience of the professional soldier and the duty of a patriot. We must never serve the enemy.' His attitude was exactly the same as mine.

Alois Vašátko and František Fajtl moved to Poland and thence to France for the short-lived aerial battle. North Africa was the next stop. From there, their gaze was fastened on the UK, the last bastion in the defence against the Nazi juggernaut. For Vašátko, language was going to be the problem. He did not know a single word of English.

Amos [therefore] bought French-English dictionaries and textbooks and distributed them to his friends. He pursued his study of English as energetically and as resolutely as he did everything else that he cared about. Day and night he laboured over the vocabulary and the grammar.

His arrival in England, where he was accepted by the Royal Air Force, was, for him, a revelation. He sensed at once – as his compatriots did with him – the Service's fighting spirit and its organisational strength. He could scarcely credit the British people's attitude to war – their calm courage, their discipline and their dedication, and, above all, their resolve, while standing quite alone, never to surrender to the superior might of the enemy. In such an atmosphere, he literally flung himself into the flying and into the fight.

The advance and promotion of such an exceptional character was probably predictable . . . The Battle of Britain with the newly-formed 312 (Czech) Squadron and its Hurricanes . . . Fresh victories to add to those he had gained in France . . . By December 1940, command of a flight in the Squadron and, by the following May, the unit's commanding officer, flying with the Kenley Wing in 11 Group . . .

Vašátko drove his followers as hard as he taxed his own endurance – 52 operational hours he flew in one month . . . His 17th kill – a Me.109, gained in a sweep over France – was a prelude to his appointment as the first leader of the Czechoslovak Air Force wing in Fighter Command . . .

Amos Vašátko was now happy and thoroughly contented. He was satisfying his aggression and his earlier yearning to fly Spitfires. But his leadership of the Wing was, sadly, to be short-lived. On that June day in 1942, he was returning from France and, unexpectedly, was engaged near the English coast by a particularly tenacious Luftwaffe pilot in a Fw.190. In a sudden break, Vašátko and the German collided. Both aircraft fell into the sea. Amos did not survive.

Here, then, was an outstanding commander and organiser – a manly fighter of exceptional intellect who commanded respect and popularity without courting it. By his achievements and moral qualities, he earned for himself the premier place in the history of Czechoslovakia's air fighting against the oppressor.

František Fajtl,
Praha,
Czechoslovakia

'Robbo'
THE ART OF GETTING IT WRONG

Jerry Monk was among those wartime volunteers – and there were plenty of them – who did all their training on single-engine aircraft, having opted for fighters, only to finish up at the controls of some multi-engined monster.

A tour on Lancasters with 630 Squadron in 5 Group of Bomber Command turned out to be Jerry's unexpected and rugged lot.

It was a solid enough base for him to build a 35-year career with Wimbledon Stadium, in south-west London, eventually heading up the company's Press office with a seat on the board. 'Retirement' brought the wheel round almost full circle with an appointment to the editorial chair of *Air Mail*, the Royal Air Force Association's journal, which circulates worldwide.

I first met 'Robbo' in March 1942 on board the SS *Mataroa*, a meat boat from the Argentinian meat run masquerading as a troopship and carrying we fledgling airmen to Cape Town. From there we were to progress to what was then known as Southern Rhodesia for flying training. 'Robbo's' hammock swung and bumped with mine in the heat and murk of C hold on that eminently forgettable five weeks' cruise and we got to know each other well. He was a likeable lad and several times we shared a place in an hours-long queue to buy a tin of condensed milk – the nearest we AC plonks could get to hard liquor.

Likeable lad though he was, 'Robbo' had an unfortunate tendency to get things wrong and my most enduring recollection of his several blemishes is of the day we were both part of the new guard being mounted at the ITW* at Bulawayo. We had done it once before and had muddled through the ceremonial of lowering the ensign, despite our scant knowledge of arms drill.

A new arrival on our course was an army bod – an officer, no less – from some posh spit-and-polish regiment, where they did things the correct

* Initial Training Wing.

way, and he was the orderly officer on this occasion. We survived his scowls and looks of astonishment as we muddled through ordering and presenting arms; but then, the ensign having been safely recovered, he bowled us a googly with the command: 'For inspection, port arms'. Porting arms was not in our limited curriculum and there was no response from our lot except an audible 'Eh' from 'Robbo'.

With steam coming from his ears our inquisitor ordered us to be marched off to our duties in the guardroom. Our corporal-in-charge quickly posted the first sentry at the gate – 'Robbo', of course – as the dark uniform and polished Sam Browne marched crisply into view, passing 'Robbo' on the way to the guardroom . . . Not a flicker from 'Robbo', standing at ease and staring Rhodes-like across the bundu. More steam from the Army's ears. 'Sentry, what do you usually do when an officer approaches you?' 'Well Sir', explained 'Robbo', with his slight stutter, 'if-if-if I hadn't got this g-gun in my hand I would salute you!'

My last memory of 'Robbo' was at EFTS* at Guinea Fowl. He was to go off on a solo exercise in the Tiger Moth and decided to start the aircraft up himself. Having made sure the Tiggy was securely chocked, and having 'sucked-in', he ran round to the cockpit, switched on, went to the front and swung the prop. He had done it well for she fired first time, but unfortunately the throttle was a little too far advanced and the tail began to rise. Dashing towards the cockpit 'Robbo' realised he would not get to the throttle in time and hurled himself at the tail of the aircraft instead. There he was, hauling down on the tail at shoulder height as the revs picked up and he vanished from our view in a cloud of dust. But 'Robbo' was never short of friends and someone was quickly on hand to rescue him from his embarrassing predicament.

Jerry Monk,
Ottery St Mary,
Devon

---

* Elementary Flying Training School.

Raoul Daddo-Langlois
CRUEL ENTERPRISE

The incident occurred on 13 December, 1941, and exposed, at a stroke, much of the man's character. The background is therefore important.

No. 66 Squadron, which Raoul Daddo-Langlois (pronounced Daddo-Longlay) and I had joined on the same day in July, five months earlier, was then based at the Royal Air Force station, Perranporth, a windswept airfield on the north coast of Cornwall. It was the Squadron's second and westernmost stop after the rigours of the Battle of Britain and the fighting over south-east England some fifteen months before.

Operations from Perranporth were humdrum. Tedious shipping patrols, flown daily in our so-called 'long-range' Spitfire IIs, were interspersed with occasional daylight sorties with Bomber Command across 120 miles of English Channel to France's Brittany peninsula. There, the German-held port of Brest and Hitler's prized warships, *Scharnhorst*, *Prinz Eugen* and *Gneisenau* – soon to make their brilliantly insolent dash through the Straits of Dover in daylight – were the prime targets.

For a fighter pilot in search of the real thing it was all pretty mundane stuff.

William Raoul Daddo-Langlois, whose family had roots in the Channel Islands, was then 19 and exactly the calibre of young officer whom the Royal Air Force wanted to attract. Public school educated, intellectually sharp, above average at games, smart, personable and determined, he came from a Service background. His father, W. J. Daddo-Langlois, had gone off to sea in boyhood and had later been commissioned in the Royal Naval Air Service towards the end of World War I. Thereafter, he had become one of the Royal Air Force's most accomplished flying boat captains, eventually retiring as a group captain.

Raoul, like his father, could fly aeroplanes – he did not allow them to fly him. The ability had become apparent early on in the training we had done together in Canada. But he was restless and impatient, easily bored and possessed of an undisguised urge to engage the enemy. From our Cornish outpost, this laudable craving was seldom satisfied.

One morning the cord snapped. Daddo-Langlois's flight commander

77

had sent him off for 30 minutes on some fairly commonplace local practice. Ninety minutes or so later he still had not returned. Then, just as concern was beginning to mount, a speck appeared on the south-eastern horizon, soon to be accompanied by the unmistakable throb of a Rolls-Royce Merlin engine.

As Raoul taxied his aircraft into dispersal, there for all to see was a jagged hole in the port wing the size of two beer barrels. The eight .303 machine guns had been fired . . .

The pilot, pressed to tell all, unfolded his story. For his authorised, local flying exercise, he had substituted a free-enterprise dash across 120 miles of sea, below radar cover, to enemy-held Brittany. There, he had had a field day, ranging widely over the peninsula and squirting left and right at any suitable target he could find. Near the end, while he was still hugging the ground to avoid detection and the enemy's flak, a sturdy telegraph pole had obstinately refused to get out of the way.

How he made it back to base, with the aircraft in that state, would remain one of the Squadron's wonders . . .

Close arrest? Court martial? The necessary elements were mostly there – save one: a conventional squadron commander who would see that the appropriate punishment was driven through.

Squadron Leader Hubert R. Allen – Dizzy Allen to one and all – 66's CO, was anything but conventional. He was 21, resourceful, unpredictable and one hell of a fighter pilot. He had fought all through the Battle of Britain with the Squadron. Experience and upbringing had taught him to recognise quality when he saw it.

He called Daddo-Langlois to his office, gave him a good-sized dressing down, and then set about camouflaging the affair as best he could. He could keep it dark principally because Perranporth was a satellite airfield and 66 was the only unit on it . . .

A month or so later, a signal came through from Group. 'Post two pilots from 66 Squadron to proceed to India for service in the Far East.' As the adjutant read it out, Raoul nudged my arm. 'Why don't we put in for it?'

In less than a fortnight, in February 1942, we were flying clapped-out Hurricane IIs not in Burma as we had expected, but in Malta, where the Luftwaffe's Messerschmitt 190Fs, flown high and fast in their well-drilled sections of four in open line abreast, dominated the Mediterranean sky.

'Raoul,' I said, 'what price Perranporth now?'

'Have no fear,' he retorted. 'It won't be long before the Spitfires are here.' His forced bravado cloaked a realism about air fighting against ridiculous odds.

When the first Spitfires did eventually arrive, and a few of us were then sent back to Gibraltar to lead in others from the carriers, Raoul settled down enthusiastically in my flight in 249 Squadron at Takali, his restlessness well curbed by the stark reality of the daily challenge. His performance in A Flight confirmed an early lesson in command – always have a linchpin in your unit upon whom you can utterly depend. Daddo-Langlois filled this role exactly. His reflected views, given necessarily in confidence, were invaluable. He became a rock for the flight commander to lean on.

We had a magnificent mix in 249, the few United Kingdom representatives blending in easily with the Australians, Canadians, New Zealanders, Rhodesians and South Africans, and the leavening of Americans who had come into the fight long before Pearl Harbor and the United States' entry into the war. Raoul played his hand easily in this galaxy of robust, international talent. Everyone liked him and respected his reserved 'Englishness'.

When, half-way through the battle, I was given command of the Squadron, A. B. Woodhall, the Group Captain in charge of Operations at the headquarters in Valletta, and the Royal Air Force's outstanding fighter controller of the war, asked me whom I wished to nominate to succeed me in A Flight.

The question was conveniently timed. It was now 25 June, 1942, and Raoul had by then completed nearly five months' hard fighting on the Island, made his mark and, at one point, had caused quite a sensation by ramming a 109 head on, and walking away from it.

'I'd like to have Flying Officer Daddo-Langlois, sir,' I said. 'I know he's still a bit young, but . . . ' Woody wouldn't let me finish. 'Tell him to put his stripe up tonight,' he interjected.

Raoul played out his time on the Island with distinction, adding to his victories and blossoming with the responsibility he had been given. As a subordinate commander, he was unforgettable, a sheet-anchor among a bunch of splendidly mercurial contemporaries . . .

Four or five months later, towards the end of our respective rest periods back in the United Kingdom, I was astonished and dismayed to find that my former flight commander had made up his mind, without reference to me or anyone else, to forsake the day-fighter role – in which he still had so much palpable potential – in favour of the work of photographic reconnaissance.

I pleaded with him to reverse his decision. Flying an unarmed Spitfire, loaded up with extra fuel tanks and cameras, reliant only upon the extremes of height and speed for defence on long and taxing missions deep into enemy territory, was totally incompatible with his restless, 'instant' temperament. This vital, specialist work required quite different qualities.

Raoul wouldn't yield. He was resolved to follow his independently chosen course; and when, at the start of my second tour of operations, I was posted to command No. 616, the South Yorkshire Auxiliary Squadron, I quickly arranged for him to be offered a flight in it. The answer came back pat. 'Not available.'

After a short attachment with No. 543 (PR) Squadron at Benson, in Oxfordshire, starting on 21 April, 1943, Daddo-Langlois was ordered to fly a photographic Spitfire IX out to Castel Benito in North Africa. Husky, the code name for the Sicilian invasion, was imminent.

Things went wrong from the start. He had trouble with the aircraft's petrol feed on the flight out to Gibraltar on 15 May and was lucky to get there. Repairs proved ineffective. The next day, the feed again played up, resulting in a forced landing in the Algerian desert.

When, eventually, he reached Castel Benito on 24 May, after an extraordinary nine-day adventure with the Arabs – engagingly recorded in his diary – he was told by Adrian Warburton, the exceptionally versatile and way-out wing commander in charge of the PR unit, to go back to England, collect another aircraft and fly it out.

Raoul wouldn't have it. 'Sir,' he retorted, 'I want to apply for an immediate transfer back to fighters.' He had had enough of photographic reconnaissance. Warburton, obviously piqued, sent him on to Cairo. Within a few weeks – on 2 July, 1943 – he was posted to 93 Squadron in Malta as a supernumerary flight lieutenant. The contrast with the standards of 249, and the great days he had known on the Island a year before, depressed him.

Eight days later, he was dead, felled on 10 July, the first day of the Sicilian landings, by US gunners while he was attacking – and hitting – a Junkers 88. After a crash-landing in south-eastern Sicily, he was taken unconscious, and hideously wounded, with a compound, depressed fracture of the skull, by tender to the hospital ship lying off-shore.

In a case of mistaken identity, the ship was bombed by American aircraft and the tender sunk. Raoul's body was recovered from the water the next day and buried at sea...

The day before he died, I was posted to command the Spitfire wing at Coltishall, in Norfolk. Within a week or two, changes had to be made in the commands of the two squadrons. Had I been able to dissuade him from his ill-starred brush with PRU, Raoul would have made an ideal fit for either. Promotion and a long-overdue award for gallantry would have followed. The poignancy of it all cut very deep and compounded the memory of a character whose friendship and constancy had meant so much to me in the two, almost uninterrupted, years we had served together.

In 1982, I returned to Malta with five other 'veterans' to help with Scottish Television's filming of the documentary to commemorate the 40th anniversary of the Island battle. One free morning, I went alone to see the beautiful Commonwealth war memorial which stands on high ground in the gardens of Floriana, overlooking Grand Harbour. There, among the list of flight lieutenants who had no known grave, the name W. R. Daddo-Langlois sprang out at me.

As I sat alone in the spring sunshine, my mind ran back to 249 Squadron and to the same month – May – 40 years before, when, after tenuous weeks of touch and go, the course of battle had suddenly and irrevocably been turned in the Allies' favour.

Raoul, whose feeling for words had pointed him to journalism and the foreign Press post-war, seemed so close he might have been sitting on the wooden seat beside me, just as he was at the peak of his time as a flight commander with the Squadron. I felt I wanted to ask him out loud about his decision to switch to PRU and his refusal to listen to my advice. My inability to prevent the virtual waste of this memorable character, whose devoted comradeship had been a bulwark in triumph and reverse, had haunted me for years.

Had my imagination taken hold? I think not. The man seemed altogether too real for that.

Laddie Lucas,
South Kensington,
London

Pelleschi

THE LOST HAND

The crews of the Royal Air Force's high-speed launches of the Air Sea Rescue Service made an unsung yet telling contribution to aircrew morale during the Battle of Malta in 1942. They were entitled to be proud of their share in the victory. Based at Kalafrana in the south-east, Sliema in the east and St Paul's Bay in the north-east of the island, the launches undertook their hazardous excursions for lost pilots and aircrews far out from port when Axis air power dominated much of the Mediterranean and played havoc with the few seaborne convoys that tried to run the gauntlet through the Narrows.

HSL 128, in those times, logged three extended searches involving round trips of 286 miles (27 hours' duration), 295 miles (16½ hours') and 302 miles (34 hours') respectively to save the lives of three Allied airmen. No task was too daunting or dangerous to attempt if any hope of recovery remained.

L. G. Head (Flight Sergeant L. G. Head) saw much of it as one of the crew of HSL 128, stationed at Kalafrana, during his long spell on the island. Inevitably there were unforgettable characters among those whom he and his crew saved. Men often exhibit hidden features when they approach the end of their tether.

Pelleschi, an Italian airman, is one of the three characters who stand out in my mind from those whom we picked up. He was one of the crew of a bomber in a formation of three, heavily escorted by a protective fighter screen of some 80 plus Messerschmitt 109s and Macchi 202s, which was attacking Halfar, an airfield in the south-east of the island on 4 July, 1942.

Spitfires of the Royal Air Force's 249 Squadron broke through the fighter screen, destroying all three bombers. Pelleschi baled out of his blazing aircraft and came down in the sea some five miles from Delimara Point. HSL 128 was called out from Kalafrana at 0919 hours to make the search. I was acting as coxswain on this trip and when we reached the area we soon spotted a man in the water, supported by his Mae West.* It was my job to keep a close eye on the man and manoeuvre the launch as near as possible to him, but not too close for fear of running him down.

As we approached he appeared to be holding his arm aloft and waving a white handkerchief. However, as we lifted Pelleschi out of the water and took him aboard the 'white handkerchief' was found to be scraps of flesh from a completely shattered hand. The sea water had washed the blood away leaving the white flesh.

It was agonising to look at the expression on the man's face. It conveyed a terrible impression of horror, utter dejection and pleading. The man's eyes seemed to be saying, 'For God's sake, what is all this about, what is the purpose of it all.' Up to that moment war, for me, had been a deadly and heroic struggle for the survival of good over evil; but now it became a terrible, loathsome and destructive thing.

I only saw Pelleschi for what amounted to a few short minutes, but in that time he had left an impression upon me which has remained to this day, a vivid and awful picture in my mind. In this dreadful context, the Italian was to become the most memorable character I encountered in the war.

It was interesting to me that Laddie Lucas, who was leading the Spitfires which destroyed the three Italian bombers that day, took two or three of his pilots to see their victims in hospital a day or so later. I am not surprised at his reaction on seeing Pelleschi. 'As I approached the bed,' he wrote years later, 'a dark-skinned, strikingly good-looking Italian face looked up at me from the pillow. It was the eyes, pleading and plaintive, which caught my attention . . . As if to emphasise his unspoken message, he held up a heavily bandaged arm. The hand was missing. Sickened, I turned away . . . resolved never again to allow any pilot of 249 to see a wounded prisoner in hospital.'

Lucas learned that Pelleschi was a violinist in civilian life. As I look back, I am struck again by the way an impression left by one wretched, pathetic man could change, in a few short minutes, an attitude to war.

I remember, too, the impact that 'Screwball' Beurling, the great Canadian fighter ace, made upon me when we picked him out of the sea, some six miles or so from the coast, on 14 October. The various stories and books that have been written about him convey the impression of a tough, hard-living, rather unruly, not-very-well-disciplined pilot who was, however, brilliant at the job.

But here was this young Pilot Officer when we found him, floating in his dinghy, wounded in the foot. He was greatly agitated and distressed because he had lost his Bible as he was disentangling himself from his

* Life jacket.

83

parachute and getting into his dinghy. As it happened, it was quickly found and handed to him, after which he calmed down.

He told us that this small book had been given to him by his mother and that he never flew without it. So here we had this man showing us, in his distress, the deeply religious side of his character – an aspect of it which he most certainly kept well hidden from his colleagues in 249 Squadron.

Then, to complete the trio of characters whom I so well remember, there was the German, Horst Gerhard, the pilot of a Junkers 88, whose aircraft had come down in the sea while on a mine-laying operation. The crew of a Wellington had sighted a red distress flare some 55 miles west of Malta and not far from the island of Lampedusa.

HSL 128 began its search at 0800. Two and a half hours later one of the look-outs reported seeing traces of smoke in the distance; we made for the area but nothing was found. At 1300 hours, with no sign of life or wreckage being seen, the search was abandoned and the launch started to make its way back to Malta.

After heading east for some miles, a man was sighted dead ahead, quietly sitting on one of the wheels of his crashed aircraft. Gerhard, who spoke fluent English (his uncle had been a professor at Edinburgh University between the wars and the nephew had paid many visits to the United Kingdom) and was a 'veteran' of the Spanish Civil War, in which he had fought with the Condor Legion, told us that he had watched us searching for him in the distance. He had fired his last distress flare (the smoke seen by the launch's look-out), but to no avail. The relief was manifest in his exhausted state. . .

And yet, of all the characters and incidents of those years in Malta, perhaps the most poignant happening occurred on 21 April, 1944. The Sicilian and Italian invasions were well behind and the Allies were advancing slowly north. HSL 128 had been ordered to take up station on the island of Pantellaria, a tiny garrison, which, in 1942, had served the enemy as an isolated strongpoint in the narrow waters between Tunisia and Sicily 170 miles or so from Malta. It was a remote thorn in the side of the Allies along the route between Gibraltar and Malta.

While there, the HSL crew visited the bombed town and the local cemetery. In a corner of the hallowed ground, among all the Italian graves, were five simple wooden crosses on each of which was carved the date – 12 June, 1942 – and a very English name. The date was significant because it was then that the famous 'June convoy' – or what remained of it – was fighting its desperate way through the Pantellarian channel on the last lap of the run to Malta from Gib.

A local lad, whom we had taken along as an interpreter, told us that these were the graves of a small detachment of Allied troops who had landed on the little island from a submarine a day or so before the passage of the convoy and had then made the rounds of military installations blowing up and sabotaging equipment and impedimenta and causing as much havoc as possible, the aim being to disrupt any further attempt by the enemy to impede the progress of the stricken ships.

All had perished, for there was little hope of escape. The sight of those crosses made a lasting impression; here was a handful of brave commandos who, unknown and unpublicised, had given their lives in the relief of Malta. I have often wondered whether those heroes are still lying there, separated from their countrymen, in a 'corner of a foreign field that is for ever England'.

L. G. Head,
Stokenchurch,
Buckinghamshire

Gianni Caracciolo
FIGHTING PRINCE

Lieutenant Francesco Cavalera (Generale Francesco Cavalera), a former cadet of the Accademia Aeronautica, was an enthusiastic 22-year-old fighter pilot serving with the Italian Air Force at Gela, in southern Sicily, when, in the summer of 1942, the Axis powers were pounding Malta in an attempt to ditch the 'unsinkable' Mediterranean island.

It was a trying start to a military career which, in the next 36 years, would take him, uniquely, to the summit of his country's armed forces, to the office of the Chief of the Italian Defence Staff – the first airman to occupy the post. Cavalera had already reached the top of the Air Force through a succession of operational commands and staff appointments in war and in peace.

In 1942, at the time of which he is here writing, he was a modest young squadron pilot concerned 'not to put a foot wrong'. But behind it all was a verve and a spirit which, coupled with a noticeable ability to fly aeroplanes, caused his contemporaries to regard him as 'one to watch'. They were right.

I first met Gianni Caracciolo at Gela, the airfield in Sicily where we were then stationed, in the early summer of 1942. He had arrived there with his *gruppo** a little before us. He was wearing summer uniform – shorts and safari jacket – but on his belt there was a large red silk sash with a band hanging from it, just like the traditional Neapolitan folk custom. It gave him and the rest of the squadron pilots who were wearing them a *scugnizzo*† look.

Prince Giovan Battista Caracciolo Carafa, 'Gianni' to his friends, was a rebel and generous with it. With his aristocratic background and unconventional and robust personality, he encouraged others to follow his lead and his ways.

---

* Roughly comparable with a Royal Air Force squadron or a Luftwaffe *staffel*.
† A quick and cunning Neapolitan rascal.

Born in Naples on 9 August, 1910, of an old and noble family, it was said that he was descended from the brave and famous Borbón naval commander Francesco Caracciolo, who distinguished himself first by supporting the British fleet against the French and then, disgusted by the flight of King Ferdinand to Sicily, by supporting the Republic of Naples. However, when the French left and the Republic fell, and Naples was then reoccupied by Borbón troops and the British fleet, Francesco Caracciolo was arrested on the orders of Admiral Horatio Nelson, who was not prepared to accept the Treaty of Capitulation. Nelson then ordered Caracciolo to be hanged on the frigate *Minerva*, of which he had once been the commander.

Perhaps because of his ancestry and military background or his adventurous spirit, Gianni Caracciolo entered the Naval Academy at Livorno at the age of 18. However, following the death of his father, Francesco, he was forced to resign in his second year at the express wish of his mother as he was the eldest son. He was not then obliged to complete his period of military service.

But the spirit of adventure was not quelled and he opted to attend a flying school, and there he obtained a first-class civilian pilot's licence. He followed this by qualifying, at the age of 24, for an international licence. Flying now obsessed him; it was a passion that he was never to lose. With his pilot's qualifications he was able to join the Regia Aeronautica as a *sottotenente** and qualify for a military pilot's licence.

Remaining in the Service, he was then posted to the 4th *Stormo Caccia Terrestre*† where he completed his training and qualified to fly operational aircraft. When the Spanish Civil War broke out and the Italian government decided to send volunteers to support General Franco's forces, Gianni, who had always been attracted to Spain, at once volunteered for service with the Regia Aeronautica's representatives.

There, on the Iberian Peninsula, he was in his element, spending some fifteen months with his Air Force comrades, winning friends with his engaging ways and making his mark with his exceptional skills as a pilot, claiming victories and being decorated for gallantry with Spanish as well as Italian awards.

Our Gianni's service in the Civil War ended on 9 March, 1938. By then he had been captivated by the graces of a beautiful Spanish girl, the Señorita Amparo Pelaez La Torre, whom he married shortly before returning to Italy. Back at home, he took his discharge from the Service to enable him to administer the family estate. This did not prevent him, however, from pursuing – and satisfying – his passion for flying, and by June 1939

---

* 2nd Lieutenant or Pilot Officer.
† The 4th land-based fighter wing.

he had taken and passed an instrument rating course at the Blind Flying School at Latina.

He was now a well-qualified operational pilot and, with the outbreak of war, he was recalled to the Regia Aeronautica on 7 June, 1940, and posted to the 51st *Stormo** based at Ciampino airfield, near Rome. Transfers between units followed and his enthusiasm was given a fillip when he was sent, first, with the 56th *Stormo* to France and the Channel Front and then, a little later, to Libya with the 155th *Gruppo*.

Gianni Cariccolo remained in the desert for virtually the whole of 1941, the aerial fighting there giving him the chance to exploit and develop all his acknowledged skills. The citation for another award for gallantry spoke of his 'solo interception of a powerful formation of bombers about to attack a naval base'. Dispersing the attack and obtaining repeated strikes on enemy aircraft, he was commended for his action. Although himself wounded, he returned to base and landed safely.

After his spell in Libya, Lieutenant Giovan Battista Caracciolo Carafa was dispatched with his *gruppo*, early in 1942, to the re-formed 51st *Stormo* based at Ciampino. With a period of hard and successful fighting behind him he was now a popular and noted figure not only in the *Stormo*, where he was regarded as being widely experienced, but to a much wider circle beyond. And yet, with his typical Neapolitan manners, he played it all down and accepted things with a philosophical and almost aristocratic calm.

But none of this was lost on the commanders of the 51st *Stormo* and the 155th *Gruppo*, Lieut.-Colonel Aldo Remondino and Major Duilio Fanali, each of whom would, in time, become Chief of Staff of the Italian Air Force. They acknowledged his worth both for the expertise he now showed in the air and for his generosity and example on the ground.

It was with the build-up of the Mediterranean fighting in the spring and summer of 1942, and the sustained attacks on 'fortress Malta', that Caracciolo came into his own, as Francesco Cavalera well recalls from his own part in these operations.

This was Gianni's outstanding time. Malta was now a well-fortified base, its fighter squadrons being equipped with Spitfires flown by experienced pilots from the earlier Battle of Britain and the current fighting over the Western Front. Moreover, they had the advantage of possessing radar to guide their interceptions – a great advantage denied to the Italian Air Force.

On 9, 14 and 15 June, at a time when the Allies were desperately trying to secure the passage of a heavily defended naval convoy through to the island, Gianni's squadron was repeatedly in action against the fighters with

* Equivalent to a Royal Air Force wing or a Luftwaffe *gruppe*.

the Lieutenant himself scoring victories against them . . . But the roll-call
also exposed losses . . .

And so the fighting went on, day after day, week after week, culminating
with the Battle of the mid-August Convoy, when the Regia Aeronautica
launched incessant attacks against the naval ships and merchantmen which
were again trying to fight their way through to the island on the last stage
of the voyage from the west.

> It was during the summer's heavy fighting that Gianni Caracciolo
> had the distinction of being decorated in the field by Il Duce, the
> Italian dictator, for gallantry against the enemy. The ceremony took
> place on the airfield at Sciacca, on the west coast of Sicily, during
> Mussolini's visit to the squadrons.
>
> Although, during this time, Francesco Cavalera was not a member
> of Caracciolo's *gruppo* and therefore did not fly in the Prince's forma-
> tions in the attacks with the bombers on Malta, there came an
> occasion in October 1942 when the two were flying together.

Gianni and I flew up to Capodichino, the airfield near Naples, in two
Macchi Mc202s to arrange for an engine change. Naturally, Gianni was
leading and I was flying as his wingman. For reasons of security, we flew
up the coast at low level and when we had landed at Capodichino it was
my job just to check over the aircraft. To my great surprise, when I got
into his cockpit I discovered that some of the more important navigational
instruments had been covered with photographs of Gianni's wife and son.

To satisfy my curiosity, I asked him why this was. He gave me the
answer rather like a schoolmaster. 'It is a fighter pilot's duty never to look
at his instruments. His head should never be inside the cockpit, but always
outside with his eyes scanning the sky.'

> Caracciolo remained on operations until the end of 1942, either in
> Sicily or Tunisia. But with the Allied landings in North Africa and
> the United States Army Air Force's ever-increasing attacks on Sicilian
> and Italian targets, the Regia Aeronautica was forced back on to the
> defensive in the face of greater and greater odds.

Gianni, promoted now to captain, was actively engaged in these last efforts
of the Italian fighter pilots to contain the growing Allied pressure with,
first, the Sicilian landings and then the invasion of the mainland. When
the armistice came on 8 September, 1943, he was in Sardinia with his
gruppo, flying protection patrols on the instructions of the Italian government against possible German attacks on military installations.

A few days before Christmas, he and his pilots and crews were ordered
to Lecce airfield in Puglia to take part in operations in the Balkans alongside

the Allied squadrons. It was a novel situation for both sides. Desperate to acquit themselves well with such equipment as they had, Gianni's *gruppo* mounted a maximum effort over the next weeks, to be rewarded in the New Year with British Spitfire Vs and US P-39s, which remained in use till the end of the war. The chivalry which, despite the rivalries of war, had existed between the Italian Air Force and the Allies in the air helped the new relationship quickly to be established.

> During these last weeks of war, Gianni was obliged now and then to return to Naples to attend to the family estate. On one of these visits there was an incident which revealed the aristocrat's ability to read the human mind and understand it. Cavalera remembers the circumstances.

Gianni was one of the few people in Naples to own a car. One morning, as he left his mansion at Riviera di Chiaia, he found his car was missing. It had obviously been stolen.

He immediately summoned the *guappo*,* reprimanded him in rough Neapolitan tones and demanded to know what kind of a — — he was to allow a car belonging to Prince Caracciolo to be stolen from 'his' district.

The unfortunate *guappo* tried to calm him. 'Sir,' he said, pleadingly, 'it is early and I think you are still sleepy. Perhaps you had a late night, and do not see so well this morning. Maybe you could now complete your sleep . . .'

Gianni understood and went away. Three hours later he returned. There, outside the front door of the mansion, stood the car, washed, polished and refuelled!

> Three decades and more later, this brave and attractive character was flying home from Switzerland in a light aeroplane. He was alone. Storms had been raging in northern Italy. Francesco Cavalera picks up the tragic story.

I was visiting a friend and I received an anxious telephone call from my personal staff officer. The Air Staff had been informed that Gianni Caracciolo had not reached his destination and must be considered missing. The Search and Rescue Service of the Italian Air Force was immediately alerted. Searches were continued for a month in collaboration with the Swiss Rescue Service, but no trace was found of the aircraft or the pilot.

Months passed and still there was no news. Then, the following spring,

---

* Local protection racketeer who, by means of physical force and intimidation, held sway in his domain. Paradoxically, he could also be generous!

a mushroom picker, looking for mushrooms on a densely covered hillside, came by chance upon the remains of a light aircraft and of Prince Giovan Battista Caraccolio Carafa . . .

Gianni had died the way he had lived – always ready to chance his arm.

Francesco Cavalera,
Roma,
Italy

Flight Lieutenant Moss
BRUSH WITH THE MO

A character could become memorable for an unlikely reason. For Clive Caldwell (Group Captain C. R. Caldwell), Australia's and the Allies' ace of the Desert Air Force in 1941 and 1942, there was an experience which produced a figure who has never since been forgotten.

Caldwell had recently taken over command of the Royal Air Force's 112 Squadron, equipped with Kittyhawks and based then at Gambut, midway between Bardia and Tobruk, in Cyrenaica. Already he was heading the Allies' top-scoring league and well on his way to an unmatched Desert total of 20½ enemy aircraft destroyed, a tally he was to increase to 28½ by the time his service in the Pacific had ended.

But strange things could happen even to the best of them.

One way and another I've been involved in a number of crashed aircraft both by day and by night. They have arisen from various causes resulting in some 50 per cent damage to total write-offs. One which did result in a total write-off I always recall with some amusement.

Early in 1942, Flight Lieutenant Moss, our new Medical Officer, had just joined 112 Squadron. He had never even been in an aircraft, much less been airborne in one. He felt badly, he said, about it. Soon, a long-awaited Miles Magister, a little trainer used as a communications aircraft, arrived for the Wing CO, Group Captain 'Bing' Cross, later Air Chief Marshal Sir Kenneth Cross.

Moss noted the aircraft's arrival and pressed me to explain his situation to the Group Captain and, if possible, obtain permission to give him a short local flight.

Sitting on our parachutes, the MO in the front seat and I in the back, and both sticking well up above the fuselage, off we went. To save time climbing for height, I foolishly flew out over the rim of the deep escarpment, thus gaining a free 600 feet. A couple of gentle stall turns went well with the passenger signalling for something more exciting.

92

I thought a little negative pressure* would be a mild start. The engine stopped immediately. Try as I might – and some of it was pretty severe for the MO, but he appeared to enjoy it – nothing had any effect. The country to which we were now committed for landing was terrible – very rough and thickly strewn with huge boulders and very large blocks of broken stone. The prop was windmilling, but of course no engine noise. I called to my passenger to hold off with both hands against the crash pad, and demonstrated it for him.

For some reason he chose to hang on to the sides of the seat instead, but I had no time to go further into that: I was able to wipe off the undercart by side-slipping into a great rock. Still under control, we then plunged into a narrow gap between other large rocks, taking both wings off. The aircraft slewed and hit a big boulder at a sharp angle, causing the loss of prop and entire engine. We then hit a small rubble area very hard, shedding the whole tail assembly, with just the bare fuselage coming to rest with my passenger out cold.

I woke the MO up and explained that this was as far as we were now going by air. Why, I asked, hadn't he held away from the crash pad as he'd been told? 'Well,' he said, 'I thought you were going to do a trick.' I asked him what more of a trick he wanted than what had just occurred – and with no expense spared, so to speak.

I told him he was well aware the engine was stopped, and as he could see the terrible landing zone, he must be a clot. Not at all, he said. The engine, on the contrary, was going very well as he could plainly see the prop turning; as to the unsuitability of the landing zone, well, yes, it did look pretty rough, but he understood that I was supposed to be a good pilot, so how was he to know that I was going to make such a cock of it as to crash the aeroplane and probably kill us both . . .

A very poor performance indeed in his view . . . If, he said, I was to watch him do an appendectomy would I know any better what was going on than he knew about my flying?

He wasn't comforted on the steep walk home, as we carried our parachutes, when I pointed out that in less than five minutes' total flying time he had now gained more experience than many had in 1000 hours and more.

Group Captain Cross wasn't pleased either . . .

Clive Caldwell,
Strawberry Hills,
New South Wales,
Australia

* Negative 'G', achieved by pushing the stick forward, often causing a non-fuel-injection engine to cut instantly – Ed.

Jack Parsonson
HORSEMAN TURNED PILOT

From Dick Clifton's (Major-General R. Clifton) reference in the study which follows to the reverse he suffered in Western Desert on 16 August, 1942, there hangs a rewarding story.

Clifton was shot down that day by the German 'ace' Leutnant Hans-Arnold Stahlschmidt ('Fiffi' to his mates), then third in the Luftwaffe's top-scoring Desert League. The South African recounted the story of his providential escape in the second of these wartime collections.* To it he added a postscript to say that Stahlschmidt was himself shot down three weeks later, on 7 September, by Flight Lieutenant Jack ('Crash') Curry, an able American pilot flying with the Desert Air Force's 601 (County of London) Squadron.

'Fiffi's' Luftwaffe comrades, who had never known what had befallen their star that fateful day, asked the editor whether Curry was still alive and, if so, whether they could be put in touch with him. After weeks of inquiries in the United States by Dick Alexander (see page 174), Curry was eventually tracked down to New Smyrna Beach in Florida, still making – and flying – light aeroplanes after retiring from the US Space Agency.

John Henry Curry was able to give his former opponents chapter and verse on Stahlschmidt's last encounter when the German's tally of victories then stood at 59.

The last time I saw Jack Parsonson (Major J. E. Parsonson, DSO) in the Western Desert was on 16 August, 1942, when he and his close friend, Rosy (Colonel S. F. du Toit, CBE, DFC & bar), flew in my section of 2 Squadron's Kittyhawks on a reconnaissance of the Alamein Line. I got rather badly hurt on that sortie and had to swim some of the way home. As a result, I was not able to witness more of Jack's memorable tour of operations, but I have often since heard him tell of these exciting times.

When Jack and Rosy were posted to 2 Squadron of the South African

---

* *Out of the Blue*, edited by Laddie Lucas, Century Hutchinson, London, 1985.

94

Air Force as supernumerary captains in July 1942, they had both seen action against the Italians in East Africa. Each went on to command a fighter squadron during those hectic months of combat from Alamein to Tunis, Rosy leading 4 Squadron right to the end of the North African campaign with Jack in charge of 5 Squadron until he was shot down just before the finish.

Jack Parsonson was, in fact, shot down three times – first, by the Afrika Korps (light flak), then by the Luftwaffe (a gaggle of Me.109s) and, finally, by the German Kreigsmarine (motor torpedo boat). It was an extraordinary story of escape, recapture and then escape. It was on the third occasion, on 30 April, 1943, that his luck ran out.

Gunfire from the E-boat he was attacking hit his aircraft in the coolant rad. As he was going down, streaming glycol, his calm voice, sounding very matter of fact, came over the R/T. 'Well boys, I've had it!' He ditched in the sea near Zembra Island, paddled ashore in his dinghy, and hid up for two nights and a day.

Confident that if he could reach the mainland in darkness he could then evade the enemy, he set out to paddle the dozen or so miles to the shore. Unfortunately, he was spotted, taken prisoner and this time they made sure he didn't get away. So, while Rosy du Toit survived four operational tours and was, in time, promoted to command 8 Fighter Wing of the SAAF as a full colonel, poor old Jack champed at the bit in Stalag Luft III.

Instead of going straight home to South Africa after his release, he came to Udine, in northern Italy, to see his friend, Rosy, who was still there with the Wing. It was typical of this memorable character. Loyalty to his friends was his highest priority. . .

Jack, like Rosy and me, was a product of the pre-war South African Military College. In those days, cadets were trained in infantry and artillery duties while, at the same time, being taught to fly. Once commissioned, he chose the Field Artillery because it promised the most exciting life. In a Horse Battery of 4.5-inch howitzers, there was ample opportunity for equestrian pursuits, and Jack loved horses almost as much as he loved aeroplanes.

He was handsome and he sat a horse superbly. On his coal black charger, 2nd Lieutenant Parsonson looked magnificent with his immaculate riding breeches and Barathea tunic, highly polished riding boots and Sam Browne belt.

His other great advantage in joining the Artillery was that once a week he could fly any of the Hawker Harts or the beautiful little Hawker Fury, whereas his fellow cadets who had chosen the Air Force found themselves on an instructor's course flying Avro Tutor trainers. However, when war broke out Jack lost no time in transferring to the SAAF.

He always had a tremendous zest for living. 'Isn't it marvellous to be alive,' was a familiar exclamation. Perhaps it was because he loved life and lived it to the full that he was determined to stay alive and would never admit that he was beaten. This comes out so clearly when he describes his escape from the Germans during their retreat from Alamein in his unpublished memoirs. Having been recaptured on his first attempt to escape, and warned that he would be shot out of hand if he tried it again, he leaves the reader in no doubt of the risks.

We sat in the well of the truck with our backs to the engine just behind the cab. The sergeant sat on my right and the sergeant major on my left. The rest of the crew – five or six of them – rested further back. The night was very dark and we were nose-to-tail in the long column.

The sergeant major drew his Luger and told me that if I attempted to escape he would be happy to shoot me. Twice during the long, boring drive I felt him raise the blanket covering the three of us and peer surreptitiously underneath. I pretended to be dozing.

Just before first light I had a curious feeling. I sensed that everyone was fast asleep and that I must get up very slowly, which I did. All that was necessary was to stretch quietly over the sergeant major, put my hand on the side of the truck and vault over it to the ground. The column was moving very slowly so it would be no great feat . . .

That is exactly what he did, and he got away with it, although within moments the alarm was raised and his captors searched for him in vain.

Jack Parsonson's reluctance ever to shoot a line often leaves one wondering just how he really felt when the chips were down. When you ask him about it, he just laughs and passes it off. 'I was terrified, old boy, absolutely petrified. But weren't we all?' And still one is left wondering.

In terms of enemy aircraft destroyed, he more than balanced his account with four confirmed – one of them in Abyssinia – and one shared. But it wasn't his personal score that distinguished him. What did make him stand out were the successes achieved by 5 Squadron and 7 Wing as a whole when he was leading the Kittyhawks into battle.

A momentous day was 22 April, 1943, when he led the Wing in the destruction of 22 enemy transport aircraft which were trying to bring fuel supplies to the beleaguered Afrika Korps. Only three days before, 5 and 2 Squadrons, with Lieut.-Colonel D. H. Loftus leading, and Jack as his No. 2 (the custom when the Wing leader flew with your squadron), had together destroyed 15 Ju.52s and SM.82s.

However, it wasn't even Jack Parsonson's success as a leader that made him such a memorable character. He had so many qualities, but there was one which, I have always thought, set him apart. This was his extraordinary generosity. As long as I have known him, in war and in peace, it has always been fatal to admire any of his possessions because he would promptly insist on giving it to you.

There was a remarkable example of this attribute years after the war when he was growing tobacco very successfully in Rhodesia. He had long since retired from the SAAF and had married a second time. His new wife's first husband, Guy Oliver, had suffered a stroke as a result of a war wound. This left him badly paralysed and quite helpless.

Jack then built a cottage on his farm specially for him to live in and where he could be properly looked after. There, Guy lived happily until he died. It was a noble act of humanity and quite exceptional, and that is why, with all that has gone before, I have selected Jack Parsonson as the most memorable character I came to know in World War II.

Dick Clifton,
Knysna,
Cape Province,
Republic of South Africa

Bert Rademan
COLONEL 'BERT'

No. 3 Wing of the South African Air Force built a reputation for itself in the Western Desert in 1942 which is secured in the records of the air offensive in that historic campaign. The Wing's light bomber squadrons, always pressing their attacks to their aggressive limit, served as a festering thorn in Rommel's side.

Kalfie Martin* (Lieut.-General H. J. Martin) rose to be its head after a successful spell leading the Bostons of 12 Squadron. With the war over, he used the base he had created for himself as an operational commander to build a professional career which took him to the summit, first, of his Service and then of South Africa's Defence Staff. To his South African decorations he added, unusually, the CBE, the DFC and the Belgian Croix Militaire.

Martin subsequently lined up with the late Neil Orpen to produce, among other works, *Eagles Victorious*,† the deeply researched history of the South African Air Force's operations in Italy, the Mediterranean and Europe from 1943 to 1945. All of which may be said to be a far cry from 1937 and his time, as an immensely powerful prop forward, in what many New Zealanders will claim to be the best Springbok rugby side ever to visit their country.

Lieut.-Colonel J. A. 'Bert' Rademan earned his wings in the South African Air Force sometime during 1936, but soon thereafter transferred to South African Airways, where he developed into an outstanding airline pilot. On the outbreak of World War II he volunteered for service in the SAAF, where he gave sterling service as a maritime pilot before being posted to a bomber squadron in East Africa. His good work here earned him a DFC.

24 Squadron, one of two units in the Desert Air Force equipped with Boston aircraft, lost its commanding officer, Lieut.-Colonel J.A. Mossop,

---

* 'Kalfie' is Afrikaans for 'little steer', a nickname which may owe something to the General's massive physique as a young man – Ed.
† *Eagles Victorious*, Purnell, Capetown, 1977.

on 21 March 1942, and, for a short while, was left leaderless. Bert, however, soon arrived and set about solving the technical problems and revitalising the aircrews. His personality had a tremendous impact. His unorthodox methods of command soon endeared him to his subordinates, but his superiors, had they known, would assuredly have taken a less sanguine view.

Dispensing with normal military procedures, he introduced a system of scaled fines for different breaches of discipline, and this soon became known as 'raiding the paybooks'. Uncharacteristically, there were no complaints – which speaks volumes for the regard in which Bert was held – but joy in the squadron knew no bounds when it became necessary to raid the CO's paybook. The crime was not divulged nor the scope of the raid.

Bert had a diffident manner, spoke in a low key and as far as is known never raised his voice in anger. He was a born leader and commanded by example. He set, and achieved, the highest standards of flying, and was scrupulously fair in allocating raids between senior and junior crew members – a policy which was to produce handsome dividends at a later stage before the Alamein battle when the Bostons were called upon to fly at an intensity never achieved before. Needless to say it became the ambition of all pilots to be given a turn at flying as one of the CO's wingmen.

Operationally, 24 Squadron reached its peak during the six-day battle when Rommel attacked the Alam Halfa Ridge feature in the 8th Army's line of defences. On 16 July the thousandth sortie was logged, a climax to the flying which started on 27 May, 1942. The occasion was fittingly celebrated by a grand dinner in the Desert at which Air Vice-Marshal Arthur Coningham was the guest of honour. He suitably lauded Bert on the fine achievement of his squadron. The Bostons, quite rightly, felt they had contributed their fair share to the victory at Alam Halfa, but the finest tribute came from Air Vice-Marshal G. G. Dawson, who stated 'that but for the Bostons the 8th Army would have been fighting in Palestine.'

The best tribute to Bert, as a commander, came from one of his navigators, Peter Atkins, who in an obituary written on the occasion of Bert's death, in 1984, said: 'No one who served in 24 Squadron in its halcyon days is ever likely to forget Bert Rademan. He was our ideal of what an operational commander should be. He was an inspired leader who led every tough raid, and frequently substituted his name as leader if the target was expected to be an unusually tough one. Aircrews soon realised that, when he led, a tough target was to be expected.

'He had great charisma and inspired intense loyalty. Although there was much to grouse about in the Desert, there never was a word of criticism of the CO. He was essentially a squadron man and when not flying was either out on the landing ground chatting happily to the hard-working ground crews, or sitting in his favourite canvas chair in the Ops Room, holding court.'

Bert was always impeccably dressed, but occasionally his 'dhobi' let him down and he would then be reduced, literally, to wearing nothing more than his identity discs round his neck and a pair of rubber-soled shoes. Once, during a lull in operations, Bert, thus attired, was lolling back in his chair in the Ops Room when Lord Trenchard, the 'father' of the Royal Air Force, appeared unannounced in the doorway. Without batting an eyelid Bert stood up, extended his hand and said: 'I'm Rademan.' The great man was struck speechless.

When the 8th Army went to ground at El Alamein, the light bombers were ordered to establish their rear headquarters in the Delta, and 24 Squadron found a home at Bilbeis, on the Sweetwater Canal. The biggest misfortune to befall the Squadron during the war occurred here one night when one of Bert's Bostons, returning from a raid, failed to locate Bilbeis. The distraught pilot decided to land at Abu Seuir, the base of 37 RAF Squadron, operating Wellington bombers.

In his confused state, the Boston pilot came in down wind at great speed and crashed into a Wellington on the end of the runway as it was preparing to take off. There was a horrendous explosion, followed by sheets of flame which enveloped three other Wellingtons ready for take off. Eighteen men died.

Bert was quite appalled the next morning when he saw the chaos, and it was with a very heavy heart that he made his way to the RAF squadron commander's Ops tent. He was at a loss to know what to say, but was overwhelmed by the warmth with which the wing commander received him. He was told not to look so dejected and was then lauded for the fine work the Bostons were doing. He returned to his base a humble and sad man.

Bert became 'tour expired' shortly before the Alamein attack commenced, and despite his most strenuous efforts failed to have his tour of duty extended. He returned to maritime operations in the Union, and ended his wartime service commanding 22 Squadron flying Venturas, PV1s, out of Malta on convoy escort duties. When hostilities ceased he returned to SA Airways, finally retiring as one of its most illustrious commanders.

He lost his last sortie against cancer in 1984.

H. J. Martin,
Glenwood Village,
Lynnwood Glen,
Pretoria,
Republic of South Africa

Jan Stam
AIRBORNE WITHOUT TRAINING!

Peter Atkins, the lead navigator of 24 Squadron during much of the Western Desert fighting, has the observant eye of the good reporter. He enjoys the knack of being able to pick out the features of the North African campaign and set them, years later, into a balanced perspective.

One lesson he learnt in the Desert was the extent to which the squadrons' ground crews contributed to the Allies' aerial victories. Indeed, nowhere was this more apparent than in the taxing and highly dangerous conditions of the Mediterranean and North African theatre.

An effective operational squadron is only as good as its ground crews. They keep the aircraft flying. In World War II, the South African Air Force was lucky in that everyone in uniform was a volunteer and, as the Navy had found about two centuries earlier, 'one volunteer is worth three pressed men'.

The drive and enthusiasm of the 'erks' was never better illustrated than in the disastrous battle at Gazala in the Western Desert in June 1942 and the subsequent uncontrolled 'gallop' back to Alamein. During the seven weeks between the opening of that battle and the consolidation of the line at Alamein, 24 Squadron flew over 1000 sorties and her sister squadron, 12, was very little short of that total. As those seven weeks entailed five moves to different airfields, it is certainly no exaggeration to say that all too often the ground crews did, literally, work round the clock.

When the 'balloon' went up at Gazala, 12 and 24 Squadrons were caught with their pants down. Between the Crusader battle and Gazala, while both armies were rebuilding their strengths, the two squadrons each kept one flight at the operational landing ground at El Baheira and the other at the base at El Daba. Changeover was made every two weeks.

Due to our usual and consistent source of 'misinformation' – Army intelligence – the squadrons were in the process of the changeover when all hell broke loose on the ground. 24 Squadron was a bit better off as

101

both its flights of aircraft were at Baheira, but only its 'A' Flight ground crews were there. 12 Squadron had just its one flight forward and, on the first day, this led to its CO, 'Kalfie' Martin, leading all six of the squadron's raids that day. Rightly, he was awarded an immediate DFC for an outstanding performance. 24 did three more raids than that and kept the lead (and a bit more) throughout.

Of course, there should have been a third squadron – the RAF's 223 – available, but a day or so earlier it had been squandered on a pointless unescorted raid and was out of action. So it was not surprising that the remaining two close support squadrons – the Army's mobile artillery, and vital in the war of movement in the Desert – were pushed to the limit. The pressure on the ground crews was enormous and to make matters worse their work was being carried out in the intense heat of an Egyptian summer when the rations were meagre and often uneatable, and there was no more than a quart of water for each man per day.

To perform at their maximum, even our magnificent ground crews had to have the right leaders. In the case of 24, it was the engineer officer, Ben Vorster, and his warrant officer, Jan Stam, who set the example. Ben was a brilliant engineer and had solved the serious 'teething' problems of the Bostons when they first came to the Desert and were using every bit as much oil as petrol! But the real driving force was Jan Stam. He was a large, taciturn man who was never happy if a single Boston was unserviceable. All the ground crews were in awe of him, but respected him because they knew he would never let up on any job until it was completed. During the entire Gazala 'Gallop', Jan Stam had damned little sleep at any time.

Soon after we settled at landing ground 99 – 35 miles east of Alexandria and our home during the whole of the Alamein campaign – there was a delightful incident involving Jan.

At the time our commanding officer was Bert Rademan, perhaps the best and most popular CO the squadron ever had. He was a gregarious man and when on the ground – as seldom as was allowed – he spent his time either listening to the ideas, groans and moans of the aircrews or wandering around chatting to the hard-pressed crews working on the aircraft.

On this occasion Jan was suffering from severe frustration. One of his beloved Bostons simply would not 'come right'. In desperation, he decided on doing a taxiing test to see if he could locate the problem. It was just as well L.G. 99 was a long field, for Jan got a bit too worked up in his test and the aircraft became airborne for about a couple of hundred yards.

When he taxied back he found Colonel Bert awaiting him. Shame-faced, he climbed out of the Boston obviously expecting a monumental 'rocket'. Instead, he was greeted by a beaming CO. 'Good show Jan!' he exclaimed, 'You're the only bloke I know to have gone solo without pilot training.'

The performances of the two Boston squadrons in those critical days

102

did not pass unnoticed. Even Radio Zeezen felt compelled to admit: 'The Bostons saved Egypt, but they will pay for it!'

Peter Atkins,
Parkwood,
Johannesburg,
Republic of South Africa

PART TWO

Maximum Effort
1943-45

By the beginning of the second half of the air war a new breed of characters had emerged. They were the amateur volunteers who had come in at the start and had quickly found that, for survival, professional forms had to be signed. Thereafter, when it was all over they picked up their cards again and returned from whence they had come.

Mostly they were the original trainees from the United States, the Commonwealth, Scandinavia and the UK. (The experienced Europeans had made a special contribution.) They had developed maximum power by mid-term and had kept the pressure going right up to the end.

They were not short of colour – or independence. They brought with them a spirit which could never be quenched, and they left behind a record which was a tribute to those who had given them their start – and to the Service which had the resilience to absorb them.

Collectively, they were unbeatable; selectively, unforgettable.

Fr Kevin
FRANCISCAN PATHWAY

The Royal Air Force can boast a select number of members, or former members, of the Judiciary who served as aircrew in World War II (see pages 35–7, 182–6 and 307–10). Judge Stanley Gill (His Honour S. S. Gill), now retired, can be counted in that eminent circle.

As a 21-year-old bomb aimer with 514 and 7 Squadrons, he flew an exacting tour with Bomber Command's Pathfinder Force and was lucky to survive. The experience, rare to the Bench, taught wisdom, judgement and an acute understanding of the often-hidden qualities of man.

It was our final training posting before going on to our operational squadron. As I entered the Mess at No. 3 Lancaster Finishing School, Feltwell, I thought I saw a squadron leader with a beard. I had never seen one before and doubted whether such a thing existed. I looked again and then I saw the padre's insignia on his lapel. A Franciscan friar.

I have to admit Squadron Leader Harrison, or Fr Kevin, OFM (Cap),* was not literally 'the most memorable character I knew in the Royal Air Force'. Obviously the other six members of my crew fall into that category, for these were the people I lived and flew with for well over a year, and came to know so intimately that even now, 45 years later, I can see and hear them talking exactly as they were all that time ago. But the same must surely apply to every other aircrew member of Bomber Command, and perhaps there is a place for reminiscences of the ordinary unexceptional aircrew without the heroics, for Bomber Command was not a scene for heroics or even overt heroism or gallantry as it is generally thought of. All that was required was unfailing efficiency in our various occupations, and a good deal of luck in escaping accidents due to too many unlit aircraft flying roughly in the same direction at the same time in the dark, and not being in the way of anti-aircraft shells bursting among them.

All this was the same for everyone, and talk about what actually happened

* Order of Friars Minor (Capuchin): the traditional designation of a Franciscan Friar – Ed.

on operations was discouraged. Anyone who started it was soon met with a chorus of 'there I was upside down, nothing on the clock but the maker's name' usually abbreviated to 'there I was — —', and someone would set the electric light swinging, and someone else might say 'Carry on, old boy, I'm a bit of a bullshitter myself'.

Others were memorable too, but not for characteristics which might qualify them for inclusion in a collection of this sort: an amazing repertoire of bawdy songs, an incredible capacity for pints of beer, an astonishing proficiency in going all round the mess without once touching the floor. Everyone's memories are full of such things.

Fr Kevin though was entirely out of the run of Air Force characters and totally different from the run of clerics as one used to get them in those days. He was a complete and normal man; not one who just put on an act of normality. He never pretended anything: and because of this, and also because he was in fact a Franciscan friar, he bestowed on anyone who knew him the kind of confidence that one might guess some of the most perfect chaplains on the Western Front must have given to the men in the trenches at the time when they needed it most – when they were actually in action.

It was not Fr Kevin's fault that he could not be with us in action. He tried hard enough to get on operations, but this was not permitted. Nevertheless what happened was that just at the time when we needed confidence there he was. It had been years since we had first mustered at St John's Wood; years since we had been put out to grass laying sewers in the fields of Ludlow; years since initial training in such recondite subjects as theory of flight and engines, Aldis lamp signalling, astro navigation, clay pigeon shooting and aircraft recognition and it had all seemed a very far cry from bombing operations. There had been a time when we supposed we would never even get our feet off the ground. Even after receiving our wings the further training seemed to stretch out for ever. Advanced Flying Unit, Operational Training Unit, Heavy Bomber Conversion Unit, and then suddenly here we were, Lancaster Finishing School and in only another week or two we would be rumbling in the transport to our squadron: there would be the first battle order with our names on it; the first briefing; the flying meal; the lunatic Dutch courage and chatter in the parachute room; the bumpy journey out to the dispersal point; the take-off. At last. . .

But nevertheless confidence was required: not the confidence that nothing untoward would happen, though it would be nice if it didn't, but simply the self-effacing recognition that it didn't really matter even if it did, that nothing in this world really mattered so long as, even if no one else knew it, one was being for oneself as much a hero as one could. Harold Nicolson, writing identically to both of his sons going off to different situations of danger in the same war, said he did not regret it at all: he envied them the chance he had never had of proving they could be heroes. That was what we wanted, we wanted the confidence to face whatever came along and not make asses of ourselves.

That was where for me Fr Kevin came in. He made all the trivial preoccupations of life seem so petty. He abounded in good humour – he saw the best in everyone. When a young couple going off on a '48' together asked him if he could marry them before they went, or if not, at least say some suitable words over them because they really did intend to be married, he was not shocked but highly delighted and amused. *Sancta simplicitas.* And when, burly and bewhiskered, walking by night in a thick sweater in the East End of London where his friary was, he was mistaken by a young woman for a sailor on shore leave, as occasionally happened, his reply would be, 'I'm sorry love (he was a Yorkshireman) I have to get home to the wife and kids.' It would never have occurred to him to say anything which might embarrass her.

None of this was an affectation. Though he read his philosophy at Oxford I never remember him preaching or moralising about anything. The only maxim or anti-maxim I ever heard him employ was Oscar Wilde's 'The best way to get rid of temptation is to give way to it', not by way of advice but as a simple statement of fact.

No wonder his chaplain's office was such a popular meeting place. Not just because he kept a precious bottle of gin in the cupboard. The smooth efficiency with which this would disappear when a knock came at the door had to be seen. He would instantly say 'come in' and before the door was open it had gone, for not everyone qualified to share the limited supply. 'A pot of tea, miss,' he would say to any of the young WAAFs who came in. I recall Paddy Holloway, daughter of Stanley Holloway, as an especial favourite, and her delight in looking after him, and making the tea. He created such an impression that, even this length of time after, no one I think could forget his idiosyncratic use of the word 'diseased' to describe anything he didn't approve of.

For years after the war in Christmas letters we were still able to discourse happily about those days, and then suddenly in 1968 the letters ceased. I heard later that he had been killed by a hit-and-run driver while out walking one evening in Providence, Rhode Island, where he was then the Provincial of his order. Fr Kevin had come into my life just at a time when I needed him – as no doubt he did into many others'. He went out long before that need ended.

Stanley Gill,
Thirkleby,
Thirsk,
North Yorkshire

109

David Holford
HE DIED SO YOUNG

Johnny Johnston (J. S. Johnston), a Melbourne Scot, began life with the Royal Air Force early – as an apprentice at Halton, aged 15 years and 179 days – and what a start those young lads got! Four years later he was in the Battle of France, a member of the permanent ground staff with 226 Squadron and its Fairey Battles. He was lucky to get away by sea – from Brest on 19 June, 1940 – after the French had collapsed.

Less than two years later, he got the chance to volunteer for aircrew duties and became a flight engineer with Bomber Command's 103 Squadron at Elsham Wolds. But he had to bale out over Galsenkirchen after a collision on 25 June, 1943. He spent the next twenty months as a prisoner of war in Stalag Luft VI, in East Prussia, before escaping.

The skipper of his usual crew was an Australian, but he flew a couple of missions – to Berlin each time – with the subject of the story that follows. In such circumstances, a crew member would get to know the captain as he really was, not as some caricature of the man.

Five years after the war, Johnny Johnston transferred to the Royal Australian Air Force and completed a six-year engagement with his new Service.

At times during the war a Bomber Command squadron suffered high losses and shaken morale. This was the case in No. 103 Squadron, Elsham Wolds, late in 1942. As ever, when things seem bleakest, a leader emerged from the pack; in this case, David Holford.

On first impression he was a typical, neatly dressed RAF aircrew officer, smallish in stature, softly spoken, inconspicuous amongst the more ani-

110

mated, exuberant personalities. On meeting him, though, this first assessment proved wrong. Perhaps his charisma is best caught in Don Charlwood's 'No Moon tonight':

'Of his words I remember very little, but his dark, staring eyes I have never forgotten. I felt that they had looked on the worst and, on looking beyond it, had found serenity.'

As a boy David Holford had walked hand in hand with his uncle, Squadron Leader D'Arcy Greig, one of the RAF team that wrested the Schneider Cup from Italy in 1927. From that day there was never any doubt as to his future.

On 8 June, 1942, he completed his second tour of operations, sixty-three in all, with the final trip to Essen – of all places. He was twenty-one, with awards of the DSO for his leadership in attacks on the *Scharnhorst* and *Gneisnau*, and a DFC and Bar. In June of that year he became Commanding Officer of the newly formed No. 1656 Conversion Unit at Elsham Wolds, and in September married a WAAF intelligence officer from the station.

In those days a tour of duty was variously reckoned as 200 operational hours or thirty sorties. In seeking to regularise this, the Chief of the Air Staff, Sir Charles Portal, called an informal meeting in his rooms, where he sought an opinion from those who best knew the aircrew limit. Representing No. 1 Group was the boyish David Holford. Two months later, on 17 February, 1943, he was promoted, becoming the youngest Wing Commander in Bomber Command. He turned twenty-two four days later.

I flew with him as his flight engineer, thrice on operations and many times as instructor on training flights. The night of 16/17 January, 1943, to Berlin, comes to mind. On operations, he had one idiosyncrasy. After the normal, 'All set, boys? Here we go!' he would sing, 'I've got spurs that jingle, jangle, jingle. As we ride merrily along', until 'Wheels up!' was ordered. I never asked him why. Maybe that was how he saw life at that time. A bunch of cowboys in the sky, riding off to shoot up some German town.

When administration demanded much of his time, he hankered to fly. Once or twice each week he would stick his head into my office with the call, 'Get your helmet, Johnny!' With only the two of us in a Lancaster, ostensibly on a 'test flight', we would take to the skies over the Humber. Alone above the earth, David Holford's commanding officer façade vanished. I soon learned that unlike other pilots who struggled to subdue heavy bombers, an aircraft became part of him from the moment he reached the cockpit. Instead of finding myself flying with a stuffy officer, I discovered in his place a devil-may-care person determined to dissipate frustrations. Most often he would seek out fat cumulus masses and then

111

dive down cloud valleys, banking round their curves as he whooped with sheer élan. Another favourite trick was to practise two-engines-out-on-the-one-side landings on the surfaces of flat, white stratus, checking minimum speeds and reactions. On one occasion, over Mablethorpe, we feathered three engines to see if it was possible to glide back to base. We managed with 3000 feet to spare. Sometimes we flew to Helmswell, where he challenged the Polish fighter boys to come get him if they could, and then demonstrated what was vintage David Holford. I was relegated to the rear turret to give evasion directions. Some days I had the huge red spinner of a Hurricane less than ten feet from where I was seated, with a wild fighter pilot peering through his windscreen and propeller arc at me, making obscene gestures. Away we would go, with an equally happy-go-lucky pilot at the other end, twisting and turning over sugar beet fields.

Green crews from OTUs, the pilots especially, were inspired by David Holford's talks. For before them was living proof that with luck and a degree of skill, survival was possible. He went out of his way to help crews having trouble in reaching operational standards, but no condemnation of them escaped his lips. But some things he would not tolerate: lack of punctuality; crew members who forgot items of gear and thus endangered their comrades; lack of discipline by aircrew personnel which was offensive to ground crews, with whom he had great affinity.

In March 1943 our comradeship ended. I was called to his office, where he informed me I was back to operational duties. As I turned to leave I read the expression in his eyes: 'You lucky b — !' When the war was over, I received a letter from the Elsham Wolds girl he married: 'David felt that at his age he should go back on Ops and not let the others "stick their necks out for him", as he put it. So he pulled a few strings and to his joy was posted to No. 100 Squadron, Waltham, as their commanding officer. In his first operation in that role he was killed. It was the night of the 16/17 December, 1943, and the target was Berlin.'

He had nursed a badly damaged aircraft back to base, but chose to remain airborne until less-experienced crews had landed. On making his approach, the Lancaster clipped a small hill. David Holford was thrown from the cockpit, suffering two broken ankles. He was not found until dawn, after lying in snow, by which time he was dead.

So his leadership ended. Or did it? On 6 April, 1945, partnered by a Canadian warrant officer, I slipped quietly away from Stalag 357. It was a run-like-hell job and not without problems. I was dirty, weary and stank of rotten potatoes when we reached safety. A British soldier handed me a mug of murky tea. To me, at that moment, it was a glass of champagne. As I raised it my first thought was, 'David Holford would have been proud of me!' His memory, plus the inspiration it provoked, must have reminded many aircrew of their pride in Bomber Command.

David Holford lies at rest in the military section of Cambridge cemetery. On his headstone are inscribed the words:

> 'Pass not this stone with sorrow, but with pride,
> And strive to live as nobly as he died.'

J. S. Johnston,
Upper Pakenham,
Victoria,
Australia

Paddy Gingles
ULSTERMAN ON THE FOOTPLATE

When George Riley, the author of the piece which follows, crewed up in 1943 with Paddy Gingles, the subject of the portrayal, it could be said with certainty that each had 'something in common'. And how!

Riley, who finished the war with 56 operations with Bomber Command under his belt, had ditched in the North Sea on 24 September, 1940, after the Whitley in which he was the WOP/AG* had been hit hard by flak over Berlin. The crew of five had all clambered into their dinghy before the bomber sank, but despite being spotted by searching aircraft within two hours, the conditions became so bad that it was four days before the Royal Navy's destroyer *Bedouin* found the dinghy. By then, only Riley was still alive.

Three years later, after spells in hospital and a period of instructing in Training Command, he was back on operations again, this time with the Lancasters of 106 Squadron. One night, while he was on compassionate leave following his father's death, his crew was lost over Leipzig.

Meanwhile John Gingles, an Ulsterman and a pilot, known (inevitably) as Paddy, was going through the fire with 9 Squadron's Wellingtons at Honington. On 7 September, 1941, then aged 19 (Royal Air Force Records made him older – no guesses why), he was the sole survivor from a crash at base after his aircraft had caught a packet over Emden. Plastic surgery and weeks in hospital under Archie McIndoe did nothing to daunt his spirit. A second tour of operations – with 432 (Royal Canadian Air Force) Squadron – took its course.

With 43 trips and two tours behind him, Gingles then volunteered late in 1943 for 617, the Dambuster Squadron, and its special duties role. A dedicated operator with an eye for the 'right type,' he quickly fastened on to George Riley, aged 22, another 617 volunteer, as a crew member. Both by now warrant officers, they found that each had earlier 'enjoyed' a spell at the Royal Air Force's Disciplinary

* Wireless operator/air gunner.

114

Centre at Brighton, known around the squadrons as 'Prune's Purgatory,' a persuasive penitentiary designed to curb the excesses of over-enthusiastic and exuberant aircrew.

It made a nice bond between them.

Paddy Gingles had converted on to Lancasters at Syerston. His farewell, before leaving for 617 at Woodhall Spa, was, to say the least, unusual. A spectacular and highly accomplished 'beat up' of the airfield resulted in his departure being delayed while he worked out his punishment – five consecutive days as duty pilot in the control tower.

However, once released, he was to grace 617 for a considerable period. He had no superior in the Squadron as an operational pilot and captain at a time when 617 could boast many a superb pilot and aircrew. He demanded the same exacting standards from his crew as he himself practised in the air, and yet, once he was away from the very strict discipline of operations, he took on all the engaging characteristics for which he will always be remembered . . . a ready and perceptive wit and an unrestrained sense of fun and humour. Eventually, under protest – and some duress – he reluctantly accepted commissioned rank; but he was never happier than when an invitation to some social event allowed him to return to the Sergeants' Mess.

Sergeant Arthur Rowell, the chief cook in the Mess, had in fact become very friendly with Paddy and often obliged him and his crew with meals and 'feeds' at all hours. To repay these favours, Paddy smuggled Arthur aboard his aircraft in July 1944 for an operation against the Wizernes rocket site. Arthur was living off the station at the time and only told his wife of his escapade after it was over. She was furious and berated Paddy for involving her husband in such an adventure. But Paddy was not at all put out by the criticism, merely permitting himself the comment that not many Sergeant Cooks had the privilege of flying operationally with 617!

The Ulsterman's capers, however, were not all confined to station life. I recall so well a soccer international which was taking place between England and Scotland at Maine Road while Paddy and I were on leave together at my home in Manchester. We had no tickets, but we joined thousands of other optimists outside the ground, hoping that somebody might take pity on a couple of Royal Air Force warrant officers.

Then, suddenly, a squad of ATC* cadets came marching smartly through the crowd, left right, left right, left, to perform programme selling or other similar duty inside the ground. Paddy nudged me. 'Come on,' he said, 'we'll take charge of these boys.'

'Right, now, you fellers,' he called out, 'pick it up, swing the arms and heads back, left right, left right, that's it, show 'em what you're made

* Air Training Corps.

115

of . . .' It worked like a charm. Within moments we were sitting beside the touchline. I could have put my foot out and tripped Stanley Matthews had I dared!

Another time our mutual love of football took us to Blackpool. The return train to Manchester was packed with never a chance of getting on board. Paddy grabbed my arm. 'Let's try the driver.'

With that, we nipped through the crowd and along the platform to the engine. A word from Paddy to the driver and we were both on the footplate as the train pulled out of Blackpool heading for Manchester. Not content with our luck, Paddy soon had the driver giving him some 'dual' on driving the engine. Within minutes, he was in charge, at the same time directing me to take over the fireman's duties.

As the driver took over for the run in to Manchester, he casually observed that we had beaten all records for the stretch between Preston and Bolton. When we reached home, with our faces and uniforms still covered with coal dust, it took a lot of hot water and a pint or two of beer to clean us up internally and externally.

Our last operation together with 617 was in November 1944, when the German battleship *Tirpitz* was sunk in the fiord near Tromso, in northern Norway, up in the Arctic Circle. By then, Paddy had taken his tally of operations to 73 and had added a DFC to his DFM. Many of the aircrew in the Squadron felt that he had deserved a higher award – but he was so proud of what he had won.

A measure of the man and what his friends and comrades had meant to him in 617 came when the Squadron's memorial fund was opened years after the war. He simply asked how many names the memorial would carry. When told, he just multiplied the total by the current cost of a pint of beer – and that became the amount of his donation . . . a beer with each one of his departed friends . . .

Paddy died in January 1988 while on holiday in Spain to the great sadness of many. Four months later, to mark the 45th anniversary of the Squadron's famous Dams raid and the historic fact that it was the Derwent Dam – a dam on Derwent Water in a valley of the Pennines in northern England – where the training had taken place, the Lancaster of the Battle of Britain Flight made a commemorative pass over the site.

The fly-past was watched by thousands of people, including a group from 617's wartime number. As the Lanc passed low over the water, one of them remembered our skipper. 'At that height,' he observed, 'Paddy Gingles would have been on oxygen!'

George Riley,
Southwick,
Sussex

116

Miroslav Vild
FLYING WITH FATE

If anyone has the experience to write about Fate and its effect upon survival, it must surely be Alois Siska, the Czech bomber pilot whose wartime activities with the Royal Air Force would have finished off all but the stoutest heart.

Three times was 'Lois shot down, the third into the North Sea in midwinter. The ditching, and six days in an open dinghy in arctic weather, had left him with but two companions as they were finally blown into captivity on the Dutch coast. Frostbite and gangrene had forced the German surgeons' decision to amputate his legs. A heart attack stopped the operation as he was about to be wheeled to the theatre. Other treatment brought limited recovery.

Three years later, Siska was taken by the Gestapo from Colditz to Prague, there to face trial by court-martial for 'treason and espionage' against the Third Reich. Only liberation by US forces thwarted the inevitable death by firing squad as the hands of the clock moved on inexorably to the final hour.

From the twentieth day of June 1940, when Mirek Vild (Flight Lieutenant Miroslav Vild) set out with me from Bordeaux bound for England in the good ship *Ary Sheffer*, until 1 November, 1944, when Mirek completed his last operational flight as a radio and radar operator, few men can have survived so many potential deaths.

On his very first operation with 311 (Czech) Squadron from East Wretham, in Norfolk, the Bomber Command Wellington in which he was flying crashed soon after take-off, eventually accounting for five killed and three more seriously wounded. Vild's escape (he was literally blown to the ground from the aircraft) was providential. 25 May, 1941, was his lucky day.

After six months in hospital at Ely and another three on light duties, recuperating with the Squadron, he was back on the treadmill. Four months later, in August 1942, after 311 had been transferred to Coastal Command, and to the airfield at Talbenny in south-west Wales, his crew destroyed their first U-boat in the Battle of the Atlantic.

117

Soon afterwards, Vild was obliged to change crews. On their very next trip, his former comrades were shot down on a patrol in the Bay of Biscay. None survived.

Vild then had a strange dream about one of his lost friends. He dreamt that, over a glass of red wine, he asked his departed comrade how he found things and what he thought about life. The message that came back was clear: forget your cares and worries, and have a drink, for all will be well.

Next, Vild was inquiring of his friend what had happened when he was shot down. Was the end very painful? He was anxious to know the answer. But, suddenly, Vild felt a strange sensation in his head; it seemed to become heavy and painful. What was this? he wondered. He wanted to rest and sleep – but he couldn't because someone was now shaking him, telling him he must wake up and get ready for the briefing . . .

Now wide awake, the radio and radar operator found it was raining outside. He didn't at all feel like flying on what would be his 33rd operation. What's more, he noticed that the comrade sitting next to him in the crew-room was looking cast down and glum, whereas normally he was a jolly, spirited and talkative fellow. Vild asked him what was wrong. It turned out that he, too, had just been dreaming and was now apprehensive; dreams, he said, can so often come true. The two remained silent, content to nurse their own thoughts . . .

As the crew were climbing aboard their Wellington, the front air gunner dropped his Thermos flask. It shattered in a dozen fragments on the tarmac. Vild looked down at the broken glass. His face came to life. 'Ah!', he exclaimed, 'broken glass! Broken glass is lucky. We shall be lucky today!'

That day they were patrolling in the Bay of Biscay, searching for U-boats leaving the south-west ports of France for the Atlantic, or returning after days at sea. Suddenly, down below, the crew spotted eight enemy aircraft, one of which was white. They were Ju.88s. Immediately bombs were jettisoned to make the aircraft safer and more manoeuvrable in a fight. The pilot climbed to 3000 feet and headed west, out into the Atlantic, at full bore. Mirek radioed the bad news of the sighting back to base.

Meanwhile the 88s began climbing for their prey with the white aircraft positioning for the initial, frontal attack. But the Wellington pilot held his course steady, meeting the approaching German head-on. As they began to close, the Czech air gunner started blazing away from the front turret. Down went the 88, plunging seawards . . .

How the 311 crew evaded the unequal attacks, none could truly say, but at the end of the engagement, which seemed like an eternity, the score sheet read: 313 Squadron – 3 German aircraft destroyed: the enemy – 0.

Back at base, the crew stepped down thankfully from the aircraft. Once on the ground, Vild sought out the front gunner. 'Are you superstitious?' he asked. 'No,' came the positive, monosyllabic response.

118

Vild brushed the negative aside. 'Have no doubt,' he said, 'the broken glass from your Thermos brought us the luck . . . '

In June 1943 311 were re-equipped with four-engined B-24 Liberators, altogether more formidable aeroplanes for the long Atlantic or northern waters patrols. One day, soon after re-equipment, Vild's crew were detailed for some rocket-firing practice. The skipper told Mirek he wouldn't be needed and could take a rest. Three or four hours later, he returned to the Squadron's dispersal. As he walked into the flight office, the Duty Officer looked up in astonishment. 'Jesus Christ, Vild, you're alive!' he exclaimed. 'We thought you were dead! Your crew have crashed and all were killed. We have reported you as dead like the rest!'

What could it be? Vild felt completely stunned. Was it luck or was it Fate? And why should he be the preferred one?

A year later, at 1400 hours on 24 June, 1944, nearly three weeks after the D-Day landings in Normandy, Vild and his crew were out patrolling the approaches to the English Channel, looking for U-boats seeking their chance to attack Allied shipping. Soon the radar operator was reporting two blips on his screen followed almost at once by visual sightings of two periscopes.

Slipping quickly down from 1500 to 400 feet, the Liberator fired its salvoes of rockets in quick succession, and a seamarker was dropped to secure the spot where the U-boats had dived. Meanwhile the Royal Navy's destroyers *Eskimo* and *Haida* were alerted and guided to the spot. Systematically, they made their searches, dropping depth charges as they went.

Twenty minutes later, the crew of the Liberator, patrolling now at 1000 feet, looked down and saw U-971 surface and surrender. U-boat No. 2 for Vild!

A couple of months later, 311 Squadron were moved to Tain, in Caithness, right up in the extreme north of Scotland, for patrols in northern waters from Iceland across to the North Cape. On 12 October, Vild's crew took off at 1300 for another long haul over the northern North Sea. The weather was atrocious, gale force winds, low clouds, squalls and turbulence. The B-24 was flying at 1500 feet; giant waves were surging and swirling down below.

Suddenly there was a terrible noise in one engine and the revs went 'off the clock'. As the flight engineer was getting to work a second engine failed. With the aircraft no more than 50 feet above the waves, spray was pouring against the windscreen and over the cabin. The captain gave orders for everything to be jettisoned – bombs, rockets, guns, ammunition – anything that could be moved, including the parachutes, to lighten the aircraft. Mirek sent out an SOS and then the pigeons were released with messages secured to their legs.

With the ground speed on two engines being held at little in excess of 90 knots into the gale, and the altitude kept steady at 100 feet, the pilot turned on to a heading of 210° for base. Eschewing the Orkneys as a possible landing opportunity in the dark and at that height, the crew struggled on for the last 100 miles to Tain ... When the wheels touched the runway, Vild had completed his 103rd trip – and still his luck had held.

When the crew flew their 30th operation on 1 November, 1944, their tour was over; for the radio and radar operator it was his 106th mission – and what sorties had this insatiable character endured since we had sailed together from Bordeaux on that sunny June day nearly four and a half years ago, following the French collapse. His Maker had, seemingly, not wanted him to die.

Flight Lieutenant Miroslav Vild was to survive another 37 years after the war's end knowing that, in his service with the Royal Air Force, Fate and Providence – and a little luck – had charmed his decorated way.

Alois Siska,
Zvole u Prahy,
Czechoslovakia

Leon Vuillemain
AN ACE OF THE STORKS

Consider the wartime background of Jean Accart (Général de Corps Aerien J. M. J. Accart), writer, and author of the next story. He had fought with special fortitude in the Battle of France, having been near-fatally wounded on 1 June, 1940, in a successful attack on a formation of German bombers flying up the Rhône Valley, south of Lyons. An enemy bullet had struck him between the eyes, pierced his skull and come to rest too near the brain to risk surgical removal. (It's there to this day.)

He recovered and, despite medical advice and all the obvious risks, elected in 1943 to take up the fight once more against Hitler. He said goodbye to his wife and five children, living then in Savoy, in occupied France, changed his name to Francis Bernard (hoping to safeguard his family) and, as he describes, made his way to the UK, where, at the head of 345 (Free French) Squadron in the Royal Air Force, he saw out the war – in France, in north-west Europe and into Germany itself.

Would you have done it with a wife and five children, and a bullet lodged a hair's breadth away from the brain?

Good question.

When the 'phoney war' began in September 1939, and continued right through the bitterly cold winter in Champagne, Leon Vuillemain, a young non-commissioned officer, was already a well-trained fighter pilot. He was a very good shot and excellent at aerobatics. He had acute eyesight, was very keen and, with a cold, hard streak mixed with an engaging humour, he had just the right temperament. He couldn't wait to engage the Messerschmitts or get at the Dornier which used to penetrate the frontier on its high-altitude, reconnaissance missions.

But our operations were by no means easy. We spent our time patrolling at between 20,000 and 30,000 feet in temperatures which, that winter, were as low as −50°C. We seemed to be covering the whole sky, back and forth. We did not then have radar to warn us of approaching aircraft and enable us to be vectored on to the enemy; nor did we have heated or pressurised cockpits.

We had read in a US magazine that, even with oxygen, standing patrols of this character shouldn't be undertaken in such conditions more than once a month because of the risk of mental and physical fatigue. However, unbeknown to the ground forces (unless they saw the vapour trails), we often flew two sorties a day, each with a pair of aircraft.

Undeterred by the tediousness of waiting, Vuillemain was still eager for the fray as dawn broke on 10 May, 1940, and the first aerial engagements were fought in the Battle of France.

Taking off as the bombs were falling, Vuillemain at once set out on a full-throttle battle climb, clambering up to meet the reconnaissance Dornier 17 with its protective screen of Messerschmitt 110 fighters. As the German aircraft, with their unmistakable black crosses, began a 90° turn to port, high up over our base at Suippes, Vuillemain picked out the enemy target and fastened doggedly onto it. . .

'Keeping close on the tail of the Dornier, he fires burst after burst into the German aircraft. Hit hard and losing height, the enemy goes into a series of violent evasive manoeuvres while the rear gunner spiritedly returns the fire, scoring hits in the engine and on the fuselage of the pursuing Curtiss fighter.

'As the Dornier goes on twisting and turning earthwards, I look down and see Vuillemain's aircraft still clinging like a leech to the prey until eventually the enemy bursts into flames and two parachutes open as the twin-engined aircraft, plunging out of control, crashes near Suippes.

'The Curtiss fighter has paid a price for victory. A heavy oil leak from the engine forces the pilot to land on our side of the lines . . .'

I wrote those words at the time – in 1940 – and quoted them in *Chasseurs du Ciel*.[*] I reproduce them now, 48 years later, because they typify the fighting flair, tenacity and sheer courage which Vuillemain possessed. After an exhausting month of almost continuous combat, his personal score stood at 11 enemy aircraft destroyed, with 5 more probables, a total he took with him with *Groupe* 1/5 'Champagne' to Rabat, in Morocco.

With the experience of the fighting in France behind him, Vuillemain, who had now taken over a flight in SPA 67 Squadron, set an ideal example for the young pilots to follow. Marin La Meslée had succeeded me as CO of the unit, which had for its crest the famous Stork of Guynemer, framed in a triangle carrying the racing colours of the Marquis de Saint Sauveur, who had been SPA 67's first squadron commander in World War I. Under La Meslée, and flying the US-built P-39, which had quickly replaced the old Curtisses, Leon Vuillemain displayed again, in the operations from

---

[*] *Chasseurs du Ciel*, Jean Accart, Arthaud, Grenoble, 1941.

Oran, all the same verve and confidence that we had come to know from the fighting in France. . .

I escaped from France in November 1943, crossing the Pyrenees and, via Spanish prisons, eventually reaching Casablanca. Once there, I found the High Command in North Africa wanted me to form the *Groupe de Chasse* 2/2 'Berry', get it into shape and then take it to Great Britain.

The day after my arrival, I met my old and good friend Marin La Meslée in Rabat. He had come there from Algeria to greet me. During a long night of exchanges and discussion, we reached, not without some difficulty, an amicable accord. Subject only to Vuillemain's agreement, he would let me take this exceptional character into my *Groupe* and come with me to England. There, he would become the pillar around which the new unit would be formed. He would, I knew, be able to take the young and inexperienced pilots under his wing and instil into them all the rudiments of the day-fighting art which he had mastered so thoroughly.

A few days later, on my way to Tafaraoui, where *Groupe* 1/5 were now stationed, I met Vuillemain again. Much matured since I had last seen him, he was ready, he said, to leave his family behind and accompany me to the UK. The prospect of being able to engage in ever-increasing aerial activity as the invasion of Europe approached offered an irresistible appeal.

Thus it was that Leon Vuillemain, then the senior warrant officer of *Groupe* 1/5, came to be the standard bearer of the *Groupe de Chasse* 'Berry' – No. 345 Squadron in the Royal Air Force – until the end of the war.

345 at once adopted the well-known Fonck crest and, with it, all the traditions of the illustrious SPA 103 Squadron with which the great Colonel Fonck, ace of aces, had fought in World War I.

Vuillemain's performance in this critical period was outstanding. Our missions ranged daily over France, Belgium or Holland and, after the invasion of Normandy and with the advance of the land forces through north-west Europe, over Germany. We went through the gamut of offensive and defensive operations – armed reconnaissances, bomber escorts, rocket and dive-bombing attacks, close support for the advancing armies, anti-V weapon sorties and the rest, often in the face of intense anti-aircraft fire.

Vuillemain never put a foot wrong, never faltered. He remained, until the end of the fighting, the same resilient, dynamic, generous leader that I had known first in the hard times of 1940. He just harboured until the end an intense personal sadness over the loss of his best friend, François Morel, one of our aces, who had once claimed 12 victories in eight days.

And so the *Groupe de Chasse* 'Berry' reached Fassberg, a base near Hamburg, now abandoned by the retreating Germans. It had been quite a journey . . .

Colonel Leon Vuillemain died prematurely in 1974. Those who served with him in wartime will remember him as a fervent patriot who did his duty as he saw it and who upheld the best traditions of the air fighting art.

Jean Accart,
Yerres,
France

R. W. Purves
CANADIAN COMRADE

There are one or two unusual features of John Gee's (Squadron Leader J. W. Gee) career in war and in peace.

In Bomber Command, he flew two rough tours of operations (and was twice decorated for them), the first – on Wellingtons – quite early on when radar aids were almost non-existent, and the second – on Lancasters – when the genius of the scientists on both sides had begotten such lethal fruits. Few spaced their tours quite so widely, or savoured the distinction of taking Richard Dimbleby on an offensive mission to Germany while the BBC's *maestro* recorded the experience for millions of listeners sitting, snug and warm, by their firesides at home.

'Hello Radio Newsreel, this is Richard Dimbleby calling you from the cockpit of a Royal Air Force Lancaster approaching the frontier of the German Reich. It is nearly 10 o'clock on a dark and cloudy night. . .' Ugh!

Then, after a lifetime in industry, Gee wrote a book – *Wingspan** – which captured with unexpected clarity those awful bombing years when, in the words of his illustrious C-in-C, 'the danger was at times so great that scarcely one man in three could expect to survive his tour of 30 operations . . . '

I first met Bob Purves (Flight Lieutenant R. W. Purves, DFC RCAF) when he came to 153 Squadron, then based at Scampton, north of Lincoln. I was commanding 'B' Flight at the time. 153 had just been re-formed as a heavy bomber squadron in 1 Group of Bomber Command and was equipped with Lancasters.

After completing his service flying training in Canada, Bob finished the operational end of it in England before being posted on 28 October, 1944, to 12 Squadron at Wickenby, north-east of Lincoln. No sooner had he

---

* *Wingspan – The Recollections of a Bomber Pilot*, SPA Ltd, 1988.

taken part in an attack on Cologne and then engaged in three training flights than he was dispatched to 153.

Our CO, Wing Commander F. S. Powley, also a Canadian, had sent for me towards the end of November and told me Purves and his crew would be coming to me in 'B' Flight. No reason was given for the early posting away from 12 Squadron, but I guessed there must have been some monumental 'black' put up. Anyway, it was clear that the CO expected me to exert the requisite measure of control when the newcomer arrived.

The story I was told was that Bob Purves had flown a Lancaster with a large consignment of whisky on board to some US Army Air Force base and had exchanged the Scotch for a load of Coca-Cola, complete with refrigerated cabinet. This he had loaded into the Lancaster's bomb bay and flown with it back to Wickenby. He had decided off his own bat that the Mess needed a good supply of Coca-Cola!

When Bob turned up in 'B' Flight office I wondered whatever I had collected. My first impression was that here was a wild and noisy young Canadian from the wild west. After a talk with him and the crew I detailed them for a training flight and sent them out to dispersal and to a waiting Lancaster. In no time Bob Purves was back in the office. He was sorry but he had pranged one of the aircraft's tail fins against a starter trolley as he was taxiing out. The aeroplane was now unserviceable.

I exploded and tore such a strip off him that he must have wondered whether he was going to be shot out of 153 Squadron there and then. However, when I had recovered my calm I decided to send him off in another Lancaster and carry on with the training flight.

That decision was probably one of the best I ever made. To be given another chance seemed to have a remarkable effect on Bob. Not only did he start to settle down, but it was also the beginning of a relationship between us that developed into a friendship which was to last for 36 years.

Naturally, after the initial experience, I kept a very close watch on him, but I soon found that provided he kept his natural exuberance under control he was a thoroughly competent pilot and able captain. Although his noisy, extrovert and somewhat irrational behaviour made him perhaps more enemies than it did friends, his enthusiasm for everything he did was compelling.

He was a bundle of restless energy, never still for a moment and going at everything with tremendous gusto; like a bull at a gate, he was always going flat out. He was, moreover, a great leg-puller and after scoring a success his laughter could be heard ringing round the Flight offices and out at dispersal.

I recall, for instance, that Squadron Leader Tom Rippingale, my opposite number commanding 'A' Flight, normally flew in Lancaster 'C' for Charlie. This aircraft had a port inner engine that habitually emitted a trail of black smoke, so much so that, in daylight, it could readily be identified in a bomber stream.

One day, Bob Purves, who had a flair as an artist, organised some trolleys and paint and when Tom next came out to his Lancaster there, to his amazement, painted on the nose was 'CLAPTRAP' and on the port inner, 'SMOKEY JOE.' Tom, a very reserved type, took it well and was genuinely amused. It was some time before he found out who had done it.

Then again I remember Bob making friends with the Senior Medical Officer, Squadron Leader Brown. Sometimes he would go and visit Doc and his wife at their house in Lincoln, where they lived with their young son, David, and have tea. He was an excellent model maker and he showed his skill carving out a model train for the boy from a chunk of wood. (I had this confirmed years later when, in 1986, I became captain of my golf club at Stratford-on-Avon and I happened one evening to have David Brown sitting next to me at a dinner. He told me then that he remembered Bob Purves visiting them in Lincoln and carving that model train for him.)

Bob became a thoroughly reliable member both of my Flight and of the Squadron, flying cast-iron missions to places like Karlsruhe, Essen, Coblenz, Ulm and Gelsenkirchen. In a Flight which contained men from South Africa, New Zealand, Australia, Canada and the UK, he very soon began to display, despite his unpredictable temperament, the Canadian characteristic of rock-solid dependability in the rough times as well as the good.

His real worth to me was demonstrated very well on 4 April, 1945, a month or so before the war's end. He was then, in any case, nearing the end of his tour. He was detailed to take part in a Gardening (code word for mining) operation in the Kattegat. Five Lancasters were dispatched from 153 Squadron, one of them being flown by the CO, Francis Powley, with my crew. The operation had been postponed three times and Francis had confided to me that he had a premonition about it.

Two of the five aircraft from 153 went missing – the CO's with my crew in 'U' Uncle and Flight Lieutenant Arthur Winder's in 'R' Roger. I was so distraught at losing Francis Powley with my crew and one of my Flight Lieutenants with his that I did not know where to turn. I felt I did not want to speak to anyone. Despite having been airborne himself on this hazardous operation for some seven hours, Bob Purves came to my room in the small hours and did his best to console me. He knew how I felt and stayed with me until it was time to report to the Flight offices. It was a dreadful reverse for the Squadron and Bob took it to heart as much as I did. There was depth and compassion in him and all that extrovert bravado hid a shy and feeling person.

If I had been asked what Bob would make of his life after the war I would have said at the time that he would make a superb salesman, but that he would probably kill himself in a car or flying accident.

127

In fact, he built up a very successful insurance broking business of his own in Toronto. Before that he had proved his worth as a salesman, winning a Cessna aeroplane in a Salesman of the Year competition. He lived with his wife, Betty, and their family on a farm at Unionville and had a delightful 'cottage' on Lake Rosseau in the Muskoka region of northern Ontario. There, he had a fleet of antique motor boats and his own float plane, an Aeronca Sedan. And yet Bob had not changed at all. When my wife and I visited him and his wife in 1974 and again in 1976, it was almost as if the intervening years since the war had been telescoped and he was still the same person I had known at Scampton all that time ago.

He was complex, unpredictable, very much his own man and yet intensely loyal, dedicated and determined. Outspoken and impetuous, he did not mind one little bit if he offended anyone. If he had his wide circle of friends, he also had his enemies. . .

One day in the winter of 1980, I got a message to telephone Canada. Betty Purves answered my call. She told me that Bob had been accidentally killed in a shooting accident on his farm. I was shattered. What a way, I thought, to go after all that had gone before . . . But what a character to have known!

John Gee,
Wellesbourne,
Warwick

Mr Vorel
THEY CALLED HIM MISTER

Few can have had such a stretch of aviation experience as Tony Liskutin (Squadron Leader M. A. Liskutin), one of the Royal Air Force's redoubtable Czechs, who fought, first, with a British squadron and then with Czechoslovak units, starting in 1941 and finishing in 1945.

Having learnt to fly in Czechoslovakia pre-war, he followed his fellow Air Force comrades' classic trail to England, slipping away from France in 1940 after the collapse. With three operational tours in his log book, Liskutin was among those of his countrymen who, full of hope, flew back to Prague at the war's end only to have to escape again as the Soviet Union fastened its cruel shackles upon the brave people. There then followed a second productive spell with the Royal Air Force.

This 40-year-old affair with the air, terminating in Zambia in 1979, is told with patriotic fervour in Liskutin's autobiography.* With that kind of record behind him and 12,000 flying hours under his belt, a man is entitled to a final look back . . .

The wild screeching of brakes on the tarmac outside the dispersal huts was followed by the pitiful yelping of an injured dog. Pandemonium, associated with a major accident, hit the tranquillity of this corner of the airfield. The driver, jumping from his undamaged vehicle and cursing the dog, had nearly collided with the parked bowser. His curses were soon drowned by the hostile protests of the pilots and ground crews who had seen the accident. They were concerned only with the fate of the well-loved but injured dog.

The poor animal was picked up tenderly and laid on a tarpaulin to await expert examination. Cries went out: 'Where's Mr Vorel, get Mr Vorel!'

Within moments the 'veterinary surgeon' was kneeling beside the Squadron's beloved pet. He cleaned its wounds and set the broken leg. The dog

---

* *Challenge in the Air – A Spitfire Pilot Remembers*, William Kimber, London 1988.

could not have had better professional treatment. It wasn't too long before it was back to normal again and none the worse for its near-fatal accident.

This was my first introduction to Mr Vorel – at Royal Air Force Station, Ayr, on the west coast of Scotland, in 1941. Here was a mild old man with a weather-beaten face, probably in his late 40s or early 50s. He could have been the father of even the oldest among the Squadron. He was from another generation. But age wasn't the reason why everyone called him so respectfully *Mr* Vorel. He was a master of all trades – physician, magician, expert cook, hairdresser; above all, he was a builder of morale.

When two Spitfires failed to return from a patrol in bad weather, there was great shock in the crew room. The sector controller confirmed the aircraft as missing, with no news from any of the neighbouring airfields. There seemed to be little hope . . . A gloom enveloped the dispersal with the pilots sitting there silently, deep in thought. The reverse was as sudden as it was inexplicable.

Just then, the door swung open and in walked Mr Vorel, his face beaming. 'Gentlemen, please, could I have your attention? I have consulted my crystal ball and all is well. One of the missing pilots is sitting on the beach, the other is further inland!'

The atmosphere in the crew room changed instantly. What an extraordinary thing to say! Some of the pilots felt it out of place, a jest in bad taste. Others smiled, thinking perhaps wishfully that the old man might be right. Certainly the gloom had disappeared. . . .

Mr Vorel was never wrong. He seemed to have some magic ability always to get at the truth and to say the right thing. In this case, the reality was just as he had said. Both pilots returned safely before last light. Mr Vorel's reputation was, of course, greatly enhanced – even if he did admit, much later, that his play-acting had been made up on the spur of the moment just, as he put it, 'to break the awful gloom'.

Among Mr Vorel's many responsibilities was the keeping of the Squadron's clay-pigeon shooting records. He put it to the CO. 'What is the difference between a clay pigeon and a wood pigeon? Surely, for the purpose of my records and this graph, they can be treated the same?'

Meat rations in wartime were meagre and some of the younger airmen complained about them, as one might expect. It was particularly galling for them to see the Squadron's periodical shooting practices, with each pilot loosing off twenty cartridges at these fragile black discs . . . just to satisfy the returns.

Always on the watch to keep up morale, Mr Vorel spotted the solution. The local woods were full of pigeons. The men would welcome the extra meat ration, but would wood pigeons count in the Squadron records as clay pigeons? To forestall any objections, he told the CO that the local farmer would be quite happy for the pilots to get in some practice on his pigeons – and his rabbits, too!

From then on the records included the bags of wood pigeons and rabbits in addition to the required clay pigeon scores. More important, the ground crews enjoyed a regular extra meat supply, imaginatively cooked under Mr Vorel's expert supervision.

Nobody really knew what Mr Vorel did in peacetime or why such an old man had decided to join the Royal Air Force. Some thought he might have been a hotel chef, others that he might have had a connection with show business, perhaps a magician-cum-illusionist! Whatever it was, Mr Vorel never spoke about his life or what had motivated it.

Corporal Otto Vorel only wanted to help the war effort . . . and this, in his own way, he most certainly did!

Tony Liskutin,
Fareham,
Hampshire

Jaroslav Himr
THE 'BLIND' FIGHT AGAINST NAZIISM

If Jaroslav Himr, the subject of the next study, was the first Czech
to command a flight in a Royal Air Force squadron in World War
II, then his compatriot, Jiří Maňák (Squadron Leader J. Maňák),
author of the portrayal, must be granted the accolade of being one
of only two Czechs actually to head up a British squadron.

Maňák's leadership of 198, with its low-attack Typhoons, based at
Manston in the Isle of Thanet in 1943, was marked by a multiplicity
of roles all of which could be relied on to attract the full blast of the
enemy's ground or ship-based defences. The leader was often the
most vulnerable in the face of such opposition.

On 28 August, 1943, the Squadron Commander was hit by flak
while on a train-busting operation in Holland. Forced to ditch in
high seas some miles off the Dutch coast, Maňák joined that small
and fortunate band of pilots who attempted the hazardous exercise
in a Hawker Typhoon – and got away with it. Hours later, a westerly
gale drove him and his dinghy back to the enemy-held shore, and
into captivity.

No. 601 (County of London) Squadron was stationed at Manston, in East
Kent, in the summer of 1941, equipped with Hurricanes. The unit was
engaged with patrols against low-flying attacks by Messerschmitt 109s
operating below radar cover; it was also taking its turn escorting Lysanders
dropping dinghies, under the enemy's nose, for aircrew shot down in the
Channel. It also had other, more aggressive, purposes.

On 10 May, one of our flight commanders, Flight Lieutenant Gregory,
did not return from a 'rhubarb', the code-name for a low-level attack by
a pair of aircraft against defended ground targets in enemy-occupied territory. Three days later, on 13 May, a replacement was posted to us – Flight
Lieutenant Jaroslav Himr, who arrived from 56 Squadron at North Weald.
He thus became the first Czech flight commander of a Royal Air Force
squadron, and may very well have been the first Allied officer to have been
given such an appointment.

Jarda, as we all called him, had been serving with the Czechoslovak Air Force before the war, but with the German occupation of the country and the outbreak of World War II, he made his way, early in 1940, through Slovakia and into the Balkans and thence to France. He was determined to continue his own personal fight against Naziism; but the French had capitulated by the time he got there and so he moved on to England. Because he spoke very good English with an almost perfect accent, he was able quickly to take his place, in September, 1940, in 79 Squadron before moving on to 56 and thence to 601; it was a remarkable performance for so recent an arrival from occupied Europe.

I remember so well, when Jarda and I were together in 601 at Duxford, later on in 1941, we were experimenting with anti-G suits, which were designed to reduce the effect of G and so help to prevent pilots from 'blacking out' in extra-tight turns. We found that we could get up to 12 G in our Hurricanes before 'greying' if not 'blacking out'. However, we were soon limited to 8 G because it was found that, beyond it, we were tearing the fairings on the aircraft and damaging the wing joints, which, hitherto, had been considered to be virtually unbreakable.

In those days, Jarda's experience and mastery over an aeroplane made a deep impression not only upon those in his flight but also upon the whole squadron. His all-round attributes made him an exceptionally memorable character. However, by the end of the year, both of us had been sent off on a rest from operational flying to spend six months as instructors at different OTUs.* I never saw him again.

In June 1942 he was back again on operations, now as the Commanding Officer of 313, the Czech Squadron. Fifteen months later, on 24 September, 1943, after a fine run with the squadron, he was leading the escort for bombers attacking the submarine pens at Brest, on the Brittany peninsula, in south-west France.

Near the target the escort encountered a mixed force of Focke-Wulf 190s and Messerschmitt 110s. When the 110s, covered by the 190s, attempted to attack the bombers, Jarda led his section straight into them, shooting one down at once. In his enthusiasm not to lose such an opportunity for a kill, he obviously forgot the rule he had so often inculcated in others – to clear one's tail before going into the attack. He was himself shot down by a 190 and reported missing. The squadron, which was following, then destroyed five of the Me.110s.

It was a sad ending to an outstanding operational career. Jarda was, by any test, exceptional. His resolution and tenacity, particularly when the going was rough, set him apart. This, allied to his obvious ability as a pilot and sheer competence as a leader, made him a most formidable commander. His friends and subordinates knew him to be very straight and

* Operational training units.

direct, but, at the same time, friendly and helpful, particularly with anyone who had problems. The squadron trusted him to a man.

As regards his last encounter, he took, in my judgement, the right decision in leading his own section straight into the Me.110s, leaving the rest of the squadron to look after the Fw.190s and follow. In this, his first consideration was for the protection of the bombers – not for his own and his section's safety. It would have been consonant with his philosophy.

Maybe Jarda's only fault was his blind determination always to fight Naziism wherever he found it; it probably deflected him from that last, critical look behind.

Jiří Maňák,
Praha,
Czechoslovakia

A. B. Woodhall

CONTROLLING GENIUS

Tony Holland (Flight Lieutenant A. C. W. Holland) saw, from a wide operational experience, the stark contrasts which could exist between the operating conditions in the various theatres early and late in World War II.

On 17 September, 1944, he was flying with 165 Squadron in the Detling Wing from Kent, led by the redoubtable Peter Powell (Wing Commander R. P. R. Powell). The Wing was covering the airborne landings at Arnhem, code-name 'Market Garden', and was part of one of the immense aerial armadas of the war.

As we went into the [designated] corridor towards Eindhoven, the first wave was coming out, and when we, in turn, came out the third wave was on the way in . . . 12,000 plus Allied aircraft . . . eyes skinned for Luftwaffe interference . . . keeping carefully to assigned altitudes in narrowed air space. The leadership had to be precise and obeyed rigidly. Thanks to Peter [Powell] and his fellow wing leaders it was.

On a reinforcing sortie to the dropping zone during the days of foul weather that progressively bedevilled Operation 'Market Garden', several glider tugs turned back half-way across the North Sea. Some of the gliders released their tow after lines had tangled in the turn. Peter Powell unclipped the dinghy pack he was sitting on in his Spitfire and threw it down to the brave struggling in the turbulent waters . . .

By contrast, two and a half years before, in the spring of 1942, Holland had been flying his first operational tour with David Douglas-Hamilton's 603 (City of Edinburgh) Spitfire Squadron in the critical Mediterranean battle to keep Malta alive.

The garrison's defence at times could scarcely muster more than six aircraft to meet the large and frequent incoming raids from Sicily . . .

How, then, were the defenders able to maintain their tenuous hold,

135

and see off the attacking Axis powers in the face of odds which were often 15 or 20 to 1 in favour of the enemy? One answer lay in the ability and brilliance of a single officer controlling the air battle from the underground Operations Room in the island's capital, Valletta – in Tony Holland's (and others') judgement the outstanding fighter controller of the air war.

Holland sets the performance of this Malta genius against the backcloth of the later Arnhem experience.

To be in the company of such vast numbers of our own aircraft at Arnhem was an exhilarating experience after the contrasting and, at times, terrifying loneliness . . . of Malta . . .

Our inspiration [on the island] had stemmed from Group Captain A. B. Woodhall, in charge of fighter operations and the senior controller. His deep, confident voice brought him and his personality into the cockpits [of our Spitfires], for me, a marvellous stimulus to my often-flagging morale.

We knew he could read, almost infallibly, the enemy's intentions as the [radar] plots [of the raids] built up [on the Operations table] in the hectic moments before interception, and how best we could tackle each situation . . .

As Tony Holland describes, Woodhall, from the ground, turned the intense aerial fighting almost into a close-knit family affair for the defenders. His nickname, 'Woody', seemed to fit the ethos.

With so few defending aircraft up at one time, squadron and ground control call signs were largely disregarded until more reinforcements could be flown in from the aircraft carriers during the summer and our numbers began to build up. And so it was to 'Woody', rather than to 'Gondar', the ground station, that we spoke and it was from 'Woody', using our Christian names, that we received our directions.

He seemed to know instinctively how to take the utmost advantage from even the weakest position as results were to prove time after time. Inevitably, against such odds, we suffered losses, but we realised that without Woody's almost uncanny foresight the victory that was eventually wrought from one of the worst air fighting situations might never have been achieved or, at best, taken far longer.

Group Captain Woodhall had the advantage of gaining his own experience as a pilot in France in World War I. To this he had added a thorough knowledge of the changed performance of aircraft and their armament from his controlling at Duxford in the Battle of Britain in 1940 and, when

136

the offensive sweeps began after it, also at Tangmere with the Wing led by Douglas Bader in the spring and summer of 1941.*

He had the complete picture. With his resultant mastery of air fighting tactics he would always come up with the best possible answers to help and guide us. There was a deep, personal relationship between Woody, on the ground, and those of us in the air.

The fact was that the ordinary squadron pilot, quite apart from section, flight and squadron commanders, drew his strength from men such as Woody, controlling a battle, unseen, thousands of feet below, and Peter Powell, leading, by example, in the air.

Each will always remain, for me, a most memorable character.

Tony Holland,
Carlton,
Newmarket,
Suffolk.

---

* Woodhall, then Sector Commander at Tangmere, was controlling the operation on 9 August, 1941, the day Douglas Bader, the Wing Leader, was shot down near St Omer, in northern France. (See Johnnie Johnson on Hugh Dundas, pages 244–9.) It fell to him to break the news to Thelma, Douglas's wife, living nearby. 'I'm afraid I've got bad news for you, Thelma,' he said. 'Douglas did not come back from the morning sortie.' Five days later he telephoned to say her husband was safe and a prisoner – Ed.

Laddie Lucas
NO BALL!

What can a feller do?

He asks Keith Miller (Flight Lieutenant K. R. Miller, 410608, Royal Australian Air Force, night fighter pilot with 169 (Mosquito) Squadron, Royal Air Force, based in 1944 and 1945 at Great Massingham in Norfolk), all-round cricketer *par excellence*, journalist and author, to write 1200 words or so on the World War II character of his choice.

The next thing the editor knows is the arrival of the piece which follows.

Spike it? Return it? No, can't do that to such an old friend. Better just treat it as truly the one 'that ran away with the arm . . . '

'Sergeant Miller!' A booming, raucous voice from the guardroom stopped me in my stride as I walked through the gates of Royal Air Force Station, Ouston, in Northumberland. 'There's an Oxford going to Northolt, only stopping here for a few minutes. You might get a lift.'

Hurriedly, I made off to the airfield's control tower just in time to see the Oxford land. I had a liking for the Airspeed Oxford, having flown the aircraft at South Cerney and its satellite, Bibury, in Gloucestershire.

It was June 1944 and I was off to London to play a one-day cricket match at Lord's for the Royal Australian Air Force against the Royal Air Force. I fancied the thought of flying instead of catching a sardine-packed train for the long, laborious trip to London.

With chocks in place, the Oxford door opened and out stepped a Wing Commander with DSO and DFC ribbons. Nervously, I saluted and asked, 'Could you give a cobber a lift to London, sir?'

'You sound like an Aussie. Sure, Sergeant, jump in. What's your name?'

'Miller, sir.' The Wing Commander struck me as a friendly sort of chap, athletic, with film star good looks.

A WAAF officer and WAAF sergeant were the only other passengers, also heading for London. I sat mid-way back on the left-hand side of the cabin, admiring the countryside. Finally, we reached the outskirts of

London and almost at once seemed to be surrounded by aircraft of all shapes and sizes.

'That's Northolt below,' said the Wing Co, 'but I'm afraid it's going to be a long wait. We're turn 22 to land.'

It was a Friday afternoon and clear that some of the high-ranking officers, and some not so senior, were flying in for a week-end in London. Round and round the circuit we went, waiting our turn.

'Won't be long now, Aussie,' shouted the Wing Commander. 'We're next to land.'

Just as we turned into wind on the final approach I saw a Spitfire suddenly slip under us, just missing our port wing; the next second it was ahead of us, wheels down, and going straight into land. The pilot had pinched our turn!

The Wing Co said nothing and carried on and landed as if nothing had happened. As we taxied in to dispersal we were marshalled alongside the Spitfire. Standing beside this beautiful aircraft was a young RAF sergeant pilot. Poor little bugger, I thought, will he get a bollocking! I knew how close he had been to colliding with the Oxford flown by our highly decorated officer.

Seeing the Wing Co and his gongs certainly unnerved him. Sheepishly he said, 'I'm so sorry, sir, about cutting in on your approach. I had to get down in a hurry, my aircraft was overheating and I had a glycol leak.'

'Well done, Sergeant,' came the immediate rejoinder. 'You were quite right to do it in the circumstances.'

I've always remembered that retort. Relief showed on the Sergeant's face. 'OK, sir, thanks very much.' He saluted, turned and walked away. He had got away with murder.

I turned to thank our pilot for the lift, but he was talking to an Air Vice-Marshal who, I thought, called him by a nickname. Knew the right people, it seemed. He spotted me standing at attention, left the AV-M and moved back to me.

'Sir,' I said, 'I just wanted to thank you for the lift.' 'A pleasure, Aussie, are you now going into London?'

At that moment an RAF flight sergeant was passing. 'Flight, could you possibly arrange transport for this Australian to Ruislip Station? He wants to get into London.' (I'd never heard of Ruislip.)

'Certainly, sir,' he said. A few minutes later I was in a van heading for Ruislip Station.

'Seems a nice enough chap, that Wing Commander,' I said.

'He's a rather famous sportsman in this country,' was the answer. I caught the name and remembered it!

Time went by, the war ended and I returned to Australia. In 1948 I was a member of the Australian cricket team captained by Don Bradman. Browsing through the papers in London one morning, I spotted a familiar name – the name of the Wing Co who had flown me down to London from Ouston that June day four years before.

I made inquiries and found where I could contact him. I sent him a note reminding him of the trip and the Spitfire incident. I asked if he would like to be my guest at the Lord's Test. He declined citing pressure of business as the reason.

Later, I met him again, and in the many years when I was a frequent visitor to London, we met at various sporting and business venues. He had become my hero and lifelong friend. Oh! I almost forgot to tell you his name. He's the editor of this book!

Keith Miller,
Newport Beach,
New South Wales,
Australia.

The entry in my log book was factual –

15 June, 1944. Airspeed Oxford No. 369. Pilot: self. Passengers: Section Officer Allen (WAAF), a Sergeant WAAF *and* Sergeant K. Miller (RAAF). From Acklington to Northolt via Ouston and Kirton-in-Lindsey. Time: 2 hours 30. Sergeant Miller kept up a running conversation with the girls throughout.

140

Sidney Seid
THE 'FRISCO INTRUDER

There are two short things to say of Dave McIntosh by way of introduction.

First, he was a Canadian journalist of international repute and long standing – foreign affairs, defence and politics forming the parish in which he moved with rare distinction for 30-odd years. He could even claim to enjoy honorary membership of the Parliamentary Press Gallery in Ottawa after watching the political scene there for some two decades.

Second, a graduate of Toronto University and born in the province of Quebec, he actually waited 35 years before publishing, in 1980, his *Terror in the Starboard Seat*,* one of the most entertaining pieces of autobiographical writing to come out of World War II. Uniquely, he admitted, as an ex-navigator entitled to wear the DFC, that he was scared almost senseless (or was he?) from start to finish of his operational tour.

Read on and maybe you'll believe him...

He came from California with a trombone in his bag. Not to play, but to fly, which was just as well, because he was a lousy trombone player.

Sidney Platt Seid (he hated his middle name – he said it sounded at least vulgar and probably obscene) was one of the American 'few'. They left the United States, before their own country entered World War II, to join the Royal Air Force or Royal Canadian Air Force. Seid came from San Francisco to Canada to enlist in the RCAF. For his purpose, which was to get into the fighting as soon as possible, he proved too good a pilot: he was kept in Canada for more than a year as an instructor. By the time he reached England for combat flying, he was straining at the leash, which so far had kept him from carrying out his self-appointed role: a Jewish St George with Hitler as the dragon.

---

* *Terror in the Starboard Seat*, General Publishing Co Ltd, Ontario, 1980, and paperback, Paper-Jacks Ltd, Ontario, 1981. Published by John Murray in the UK with the title, *Mosquito Intruder*.

His navigator became *me*, Never-ready the Nervous. ('Ah,' said my late friend, Dave Stockand, years later, 'derring-do and derring-don't.')

We crewed up, not by choice (his or mine), at High Ercall in Shropshire, an operational training unit for Mosquito squadrons. We were headed for 418 Squadron, the only RCAF night intruder outfit. Pilots and navigators didn't know each other, even casually, and crewing was done by a sort of lottery. Sid must have been late for the draw because he ended up with the last available navigator.

We met in the bar for the first time. He was tall, dark and handsome and ogled by women (as the barmaid was doing right then). He had huge hairy hands, all the better for gripping stick and throttles, and drank only Scotch, which meant I was going to have a sober pilot because any Scotch supply in wartime Britain ran out in five minutes.

Sid was also blunt. 'Look,' he told me, 'I've waited a long time to get to a squadron. I got stuck as an instructor for months and months and I don't want to hang around at any goddam OTU for one minute longer than necessary.' Well, that explained why he'd accepted me as navigator. He would have taken a reasonably clever dog, which was closer to the mark than I thought (see below).

Our flying career as a crew started inauspiciously. The first flight lasted only ten minutes because a wing tank fell off. On our first map-reading night exercise, I guided us back to the wrong field. On a day trip, our radiators boiled over on the tarmac. We stripped the tyres. And as a crowning achievement we wrote off a Mosquito completely in a belly landing because I couldn't work the emergency pump properly to lock down the undercarriage.

418 must have been anxious for replacements because High Ercall gave us a passing percentage of 50.000001, I would say. Sid informed me: 'If I re-crew, I'll have to go through this whole goddam course again and the war'll be over before I get into it.' We joined 418 at Holmsley South near Bournemouth on D-Day, June 6, 1944. He had made the war in time.

It didn't take me long to find out just how keen Sid was. He was incensed that for our first trip – called a 'nursery op' – we were assigned a quiet little German airfield just inside the Brittany coast, while another newcomer got a busy field near Paris. Our patrols – called 'flowers', of all things – were two-hour night watches on enemy fields designed to pick off their fighters taking off to engage our bombers or landing afterwards. We carried no radar and our sightings were for our eyes only.

On our third op, we were coming back from the east side of Paris when Sid spotted some lights on a road (we nearly always operated at low level, night and day) and dived at the convoy with all eight cannons and machine-guns (four of each) firing. As we bottomed out, I glanced to starboard and saw the tops of some trees – above us. After that, on the way home from patrol, Sid went after any ground or water transport we could see.

Trains were easiest to spot, especially on moonlit nights. We had orders to shoot them up lengthways in the hope of hitting an ammunition car. We were on our way back one night from Munich, where we'd been suckered by a dummy field and nicked by flak, when Sid stopped a train by blowing up its engine. There was only one passenger coach among the freight cars. Sid went at it broadside and set it afire. We could see passengers jumping out and being hit. We kept going around for more broadside bursts until the ammunition gave out. I had arrived willy-nilly in the middle of a one-man Jewish war against the Germans.

Sid didn't make a thing of being a Jew. Many of his colleagues found out the hard way. There was, I think, a strong streak of anti-Semitism in Canada in those days and Mess or Ops Room talk sometimes got around to the subject of Jews, usually derogatorily. Sid would let such a conversation run on for a while, then drop his bomb: 'I'm a Jew, you know.' Depending on the next words, Sid took out a little notebook and made a tick in it. One column of ticks was for those who said, 'Some of my best friends are Jews,' (about 70 ticks by war's end), and the other for, 'But you're different,' (about 65).

Sid wasn't resented for this score-keeping; indeed, some volunteered to collect ticks. Sid said this wouldn't be fair: the offending remarks had to be made in his hearing. Besides, there were much more important listings in his notebook – and he temptingly flourished pages of addresses and telephone numbers.

Sid's sally one Sunday morning became a favourite squadron story. We all liked the tippling padre, but few attended his services. A chagrined CO one Sunday dragooned some aircrew for a hangar service, and as the trucks pulled away from the mess, Sid emerged and we offered him a lift to the field. 'No thanks,' he called out, 'but you guys go ahead; some of my best friends are Protestants.'

Sid soon acquired a reputation as a train-buster and general shooter-upper, but an even greater asset to the squadron was his story telling. He claimed, for instance, that he blew a Jerry convoy so high that he saw one truck driver bail out. Every trip we made, routine or otherwise, was grist for his self-propelled story machine. He was an entertainer in the Mess and the Ops Room and the flight hut. All the stories were fairly accurate accounts, or mild exaggerations, of Sid's and my failures at pilotage and navigation. Most of these errors were mine, but he didn't spare himself. 418 is the highest-scoring squadron in RCAF history and was chockful of aces. Pilots did not strew their mistakes publicly before their comrades, except for Sid. He talked like no other pilot, I venture to say, in the history of aerial warfare.

Let me try to give a couple of examples.

We had one hell of a time shooting down our first flying bomb, or V-1, at night. First, we couldn't catch up with one, then we screamed by another before we could get a shot. When we finally hit one, we were much too close and the blast took all the paint off the Mosquito. This is how Sid reported to the Ops Room:

'Jaysyz. There we are going down like a stone in a well and my alligator* sitting there with his balls in his mouth he's so scared and I'm fingering the tit to get ready for a burst when we go tearing by as if that goddam thing had stopped to let somebody off. Then my alligator lectures me on tactics.

'Back up we go with my alligator twitching like a dry leaf on the end of a dry twig in a dry wind because he's afraid a Jerry is going to crawl up our ass while we're trying to get up a doodlebug's ass. Well, we spot another, though my alligator pretends he doesn't see it and says we should go home another way, like the three wise men. Down we go again. I don't know how you're supposed to tell how far away you are. I thought we were about three hundred yards away when I fired. Jaysyz, we weren't three yards away. I'm going to wear dark glasses at night after this.'

One night, I unthinkingly mistook smoke for cloud and took us directly over burning Wiesbaden, the RAF's target for that night. This misadventure produced this story for the mess the next day:

'Have you heard the latest about my resident genius? The shit is coming down on Wiesbaden, and the shit is coming up from below. And guess where we are. Smack in the middle, the bombs coming down and the flak coming up. A couple of tourists rubbernecking around. "Why, there's a bit of cloud," says my alligator. And he steers me into the smoke. We damn near smothered to death.'

His descriptions of me in these situations were bang-on. I never thought that he was ridiculing me, though, or himself. He was simply entertaining the squadron, and telling the truth while he was at it. He was Everyman of aircrew, exposing, and perhaps lessening, our terrible fears. I don't maintain that Sid was the only flier who told the truth. But he was the only one I knew of who broadcast it.

On the long over-sea hauls to and from Denmark, Sid would get peeved because, especially in cloud, he had to fly every second while I sat twiddling my thumbs. One night, on our way home from an uneventful patrol near Copenhagen, Sid said suddenly; 'Christ, I put red on black.' This meant he had put the compass on reverse course and that we were flying east instead of west and home.

'We must be over Finland somewhere,' he said.

My knees knocked convulsively. But I looked up at the North Star (thank heaven there was no cloud) on my side, the starboard side, the side it should be on if we were going home.

'Just checking whether you were awake,' he chortled.

* Navigator to you, sir – Ed.

144

But our tour was going by and we hadn't knocked off a single German plane. We hadn't even seen one. Sid began to badger the CO about a daylight ranger. This was the type of operation which had enabled 418 to run up its score. Daylight rangers were deep penetrations at low level – treetop height – into Germany and occupied Europe. Some of our crews had successfully preyed in daylight on remote and unsuspecting fields in the deep south of France, in Czechoslovakia, in southern Germany and Austria, and in Denmark. Success depended a great deal on the quality of Allied intelligence.

Sid persuaded Russ Bannock, the CO, to take us with him on a daylight raid to Vaerlose, near Copenhagen. We actually saw enemy aircraft – on the ground, praise be. Bannock destroyed two and Sid damaged two, cursing himself for poor shooting. Then Sid led a two-Mosquito foray into Norway. We went up fiord and down valley to reach a field behind Oslo. There wasn't a single plane on the field or in the open hangars. We fired at a man fleeing across the tarmac and missed.

Sid was fit to be tied, particularly because he had made a special trip to London to seek out the best available intelligence on enemy airfields. The Oslo field, he had been assured, was packed with planes, wing-tip to wing-tip. After this embarrassment, Sid vowed that we'd go alone next time.

The Allies meantime had reached Belgium and Sid doped out a plan to refuel at a Belgian field so that we could reach Poland. When we reached our Belgian sanctuary, the RAF had moved out and it was deserted. Undaunted, Sid scrounged gas from a US Army engineering unit. What it was doing with aviation gas, it didn't say.

We took off from a flareless runway before dawn, using a Jeep's head-lights to give us the direction and the gas bowser's lights to mark the end of the runway. At first light, we attacked Stargard and Kolberg east of Berlin, destroying eight German planes and damaging five. We stalled just off the deck over Stargard and the stick flew out of Sid's hand, but the plane recovered itself. When we left Kolberg, on the Baltic coast, we ran into a flock of birds and were badly holed.

At the English coast, a patrolling Spitfire pulled alongside to look us over – the bird hits made it appear we were badly shot up – and I signalled to the Spit pilot with my fingers, eight and five.

'Cut it out,' Sid said sharply. 'They were all on the ground, for Christ's sake.'

As usual, Sid had a story for the mess:

'You wouldn't believe the abuse I have to take from my alligator. "What in hell do you think you're flying, a yoyo?" he says to me. Just because we're over on our back, ten feet off the deck, and the stick flies out of my hand. I mean, none of you guys would put up with shit like that from your alligator.

'My alligator says he doesn't want me to touch the stick from now on.

He says I fly a hell of a lot better letting the machinery do all the work. And my boy here can navigate circles around your alligators. If he doesn't take me right over a burning city, he takes me right into a flock of birds. It's not easy to pinpoint a flock of birds and work out an interception course as quickly as my boy did.'

And he'd put on a paternal look of pride. (We were both 23.)

Near the end of our tour (41 trips) we did get a glimpse of a Jerry plane at night in the circuit. We were way out of position, but Sid fired anyway. Moments later, a plane crashed on the runway, exploded and burned. We figured the poor bugger must have panicked when his control tower told him somebody was shooting at him.

Sid's story-telling was not confined to the aircrew; he always filled in our ground crew as soon as we got back. The groundcrew hours were even longer than ours, but at least one of the crew was always at the dispersal to open the Mosquito door when we got home, no matter the hour. Sid had made a point of meeting and learning the names of our ground crew before our first night flying test on the squadron. We shared food parcels and cigarettes from home and drinks in the pub, Sid usually sitting drinkless because there was no Scotch.

Not once in our tour did we have a mechanical failure on our own plane attended by our own crew. We did have such failures when our plane was undergoing major overhaul and we drove somebody else's. On one trip, Sid's pee funnel plugged during use. He didn't ask the ground crew to mop up when we got back, he got some rags and did it himself.

Sid had a spaniel-sized mongrel he called Mozzie or Mostitch and which roamed at will. Sometimes Sid took the dog on night flying tests, but I had to hold the damn thing on my lap most of the time so that, Sid said, it could see the countryside properly. He told the Ops Room that Mostitch's navigational skills compared favourably with those of his regular observer.

Sid could have doubled his pay by switching to the US Air Force while staying with 418. That would have been disloyal, he told me. His only concession to Yankeedom was to wear a Canada-USA flash on his shoulder.

On our second-last trip, we were assigned airfields near Kassel on a particularly miserable November night. We flew through a heavy front and were up and down like a bird in the chimney. We bumped around for two hours on fruitless patrol and flew back through the front. When we got back to base, all the other crews which had been out were still in the Ops Room, which was unusual. The normal thing to do was to report to the intelligence officer, bolt bacon and greasy egg, and scram, to pub, Mess, barracks, or wherever. All the other crews had turned back because the weather was so foul and were waiting in the Ops Room for news of Sid.

In obvious joy, the pilots clapped Sid on the back and offered to stand drinks. They didn't say so, but they had wanted him back. Sid was a bit

146

bewildered by the compliments about his flying, and didn't realize what a rare tribute it was for all the crews to hang around for word on one lone stray. I had to tell him that they liked him. I should have said loved, but was too shy to use such a strong word among men.

Sid volunteered our services, without asking me, for the Pacific war.

'You know I couldn't fly without you,' he said. He had to spoil it with a huge wink.

We never flew together again; we became instructors at separate operational training units in Nova Scotia in January 1945. At the end of the war, I took the train to San Francisco and blew all my savings in ten glorious days with Sid. His mother fawned over me: she knew who had brought him back alive.

When my wife and I went to San Francisco on vacation in 1951, Sid turned over his apartment to us. It was the last time I saw him. We continued to correspond – he signed himself 'your pilot' – but his letters came from places like Sierra Leone and the Caroline Islands in the far western Pacific.

He was working in the Palau Islands in the Carolines when, on 6 December, 1965, he was asked to search for three men missing in a boat. He went up in his own plane that morning and was never seen again. The three men were picked up a week later in good condition.

Sid left his widow, three sons and a daughter, born after he vanished. The search went on for weeks, hundreds of Palauan canoes assisting. The Palauans loved him as much as 418 did.

Dave McIntosh,
Ottawa,
Canada

John Deall
WING COMMANDER TO CORPORAL –
AND BACK

'Jock' Hilton-Barber (Group Captain R. Hilton-Barber) was one of the 'old' Rhodesians who made a notable and lasting contribution to the Royal Air Force at war. In an extensive operational run, he was flying a specially adapted, long-endurance Hurricane II on photographic reconnaissance from Malta at the same time as Adrian Warburton (see pages 372–7) was starting his activities on the island in the early days of the Siege.

'Jock' had already played his idiosyncratic part in one of the most bizarre ferries from the UK to the Middle East in June 1940. One of the Blenheims which was 'navigating' the Hurricanes down through France to the south in zero weather crashed on high ground in the French alps. It had all 'Jock's' kit, including his passport, on board. 'After the war,' he recalls, 'the Maquis found the aircraft – and the passport. They returned the document to the Air Ministry, mystified, asking for details!'

'Jock' Barber was still taking pictures with 540 (PR) Squadron and its Mosquitoes towards the end of the war in Europe, when the unit was sharing the airfield at Coulommiers, west of Paris, with the Americans. It was then that he had his encounter with two specimens of the Luftwaffe's latest jet – the Me.262: quite a change from ferrying a Hurricane I 'blind' in and out of the mountains, four years before . . .

John Deall (Air Commodore John Deall) was born in Umtali, on the border of the 'old' Southern Rhodesia and Mozambique, son of a father who had come out to the country in 1900 to farm – a true pioneer. John's problem on the outbreak of war was to get into the conflict at all. He had begun

his working life as an apprentice electrical fitter with the Salisbury Municipality – a reserved occupation, and they didn't want to let him go.

However, when eventually he was accepted for pilot training with the
Rhodesian Air Training Group, he advanced quickly, becoming, in time,
a flight commander and then commanding officer of the famous 266
(Rhodesia) Squadron, equipped with Typhoons. Between 1942 and early
1945, it was, apart from a rest in the middle, a continuous operational
progression which brought him the DSO and the DFC, to which there
were later added the OBE and AFC.

It was early on Christmas Eve 1944 – a freezing morning – when John
was commanding 266, then operating in a ground attack role with 146
Wing from Antwerp in support of the advancing Allied armies, that he had
one of his most poignant experiences of the war.

He and his trusted No. 2, Flight Sergeant Morgan, flying as a pair, had
been attacking military transport in the front-line area when his aircraft
was hit in the oil and coolant radiators by the enemy's intense and accurate
ack-ack fire. Struggling back behind our lines, John had managed a wheels-
up, forced landing, then was met by a helpful old Dutchman, who at once
offered him his bicycle to ride up the road and make contact with the
Army, two or three miles away.

When he returned, he found quite a crowd of locals gathered round his
aircraft and, to his great distress, a body, covered with a blanket, lying in
front of the starboard wing. A young girl, a doctor's daughter, who spoke
good English, told him of the tragedy. Let John pick up the story.

'Apparently, a young man had got into the cockpit, defying the protests
of my old helper, strapped on my parachute and donned my flying helmet.
He had then started playing around with the switches and controls until
he put a thumb on the firing button, which loosed off two of the four 20
mm cannons, which hadn't been damaged. The old man, who had been
standing in front of the aeroplane, was killed stone dead.

'It was a dreadful affair, but the young girl was wonderful, as was the
crowd, consoling and comforting me, which helped a great deal. A guard
was mounted on the aircraft and I was taken away to the nearest airfield,
where I made my report. I then travelled back to Antwerp by road, cast
down, arriving just before dusk. As I passed through the dispersal area I
was touched to see a new Typhoon standing in my aircraft's usual place
with my initials, JHD, emblazoned on the fuselage.'

On that final tour alone, John Deall flew 116 operational sorties with
146 Wing of 84 Group in the 2nd Tactical Air Force. Some idea of the
devastation wrought by the Wing's five squadrons – 266, 193, 257, 197
and 263 – may be judged by the attack on the Headquarters of the 15th
German Army at Dordrecht.

It was a brilliantly executed affair requiring pinpoint accuracy, as the
HQ was in the middle of a town. Attacks had to be made at an angle of

some 70°. John went in first with 266 and its rocket-firing aircraft followed by the rest of the squadrons with bombs. There was a succinct comment in John's log book. 'Very good results – flak hot.' A postscript was added on 31 October, 1944. 'Report in today: 2 generals, 55 officers and 200 other ranks killed [at Dordrecht].'

Soon after this stunningly successful attack, the Wing was visited by 'Boom' Trenchard – Marshal of the Royal Air Force Lord Trenchard, the 'Father' of the RAF. Again, John recalls the visit vividly.

'During drinks in the Mess, one of the young pilots put on the Marshal's heavily 'scrambled egged' hat in the cloakroom and, grabbing the famous baton, engaged in a good-natured demonstration of supreme authority for the benefit of a few of his friends. Unfortunately, he broke the baton in the process!

'It fell to me to break the news to the Marshal and offer humble apologies. Having once been young and spirited himself, he took it all in quite good heart, but added that he expected the baton to be suitably repaired. It was – with pure silver-wire binding!'

Before the war's end, John Deall was promoted to Wing Commander and became 146 Wing's Operations Officer. It was a fitting finish to a wartime run of remarkable endeavour. On his return to Southern Rhodesia and Salisbury, he found that the City Municipality had named a road after him – Deall Road – just as they had done for Johnny Plagis, the brilliant Rhodesian who had fought through the Malta Battle. 'Yes,' said the former 266 Squadron CO, 'a fine tribute, but they called Johnny's road a *street*!'

After World War II, some of the old Southern Rhodesia Air Force stalwarts, who had survived the fighting, were determined to resurrect the Force. In 1951, John was inducted into the Southern Rhodesian Staff Corps Air Unit – as a corporal! It was the policy that all ex-servicemen who rejoined should start again from scratch.

Gradually, the tiny air force began to grow and, with the acquisition of new aircraft, started operating with the Royal Air Force in Cyprus and Aden, such was its spirit. When he reached 50, the compulsory retiring age, John had been promoted to Assistant Chief of Staff with air rank. But well before that elevated point had been reached, he had had an amusing episode when, with others, he returned to the UK to ferry back to Southern Rhodesia from Britain some Spitfire Mk XXII aeroplanes. He was then an acting warrant officer, having just been promoted from sergeant. During their stay, he and his friends visited the Prospect of Whitby, a famous old pub on the River Thames. He'll never forget it.

'The pub was frequented by servicemen, most of whom were still then in uniform – as we were. I was standing next to a British Army officer.

Glancing from the DSO and DFC ribbons* on my chest and then at the Warrant Officer's coat of arms on my sleeve, he murmured in my ear: "My God, old boy, you must have put up a terrible black!" '

Jock Hilton-Barber,
Alexandra Park,
Harare,
Zimbabwe

* Only awarded to commissioned rank.

Peter Andrew
FANCY KIT!

General Rogers (Lieut.-General R. H. Rogers) was the youngest lieutenant-colonel in the South African Air Force in World War II, serving right through the operational mill both with his home Service and with the Royal Air Force . . . Western Desert in 1942, Sicily and Italy in 1943 to 1945 and then, when the North Koreans invaded South Korea in June 1950, and the United Nations came to the aid of the oppressed defenders, he flew another tour with the multi-national force, this time on P-51 Mustangs.

Small wonder that, with that lot, he picked up a DSO, two British DFCs and an American counterpart. Nor was it any surprise that with that kind of record behind him he should, in the next 30 years, rise to the pinnacle of his own Service.

Bob Rogers inevitably attracted some outstanding characters to his side; from such a galaxy, he picks two – for rather special reasons . . .

While commanding No. 225 Squadron, operating from an airstrip North of Naples in early 1944, a vacancy occurred for a second-in-command. After discussions with 285 Wing Commander and OC 40 Squadron, it was decided that Major Peter Andrew, an experienced operational pilot, should be transferred from 40 Squadron to fill the post.

On the day of his arrival, I arranged to meet him with the Squadron Adjutant and the Flight Commanders.

Major Andrew duly arrived in a Spitfire and taxied to the dispersal area, where the reception committee was drawn up to meet him. He switched off his engine, completed his checks, removed his helmet and climbed out of the cockpit.

I couldn't believe my eyes! I beheld what appeared to be a civilian, dressed in a rather scruffy brown suit and, to add insult to injury, he placed an even more dilapidated pork pie hat on his head. This, he courteously doffed as he advanced towards me with outstretched hand: 'Good morning Sir!' he said, 'glad to be joining your Squadron.'

'Peter Andrew,' I rejoined, 'what the hell do you think you're doing?'

Dammit, I thought, I'd been singing his praises to the chaps in the Squadron and he'd let me down horribly.

The expressions on the faces of the rest of the reception committee varied from incredulity to amusement and the erks who were now attending to his aircraft could make neither head nor tail of what was going on.

Peter stopped in his stride, looking hurt and puzzled and then a smile lit up his face as he answered, 'Oh, you mean my flying kit?'

'Flying kit be damned! Explain yourself,' I growled.

'Well Sir, it's like this: one of these days I'm going to be shot down across the lines and I'm going to have to crash-land in enemy-held territory. I know I'm not going to have much time to make good my escape, so what I intend doing is to jump out of the cockpit and stand looking at the wrecked Spitfire as the Jerries come rushing up. On their arrival, I'll point into the distance and say: "He went that-a-way!" '

Needless to say, the welcoming party exploded into fits of laughter and Major Andrew continued to fly thereafter in his instant escape kit.

He successfully survived the war and never did have the opportunity of putting his theory to a practical test. I often half-wished that he would be shot down, but on condition that I was near enough to watch and listen to what I was sure would be an Oscar-winning performance.

Looking back, another character who stands out in the memory from the war years is Jan Blaauw – Johann Philip Derk Blaauw – who was born and bred in South-West Africa, a vast, sparsely populated, arid yet fascinating land on the west coast of southern Africa. I have no doubt that his formative years in South-West had much to do with the development of his self-reliance and independent spirit.

Ever since I've known him, he has gone his own way, with seldom a glance to left or right; completely self-sufficient and well prepared, both physically and mentally, to meet any eventuality. Tall, dark and handsome, he has broken many hearts in his travels.

Jan joined the South African Air Force in April 1939 and, after being commissioned a year later, spent most of the war years flying operationally. Although he took more chances and dared more than most, he seemed to bear a charmed life. He was quite fearless and confident of his ability to survive.

He started his operational career in East Africa with 40 Tac R Squadron,* one of the first SAAF Squadrons to be committed to operations. After eighteen months in East Africa with 40 and 41 Squadrons, he accompanied 40 Squadron to the Western Desert as a Flight Commander. Shortly thereafter, in September, 1942, at the age of 21, he was given command of 7 Fighter Squadron and thereafter, in turn, he commanded

* Tactical Reconnaissance Squadron.

40 and 203 Squadrons. He also served a spell as Officer Commanding the Tac R OTU† in Palestine. In all, he flew close on 500 combat missions.

After World War II, his next taste of 'operational flying' was in 1949, when he took over command of the SAAF contingent flying in the Berlin Airlift. Flying Dakotas was a change which he took in his stride and, moreover, his fluency in German was of great value both on and off duty.

When the Korean war broke out, Jan decided that he had not yet had enough and volunteered for duty with 2 Squadron. There, he completed over 100 missions on P-51 Mustangs, although the normal, official tour required only 75 missions to be flown. It was in Korea that he set the seal on a brilliant operational record by carrying out a deed of extraordinary heroism in which he literally offered his life to save that of a fellow airman.

On 11 May, 1951, he was flying No. 3 in a formation of four Mustangs on an interdiction mission west of Singye. The leader's aircraft was severely damaged by ground fire and the pilot, Lieutenant V. R. Kruger, was forced to bale out not far from the target. The remaining three members of the flight 'capped' the downed pilot, keeping the enemy from reaching him by strafing. At the same time attempts were made to alert the rescue organisation. (These people were responsible for some amazing rescues in Korea, often in the face of great odds.) Unfortunately, there was some delay before contact was established and assistance requested.

After more than an hour, the expected rescue helicopter had not yet arrived and fuel in all three aircraft had reached a critical state. Jan accordingly instructed the other two pilots to return to base.

He continued to cap the downed pilot until his own aircraft ran out of fuel two hours after the leader had baled out. He crash-landed without serious injury in a paddy field on the side of a mountain (no mean feat in itself) and went to the aid of Lt Kruger, who had sustained second-degree burns and a dislocated shoulder.

A little later, the rescue helicopter arrived with fighter escort and picked up both pilots, returning them safely to base.

During his career in the SAAF, Jan Blaauw's exploits, in war and in peace, were legendary. When he retired at the end of 1975, as OC Strike Command, he left a gap that could not easily be filled. You just don't get many people like Jan; but the legend lives on.

Postscript: Regrettably, Jan Blaauw could not be adequately rewarded for this deed. South Africa had no awards and decorations of its own and, by agreement, had always rewarded deserving cases with British decorations.

Later, however, it was decided to do away with this practice and introduce our own awards. Unfortunately, when 2 Squadron were sent to Korea our awards were not yet ready and arrangements were made with the

† Operational training unit.

United States government to award American decorations. Subsequently, it was found that foreigners were not eligible for the award of their highest decorations.

R. H. Rogers,
Leisure Isle,
Knysna,
Cape Province,
Republic of South Africa

Don Jandrell
TAXI!

Peter Bagshawe was one of those rare Royal Air Force officers and squadron commanders who started life in the British Army – Royal Military College, Sandhurst, and then the 2nd Battalion of the South Wales Borderers. But having transferred to the junior Service in 1941, he certainly made up for lost time.

26 Squadron on Allison-engined Mustangs . . . 175 on Typhoons, both in the UK. . . Then the Desert Air Force in Italy – flight commander of 260 Squadron with its P-51s followed by command of 250 with Kittyhawks during the inexorable northern advance . . . None could deny the merit of the award that was conferred upon him.

Bagshawe lives now in Natal, having spent a lifetime in aviation and the hotel and catering trade. Maybe his experience with 239 Wing in Italy had something to do with his choice of domicile. When he arrived with the Wing in 1944 it was commanded by a South African, Colonel Laurie Wilmot, whose No. 2, Eric Baker, was also South African. Then half the pilots in 260 Squadron were South African – as they were when Bagshawe commanded 250, where his two flight commanders were seconded from the SAAF. It was a measure of the South African Air Force's support of the Allies in the North African, Mediterranean and southern European theatre.

Peter's hobby? Writing books – and newspaper and magazine stories – and securing first-hand witnesses of the air war.

I was fortunate to have operated during World War II under a variety of leaders and commanding officers who flew their way into the history books through brilliant leadership and outstanding courage. An exceptional character I recall from among these unforgettable men is Don Jandrell (Squadron Leader Don Jandrell), a South African from Johannesburg who, like his illustrious countrymen, Malan, Hugo and Pattle, joined the Royal Air Force instead of the South African Air Force. There was a waiting list for aircrew in the SAAF at the start of the war and the RAF was the quickest way into the fight.

Don was the CO of 260 Squadron in 239 Wing of the Desert Air Force when I joined the unit at St Angelo, a few miles south of the smouldering ruins of Cassino and 95 miles from the capital city. It was May 1944, and the battle for Rome was in full swing with the Squadron's pilots flying three sorties a day, hammering the retreating German armour.

I was first introduced to Don in the pilot's Mess pub and I warmed to him on first sight. Here was a handsome, flamboyant character with light brown hair, sincere hazel eyes, a healthy complexion and a huge handlebar moustache which curled at the ends like a couple of Catherine wheels. Now and then he would gently stroke the curls, a satisfying concession to his palpably friendly features. His impressive charisma, engaging smile and firm handshake left me convinced that he would be a man to trust in a jam.

I sensed the Squadron's high morale and spirit at once; it was obvious from all the cheerful and enthusiastic chatter. The pilots were a mixture of South Africans and Anglo-Saxons with a few other nationalities thrown in – the perfect example of how men of different races can work together in harmony in support of a common cause.

Rank was of little importance in these circumstances, but the CO was respected by all as the head of the family. If this allowed a relaxed attitude on the ground, it also made for very strict discipline in the air.

I flew as Don's wingman on most of 260's operations during the battle for Rome. Not only did this let me learn plenty from his aggressive, but responsible, leadership, it also enabled me to witness at first hand his incredible accuracy with bombs and guns. His briefings were direct, clear and concise, and, once in the air, his orders were given in a calm but certain voice which gave confidence to those whom he led.

I shall always remember the day when he led a dive-bombing and strafing attack on a transport bottleneck on the outskirts of Rome. The road was aflame with burning vehicles, the flak was intense and accurate, but Don, fully in command, led and encouraged us as if he was in charge of a Sunday school treat.

When his tour with the Squadron was over, he was posted to the front line as 'Cab Rank' controller. 'Cab Rank' was a system, perfected by the Desert Air Force, as a means of providing instant support for the Army. The control post was well chosen to command a panoramic view over the battlefront and behind it patrolled a flight of aircraft between two given points ready for instant call-up. The controller was in touch by radio telephone both with the Army commander and the flight leader. All three participants carried topocadastral maps which enabled them to pinpoint targets.

Don became an expert controller. On many occasions, I was the flight leader in the 'Taxi Rank' and he never failed to guide me on to a target, whether it be a troop concentration, tank or just a lone gun position. What's more, there was always a touch of humour in his directions.

One morning, when we had just completed a sortie, he called me on the RT. 'Why don't you come and visit me on your day off? You could then see this outfit operating and after that we could down some "high octane" together from the selection of liquor in this villa's cellar.'

Taking him up on his invitation, I spent a few fascinating hours watching Don controlling six successful operations. His observation post was situated in a villa straddling a koppie* which overlooked an active battlefront. But the Germans must have twigged its purpose. We were just enjoying a choice bottle of Italian Chianti when shells started bursting all around us. It was pretty clear that the villa would soon be clobbered.

Don shrugged off the attack with a nonchalant grin. 'Let's down another bottle of vino,' he quipped, grabbing a corkscrew, 'before locating an alternative hideout.'

'Bugger you, mate,' I retorted, 'you can drink on your own.' With that, I scrambled out of the front door, jumped into my Jeep and drove off, with my foot flat down on the accelerator.

So dynamic and fearless a character seemed destined to live on. Yet, sadly, Don died in an unfortunate accident soon after returning home to South Africa. He was one of the unsung heroes of World War II whose leadership was undoubted... and whose service passed without reward...

Peter Bagshawe,
Durban,
Republic of South Africa

* Small hill.

Bertie Mills
A LIGHTER BLACK ROD

There is a small and dwindling, but nonetheless devoted, band of men who, in the wartime Royal Air Force, served on the staff of Group Captain T. N. McEvoy (Air Chief Marshal Sir Theodore McEvoy) in the Day Operations Branch at Headquarters, Fighter Command. Its members will tell you (and expect no contradiction) that their Master was, quite simply, the most accomplished staff officer whom the Service produced in World War II.

Mac's paperwork was a marvel of clarity and construction, the ultimate answer to verbosity, pomposity and convoluted English. His minutes on the files, often written in his own exquisitely formed calligraphic hand, were an amalgam of brevity, levity and devastating common sense. Occasionally, his comments would be returned in the form of verse – as witness the case, recalled by David Scott-Malden,* of a Mr Robinson, a member of a Rescue Squad, who had written in advocating more airfields as the answer to the enemy's current Fw.190 and Me.109 tip-and-run raids on coastal resorts. He and his mates offered to 'run up a few of these 'ere airydromes in no time . . .' The Group Captain's rejoinder on the file was to the point:

> If Robinson's Rescue-men try,
> Our fighters will darken the sky:
> They'll have strips to alight on,
> At Bournemouth and Brighton
> And Ramsgate and Romsey and Rye.

* Wing Commander Ops 1(a) on McEvoy's staff in 1942, with a First in Classics at Cambridge, leader of the North Weald (Norwegian) Wing and, later, Air Vice-Marshal – Ed.

In 1938 a branch in the Air Ministry called FO1, under Wing Commander John Whitworth Jones, dealt with policy for all flying operations. 'Bertie' Mills, a squadron leader, was FO1a and I came in from the Staff College to fill a new post (FO1b) for fighter policy so that Bertie could concentrate on the bombers. The main impression I got was of jolly common sense. Hitler and Mussolini were on the rampage; war could come at any time; we had no modern aircraft or airfields and no money to buy any with. There was a good deal of undisguised gloom about, but the late hours and heavy burdens could never subdue Bertie's humour or make him flap. We sat opposite one another in a small back room in Kingsway. One day a shorthand typist came in to take dictation from me. While I was casting about in my disordered mind how to begin the minute, the typist, to break the embarrassing silence, said: 'Wouldn't it be a lovely day for flying?' Bertie looked sternly at her and said: 'When you've been here longer, Miss Bates, you will know that in the Air Ministry we don't *think* about flying: we write about it.'

But Bertie did a good deal more than write about flying. The days being bung-full of work, Bertie arranged that we should fly at night. He would often go off in a Tiger Moth from Hendon to such places as Finningley, getting back in time to be at his desk next morning. This was all done without radio or any navigational aids other than some recently established 'pundit' beacons. One night, after the black-out had been introduced, and all sign-posts and place-names removed from the face of the country, Bertie was trying to get home to Woking after landing back at Hendon. He became as lost as a German parachutist was intended to be and had the bright idea of popping into a telephone kiosk and asking the operator: 'Where am I?'

In preparing air-raid precautions policy we had to study the effects of decisions taken during World War I and discovered that the blackout then had led to a marked increase in loot and rape. 'That gives you ideas, I suppose,' said Bertie, 'I know what you'd go in for, of course, but I think I'd go for the loot: there's a pair of boots in Randall's window that I've had my eye on for some time'.

About then, Bertie was promoted and, as a wing commander, qualified for a room to himself. In those days a familiar advertisement carried the message: 'There's enough acid in your stomach to burn a hole in the carpet.' One day I was in Bertie's new office and complained that while a pampered wing commander was allowed a carpet, a poor downtrodden squadron leader had to make do with a worn-out bit of lino. 'Don't worry, chum,' Bertie said, 'you'll never get one. They know there's enough acid in your stomach to burn a hole in it.'

Our master (later Air Chief Marshal Sir John Whitworth Jones), another man of unswerving integrity, was a tornado of energy and dynamic initiative with a brain that left us limping yards behind. He not only thought things up but put them into effect. My recollection of project 'Starfish', for instance, is that Whit thought before breakfast of the idea of bonfire decoys, went out with Conky Bill (Director of Works) setting them out by about lunch-time and while the Germans were raining their bombs on them that night, Whit was busy with his next scheme. We sometimes felt we had to pour cold water on some of his ideas and I remember Bertie coming in exhausted after an hour with him and saying: 'Whit always makes me feel the enemy of progress.'

When war did come, Bertie's main aim was to get out and fight in it, despite his being beyond the age generally accepted as suitable for taking up active operations and despite his great value as a staff officer in the CAS's* Department. He got his way early in 1940 and was posted to command No. 115 Squadron on Wellingtons at Marham. From there he took part in raids across the North Sea, many of them to attack the enemy airfield at Stavanger. For his leading part in these operations he was awarded the DFC.

At the end of his operational tour he was inevitably taken back for another spell of staff work: this time at HQ Bomber Command, as DS† at the Staff College and then back to the Air Ministry, but before the war ended he got out again and took part in operations in the Balkans. I took over the post he had left in the Air Ministry and found his staff still with the smiles he had left on their faces.

After the war Bertie was AOC‡ in Malaya and then C-in-C Bomber Command, but the next time I served with him was at Fontainebleau from 1956 to 1959. He was Commander, Allied Air Forces, Central Europe and I went there as his Chief of Staff. With three services of seven nations, differences of opinion were inevitable, but with Bertie and other equally well-chosen commanders, these were settled satisfactorily with a minimum of rancour and no sacrifice of principle.

Our lives were brightened by Bertie's quips. He and Molly lived in a house called the *Hotel Bellune* (occupied in Napoleonic times by Marshal Victor, duc de Bellune). They had a most obedient and well-trained collie, Geoffrey, who was a favourite with us all. For some legal reason it was deemed advisable to put on the front gate a notice saying: '*Chien méchant*'. Bertie said he found Geoffrey reading this notice one day and could never look him in the eye again. Bertie and Molly kept hens and Bertie told me he used to go down before breakfast and talk to them. 'Do they speak French?' I asked. 'Oh yes' said Bertie, 'they say: "*heurrrreuses, heurrrreuses*".'

* Chief of the Air Staff's.
† Directing Staff.
‡ Air Officer Commanding.

One day we were picnicking in the forest and saw a notice prohibiting trespassing '*sous peine de poursuite*'. We meditated over this for a while and Bertie said: 'So you see, chum, if you come here to do the sort of thing *you* do in forests, you want to be sure you're wearing your gym-shoes.'

Under his light-hearted approach to all things was a quite inflexible devotion to principle. This was shown at a memorable exercise-conference at HQ Allied Forces. The Commander-in-Chief, Allied Forces, the late General Valluy, whom we all loved dearly, was (I suppose, naturally) inclined to follow the French custom of being briefed, not by his Service Commanders, but by his 'Cabinet', who did not always consult the people they ought to have consulted. Decisions made as a result of such briefings were sometimes unfortunate. On this occasion, General Valluy, in full session before all formation commanders and staff, announced a decision which Bertie saw would prejudice all future planning. He rose at once and said: 'Sir, I cannot accept that decision.' Whether or not such a thing had ever happened before on the Continent of Europe I don't know, but from the silence that followed Bertie's words I should say not. General Valluy, to whom must go full marks, smiled, took Bertie by the arm and said: 'My friend, let us go and discuss this.' Later, when the conference had reassembled, the General had the moral courage and good sense to give a new decision and I think his stature was not diminished. Bertie's could not have been higher.

Of Bertie's time in Washington I cannot tell at first-hand, but I recall that he reintroduced the Victorian ear-trumpet for use at cocktail parties, not to aid his own hearing but the reverse, as it were, so that he could talk to his neighbour without making himself hoarse, after suffering from the sort of conversation that went: 'I died this morning!' 'Yes, isn't it.'

When I asked Bertie to propose the toast of 'The Bride' at our daughter's wedding, he agreed to do so as it would, he said, give him the opportunity to unmask me publicly. This he did to such effect that guests were heard to murmur that they hadn't realised I was that sort of chap.

Bertie's tour of duty as British Military Representative in Washington was his last before he retired.* He had then served longer than any other air force officer in the world: he had gone to Cranwell when the Royal Air Force was the world's only air force and had out-stayed all his contemporaries.

Of his spell as Black Rod others are more qualified to speak, but the letters I used to get from him, written during debates in the House of Lords, made Hansard seem a colourless production.

Others who knew him – at Cranwell, in No. 12 Squadron, as C-in-C Bomber Command and everywhere else – no doubt treasure equally happy

* He retired as Air Chief Marshal Sir George Mills – Ed.

memories of his courage, humour and originality. This note is just to record some of my memories and to express the delight I had in his guidance and friendship.

Theodore McEvoy,
Bognor Regis,
West Sussex.

George Whitehead
THE HEART OF POLAND

The Whiteheads were the most English Poles, and the most Polish Englishmen under the Sun.

Group Captain Stan Wandzilak

If there was one job which the majority of operational pilots did not want in World War II, it was the clandestine work which came under the broad heading of Special Duties. This involved the depositing and picking up of secret agents in moonlight in some part of the enemy-occupied world or the dropping of them at low level by parachute on some pinpoint target – or some other variation of the theme . . .

If a pilot or a navigator engaged on one of the more conventional operational roles had been asked what he thought of it, ten to one the retort would have been 'they can have it'. 'They' were courageous and utterly dedicated operators from 138 and 161 Squadrons based at Tempsford in Bedfordshire.

Bob Hodges – the embryo Air Chief Marshal Sir Lewis Hodges – a fine St Paul's and Cranwell-educated officer, was such a one. He flew these operations to France in one form or another for some four years and in the process collected a pair of DSOs and two DFCs as well as the *Légion d'honneur* and the *Croix de Guerre* from the French. 'They' would say he was entitled to them – period.

Scaling the heights afterwards of the peacetime Service, Hodges knew the worth of the incredibly brave 'passengers' he carried in those exacting times.

George Whitehead was born in Poland at Marki, some 15 miles east of Warsaw in 1908. Whitehead is an English enough name, but George was a Pole at heart and his early upbringing in Poland made a deep impression on him, and although he spent most of his life outside Poland his roots were firmly there.

His father was a Yorkshireman from Bradford who went out to Poland

164

as a young man to help his uncles, who managed the textile factory of the family firm of Briggs Brothers & Co. The Briggs brothers had originally set up in business in Bradford in the middle of the last century and had become famous in particular for the manufacture of the textile cloth for umbrellas – hence the name of the Briggs umbrella which we know to this day. By the 1890s they had developed a considerable business with Russian merchants and it was this that led to the establishment of a factory in Poland to service the Russian market.

George Whitehead's father, having settled down to work at the Marki factory, married into a Polish family – the Wedel family – a well-known firm of chocolate manufacturers in Warsaw, and it was through his mother that George developed his strong Polish characteristics and love of the country of his birth.

He and his brothers grew up at the Marki factory, the family occupying the manager's house. Then, in the summer of 1914, they all came to England for the holidays. While here World War I broke out and they were unable to return to Poland – in fact, the three eldest boys did not return until 1922. The years of the 1914–18 war were spent at preparatory school in Bournemouth and this was followed by public school at Oundle and then Oxford; but in 1922 the three brothers returned to Poland for the summer holidays at Marki.

The journey to Poland was certainly an exciting and interesting experience for a young man, and George has himself described the first of many such journeys most vividly.

'We went by the boat train via Zeebrugge, and a foreman from Bradford, who was going out to the mill, took us in charge. It was quite a complicated journey, taking nearly 48 hours and involved getting out at the Belgian and German borders and having our passports and luggage checked and then going through the same performance at the Polish frontier at Zbaszyn, where my father met us and accompanied us on the last stage to Warsaw.

'On the train journey through Poland what struck us most was that the countryside was not only flat but empty. There did not seem to be any towns or villages as one saw going through Belgium and Germany. When the train arrived at Warsaw station we were met by a whole host of relations and we went to my grandmother's house for lunch.

'The journey to Marki was by car – a T model Ford – and we went bumping along on the Radzymin road. The state of the roads was awful and the cobble stones a real bone-shaker. When we turned into the gates of the factory the rest of the family were there to welcome us.'

After leaving Oxford, George Whitehead spent a year in France with a French family to perfect his knowledge of the language before returning to Poland to complete his military service with the Polish army. He was obliged to do this as he had a Polish passport, his father not having registered his birth with the British Consul in Warsaw.

165

There then followed a period working in France in the confectionery business, as the Wedel family firm had opened a branch in Paris. From Paris, in 1939, he went to the United States to represent the firm at the New York World's Fair and it was while he was there that Hitler marched into Czechoslovakia and the ring closed in on Poland. Before the exhibition ended, World War II had begun, and once again, as in 1914, George found himself away from his homeland.

To get a passage across the Atlantic in September 1939 was not at all easy. The Americans had stopped their ships sailing to the countries at war, but sailings to neutral countries continued and he managed to get a passage to Genoa as Italy had not yet entered the war. On arrival at Genoa he made for Paris and eventually reached England, where he volunteered for military service.

Large numbers of Polish airmen had escaped from Poland and had come to England from France. There was therefore an urgent need for liaison officers to work with the Polish squadrons and George Whitehead, with his fluent Polish, was appointed adjutant of No. 308, one of the Poles' fighter squadrons. And so there began a close association with the Polish fighter squadrons throughout the Battle of Britain and it was while he was serving with 308 that he met Squadron Leader Tommy Yeo-Thomas, an intelligence officer working with the Poles, who became a close personal friend. Yeo-Thomas had worked in France before the war and spoke fluent French. He had volunteered for Special Duties with French intelligence and, after being given parachute training, was sent to France on a special intelligence mission for General de Gaulle.

At the beginning of 1943, George decided to follow his great friend into the Special Operations Executive (SOE) and volunteer for Special Duties on the Continent. With his knowledge of Polish and French he felt he could be of more use to the war effort working for SOE. Initially, he worked with the Polish section of SOE in London, planning the support of the Polish resistance groups, with air supply mounted from England and Italy.

Then, towards the end of 1943, there was an urgent need for French-speaking officers who would be able to work with Maquis groups close to the Belgian–German border and to co-ordinate their activities. George Whitehead volunteered and, after special training, including parachuting, he was assigned to an SOE mission going into the Ardennes region of Belgium.

The mission was code-named 'Citronnelle' and their task was to make contact with the Maquis groups in the area and to organise them into fighting units, to receive supplies of weapons by parachute and to be ready to give support to the advancing Allied armies following the Normandy landings.

After two false starts, the 'Citronnelle' team parachuted into the

Ardennes in April 1944. There they were greeted by a host of untrained and virtually unarmed and physically exhausted young men who had little or no idea of military discipline, and whose ranks had been penetrated by traitors. The team therefore had a formidable task before them. For the next two months they were continually on the move and were successful in organising the reception of deliveries of arms by parachute, and in instilling some sense of military discipline and training into the scattered Maquis groups and welding them into fighting units.

However, their task was made more difficult because the advance of the Allies from Normandy was taking much longer than originally planned. The 'Citronnelle' mission was consequently subjected to a very damaging German attack in which their leader was captured; there were many casualties besides.* As a result, the mission was eventually forced to withdraw towards the Allied lines.

For his part in the action George Whitehead was awarded the Military Cross, having proved himself, in the words of the citation, 'to be a fearless and capable leader'. He was also awarded the *Croix de Guerre* by the French government.

Because of the war the family business in Poland suffered greatly and George, a squadron leader at the finish, decided to settle in Jersey, where he carried on with his various business interests. Nevertheless, he continued to visit his surviving relatives in Poland as often as he could, visits which he much enjoyed.

In the post-war years he never forgot his wartime colleagues. He was always a regular and loyal supporter of Special Forces reunions in this country, particularly those of the Tempsford Association, and, in France, *Amicale Action de la France Combattante.*

It was after the war that we all got to know him best, a staunch colleague and a quiet, unassuming and lovable man. He died, aged 77, in 1986.

Lewis Hodges,
Plaxtol,
Sevenoaks, Kent

Postscript: Before his death, George Whitehead wrote a private account of his experiences which confirms Sir Lewis Hodge's contention that he was at heart a Pole. In it, Whitehead recalled that he had a cousin who was a writer and wrote under the pen-name of Alexandra Orme. 'In a book called *From Christmas to Easter* she wrote:

---

* A number were shot out of hand. Whitehead's English colleague, although in uniform, was taken by the Germans to Buchenwald and later hanged. Yeo-Thomas, who had been picked up in Paris earlier in 1944, was also sent to Buchenwald, but survived – Ed.

"I am not a Pole by blood, but by sheer frantic habit. Once you start being a Pole it's terribly hard to stop. Try it – hopeless struggle." '

Whitehead's comment is conclusive for those who remember the Poles' spirit in the Royal Air Force in wartime – and latterly. 'I think there is a lot of truth in what my cousin has written. But the question is: "Does this process work quicker in Poland [than with other countries]?" The hold of Poland is not one of materialism, but of the simple, genuine qualities of life. . . If a minimum of independence is given to Poland these qualities [will always be sustained] by her attachment to the things of the Spirit . . .'

Bill Kemp

THE KATZENJAMMER KIDS*

When Ben Drew (Major Urban L. Drew, USAAF (Ret)), a 20-year-old 1st Lieutenant from Detroit, Michigan, took his place in the 375th Squadron of the 361st Fighter Group early in 1944, the US Eighth Air Force's great daylight offensive against precision targets in Nazi Germany was reaching its magnificent peak.

The P-51D Mustangs, of which Drew was then an undoubted exponent, were ranging throughout the length and breadth of the Third Reich. Products of US and British design and manufacturing genius, they helped to turn the air war decisively in the Allies' favour. Drew's destruction of two Me.262s, Germany's newest jet, in one sortie on 7 October, 1944, and confirmed years afterwards by Major Georg Eder, himself a Luftwaffe ace (42 B-17s and 6 B-24s were among his 'bag'), assured the American a place in military history.

The award of the US Air Force Cross, the country's second highest decoration for gallantry, was uniquely bestowed upon Drew thirty-eight years and eight months after the event by Secretary of the Air Force Verne Orr.

One early morning, late in 1943, I was scheduled to take three P-51-commissioned students on a ground gunnery mission to the Gulf of Mexico. I was then based at Bartow, Florida, with the 54th Fighter Group. On the way to my aircraft I was told that my buddy, 1st Lieutenant William T. Kemp, had been confined to quarters according to the disciplines of the 104th Article of War. The reason given was an altercation in a bar the previous night, when Kemp had fractured the jaw of a Captain. I should mention in passing that Bill Kemp had been the Golden Gloves Heavy-

* With due acknowledgements to the originator of the (then) famous US comic strip cartoon.

weight Champion in the United States prior to his military service.

On the way to the gunnery range all three of my students aborted, for one reason or another, and I ended up shooting at the target all by myself. Being at tree-top height I stayed at that level and headed for Bartow. Suddenly, an airfield appeared before me and I was heading directly for a reviewing stand with a whole squadron on parade. I firewalled the throttles in an effort to get across without being identified. Unfortunately this was not to be the case. The formation I had forced to 'hit the deck' was Colonel Cochrane's Commando Air Group on its final parade before proceeding to the China-Burma-India theatre, where it was to become one of our famous groups. On arrival at Bartow, my Commanding Officer was waiting for me in Flight Operations. When I confirmed to him that it was I who had 'inadvertently buzzed' the field at Lakeland, the Colonel told me that according to the disciplines of the 104th Article of War I was confined to quarters until further notice.

Three days later, the Sergeant of the Guard informed Kemp and myself that we were to dress in Class A uniforms and present ourselves to the Commanding Officer within 30 minutes. Colonel Harker, our CO, read the long list of charges against both of us as well as what could happen to us if the charges were pressed. However, the Colonel advised us that in the light of our service as Instructors with the 54th Fighter Group, and the fact that many of our student pilots had gone on to claim fame overseas, he would enter in our personnel records that we had been recommended for punishment, but that he would also issue orders immediately for both of us to be transferred to the European Theatre of Operations.

Once in England, Kemp and I were assigned to the 361st Fighter Group, then stationed at Bottisham, in Cambridgeshire. We reported to Thomas J. J. Christian, the Group Commander, who advised us that due to extremely heavy losses in the 375th Fighter Squadron that very day (they had lost their Squadron Commander, Operations Officer and a Flight Commander), he was assigning both of us to the 375th and, as most of its pilots were our former students, he asked us to assist in raising the morale of the Squadron and giving it some effective leadership. Effective leadership we were indeed to give it, but not necessarily to the liking of everyone!

While I destroyed a Ju.52 on the ground on my first mission, Kemp decided he would not give me any credit for that, even though the Eighth Air Force did! This started what was to be some good-natured and intentional banter between us. Kemp shot down his first Me.109 five days later, but, in reviewing the combat film, I decided not to give him personally any credit for the victory since it appeared much too easy a 'kill' to earn him any points.

At this time I was given command of 'A' Flight in the squadron and received my new P-51D Mustang which I called 'Detroit Miss'. Kemp was given command of 'D' Flight and was allotted a new P-51D which he called 'Betty Lee', after his wife. It was now the summer of 1944 and the US Eighth Bomber Command was escalating its daylight missions to enemy-occupied Europe. Losses were heavy on both sides. Our North American P-51D Mustang now had the range to escort our B-17 and B-24 bombers all the way to the target on their deepest penetration missions into Germany. My first aerial victory, an Me.109, was a piece of cake. I destroyed it from dead astern with the pilot taking no evasive action at all. Kemp reviewed the combat film and said laughingly: 'Drew, not only would I not discuss that victory if I were you, I would throw the film away and forget it. In my book you get no credit for that one.'

About that time, the Squadron Commander of the 375th, Major Roswell Freedman, when talking to British and American newspapermen, said that if the Squadron wanted to engage the Luftwaffe on a mission, all it had to do was send the 'Katzenjammer Kids' out ahead and they would sure find the enemy. The Press asked the CO who the Katzenjammer Kids were, and Major Freedman identified them as Kemp and Drew. They were so named, he said, after a then famous comic strip in the US bearing that name. The strip was known for the fact that the kids were always in trouble.

Shortly after the interview, Kemp and I were assigned to the same flight on a mission. I ended up flying Kemp's wing. As it was rather a dull operation, Kemp asked for, and received, permission to go after 'targets of opportunity' – a simple ruse to get us down to the deck to look for trouble. After shooting up all the vehicles we could find in a 30-mile radius, Kemp called out that there were some 50 to 60 'Bogies' dead ahead, down on the deck. We had run into two squadrons of Me.109s taking off from their aerodrome.

Kemp barrelled in and shot down one, immediately forcing a second to force land and fly into a row of trees. He then ran out of ammunition. I pulled up within 20 feet behind a 109 and thought here is a very easy one, but when I pulled the trigger I sadly discovered I, too, was out of ammunition. The rest of the story gets more 'hairy'. It wasn't long before the Germans realised that the three Mustangs flying among them had no ammunition left; the 'dance' then became very exciting.

Kemp led the three Mustangs in some of the finest display flying I have ever witnessed and managed to extricate all three of us safely from the mêlée. We stayed down on the deck and barely had enough fuel to make it to Manston. This episode made the *Yank*, the US service paper in Europe, and served further to publicise the existence of the Katzenjammer Kids.

Three weeks later, I was leading my 'A' Flight and Kemp was leading his 'D' Flight on a difficult strafing mission in northern Germany. Our

171

bombers had attacked an airfield, and immediately after the bombing the entire squadron went into 'line abreast' to strafe any targets we could find remaining. Just after passing over the aerodrome Kemp called out, 'Drew, I'm hit.' In a short radio exchange, Kemp told me that a shell had exploded in the cockpit and that he was bleeding profusely from one arm. I asked if he needed help from other fighters to take him home. 'No,' he said, 'I can make it alone.' It was not guessed at the time (except by me) how heavily he was bleeding. I was terribly worried that he would not make it home.

En route to England, he observed 50 B-24s without escorting fighters and at the same time spotted some 40 Me.109s and Fw.190s positioning for an attack. With no thought for his own safety, Kemp turned and met the Luftwaffe formation head on, shooting one Me.109 down almost immediately, and succeeding in breaking up the attack on the bombers altogether. He then continued his lone escort of the entire bomber division all the way to England.

After Kemp had landed back at base he became unconscious and had to be lifted from the cockpit. He had lost a great deal of blood. After many days in hospital he was called to London. There, in an impressive ceremony, Lieutenant-General Spaatz awarded him the United States Distinguished Service Cross for extraordinary heroism against an armed enemy of the United States.

Throughout the summer and early fall of 1944 both Bill Kemp and I became 'Aces' and among my victories were two Me.262s which I surprised taking off from Achmer aerodrome on the first operational mission of the Kommando Nowotny, equipped with the Luftwaffe's new jet fighter. When Kemp read the de-briefing on the mission he said 'Drew, you get no credit from me whatsoever on these two aircraft, jets or no jets, I don't count as victories airplanes just having taken off.'

I argued vociferously with Bill, but to no avail. So while, in the final analysis, we were both credited with six victories apiece by the Eighth Air Force, according to the 'authoritative' record of the Kemp-Drew logs, each pilot had only given the other credit for two kills.

But Kemp and I had done what Colonel Christian had asked us to do when we joined the 361st Fighter Group. We had reinstalled an *esprit de corps* in the 375th Squadron, making it the leading-scoring squadron in the Group; and when all the tallies were added up, 39½ aerial victories had been credited in total to Kemp, Drew and the other four Aces in the Group, who had all been either Kemp's or my students in Florida.

Bill went on after the war to start the Arizona Air National Guard, becoming a Squadron Commander as well as the personal pilot of Senator Barry Goldwater, the senior Senator from Arizona. Sadly, he was killed, as so many other of the air war's characters have been, in a motor car

172

accident in the late 1960s after attending an Arizona Air National Guard meeting. Today I live in the Republic of South Africa with my South African wife and think many times about Bill Kemp.

Urban L. Drew,
Waterkloof Ridge,
Pretoria,
Republic of South Africa

Sully Varnell
THE ACE FROM TENNESSEE

Dick Alexander (Major R. L. Alexander) had what in Britain some were once apt to call 'a very good war'. It was certainly extensive. He was one of the enlightened Americans who travelled up to Canada to volunteer for service with the Royal Canadian Air Force many months before the attack on Pearl Harbor. After training in Canada, he crossed to England and joined 133 Squadron, one of the three American Eagle Squadrons which, in the early years of war, fought under the operational control of Fighter Command of the Royal Air Force.

When the US Eighth Air Force was starting out on its sustained daylight offensive against Nazi Germany in the autumn of 1942, Dixie Alexander, along with the other Eagle Squadron volunteers, transferred to the USAAF. Thereafter, for much of the next two years, he flew, first, with the US Eighth from the United Kingdom and then with the US 12th and 15th Air Forces in the Mediterranean theatre, in Sicily, Corsica and from the Italian mainland.

It all represented a long and varied operational stretch which Dixie recaptured with colour and reality in his autobiography *They Called Me Dixie.**

Of all the people that I met during World War II, Sully Varnell is, for me, probably the best remembered. Sully was from Tennessee, and had gone to college for two years before enlisting in the Air Force. He was my element leader on 31 May, 1944, when I was shot down by one of our own B-24s over Austria. On that day, Sully destroyed two Me.109s – his first and second victories.

During the month of June, he went on to shoot down 15 more enemy planes, running his total to 17 before he was rotated back to the United States. He died in a plane crash while serving as a gunnery instructor shortly thereafter.

* (Robinson Typographics, Hemet, California 1988)

I did not see Sully after our take-off on 31 May although, of course, I observed him in the air. I was not around to see him become a great fighter pilot, but the statistics are all there, and I was not surprised. It just had to happen . . .

I was attracted to Sully in a way that I have seldom experienced with others. We related so well in thought. While flying together, either of us could break in with radio transmission and answer a question that was floating about in the other's mind. We did this a lot and it gave both of us a strange feeling.

Sully would have been at home with Daniel Boone, Jim Bowie or Tom Jefferson. He was tall and slim, easy-going, shy on first appearance, and quiet. His sense of humour was delightful; his dry wit and quick mind could shock an audience into complete silence. He had that great perception and depth in his reasoning that makes for great horse traders, and he could stand back, listen at length, and destroy all arguments with a few well-chosen words. He was never vicious, but his little barbs were always to the point.

In the air he had everything. While I did not stay around long enough to see him become a great Ace, I knew it had to be. He flew superbly, shot exceptionally well, had good airmanship, excellent discipline, great eyes and co-ordination, and could anticipate and plan in the air.

During the many years that have passed, Varnell's memory has always remained with me. There was just so much good in the boy. Through the years since the war, I had long wished to call on his family and visit his home town. I was unable to write because I did not know them . . . but I did know that he came from Charleston, Tennessee, a little mountain town north-east of Chattanooga.

A few years ago, I was *en route* to Alabama by way of Chattanooga on business. I decided to make this the trip that I visited either his family or his grave. I located the turn-off from 75 to Charleston just before noon on a warm, beautiful Sunday morning. The area was lovely, as only Tennessee in the spring can be, with the many dogwoods and flowers in bloom. Sunday in a little mountain village finds few residents afoot, or places of business where one might seek information about a friend from many years past.

I began with the country grocery and went on until finally a minister's wife directed me to a lady who had gone to school with Sully and was married to one of his cousins. The woman told me where he was buried and explained that Sully's mother was visiting in Carolina. She informed me that Sully was buried in the cemetery at Calhoun, another wee town separated from Charleston by a little river. Calhoun by auto was only a few minutes, and I had no trouble finding the church and the cemetery. I parked and began my tour, looking for Sully's grave. It is a large cemetery that, no doubt, has served the entire community for many years. I had the place completely to myself, and during my entire time there I saw no one.

I must have spent at least two hours searching, and had not covered a good half of the cemetery, when I realised how late it was getting, and how far I had yet to drive. I was tired, and the warm day had turned hot. I sat down on a tombstone, asking the unknown occupant of the grave for his forgiveness and offering my thanks for the accommodation. I was thinking about Sully – the nearness, and the immensity of everything – and I knew that he had to be somewhere close by, knowing my feelings. I did not wish to give up the search; and yet I knew that I did not have the time to cover the rest of the grounds. There was also the possibility that I might have walked right past his grave without knowing it. In frustration, I said out loud: 'Damn it, Sully, if you're here, let's quit playing games and show me something!' I knew that was the sort of thing he would have enjoyed doing. Sully and I were close, but he loved to tease, usually in a respectful sort of way.

I had no sooner uttered the words than my eyes were directed to a stone standing upright, off to my right, about 100 feet away. With no hesitation at all, I rose and walked directly to Sully's grave. There was a cluster of pines shading it. It might have been an area which I had already passed by, but there it was: 'James Sullins Varnell Jr, Capt, USAAF'.

I sat for possibly a half-hour, thinking and enjoying a couple of cigarettes, and then rose to leave. I felt a great feeling of accomplishment and peace of mind; it was as though I had finished the last chapter of a very fine book, and closed the cover. Something that was finished, and yet would always remain with me, or could be opened and re-read at any time.

Dick Alexander,
Piper City,
Illinois,
USA

'Cookie'
FOOTPRINTS ON THE BLOTTER

Professor Robin Higham of the Department of History, Kansas State University, and editor of *Air Historian* in the United States, was a flight sergeant pilot of the Royal Air Force's 48 (Transport) Squadron flying DC-3s from Chittagong to points along the Arakan coast, and to airfields in the Irrawaddy plain from Mingyang to Rangoon and beyond, in the later stages of the Far Eastern conflict.

It was the collective character of his fellow senior NCOs on the ground staff which made a treasured memory from his Canadian and Burmese days and nights. Applying the historian's mind to these men, he sorts them, in easily recognisable relief, into their irreplaceable categories.

Looking back over 40 years to World War II and those impressionable years when, as a lad of 17, I accepted the King's shilling and was given my Notice Papers at No. 31 PD, Moncton, New Brunswick, Canada, the most unforgettable characters I met in the next four years were an assortment of ground-based, senior NCOs.

These rulers of the Air Force fell into several categories. First came the smart, Brylcreemed, usually moustachioed flight sergeants and sergeants of the General Duties ilk. They handled everyone from young gentlemen to permanent aircraftmen, 2nd class, with firmness, precision and authority.

Then there were the mixed group of technical specialists – some, like the disciplinarians, who had 20 or more years in the Service, and others who were in for Hostilities Only. They ran the gamut from fitters and riggers through storekeepers to armourers (the latter being also normally the best cooks in the squadrons with which I served).

177

Lastly, there was a much less smart crowd – definitely HO – who served in a variety of posts from staging-post manager to orderly room clerk and were, in my experience of them in India and Thailand, distinguished by their casual scruffiness, which almost matched that of we NCO aircrew.

But all these worthies, with their crowns and chevrons, and sometimes good-conduct stripes for, as the Service put it, 'five years' undetected crime', had one great thing in common – a wonderful sense of humour.

There was immaculate little Sergeant Russell, bouncing into the barracks at the crack of a June dawn 'wakey, wakeying' us for PT in his white turtleneck sweater; or his friend, 'Tiny', heaving 12 stones through the door on a like mission, or Flight Sergeant LeNoir at Victoriaville breathing garlic into our faces and calling for volunteers for the boxing team – then having them shadow-box with pails and mops around the bunks to get the place clean.

And, at the other end of the spectrum in Bangkok, there was our grounded Halibag* pilot, entertaining us by lofting a smoke-grenade, which he had filched out of his stores, into the Thai guardhouse; and young, portly Sergeant Peachem telling us wonderful tales of his sex life in Egypt. At another moment it was sheer joy to watch Peacham appearing to be absolutely serious in responding to the fatuous request of some officer whom we all knew did not know what he was talking about.

That sense of humour even carried up to that most exalted of all personnel, the Station Warrant Officer, although, as NCO aircrew, making a habit, on principle, of staying well out of his way, we never had much chance of seeing that side of him in action.

The Royal Air Force in World War II was a Commonwealth force. While learning to fly in the Air Training Scheme in Canada, I had two flight sergeants as instructors. The real prize – and the more unforgettable of the two – was 'Cookie'. Not only did he have a wonderful Aussie accent, he also had a direct frontier manner to go with his purple uniform.

One day we got a new Canadian flight commander, a flight lieutenant known as the 'Little Eagle' for his absolute adherence to regulations, including the stiff wire in his cap. Shortly after he had set up his desk – with a clean white sheet of blotting paper neatly squared upon it – 'Cookie' came in from a damp early morning flight. With his parachute still slung over his shoulder, he looked into the CO's office. Seeing the blotter, he marched right up to the desk, jumped up smack into the middle of the white rectangle, left two muddy footprints, jumped back off, turned about and stomped out.

* Halifax aircraft.

Professor (Flight Sergeant) Robin Higham

The story spread like wildfire, and deservedly so. And although 'Cookie' was commissioned soon afterwards, he never became pompous – especially not after a couple of beers!

Robin Higham,
Department of History,
Kansas State University,
Manhattan,
Kansas,
USA

Sadaaki Akamatsu
BLACKSHEEP AKAMATSU – ZERO ACE

Yutaka Morioka (former Navy Lieutenant Yutaka Morioka) graduated from the Japanese Navy Academy at Etajima in November 1941, and because of his proficiency as a pilot became a dive-bombing instructor. When, some two years later, he converted on to fighters he had what many a successful Zero, Spitfire or P-51 pilot had originally had – an impressive mentor or leader to impart the fundamentals of the arts of combat and leadership.

In the case of Yutaka Morioka, it was Japan's 'legendary blacksheep', Lieutenant Sadaaki Akamatsu, whom Saburo Sakai (no less) regarded as one of the Japanese Navy's exceptional pilots in the Pacific war, who provided the example.

Morioka, who later became a public accountant living in Tokyo, profited to the extent that, before the war's end, he had advanced to command a Zero squadron in the 302 *Kokutai* (Air Group).

The editor is indebted to Henry Sakaida, the air historian, living now in Temple City, California, for the translation and arrangement of the short study which follows.

Although former Navy Lieutenant Sadaaki Akamatsu died in 1980, I shall never forget the man, his expertise or the example he set. I was originally a dive-bomber pilot, but due to the operational needs of the war I converted to Zero fighters in April 1944 while based at Atsugi airfield in Japan.

At that point I knew nothing whatever about dogfighting or the tactics of air combat. But Akamatsu was a master of air fighting and he became my instructor, the man from whom I learnt such skills as I was able to develop. For me, he was certainly the Number One!

I remember so well the first time he took me up for a mock combat training session. It was an extraordinary experience. Here was I employing all the evasive tactics I knew and yet Akamatsu spoke to me over the RT: 'Lieutenant Morioka! I've shot you down already at least four times.' And that, I may say, was after no more than ten minutes' dogfighting.

We did these training sessions every day and after two months of it

Akamatsu complimented me on the advances I had made. He then presented me with a certificate confirming that, after all this work together, I was now a skilled Zero pilot. I haven't any doubt that the reason I am still alive today is because I had Akamatsu as my mentor and model in those first critical weeks. That was my good fortune!

He was, of course, a real outlaw when he was younger and fairly lived it up. He liked to drink *sake** and he was never averse to concentrating his attentions on the opposite sex. All the same, those stories about him wearing a kimono and wooden sandals while taking part in fighter interceptions are just ridiculous. In any case, when he became an officer he also became a reformed character!

Looking back over all these years, I'm quite sure I never knew another character quite like Akamatsu, the one and only!

Yutaka Morioka,
Tokyo,
Japan.

---

* A Japanese fermented liquor made from rice.

181

Wing Commander Rodber CSO
THE SIGNALS SAID 'GO'

Eric McLellan, one of the four members of the Judiciary to grace this collection (see pages 35-7, 107-9 and 307-10), entered the Royal Air Force after Oxford with difficulty. Given the chance, he would have opted to be a pilot. But, healthy though he was, his eyesight was such that not even as a volunteer for ground duties could he match the Service's early wartime requirements. Later, however, pertinacity paid off when, with some easing of the visual standards, volunteers were sought with the necessary intellectual qualities to serve in the Technical Branch in a capacity which, in the event, would bring the embryo advocate many hours' flying.

McLellan, with his eventual Signals expertise, could have mustered with the Ultra* force, but he preferred the contact with the air. This he got with the Royal Air Force's 205 Group from North Africa, across the Mediterranean, to the Italian mainland and thence to the Balkans before returning, finally, to the Canal Zone of Egypt, in a three-year overseas stretch.

Post-war at the Bar, in one of life's strange twists, he found himself spending weeks in court at Aylesbury, ranged with prosecuting counsel, in the celebrated case of The Great Train Robbery. Two decades earlier, the notorious Leatherslade Farm House, hideout of the Robbers, had been a haven on the airfield perimeter 'where the initiated could get a cup of tea for a penny', while the Signals volunteer was doing his OTU† flying at Oakley, the satellite, less than 10 miles north-east of Oxford.

' . . . There I was, in the middle of a case which, for months, made front page news . . . Most members of my profession would have envied me, and I was ungracious enough to find it tame compared to the great events I had lived through when I was young . . .'

---

* Enemy code-busting organization based at Bletchley Park.
† Operational training unit.

Since I spent the war in the Technical Branch, it is not surprising that I draw my Most Memorable Character from the ranks of its senior officers. What I find decidedly difficult, however, well over 40 years on, is to convey to anyone not engaged at the time, and indeed to many who were engaged, but concerned only with the end product, the nature of the Branch or the precise qualities that made one of its members memorable. It was accorded plenty of respect, but very little comprehension.

Those who commanded wings and squadrons and flights and who experienced at first hand the unforgettable qualities of the officers and senior NCOs who served the Technical Branch, in its various trades, will comprehend precisely the Judge's problem.

They were an utterly professional lot, proud, exceptionally well trained in peacetime, disciplined, confident and often tersely critical, whose catechism rested upon obtaining an affirmative answer to the primary question: 'Is the aircraft operationally serviceable to fly?'

They did not court publicity nor did they expect it. It would have been distasteful to them. They serviced the heroes – and that was good enough for them. Their unquestioned ability made the vast expansion of the wartime Service – and victory – possible.

That is the background against which Eric McLellan selects his archetypal character, Wing Commander Rodber, Chief Signals Officer of No. 205 Group during the Italian campaign and after . . .

As Rodber is hidden in the anonymity surrounding his calling, I had better introduce the man and his job. First, the job.

The Group had had a most distinguished history in the Desert from beginning to end. It did as much as any unit to save the Delta and conquer North Africa by bombing Rommel's supply ports. The fine weather of the eastern Mediterranean and the sturdy simplicity of the Wellington made it ideal for the task, even when it was obsolete elsewhere. In particular, the weather made adequate for present purposes the robust methods of navigation immortalised in the 70 Squadron song [sung to the tune of 'Clementine']:

> 'Have you lost us, navigator?
> Come up here and have a look;
> Someone's shot our starboard wing off!'
> 'We're all right, then, that's Tobruk.'

It was all heroic and it gathered as much myth as the Trojan War. If I may be allowed a personal note – they were the finest body of men I have ever had the honour of serving with, and remained so after action from Mersa Matruh to Warsaw and back again to the Delta.

Having said this, the sobering consideration remained that the techniques that had led up to the thousand-bomber raids would have to be digested and applied in very different conditions and much worse visibility if the Group were to survive in Europe.*

Now for the man. Rodber was in most ways a typical senior officer of the Technical Branch. He was a regular, and his 'long distance' medal showed that he must have served at least 17 years in the ranks before being commissioned. He was older than most – I should think in his early 40s – but with a decidedly venerable appearance and a good deal of silver hair. He was tall and robust with a fresh complexion and very blue eyes. He had a benevolent expression and a very even temper, which I never saw him lose.

To me, he looked like Methuselah and, as an irregular in my middle twenties, I wondered how I should get on with him. I need not have worried . . . for his looks did not belie him . . . and he was one of the nicest men I have ever met. Indeed, it is a gratuitous act of kindness by him after the end of hostilities that fixes him most indelibly in my mind.

There was never any doubt that he was a nice chap, but, as Clemenceau said, it is not enough to mean well. It is necessary also sometimes to be right. The question remained as to whether he would be up to playing a leading part in the adaptation . . .

Confirmation of Rodber's quality under the whip was not long in coming, for 205 Group, commanded from the late summer of 1944 onwards by the South African, Brigadier J. T. (Jimmy) Durrant, with its strong South African Air Force presence, and based at its Foggia complex of airfields hard by the spur of Italy, was now in the thick of the aerial activity . . . The round-the-clock Anglo-US bombing offensive . . . The brilliant mining of the Danube, vital German artery, which required the Naval sea mines to be dropped from a height of 50 feet to avoid disintegration – its success was a potent factor in the Russians' recovery of the Crimea . . . The hazardous supply-dropping operations in support of the tragic Warsaw Uprising in August and early September 1944, which involved the B-24 crews in round-trip missions of some 10–11 hours . . . And then the attacks associated with the Allied invasion of the south of France, one of the most

* McLellan has here in mind, among radar and other 'air electronic' devices, 'Window' (tin-foil strips scattered from aircraft to confuse enemy radar and, therefore, night-fighter defences) and 'an alleged night-fighter detector called "Monica" which the Luftwaffe could detect much earlier than we could – the cause of nightly losses in the seventies at Leipzig and Berlin early in 1944 . . . After the war, I was shown captured German Signit reports praising our swiftness and secrecy and our silence on the ground and in the air, making it difficult to determine our intentions . . . They ascribed this to our long operational experience and our rigid and undeviating Signals discipline' – Ed.

ill-conceived and senseless operations in the last year of war . . . It was a period of relentless pressure which took its toll in aircraft losses.

One day, during a short-lived lull, Eric McLellan visited 205 Group HQ for lunch.

I was with Rodber and a couple of other Technical officers, old in my terms and much senior in rank. I said something cautious about the shocking losses of the last months. I was surprised and impressed by the glimpse of iron that my remark brought out in Rodber.

'We've got the Crimea back,' he said, 'and the only price we had to pay was less than a hundred obsolete kites and the equivalent of a couple of companies of infantry.' And he added, 'If you go to war to help people and then do nothing when they fight, you don't add up to much.'

[The mining of the lock gates on the Danube] was not, of course, an individual, but a corporate success, but we felt confidence in Rodber's part in it and his powers to direct his inferiors and to maintain his side in any contest with his equals and superiors.

Early in 1945, [the Balkans], and the political side of the war, knocked firmly at my door. One of my radio stations received a call from General Mihailović* quite out of the blue. It was a proposal to return to the Allies 200-odd aircrew, prisoners of war or on the run. I had the sense to see that it was red hot and, after returning a purely formal answer, asked for instructions.

The only instruction I got was that if the Jugs wanted to talk to me they had better talk to me. They did and in the end a rendezvous was arranged at the back end of Yugoslavia and the aircrews were all flown out. I was never bothered with advice or fuss. I knew, however, that had I needed advice it would have been good, and if I had asked for an order I should have received it clearly and unequivocally. Anyone with experience of the Service will realise that the greatest compliment I could pay to my boss was not to ask for an order. That was the way we did things . . .

One last experience must suffice. The final land offensive in Italy against the Germans began in April 1945. It involved a plan to drop bombs at a place called Lake Comacchio at night, 1000 yards in front of our advancing infantry, a feat never attempted before, nor, as far as I am aware, since. It was a set-piece battle with plans complex and comprehensively timed, and leaving no room at all for error.

So far as we were concerned, it involved getting about 25 Liberators [B-24s] off our primitive airfield at intervals of 30 seconds . . . Any hitch was liable to trigger off a serial blowing up of fully bombed-up aircraft. We knew it could be done because we had tried it, but there was a last check that had to be reported from one end of the airfield to the other.

---

* General Draga Mihailovic, guerilla leader of the Cetniks in Yugoslavia.

Lights did not do because it was already like Piccadilly Circus on a Saturday night and telephone wires were liable to be broken . . .

For once, I asked for advice. I got a reminiscent look. 'You never served in seaplanes, did you? What with the wind and the sea you couldn't hear yourself think. They used a lot of semaphore.'

With the ending of the war in Europe, the Group started to contract on Egypt, first to Alexandria, then the Canal. . . By this time I was about as war-sick and homesick as a man could well be. But Alexandria was a paradise full of nice people and pretty girls . . . I took up with one of the prettiest – an Alexandrian Greek . . . But she was due to go to England on her own affairs before me . . . so I got some leave and made arrangements to see her off.

I duly went to Port Said and, after a fruitless search, found no sign of her . . . It seemed like another kick in the teeth from fate, and I returned to the Canal reconciled to never seeing her again.

On reaching my room, I found to my astonishment a note from Rodber telling me that she was now sailing from Suez tomorrow and that I was to meet her and have lunch at Shepheard's Hotel in Cairo. If I would be on the tarmac at 0930, a pilot and aircraft would take me there . . . I was and it was. We did have lunch together, made firm arrangements to meet in England and in due course married, and have remained so.

I found out later that one of the bevy of pretty girls – a Wren – had had the brazen cheek to ring up Rodber and tell him of the crisis. He had done what he always did – the simple, obvious, and effective thing.

Perhaps it is not surprising that I find him memorable . . .

Eric McLellan,
Hambledon,
nr Portsmouth,
Hampshire

'Digger' Hassell
AUSSIE NAVIGATOR

Tom Bennett (Squadron Leader T. Bennett) was a navigation leader with 617 Squadron at Woodhall Spa, in Lincolnshire, and widely experienced at the job, having served previously with 49 Squadron at Scampton. He was navigating during 617's famous attack on *Tirpitz* on 15 September, 1944, when the German battleship was lying alongside in Kaa Fiord, an offshoot of Alten Fiord, up in the North Cape area of Norway.

Led by the irrepressible Willie Tait (he headed all three of the Squadron's attacks on the ship), 617 had flown to Yagodnik, 20 miles south-east of Archangel, in Russia, to deliver a surprise attack from the east.

Tom Bennet is now Keeper of the Archives for 617 and a dozen years ago published an arresting account* of some of the Squadron's equally daring, but less heavily publicised, operations.

I came to know Flying Officer 'Digger' Hassell, the Australian, in May 1945, when, after leaving 617 Squadron and its base at Woodhall Spa, I joined the staff of the Prisoner of War Rehabilitation Unit at Royal Air Force, Cosford, in Staffordshire.

Digger cut an unconventional figure. He was barely five feet tall, very square, balding with a moustache and, seemingly, hewn out of granite. Then in his early 30s, he was one of the returned 'Kriegies' and had somehow contrived to get himself a permanent job on the Unit's staff. His story was as unusual as his appearance and personality.

He had won himself the distinction of having been *twice* taken a prisoner of war. Originally, he had served for two years as a private with the Australian Expeditionary Force in the Middle East and was one of the thousands of Aussies who, in 1941, had been flung into the battle for Crete. When the island finally fell and he was taken prisoner, Digger was kept there to help with the clearing-up operation. He was not at all

---

* *617 Squadron – The Dambusters at War*, Patrick Stephens, Wellingborough, 1986.

complimentary about the rough treatment he received at the hands of the German guards.

One day, he chanced upon an undamaged rowing boat, which he found lying on one of the beaches. With the help of an Australian friend, he was able to drag it to a secure hiding place. It wasn't long before the two had 'acquired' a pair of oars and hidden them beside the boat.

Seizing their chance, the two Aussies slipped out of their camp on the first moonless night, dragged the boat down the beach to the water's edge and launched themselves quietly out into the Mediterranean. Their luck held. Two days later, they were picked up by a Royal Navy destroyer and later returned to Egypt. Rumour had it that the hitherto cordial relations between the Royal Navy and the Australian Army 'brass' were never quite the same after Digger and his equally outspoken countryman were returned to a less-than-grateful Army!

However, like other Aussies who had returned from the maelstrom of Crete, they soon found themselves rewarded with what they called 'cushy numbers' in which to see out the war. Digger took advantage of an opportunity which was offered to transfer to the Air Force and to what he called a 'welfare commission' with a squadron of light bombers. There, his prime concern was with the fair distribution of cigarettes and parcels which arrived regularly from organisations back home for all the Australians on strength, ground crew as well as aircrew.

While with the squadron, he was able to engage in some non-operational flying – air tests, local flights and so on – after which he considered himself 'quite as capable as those other jokers who flew next to the pilot'. He therefore summarily awarded himself a navigator's brevet. (I only learnt of this 'sacrilege' when Digger and I were on a business trip together to Glasgow on behalf of the Mess at Cosford. Then he was wearing his best blue uniform, complete with navigator's wing. He never sported the brevet on his battledress!)

When Italy surrendered in September 1943, and the Germans, in response, began to turn their attention to the Aegean, the squadron and supporting personnel were moved to an airfield on the island of Cos. The enemy, however, had other ideas and a month later, in October 1943, the island fell and for the second time in as many years, Digger Hassell became a prisoner of war.

Again, fortune favoured him. As a result of his transfer to the Air Force after Crete, there was little likelihood of him being identified as the Australian private who had escaped after the earlier island battle. As Digger was now wearing a flying brevet, he was quickly despatched with a group of aircrew to Germany and to the Dulag Luft interrogation camp, near Frankfurt-on-Main. This tickled his fancy. 'Christ, Ben!' he grinned, as he related his story a couple of years later, 'I couldn't have told the bastards a bloody thing about the Air Force even if I'd wanted to!'

The group finally arrived in Frankfurt at night and soon began the trek to Dulag Luft in the charge of a young German guard armed with rifle and fixed bayonet. After about an hour, with the guard obviously unsure of the route, Digger put it to the man straight. 'Have you got any idea where the hell you are?' The guard shrugged.

Digger then turned to the rest of the party of aircrew. 'All you fellers sit down until this rooster finds out where we are and where the camp is.' The group happily complied and the guard then began to get agitated, pacing up and down and making threatening lunges with his bayonet without actually touching any of his charges. He periodically fired a shot into the air. Eventually, help came and the party was then duly marched off to Dulag Luft, but not before the guard had made his report on Digger, who was then sentenced immediately to fourteen days in the camp's solitary confinement 'cooler' for 'insubordination'. He assured me that, after some two years with the Australian Army in the Middle East, 'that German "cooler" was like a holiday camp!'

After completing his term, the Aussie 'navigator' was returned to one of the usual cells. Then, one sunny morning, he was marched off to a large, comfortable, book-lined study where he was confronted by the sole occupant. 'Ben,' said Digger, as he recounted the incident to me, 'this Kraut spoke perfect English – just like an Oxford don.' (I discovered that Digger regarded anyone who retained his aitches as 'gentry'.) 'He looked at me and said: "Ah, good morning, Mr Hassell, what a lovely day you have brought. Do you know that everyone here in Germany will be feeling very happy and joyful on this lovely morning?"'

'Oh yes?' queried Digger casually, showing a disrespectful lack of interest . . . But there was no stopping his host.

'Why yes, Mr Hassell,' he beamed, 'you see, the Führer made a glorious speech last night to the German nation – so inspiring, so optimistic! He spoke about "vengeance" weapons and other war-winning inventions which will soon be launched against Germany's enemies. Herr Hitler has so very obviously got something up his sleeve . . .'

'He'd better have,' cut in Digger dryly, 'otherwise he'll get something up his bloody arse!'

The German eyed Digger incredulously, hardly able to believe his ears. A shout for the guard and the Australian 'navigator' was soon being escorted unceremoniously back to the 'cooler' – this time for the full 28 days. Eventually to be packed off to Offlag, the prisoner was glad to find this was the end of his interrogation.

Digger Hassell epitomised for me the inimitable independence and strength of the Australian character. There, in 1943, in the heart of the Fatherland, a prisoner in the midst of 80 million hostile Germans, he had exercised what he regarded as his 'fundamental and inalienable right' to comment on affairs *exactly* as he saw them.

It was my good fortune, from my earliest training days in the Royal Air Force, to come to know a succession of 'characters'. Even with the passage of 40 years and more, the memory of their attitudes and antics still brings a smile. They lightened our load in the dark days with their natural and uninhibited humour. They never realised the fillip which their pungent, uncompromising statements gave.

This was the mould in which Flying Officer 'Digger' Hassell, 'navigator' extraordinary, was cast.

Tom Bennett
Westcliff-on-Sea
Essex

PART THREE

1 The Commanders
2 The Families

1
The Commanders

There were some charismatic characters among the commanders in the various air forces of World War II. They differed as widely in personality as they did in method. Each had his own style and idiosyncrasies; and those whom they commanded – the aircrews and the ground personnel – all formed their own impression of the senior officer who, at critical times, could well hold their destiny in his hands. The media added the colour and the spice.

The eight operational commanders who are here portrayed differed, like all the rest, from one to another. There were, however, certain denominators which were common to all – decisiveness, courage and confidence. Without these essential attributes authority and, therefore, command would have suffered.

It may be no more than a coincidence that in each of their biographers there was irrefutable evidence of similar traits.

Sir Arthur Harris
THE BURDEN HE CARRIED...

It is probably sufficient to say that Marshal of the Royal Air Force Sir Michael Beetham was the last Chief of the Air Staff to fly operationally against the enemy in World War II. But one further fact may as well be added.

There was a dark night late in December 1943 when 50 Squadron, of which he was then a member, was among a strong Bomber Command force briefed to attack Berlin. It was Beetham's seventh trip and, with his crew, the fourth to the Big City in that short spell.

In the turmoil over the target, and unbeknown to the future CAS, an incendiary bomb, dropped from an aircraft above, passed straight through the starboard wing outer fuel tank of the Lancaster, leaving a massive hole in its train. It wasn't noticed until the ground crew saw it on return to Skellingthorpe, the Squadron's base near Lincoln!

Providence dealt some lucky hands...

There can be no senior Commander in the Royal Air Force in World War II better known universally than Marshal of the Royal Air Force Sir Arthur Harris. At centre stage directing the strategic bombing offensive from Britain for more than three years, he wielded a force which played a decisive role in the defeat of Germany. Such though was the destruction of Germany by the end of the war, that the mere mention of his name still arouses deep passion and controversy. No other wartime commander has had to endure such vilification as he has for the bombing.

Yet everything he did was in accordance with his political directive from the War Cabinet. What he did do was to carry out that directive to the letter and with a single-minded determination to achieve the objective – the destruction of Nazi Germany to the point where the capacity of the German people to resist was fatally weakened. Where perhaps he over-estimated, and he was not alone in this, was in believing that the war could be won by bombing alone, but few detached analysts would argue with the conclusion that the bomber offensive made a major, indeed indispensable, contribution to the defeat of Germany.

194

When he took over Bomber Command in February 1942, the bombing campaign had had little significant effect on the German war machine. There had been some successes, but crews had often had great difficulty in finding their targets at night and in the prevailing poor weather. There were deficiencies in aircraft, weapons, navigation techniques, training and the support organisation. But by then the foundation work for improvement had been laid, the force was building up and what was needed was a leader to inspire the Command and give it a new dynamism.

Bert Harris* was the ideal man for the task. He managed to transform the Command in the space of a few short months and to launch a devastating 1000-bomber raid on Cologne – a tremendous psychological boost not only to everyone in the Command, but also to a hard-pressed British public, not to mention its effect on the enemy. And from that point on, under his direction, the weight of the bomber attacks and the effectiveness steadily and relentlessly increased.

The strain on him personally must have been immense. He personally directed the campaign night after night continuously for 3¼ years. He always insisted on being informed immediately, whatever the time of day or night, as to the result of each raid and the losses. He had to cope with a constant stream of visitors to his Headquarters at High Wycombe; ministers, politicians, foreigners and numerous so-called experts anxious to influence him as to targets to attack. And he had to fight off many attempts to divert the bombing effort and the resources devoted to it to other tasks.

The losses of aircraft and crews were heavy, running into many thousands, and he felt those losses deeply, for he was a very compassionate man. But every member of the Command had faith and confidence in him in spite of those losses. How did he achieve this when few of the people he was commanding ever saw him? For, understandably, he did not have time to visit his stations and squadrons. He said himself, 'As Commander-in-Chief I had to lay on every day in ever-changing weather conditions a major battle whether it happened or not. There came a point every day when as Commander-in-Chief I had to say yes or no subject to various conditions, including the met report. In those conditions I could not jaunt around the country and keep everything in mind.'

Nevertheless his personality reverberated through his staff and his commanders at all levels. Everyone knew who was Commander-in-Chief and felt his presence. His blunt and outspoken views permeated the Command. It was a remarkable feat of leadership.

What was it in his character that gave him such drive and determination?

* The Royal Air Force knew Sir Arthur Harris as 'Bert'. 'Bomber' Harris was the invention of the media. Ed.

Imaginative, farsighted, inventive and forceful, he was held in deep respect and affection by his staff and all who served with him.

His early life gives the clue to the moulding of his character. With parents in India he was thrust into the British boarding school system at the age of five and, seeing little of his parents, he soon learnt self-reliance, resourcefulness and an independence of mind.

He was fortunate that his prep school, Gore Court, adjoined a farm, the distractions of which appealed to him, and he proved adept at handling animals, particularly horses. Indeed, he always said one of the proudest days of his life was when he was allowed to drive the Governess's cart down to the station to fetch a guest. What the guest thought of being entrusted to a 10-year-old we do not know, but for him it was a great occasion.

When the time came to leave school his father wanted him to join the Army, but he determined to go farming in Rhodesia. For four years he tackled all manner of jobs – farming, tobacco planting, mining and driving a mail coach among them. One of his first jobs was to help a farmer build a house. There were no building contractors in that land of pioneers, and he even had to make his own bricks. After learning how, he enjoyed the task immensely and became a proficient brick-maker and, as he said, learnt to drop a number in later life!

Those years taught him to stand on his own feet, to turn his hand to almost any trade, to live rough when required, to live by his own wits and his own labour. When war broke out in 1914 the young Harris joined the 1st Rhodesian Regiment to fight the Germans in South-West Africa, a hard foot-slogging campaign over tough terrain that lasted a year. With the regiment disbanded Harris came to England and, swearing never to march again, joined the Royal Flying Corps. Thus he set out on his Air Force career with a uniquely varied background of life, a background which did much to mould his character and teach him how, as a Commander, to bring out the best in his men and inspire them.

Corporal Thomson, his fitter on 45 Squadron in Iraq in 1924, wrote of him recently, 'We called him Blood Harris – I'm talking about the riggers and fitters – because he was inclined to be red-haired. It was nothing to do with his temperament, though he could be irascible, as we all were in that climate. We would do anything for him, we loved him.'

Arthur Harris's close involvement in every activity of his men and his understanding of their needs earned him that same respect and affection throughout his career. His pioneer work on night fighting and night flying when a Home Defence Squadron Commander in World War I, his inventiveness and enterprise in Iraq in the 1920s when he showed that his transport squadron could outperform the bomber squadrons at their own game, his work in the Air Ministry as Director of Plans, where he laid the foundations of the future Bomber Force, and the rapport he established with the American political and military leaders when Head of the newly formed wartime RAF delegation in Washington, were all destined to prepare him for the mammoth task with which he was entrusted in February 1942.

His critics concentrate their attacks on the policy of area bombing. What those critics choose to ignore is that, up to 1944, precision targets could not be identified at night, and our weakly armed bombers could not survive over Germany in daylight without prohibitive losses. Harris was not the originator of the Area Bombing Policy, although he did fervently believe in it. There was no alternative for us as a nation other than to come to terms with Hitler, or to fight a purely defensive war and hope for something to turn up. The critics forget we were fighting a total war, we were back on our heels and there was no other way in which we could carry the war to Germany. And the British people, themselves bombed in London and many other cities, desperately wanted to hit back.

Bert Harris gave the nation the psychological boost needed to counter the reverses we had suffered in France, Egypt and the Far East. At the same time he strove relentlessly to improve the accuracy and effectiveness of the bomber force to the point where, by 1944, precision attacks at night were possible, and indeed were carried out with devastating effect. Harris has often been accused of a lack of flexibility. True that he argued with great determination against the diversion of his force to other tasks, but when he was overruled – for example, when ordered to support General Eisenhower in the Normandy campaign – the support he gave was unstinted. Eisenhower wrote to General Marshall in September 1944, 'Harris actually proved to be one of the most effective and co-operative members of my team, he met every request.'

Much of the critics' venom against Harris focuses on the bombing of Dresden. Yet Dresden, together with other cities in eastern Germany, was on the target list from Eisenhower and the Chiefs of Staff to give support to the Russian front, as it was being used as a focal point for communication in the transfer of troops and supplies between the Eastern and Western fronts. It was bombed by both the British and Americans and received specific political approval. The outcry was fuelled because the raid was so devastatingly effective. [Editor's italics]

Over the 40 years between handing over Bomber Command and his death at the age of 92 he bore all the controversy and criticism with great dignity. He was not treated well by the nation after the war. He was not, at the immediate post-war stage, offered the peerage given to many whose contribution to victory had been far less. In fact at that stage he received more honours from foreign countries than he did from his own; in particular from the United States, with whom he had worked so closely and harmoniously in co-ordinating the operations of Bomber Command and the United States Eighth Air Force, where President Truman awarded him one of America's highest honours, the Distinguished Service Medal.

Churchill, by then out of power, said to Harris, 'You fought a thousand battles, a record for any commander, and won most of them. Jellicoe fought one, lost it, and they made him an Earl!'

Churchill tried to correct the injustice and offered Harris a peerage when he returned to power in 1951, but Harris turned it down, although he accepted a baronetcy. Typical of him, he was not concerned personally, his only concern was for his bomber crews who, he felt strongly, should have been given a special Bomber Campaign medal.

The respect and affection in which he was held by all who served with him has endured to the present day. At the annual Bomber reunions, which he attended right up to the last year of his life, he was always received with the greatest warmth; he retained his pungent, witty style and captivated everyone. He continues to be revered and remembered at every Bomber function.

Typical of his style are the words he spoke to the Canadian aircrew of 4 Group when, the war over, he was able to find time to leave his Head-quarters and say farewell to them. 'When you get back home,' he said, 'and they ask you what you did in the war, you can say "We won it." '

He was the very man epitomised by Kipling. He could walk and talk with kings and queens, but he never lost the common touch. He was for me the most memorable character of World War II.

Michael Beetham,
South Creake,
Fakenham,
Norfolk

Sir Hugh Pughe Lloyd
AGGRESSIVE ISLAND DEFENDER

Those who survived a devastating operational run in wartime may well have felt at the end of it that they were 'being kept for something'. Such a one could well have been Ivor Broom (Air Marshal Sir Ivor Broom).

A product of 2 Group in Bomber Command and of Malta's siege in 1941, he was one of the few Blenheim pilots to emerge from this tortuous time when the mortality rate from the low-level daylight attacks against shipping and other targets was as high as, if not higher than, any other comparable activity in those cataclysmic days.

After senior command in the Royal Air Force post-war, Broom became Controller of National Air Traffic Services and a member of the Civil Aviation Authority – just the type to sort them out over Heathrow and Gatwick.

Hugh Pughe Lloyd, who as a very junior pilot in World War I earned the Military Cross and Distinguished Flying Cross, was 45 years old at the outbreak of World War II. From May 1940 to late May 1941 he was the Group Captain Senior Air Staff Officer in No. 2 Group of Bomber Command, which at that time operated mainly Blenheim aircraft from United Kingdom bases. Ten days after leaving No. 2 Group he arrived in Malta as an Air Vice-Marshal – rapid promotion by any standard – to command the Royal Air Force in Malta.

Historians have, justifiably, written at length about the remarkable defence of Malta during World War II, but Hugh Pughe, as he was affectionately known, was never purely defensively minded. He regarded the island as being in a strategically perfect position to harass and sink shipping carrying supplies to German and Italian troops in North Africa. He was the ideal man to implement that part of his directive which said, 'Your main task is to sink Axis shipping sailing from Europe to Africa.' The outstanding defence of the island by his very limited fighter force provided the capability for his bomber and reconnaissance aircraft to seek the enemy by day and night. So successful were he and his small force that Malta eventually became the springboard for the first assault on Nazi-occupied Europe by Allied forces.

It was in September 1941 that I was first to learn of the decisive manner in which he commanded his forces – without always paying too much regard to normal staff procedures. My crew and I (all sergeants at the time) were flying a Blenheim *en route* from England to the Middle East and thence to Singapore, and landed at Malta for a refuelling stop – but we were to go no further. His two Blenheim squadrons, which were on detachment to Malta from his former Group in England, were suffering heavy losses in their mast-high attacks on ships carrying supplies from Italy to Rommel's forces in North Africa. He replaced those losses by 'hijacking' aircraft and their crews who landed to refuel. Within 48 hours of landing for our refuelling stop we were operating with the Blenheims based in Malta.

The squadrons under his command in 1941 were a mixture of day bombers, night bombers, reconnaissance and the wonderfully effective fighter squadrons, so activity continued on a 24-hour basis. I don't know when Hugh Pughe ever slept. He never seemed tired, and his bulldog manner bred a similar spirit of resolve in his air and ground crews. Nothing seemed to shake him personally. He instilled confidence in his men and developed the spirit, ability and determination to overcome odds which any rational person might have been excused for considering overwhelming. I always felt that he had a special regard for the Blenheim squadrons, but I learned later that other squadrons also felt he had a special regard for them – the art of a true Commander, who made each unit feel special.

One day after we had suffered some heavy losses he visited the squadron at Luqa airfield (now Malta airport). We were lined up for a pep talk when an air raid warning sounded. Calmly he went on talking. The camp siren sounded, but he continued talking until his aide said, 'They are diving on the airfield, sir.' He looked up, and then casually and slowly said, 'I think we had better take cover.' The bombs fell as the crews dived for cover almost before he had finished his sentence. Within seconds he was back on his feet and quickly started touring the airfield to inspect the damage.

He exhibited a delightful human touch one day when my observer and airgunner, both sergeants in uniform, were walking from Luqa to Valletta. A car stopped, a corporal driver got out of the car, and told them to get into the car. Inside the car was the Air Vice-Marshal, who, when he found they were a Blenheim crew, immediately started talking about the important role of the Blenheim. He took from his briefcase a signal of congratulations for the Blenheim crews which he had received from the Air Ministry that day and showed it to them. My air gunner was not wearing a hat and in response to Hugh Pughe's question he replied that he had lost it and the storekeeper would not give him a replacement unless an old one was produced. Immediately the Air Vice-Marshal produced a sheet of paper, wrote an instruction to the Stores to issue my air gunner with a new hat, signed the paper, handed it to my air gunner and asked if that would satisfy the pedantic storeman! My air gunner, a cheerful Londoner, replied 'I hope so, sir, but they are a strange lot in Stores!'

I only served in Malta under Hugh Pughe's command for four months, but as a 21-year-old sergeant pilot I first learned from him the importance of senior officers identifying themselves with their units. In 1941, Malta was in the midst of a life and death struggle, yet I felt no apprehension about the future. He generated both individual and collective courage and a trusting faith that we would win through. Defeat was not a serious option, and it was fitting that this very operational commander should be knighted by King George VI in a tent in Tunisia in 1943. He was the first Air Marshal I had ever met and he not only altered the whole course of my life, but gave me, by example, my first lessons in leadership and the role of a commander. Having hijacked me in September 1941, he commissioned me in November 1941, when my squadron had lost all its officers except the Wing Commander and later in life our paths continued to cross at brief intervals.

In 1947–48, when he was the Commander-in-Chief of the South-East Asia Air Command, I commanded one of the two Spitfire squadrons in Singapore (the last two Spitfire squadrons in the front line). He never forgot that I had been one of his pilots in Malta in 1941 – and I was merely one of many hundreds who served under him. In 1948 the three British Service Chiefs in Singapore were invited to Australia and New Zealand as guests of the Governments concerned. He plucked me out of my squadron for a couple of weeks, made me Staff Officer to the party, a role about which I knew absolutely nothing, and said that if anyone asked him to speak about operations from Malta he would hand over to me. That was my briefing. Short and sweet. I fear I was a very inadequate staff officer on that trip, but I had the great privilege of being with him for two whole weeks.

In the early 1950s he commanded Bomber Command. At that time, bombing accuracy fell short of his high standards and he set himself the task of improving the accuracy in all weather conditions. He constantly sought the precision with which a rapier strikes its target, and although he did not achieve his objective for all his crews, he set in train the groundwork for his successors to do so.

In those days Command Headquarters still had communications aircraft to keep staff officers in limited flying practice. He was always keen that his air staff officers should maintain close contact with stations and squadrons, and I recall him saying to me once, 'There is only one way for an air staff officer to arrive on a visit to a flying station – and that is down the centre of the runway.' He had little time for air staff officers who failed to maintain a practical operational approach to life. Paper tigers were not popular with him. I recall the occasion when he attended a guest night at Manby, in Lincolnshire, in the early 1950s shortly before he retired. He left just before midnight, and although he had a professionally qualified crew in charge of the aeroplane, he sat in the left-hand seat and taxied out for take-off.

We did not meet again until 1971, when I was an Air Vice-Marshal commanding No. 11 (Fighter Group) in Strike Command. He lived some 30 miles away and I invited him to a dinner party. He demured, and said he was now too old to go out at night, but I pressed him hard and insisted on sending a car for him. We had a marvellous evening, the old sparkle was still in his eyes, the quizzical look still present, and he kept my other guests enthralled with his stories at the dinner table. As we rose from the table he turned to my wife, pointed to me, and said with a grin, 'To think I am responsible for that!'

We never met again. My relatively lowly rank at the height of Sir Hugh's career meant that my personal contact with him was always fleeting, but the impact was always lasting. Most people meet in life a few – very few – unforgettable characters who make a big impact on their lives. Air Marshal Sir Hugh Pughe Lloyd, Air Force Commander Extraordinaire, was one of those for me.

Ivor Broom,
Loudwater,
Rickmansworth,
Hertfordshire

Sir Keith Park
THE IMMACULATE IMPRESSION

Sandy Johnstone (Air Vice-Marshal A. V. R. Johnstone), a blatantly patriotic, golfing Scot and one of the original members of the Auxiliary Air Force, joined 602 (City of Glasgow – 'his' city) Squadron in 1934 and remained with it for seven years, rising to command it during the Battle of Britain.

At one point during the battle, 602 was based at Drem, hard by the shores of the Firth of Forth, when the astonishing Dick (Batchy) Atcherley, the arch-joker, was commanding the station. Batchy got his Signals Section to install a public address system to which, as Sandy relates, the station commander had frequent recourse.

One morning he spotted an airman sloping along the perimeter track, hands deep in pockets, looking thoroughly unmilitary. 'That airman there, with his hands in his pockets,' boomed out the unmistakable voice, 'take them out at once.'

Not only did the unfortunate object of the admonition jump a mile at the 'unseen' voice, but a hundred other 'culprits' all over the airfield leapt to conform.

Two years later, Sandy Johnstone was leading a Spitfire wing in the thick of the Battle of Malta. Thus he became one of the few who saw Keith Park through the eyes of both a squadron and a wing commander in two of the great aerial conflicts of history.

We had heard of Keith Park before our squadron moved south from Scotland to take part in the Battle of Britain. But who hadn't? As Air Officer Commanding No. 11 Group, Park was the man in tactical charge of the Hurricanes and Spitfires about to become locked in mortal combat in the greatest air battle of all time, and soon to become a household name.

I was in command of a squadron of Spitfires operating from West-hampnett, a small satellite airfield in West Sussex, but, although we had been there from the second week of August 1940, it was not until 7 October that I first met our AOC; hardly surprising, I suppose, as he could not have been expected to move far from his Headquarters at Uxbridge while the Group was so heavily engaged. Nonetheless, in spite of his absence, we had quickly appreciated his firm hand and had already built up our own image of this, so far unseen, master as a small, tough, operator – something of a fire-eater; an awe-inspiring figure and one who would not suffer fools gladly. It was therefore with some trepidation I awaited our first meeting at Westhampnett on that unforgettable day in early October.

The days had long since gone when fighter pilots kitted themselves out in light-coloured overalls and flying helmets. Now we had adopted darker, more sober hues to blend with the camouflage of our aircraft to avoid making ourselves any more conspicuous in the air than was necessary. After all, no one in his right mind goes deer-stalking wearing a bright scarlet anorak! So we watched with curiosity as the Hurricane taxied towards the dispersal, its white-helmeted pilot giving a casual wave of the hand in friendly greeting before switching off the engine and unbuckling his safety harness. Then, when a tall, slender figure, dressed in an immaculate suit of white flying overalls, climbed from the cockpit, my preconceived impressions immediately went straight out of the window in the warmth of the greeting which followed.

'Sorry to have been so long in paying you a visit, Johnstone . . .' he began, ' . . . I have wanted to meet you and your boys for a long time, to express my thanks for all your hard work . . . May I talk to those on Readiness first, then meet the others in the Mess? However, if that's not convenient . . .'

The informality was a refreshing change for, as members of the Auxiliary Air Force, most of our previous contacts with senior Air Officers had been remote affairs when, after an exchange of expected platitudes, the great men usually departed soon after, leaving the impression that, having been seen to have done their duty, they could return to the fastness of their offices to continue deliberations on an altogether higher plane. But not so Keith Park.

Here was a man who was remembering what it was like to be at our level; one who was genuinely interested to hear at first hand about our brushes with the enemy; who listened carefully (Park was a good listener); could lend a sympathetic ear to the odd grumble, yet quick to pounce on anything trivial. Then, having first allowed us our say, he went to much trouble to explain in detail the problems he himself was having to face at his Headquarters. It was a lively encounter and, after his departure, we were left with the impression that it was we who were in the driving seat and that he, the AOC, had been there to learn. It made a lasting impression and taught me a lot.

Deep down, however, I think Park envied us for being so much in the limelight and was not above trying to grab some of the kudos for himself whenever the opportunity arose. Once he even claimed to have been in combat with enemy aircraft during one of his Hurricane transit flights, although I don't think Intelligence sources were ever to substantiate the claim. It was an understandable vanity.

Park **was** a vain man, and there may have lain the cause of his unpopularity with some of his colleagues in the other services. There was a bit of the peacock in his make-up and he loved to be the centre of attention, a foible I was to notice while serving under him again as a Spitfire Wing Leader during the Siege of Malta in 1942, when Park was once more in charge.

At the time, there was a desperate shortage of fuel on the island, when all forms of motor transport were banned, other than a few vehicles for strictly essential purposes. Nevertheless, on the pretext of urgent operational necessity, Keith Park was to be seen daily, driving about in a flashy, bright red, sports MG long after the Governor, Lord Gort, had made it his practice to forego the Rolls-Royce in favour of a bicycle as his normal mode of transport. Moreover, when most were reduced to wearing old battledress uniforms, our AOC would invariably turn up immaculately attired in tunic and slacks as if ready to step on to a parade ground.

One can perhaps further understand the frustrations of the Navy and Army commanders in Malta during the siege for, throughout this critical time, their forces, other than the anti-aircraft units, had been reduced in effectiveness through lack of outside support and could do little more than perform subsidiary duties in support of the air defences on the island. Worst of all from the Navy's point of view, The Union Club, that traditional centre of its social life, was now monopolised by Royal Air Force officers who had not yet learned to respect such hard-won privileges! Regretfully, the RAF was still largely regarded by our sister services as a gaggle of precocious upstarts!

While the battle raged, however, we were much too busy in the air to spare any time to analyse the causes of friction among the higher-ups, even if we had been aware of it in the first place. To us, our AOC could do no wrong and we much looked forward to his frequent visits to the airfield. In return, Park greatly valued the loyalty of his aircrews and seldom lost an opportunity to foster it. For instance, at the meetings with his Wing and Squadron commanders held regularly in his office in Valletta, the AOC always managed to conjure up a full bottle of gin which he would circulate among the gathering to free it of any inhibitions during deliberations with the boss. As a result, he learned far more about the 'sharp end' than otherwise he might have done, while we, in turn, derived much added pleasure whenever summoned to 'Father's Prayers' in his office in Valletta. Park was a good psychiatrist.

I never heard anyone question the wisdom of the AOC and, rightly so, for we believed implicitly in his direction of our affairs. Yet, in retrospect, one wonders whether much of his success could not be put down to his capacity for listening and then inwardly digesting what he had heard, before distributing others' ideas as products of his own inspired thinking. Even so, it required a clever man to use the brains of others to further his own advantage.

In many respects Keith Park resembled Montgomery in his use of flamboyance, and Eisenhower for the manner in which he traded his personal charm for the knowhow of his subordinates. But most of all, I believe Park's greatest strength lay in his ability to inspire loyalty and one wonders how much of this had rubbed off on his erstwhile boss, Dowding, two years previously when he too, in spite of being little liked by his contemporaries, was able to inspire a remarkable degree of loyalty from those privileged to serve under him.

I shall always remember Keith Park with affection. Suave, immaculately turned out, ever courteous and friendly; nor will I ever forget our first meeting on the muddy little airfield in Sussex in 1940; nor, indeed, when I went to his office on first arriving on Malta in 1942 and he went to great pains to explain why I would have to wait a few weeks before taking over a Spitfire Wing as the fellow who had been running it while awaiting my arrival was doing an excellent job and ought to be allowed to continue. He was aware of my disappointment.

'I promise you will have the very next Wing that arises . . . ' a promise I knew he would keep. And, after my repatriation early through illness, the AOC was genuinely upset at my misfortune and took the trouble to write a long personal letter after my return to the UK to give me up-to-date news of my old Wing. This was the act of a man who cared. It was also the act of one who well understood the value of human relationships. They were but two of the ingredients which made Keith Park a great leader.

Sandy Johnstone,
Framlingham,
Woodbridge,
Suffolk

Werner Mölders
MASTER TACTICIAN

There weren't many in the various World War II air forces who became generals, or the equivalent, before they were 30. Two, three, four? Maybe; but, surely, very few more.

Adolf Galland, 'the man who', according to his official British interrogators in 1945, 'more than any other shaped the destiny of the German Air Force's Fighter Arm and led it,' was one. He was 29 when Hermann Göring promoted him to be *General der Jagdflieger* – General of the Fighters – in late November 1941. He held the job until January 1945, when, because of an open and outspoken disagreement with Hitler and Göring, he was dismissed.

Then, in the closing weeks and months of the war, he raised and led the most advanced and accomplished fighter unit of the whole conflict – the illustrious JV 44 – staffed by a handful of Pilots of All the Talents – Bar, Lützow, Barkhorn, Hohagen, Herget, Schnell, Steinhoff, Schallmoser, Krupinski and others – and equipped with Germany's brilliant new jet, the Messerschmitt 262. No other air force had a jet-engined aircraft to touch its performance or handling qualities. God knows what would have happened to the US Eighth Air Force's great daylight offensive in Western Europe if Hitler, in his deranged state, hadn't interfered and tried to turn this beautiful fighter into a bomber, thereby delaying its entry into service. With greater numbers and earlier availability, the carnage could have become unacceptable.

Descended from an old Huguenot family, the first Galland came to Germany in the 17th century to set a standard for toil, application, devotion and sacrifice which subsequent generations were, by tradition, trained to emulate. Adolf Galland, 'Dolfo' to his British friends (it was Douglas Bader's nickname for him) and 'Mufti' to his old Luftwaffe comrades, is a proud descendant of a respected family.

Werner Mölders was born on 20 March, 1913, and was therefore exactly one year and one day younger than I. He was a man of undoubted ability and talent. For my part, I first met him in Seville, in Spain, in 1938 during the Spanish Civil War, when he was sent by the Air Ministry in Berlin to take over from me as the CO of No. 3 Squadron of JG 88, the Mickey Mouse unit which, at the time, was the only one still to be equipped with the obsolete Heinkel 51 biplane. The other two squadrons in the *gruppe*, No. 1, commanded by 1st Lieutenant Lützow, and No. 2, commanded by 1st Lieutenant Schlichting, had by then switched to the Messerschmitt 109.

We used the He.51s strictly in a ground-attack role, giving direct support to General Franco's forces and trying, as far as we could, to avoid air combat.

I well remember the difficulty I had in finding a successor until Mölders was sent out to follow me. I would not accept the first replacement because I did not consider him to be suitable for the job. The second was killed while he was being groomed to take over, ramming Lieutenant Michaelis, one of my best pilots, in a mid-air collision. It was in the face of these reverses that Werner Mölders, an exceptional choice and specially picked, was selected to take my place.

As the Squadron was almost at once to be equipped with the 109, Mölders was quickly able to bring it back to its primary role as an air combat entity. In this, he was manifestly successful, gaining for himself 14 victories in Spain, and topping the Condor Legion's scorers, before adding another 101 to his total in World War II. Beyond this, he was a brilliant tactician, developing revolutionary fighter tactics of which he was the recognised master. I was personally able to benefit from his grasp of these skills before the start of the campaign on the Western Front.

Werner and I became friendly competitors during the Battle of Britain after Hermann Göring had called us to his country house at Karinhall and given each of us a wing of nine squadrons. Unlike Mölders, I did not care much for this promotion, particularly when Werner had said to me afterwards: 'There you are, now you can become the new Richthofen of our Fighter Arm while I will be the new Bölcke.' What he meant was that I would be the one who would score the victories while he would be developing the tactical side of the fighting.*

Mölders was 28 when, in 1941, Göring promoted him to be the first General of the Fighter Arm. This was a tribute to his achievements not only as an individual fighter pilot and to his capabilities as a squadron, group and wing leader, it was also to mark the respect in which he was held within the German Air Force both as a tactician and as a man of outstanding character. He was an individual who stood by his principles and was resolute in dismissing the polemics of Party politics, particularly

* In the First World War, Oswald Bölcke was regarded by the German Air Force as being the unrivalled fighter tactician, far superior to all his contemporaries in this respect. Baron Manfred von Richthofen, on the other hand, was seen to be the outstanding individual pilot, arguably the best on either side in the first conflict – Ed.

when they conflicted with the tenets of the Catholic Church. He had all the qualities which enabled him to settle easily into his role as the overlord of the fighters. The job came naturally to him.

The only time when I had small differences with Werner was when, in his position of authority, he began to interfere with the combat tactics which *Jagdgeschwader* 26, under my direction, was following with notable success in the west. But this was no more than a short-lived interlude, for we quickly devised a simple and compelling method of disposing of the problem.

Some of my younger officers organised, with obvious good taste and judgement, a party for him in Paris to which they invited a number of attractive and carefully chosen girls of undeniable good looks and charm. We felt this would be an unobtrusive way of calming his ambitions.

Werner was, by this time, well regarded as a pillar of the Roman Catholic Church. However, this did not appear to prevent the party from achieving its object. After it had got nicely under way, he was one of the very first to find himself unable to resist the overtures of one of the most attractive of our guests. After that, we felt we were on a winner. Certainly we had no further cause to worry about interference with our fighter tactics.

There was, of course, the remarkable meeting that Mölders and I had earlier had with Hermann Göring in the Pas de Calais in 1940, when, after an inspection of the squadrons, the Reichmarschall finally asked each of us what we would need to become more successful with the escort of our bombers operating in daylight against targets in England.

Werner at once gave his answer. He said he would like more powerful engines for the Me.109. Göring then turned to me. 'And what about you,' he asked, 'what can we do for you?'

I decided to chance my arm. 'Herr Reichmarschall,' I replied, 'I would like you to equip my wing with Spitfires!'

Mölders did, in fact, get his more powerful Daimler-Benz engine for the 109, while I never got the Spitfires!

His sudden and unexpected death in late 1941 came as a hammer blow, following, as it did, so soon after Ernst Udet's tragic suicide. The Heinkel 111, in which he was being flown by Lieutenant Kölbe, an experienced pilot who had been with the Condor Legion in Spain, developed engine trouble *en route* to Germany from the Crimea.

Having feathered one engine, the pilot decided to attempt a single-engine landing with the other at Breslau in appalling weather. Coming down through cloud and fog, he was forced to try to land the aircraft virtually blind. Finding that he was undershooting, he at once opened the throttle, but then the 'good' engine didn't respond and the aircraft crashed, killing Mölders and the flight engineer instantly. The pilot died on the way to hospital, but Werner's aide-de-camp and the radio operator survived and were able to describe the terrible circumstances in detail.

209

The loss of Udet was tragic enough. As a World War I pilot of evident skills, he had had 62 kills to his name. Everyone liked him and he was especially popular with the active pilots. But then, eight days after standing with other holders of the Knight's Cross in the Fighter Arm as the guard of honour at Udet's state funeral on 17 November, to have to repeat the same depressing service beside my friend Werner Molders' grave in the Invalidenfriedhof in east Berlin, was a searing experience. We laid him to rest close to where Udet and Manfred von Richthofen had been buried.

It was a sad ending to a short but glittering career. I had lost a close friend and respected competitor and the Luftwaffe mourned the passing of one of its great characters.

Adolf Galland,
Bonn (Bad Godesberg),
Germany

Sir Ralph Cochrane
CLEAREST MIND IN THE AIR FORCE?

Leonard Cheshire (see pages 19–23) saw Bomber Command's leaders from the vantage point of a squadron commander with a resilient and far from conventional mind. As the CO of the famous 617 Squadron he was specially placed to assess the worth of Sir Ralph Cochrane, his AOC in 5 Group, an appointment which the Air Vice-Marshal held for two years from February 1943, a critical time in the great night offensive against Nazi Germany.

In the twilight of his life, Cheshire looked back and put Cochrane's contribution to victory in historical balance.

Well do I remember the October day in 1943 when I was driven down from Marston Moor, near York, to the AOC's headquarters at Moreton Hall near Swinderby. Indeed, how could I forget, for not only was it going to be one of the most crucial interviews of my Service career but, in more senses than one, I was in for a great surprise.

For the past eight months or so, I had been languishing as a prematurely appointed Station Commander, doing a job for which I was ill-equipped and for which I had no liking, other than the personal contact with the men and women on the Station. It was a far cry from operational flying, the only job for which I had been trained and, strange though it may sound, the only one in which I felt at home. For weeks I had thought up one scheme after another for obtaining my release and getting back to a front-line squadron, but without success. My own AOC had firmly declared that I would never be allowed to return to ops, and had gone to considerable lengths to get me promoted to Group Captain before my time – thereby, I suspect, opening himself up to considerable criticism should anything go wrong. Only if a Special Duties post suddenly appeared for which I could put myself forward, as having just the experience and the qualities that were needed – and this latter, let alone the former, was highly dubious – could there be the slightest glimmer of hope. I used to pace up and down my office, looking out of the window at the airmen and WAAFs walking by, and wish that I could be as free as they.

Then, suddenly, 617 Squadron lost its acting CO, the talented and outstandingly brave George Holden, once my fellow instructor on an earlier tour of duty at Marston Moor, and, through an intermediary, I applied to Ralph Cochrane. He agreed to see me, as a courtesy, but I was left in little doubt that the odds were against. There was the further problem of getting my own AOC to allow me to relinquish the rank he had struggled so hard to get me and so, without causing offence, release me.

I was told that Sir Ralph Cochrane was probably the most efficient of all Bomber Command's AOCs, but totally humourless, devoid of any human feeling, and that I would not enjoy working with him. This I took with a little pinch of salt for, after four years in the wartime Air Force, you come to know the exaggeration of junior officers' judgements of their superiors; in any event, my sole preoccupation was presenting my case in a way that I thought held the best chance of acceptance. All the same, I was preoccupied and edgy on the journey, loosening up only now and then to exchange a few words of banter with my WAAF driver.

From the word go, I knew that here was a man to be respected, perhaps even feared. But he was also a man whom I knew I could get on with. He clearly knew exactly what he wanted and, if I had any prepared arguments in my mind, I soon dismissed them, knowing that he would quickly see through anything that he thought was not genuine. Contrary to what I had been told, I had the impression of a slight smile about his lips every now and then, though from the content of what he was saying you might not have thought so. Still, it was definitely there; and in the months that were to follow I came to admire, even at times to love, his moments of real wit and humour. Yet, I suspect, one had to know him and to gain his confidence before he let it shine through. The interview exceeded my wildest dreams. He gave me the job there and then, but threw me completely into confusion by saying that I would do a fortnight's conversion course onto Lancasters before taking up my command. I protested vigorously, pointing out the number of tours that I had done, both as an operational pilot and as an instructor; but he gave me just one look, and I knew it was no use saying any more. In fact, he probably did me the best turn of my wartime career.

During my time in 4 Group, I was blessed with a good AOC, a New Zealander, Roderick Carr. But Cochrane – 'Cocky', as we came to know him – was in a different league altogether. Arguably, he had the finest and the clearest mind in Bomber Command, if not in the entire Royal Air Force of the day. Above all, he had the ability to think for himself and from a wholly new perspective, instead of accepting current strategy and seeing how it could be improved. But for this, there would probably have been no 617 Squadron, as built up by Guy Gibson and then developed throughout the remaining phases of the war. When you presented him with a new idea for precision bombing, he looked at it rather as he might at something the cat had brought in the door. But you knew that, beneath that mask, his brain was working, digesting the various elements and sorting the less from the more important. It might take you three weeks of continuous, concentrated argument and visual results to convince him. But you knew that, once convinced, he would back you totally and irrespective of the cost to himself. More than this, he would probably come up with his own suggestions for improving the basic idea that the Squadron had developed. On the other hand, woe betide you if the proposal did not stand and you had wasted both your time and his.

I have to say that I like it that way; World War II was too serious a business to waste time on hare-brained schemes, yet it was won more by imaginative thinking – I would go further still, and say that it was in essence won by the 'backroom boffins': therefore new thinking was needed and, if an idea really had merit, then somebody in authority had to stand behind it and guide it through the dark and murky corridors that are the characteristic of some sections of the Establishment.

Somebody once said that Cochrane was probably the man who should have taken over Bomber Command in the late autumn of 1944. Looking back, with the advantage of hindsight, I have begun to think that this could possibly be right. The bomber offensive acted as a second front, by virtue of the huge quantity of men, equipment and national resources that it diverted from the battlefields to the defence of Germany. In addition, together with the US Eighth Air Force, it forced the Luftwaffe to come up and fight and finally defeated it, so that at D-Day the Allies had total mastery of the Normandy skies. Without the bomber offensive, there would undoubtedly have been no re-entry into Europe in the summer of 1944; and without Bert Harris* the bomber offensive would not have achieved this crucial role.

Nevertheless, once the Allied forces had begun to penetrate Germany itself, there was no need to continue bombing cities. That we did so remains something of a mystery, to be explained in part by Sir Arthur's conviction that bombing alone could bring the war to an end – so nearly right, but in fact never an achievable goal – and partly by the fact that in major wars strategies seem to carry their own momentum and are reversed only with the greatest difficulty. Cochrane, in my view, was the one man who had the intellectual vision and flexibility of thought to have recognised that the time had come to switch targets. Harris, after all, had worked himself to the limit of his resources. He had faithfully carried out the task given to him by the War Cabinet and, like Churchill himself at the end of the war, he should have been relieved. Had 'Cocky' stepped into his shoes and seen that the need now was to go for oil and for close support to the Army, the war might have finished earlier; there would have been no

* Air Chief Marshal (later Marshal of the Royal Air Force), Sir Arthur T. Harris, C-in-C, Bomber Command, from 23 February, 1942.

Dresden – though this, it has to be said, was not Bomber Command's choice of target – and both Bomber Command itself and its outstanding Commander-in-Chief would have been judged differently by the post-war generation.

It was my privilege to remain in touch with 'Cocky' after the war. I think that I remained until the very end somewhat in awe of his mental sharpness and his insistence on correct behaviour, total commitment and professionalism. But it was the caring, human side of him that left its mark on me more than anything else. Perhaps it was the depth of this side of his character, added to a natural shyness, that made him feel he must conceal what was going on inside by a slightly stern exterior. During the war itself, he drove himself mercilessly and was forever thinking of how he could better discharge his responsibilities, both to the welfare of the men under his command and to the prosecution of the war effort. But, once this was all behind, it was easier for him to display his true nature. On many occasions I was touched to discover how interested he was in certain aspects of my activities and by the trouble he would go to in helping or advising me. On my side, I felt that he was never really acknowledged in the way he should have been, and that the RAF was the loser in consequence. He, I think, felt this too, though he never betrayed as much.

At one of the 617 Reunions in the RAF Club, a major occasion attended by Bert Harris and several VIPs, a most unfortunate thing happened. Harris had received a standing ovation at the end of the toast to him and, during the following toast, when a reference was made to the part played by A. V. Roe's, one of the Squadron members sitting just in front of the head table unexpectedly jumped to his feet, waved everybody else up and urged them to give the A. V. Roe's representative a similar ovation. But, when Cochrane's turn came to be mentioned, the audience merely clapped. It was partly because to repeat it a third time may have seemed overmuch, and partly because the toast did not come to a satisfactory conclusion, catching us by surprise. Many of us felt deeply embarrassed and, though there was not the slightest sign that Cochrane noticed the omission, I cannot help feeling that he did.

Then five years or so later came another reunion, near Weybridge, to honour Barnes Wallis, to which Sir Ralph came despite feeling not at all well. It fell to my happy lot to give one of the speeches, an occasion which I vowed to use in order to make up for our lapse. The ovation 'Cocky' received was overwhelming, almost more than any I have witnessed. It is reported that, as he got into the car to be driven home, he turned to his son and said: 'I am rather pleased that you now know what my wartime aircrew thought of me.'

Perhaps it was a blessing that the first occasion went wrong, for in this short off-the-cuff remark is summed up the loneliness of the man who, throughout those long war years, submerged his personal and inner feelings in order the better to discharge his duties and protect his crews, yet who must have yearned to let others see him as he really was.

Leonard Cheshire,
Cavendish,
Suffolk

Eduard Neumann
DESERT COMMANDER

Few can be better equipped than Gustav Rödel, a retired Brigadier-General living in Bonn, to provide a picture of Eduard Neumann, the highly regarded commander of *Jagdgeschwader* 27, the Luftwaffe's air component which provided support for General Rommel's Afrika Korps in the fluctuating fortunes of the Desert war of 1941 and 1942.

Rödel was flying alongside Neumann in the Battle of Britain in 1940, then he served under him as a squadron commander in North Africa, becoming one of the Luftwaffe's most successful Desert leaders in 1942. When, in the spring of 1943, the time came for Neumann to relinquish command of JG 27, Rödel was by experience and bearing the obvious successor. Still 'in play' at the end of the war, his personal score stood at 98 Allied aircraft destroyed, 52 of them falling to his guns in the North African fighting.

Of all the exceptional commanders and leaders I served with in World War II, Oberst Eduard Neumann stands out in my book from the rest. I would place him at the top of my list of wartime characters. There will be many who also served with him in the famous *Jagdgeschwader* 27, which Neumann commanded with rare distinction in North Africa from June 1942 to April 1943, who will share my judgement.

Our Edu's experience on the Western Front in 1940 and 1941, both as a pilot and as a formation leader, gave him an acute understanding of tactical warfare and the ability to judge a man's worth and, beyond that, his potential as an operational commander.

Aged 29 when the fighting began in the West, he had already become matured by experience in the Spanish Civil War. He had developed his own style of leadership in the air, creating for his followers the opportunities to score rather than seizing them for himself. His own individual total of 13 aircraft destroyed would have been immeasurably increased had he pursued a more individual role. But that was never his way, for Edu was essentially a 'team man'.

216

These were qualities which were to stand him in special stead when he became the Kommodore of JG 27 in the Western Desert, working in close support of Erwin Rommel's forces. But it was not purely as an operational commander that he shone. By his own example he set standards from which, even in war, he was not prepared to depart.

I recall an incident when, at about 19.30 on 20 July, 1940, I was flying as Edu's wingman during the fighting over south-east England and the Channel. We had intercepted a formation of Blenheim bombers some 30 kilometers south of Portland. My leader, having closed the range and made an instantly successful attack on one aircraft, watched its occupants bale out; he then proceeded to follow them down and stay orbiting just above the water until he was satisfied that the survivors had made contact with the lifeboat.

Having to stick with my No. 1 had prevented me from attacking a second bomber. After we had landed, I could not hide from Edu my intense disappointment at having to surrender whatever chance I might have had of destroying the second aircraft simply because he had elected to see the survivors from his bomber safely into the lifeboat.

'Yes,' he said, nodding, 'I quite understand. But do you not feel better now that we know the crew of that first aircraft are safe in the lifeboat?'

There are some who will say that there is no such thing as chivalry in the air. Edu, by his example, taught me otherwise. It was one of the many lessons I learnt from him during our service together.

Then again I noticed the trouble he used to take to get to know his pilots, to discuss with them their problems as well as their successes and to encourage them to talk about their families. When we all sat down together in the evenings after the day's fighting was done, he would make a point of stimulating this feeling of comradeship and human understanding. I recall how struck I was by the importance he attached to the need to understand the psychological side of the pilots' attitudes to combat and by the trouble he took to help them control their thinking and emotions. It was a distinct feature of his leadership and I witnessed it through the different stages of his advance right up to his command of JG 27 in the Desert.

I have no doubt that this was one reason why he was able to bring out the best in the squadron pilots ... and why, in North Africa, JG 27 possessed, under him, so high a proportion of outstanding performers, including the star of all, Hans-Joachim Marseille. Indeed, it is arguable whether there was another *Jagdgeschwader* in the German Air Force where the percentage of exceptional pilots and leaders was as high. Much of it stemmed from the brand of leadership which Edu offered.

Even now, nearly half a century later, it is a noticeable feature of our annual JG 27 reunions that this spirit still prevails. It is, moreover, true of the Italians who attend just as much as it is of their German counterparts, for Neumann's relationship with the Regia Aeronautica, as a commander in the Desert, was deliberately close. He made a conscious effort to encourage the blending of the squadrons of the two countries into a united force. This spirit even extends to the offspring of the Italian survivors just as much as to ours, for these annual gatherings have now become essentially family affairs.

It is one of the reasons also why the President of the German Air Force Fighter Pilots' Association always tends, whenever he addresses our reunions, to refer to this spirit and to say that, in this matter, JG 27 is still on its own. The implication is that all this stems from the lead which the unit's Desert commander has always given.

Eduard Neumann was born in 1911 in the dukedom of Bukowina, which at that time was in the keep of the Austro-Hungarian Empire, the Kaiser being Franz Joseph I. His ancestors had emigrated there in the 18th century as, indeed, many other families had ventured to do. However, after the signing of the Treaty of Versailles, following the ending of World War I, many families of German extraction were subjected to political revenge and, as a result, decided to make their future in Germany.

Edu was one who emigrated to enable him to continue his engineering studies in Berlin. Then he joined a students' flying club and qualified for his wings. And so, when the General Staff of the Reichswehr became intent on rebuilding the German Air Force in 1935 – despite the problems posed by the Versailles Treaty – those with flying ambitions and the right background found themselves being hand-picked for service with the air arm.

Thus did Neumann enlist as a member of the German armed forces and get the chance to put one foot on the first rung of the Luftwaffe ladder. At the end of the French campaign in 1940, he was posted to the headquarters of JG 27, being earmarked for leadership of a fighter *gruppe* when an opportunity arose.

I was also serving at this time on the same headquarters staff with responsibility for the technical back-up. Adolf Galland was likewise a member of the same staff. The three of us, together with the Kommodore, Max Ibel, were soon to fly sorties together during the Battle of Britain. And so I began my service with Eduard Neumann, which was happily to endure until April 1943, when I followed him in command of the *Jagdgeschwader*. It was a privilege for me that he should have recommended me for the job.

Edu was, in fact, General Galland's right-hand man for virtually the whole of 1943 and never really left his staff. Because JG 27 was partially involved with the fighting in the Balkans, he and I remained in touch, even when, in 1944, he was Chief Controller of Fighter Command and responsible for the day and night flying until the collapse of the front in Rumania. Moreover, from the autumn of 1944 until the end of the war, with only one very short break, Neumann was also head of Fighter Command in northern Italy, where he only had very few Italian fighter pilots under his command; these, however, were very good and he had a high regard for them.

It did not please him particularly when he became a prisoner of war right at the end. Nevertheless, he certainly had nothing to moan about for his treatment was exemplary. His guards were always correct in their behaviour and understanding towards him, which was more than could normally be expected in an interrogation or prisoner-of-war camp.

We used to pull Edu's leg after the war when he founded his own technical company concerned with the manufacture of cranes. As far back as 1933, he had once landed by mistake on a crane near Berlin. 'Just magnetised by cranes,' we said.

But looking back to the war years, I realise full well what I owed to this memorable character. Our time together was to leave an indelible impression.

Gustav Rödel,
Bonn (Bad Godesberg),
Germany

Sir Harry Broadhurst
THE BROADHURST LEGACY

Charles Mrázek (Group Captain Karel Mrázek) was one of the 'special' Czechs. By his leadership and fighting qualities he made a lasting (and well-decorated) mark with the Royal Air Force.

Apart from his later service, he had one signal distinction in November 1940, right at the end of the Battle of Britain. He was flying with 46 Squadron, based at Stapleford Tawney in the North Weald sector of 11 Group, when, high up over Maidstone and the Garden of Kent, the unit's Hurricanes encountered Mussolini's contribution to the Axis powers' attack on Britain – a formation of Fiat BR 20 bombers, supported (at a distance) by a gaggle of CR 42 fighters.

It was just Charles's luck that on that, of all days, the Rolls-Royce engine in his Hurricane began to play up and lose power. Inevitably, he started to lag dangerously behind. 'All I could do,' he said later, 'was to hang about, keep my eyes open, and see if I could find any stragglers making for the Channel and home . . .'

He did, two CR 42s falling to the guns of his largely unserviceable aircraft. But he couldn't claim them. The Squadron, together with 249 and 257, had had a field day and he, all by himself, had no witnesses as he made his way, almost out of fuel, back from the Straits of Dover.

In his excitement, he had forgotten to switch on his camera gun . . .

To write fairly about Broady – for that's how we Czechs and everyone else who served with him always referred to Air Chief Marshal Sir Harry Broadhurst – I must go back a little and provide some background. It is important to the picture of the man whom I came to know – and so much respect – in the early war years . . .

After the fall of France in 1940, practically all our aircrew came to England by whatever means we could find. Listening to Winston Churchill we were certain that it was the one country which would fight Hitler until the death – or victory was won.

I had been a 28-year-old fighter pilot, a regular officer in the Czech Air Force, in the run-up to the fighting in World War II. I was commanding our 33 (Fighter) Squadron. The professionals among us were, of course, well trained and experienced pilots by the time we came to Britain, having flown many operational hours already in both Poland and France.

But coming to England to fight presented us with real problems. The country was completely unknown to us. Only a very few of us could speak the language – I couldn't speak a word! This was our biggest handicap. The understanding of Service phraseology and getting to know the slang and the coded messages over the RT was of vital importance if we were to operate successfully – and survive. It was literally a matter of life and death for us . . .

We had no idea of the organisation of the Royal Air Force . . . We had never heard of operations rooms, radar cover, the control of airborne operations from the ground by means of a controller speaking to the leaders over the radio . . . We had to accept and become familiar with new procedures and tactics in the air, and become adept at handling strange, yet beautiful, aeroplanes. And what's more, it all had to be done quickly. The Royal Air Force in 1940 and 1941 could not carry passengers for long.

But one of the great strengths of the Service was its ability to absorb into the squadrons those of us who had escaped from German-occupied Europe. It says much for its organisation and for the basic standards in the fighting units that we could be embraced so fast – despite the difficulties which we posed.

As a former commanding officer of an operational squadron in our Air Force, I could see at once that it was primarily due to good leadership. The Royal Air Force, for the most part, had fine operational leaders – squadron commanders, wing leaders, station and sector commanders. They had flair and personality, and the ability in the air to gather the 'displaced Europeans' under their wing and blend us into what was there already. This capability made a deep impression upon me. Even now, as I look back over nearly half a century, this was one of the features of those early, difficult days which I remember most vividly.

This, then, was where Broady came into my own service experience. It was 1941, the Battle of Britain and my eight months as the only Czech among all those English fellows in 46 Squadron were over. I had been given command of 313, the Czech fighter squadron, and we were then posted to Hornchurch, the airfield north of the River Thames in 11 Group of Fighter Command. Broady was the station commander, but he also led the Wing as frequently as he could. I shall never forget what he did to dovetail 313 into the Wing (with all the problems he must have had with us). I truly believe, with the experience I was later to have myself as a wing leader, that only a great commander could have done it in those circumstances and at that stage in the war.

What, then, of this legendary figure? What impression do I still retain of him after all this time?

Let us be quite clear of one thing: Broady was not an easy man. You could not cross him and expect to retain his support. He had a discipline and a strong personality and, when he wanted to turn it on, a charm which made people respond to him and follow him.

I will never forget the image he created for me on 313's arrival at Hornchurch. He was only some five years older than I and yet, when I reported to him in his station commander's office and glanced at the decorations on his battledress, I knew at once that this man was 'somebody'. His welcome was friendly, but not particularly 'matey'. He did not know much about us and I knew nothing about him. He had no idea what he might expect from us and I, in turn, did not know what to expect of him. Here we were trying to size one another up.

He promised nothing save that we could expect hard work. He would require military discipline from the whole Squadron not only on the ground but, more so, in the air. I had no difficulty in giving him the assurance he wanted. With that the welcome ended – and our co-operation began . . .

Broady led the Wing on many occasions over France, Belgium and Holland and what struck me was the way that he did it. You got the feeling that he had the squadrons firmly within his control. There was one example which I particularly recall.

We were flying one day as the top cover for a few light bombers attacking St Omer in northern France. Broady was leading the close escort around the bombers at 10,000 feet. Just as we were about to turn away from the target and back towards Calais, he suddenly called me and drew attention to Huns above us. I had already seen the Me.109s preparing to jump us from out of the sun, but Broady also pointed out to me that one of my aircraft was lagging behind the formation. When I saw my Blue 4 falling behind, I slowed down to give him the chance to catch up while at the same time keeping the 109s well in view.

A small incident? Yes, but it taught me one of the lessons of good wing leading for the future – always keep the two or three squadrons well within sight and watch out for the stragglers before they became a prey for enemy fighters. After this, I regarded Broady as my mentor, although he never knew it.

I remember one evening in the local pub he came up to me and said: 'Charlie, you know I feel quite safe down below when I've got you Butchers (the Squadron's call sign) above us.' In a sentence it gave me a warmer feeling than the whisky in the glass which had just been handed to me. I then knew instantly why it was that 313 was so often chosen as the 'top cover' or the 'freelance squadron' as he called it.

To sum up, Broady was a brilliant pilot and a master tactician. He was always cool-headed – I never saw him off balance. He anticipated well and he had an undeniable gift of being able to appraise a battle and keep it all within his grasp as it developed. Things moved very fast, as we know, but despite it he seemed always to be able to keep everything in perspective. He was quite simply a natural commander in the air as well as on the ground.

As a man, he had a friendly and human approach to everyone. He could be a tough customer – oh yes! At the same time he was a welcoming, jovial, sociable partner in whose presence no one felt inferior or overlooked – even those of much lower rank.

I salute you, Broady. You gave me experience and confidence which I was able to exploit when eventually I became the leader of the Czech Wing. It was my special luck that in those early days in England I had you as a model.

Karel Mrázek,
Jablonec n Nis,
Czechoslovakia

Sir Basil Embry
MAN OF FIRE

Air Marshal Sir Peter Wykeham was cast in much the same operational mould as the idiosyncratic character whom he here portrays.
It is as well that this should be so, for only someone who went through
the gamut of wartime flying – and commanding – in the Desert,
Western Europe and, later, in Korea, and who served and flew with
his compelling subject, is really fitted to make a complete judgement.

Between the two of them, Wykeham and Embry won six DSOs.

There is one other feature to mention. The author writes for his
own as well as other people's pleasure – as befits one who married
into J. B. Priestley's family 40 years ago.

War discovers strong characters: even in peacetime the flying services
attract eccentrics: so the flying services at war effortlessly produce dynamic
and unusual leaders. But even in this company Basil Embry was special.

When I first met him, in North Africa in 1941, I thought I had lost the
capacity to be surprised by my fellow-combatants. He arrived from
England, posted as Senior Air Staff Officer of Desert Air Force. Thus he
was my immediate boss. He was already celebrated for a spectacular escape
from France. Shot down when leading his Blenheim squadron, he was
picked up by the Germans, escaped, and captured again. He escaped again,
his second burst for freedom launched by a murderous assault on his
guards, after which he bicycled across France, crossed the Pyrenees, and
finally arrived at Gibraltar clamouring to be restored to his squadron.
Instead he was sent to command a night-fighter base and later detached
to North Africa, and now we dusty airmen of the Desert Air Force, who
thought all European operations somewhat suburban in character, could
get a close look at this one-man tornado.

We saw a small, wiry man, with a dark-complexioned face crumpled like a dried apricot. He had a shock of black hair, and a wandering nose which would, in earlier times, have marked a genial addiction to port wine. His eyes were very dark blue, and seemed to crackle with electricity. I know that eyes cannot do this, but his did. He had a disconcerting habit, even in quite amiable conversation, of advancing his face to yours until his nose was a couple of inches away, while his eyes bored into you. It was an unnerving trick. Whenever Basil spoke to me with real animation, which was often, I had great difficulty in keeping his face in focus, but it certainly gave considerable emphasis to whatever he said, important or trifling.

This short figure, with an expression which changed in a second from ferocity to delighted laughter, radiated dynamism to an almost frightening degree. He set about his work with a fierce energy, tempering ruthlessness with a strong sense of humour. Basil was the first senior officer I had met in the British Armed Services (the Americans, later, shared the gift) who gave me the comforting feeling that war could be better endured by applying to it a powerful sense of fun. My fellow-pilots knew the secret, but here was an Air Commodore who knew it too. It was a revelation.

We knew that Basil was deadly serious at heart, but his technique was to appear to treat everything warlike, including the enemy and our own High Command, as a continual running joke. Our service together in North Africa was brief, and the next time I met him, in England, he was the Air Officer Commanding No. 2 Tactical Bomber Group, and he had caused me to be posted to command No. 140 mobile Mosquito Wing under his command. Basil was ruthless in getting the people he wanted for this post or that, hammering down the objections of Personnel staffs in a way that must have been very distressful for them. He was equally rough on those he wished to discard. I quote his memoirs:

'One day I was sitting opposite an air-sea rescue control officer at lunch when I heard another officer say to him, "Will you please go to the Ops room at once. A pilot has bailed out over the sea." He replied "Yes, I will be there in a minute, I will just finish my soup." I shouted at him across the table "Do you realise there is a boy in the sea fighting for his life? What you will do is to pack your kit and get out of this Group before I lay hands on you." '

Basil's philosophy of command was simple enough – he led from the front, even at Group Commander level, on all possible occasions. Whether it was in air operations, or in dealing with officialdom (including his own superiors) his policy was to get so far in front as almost to be out of sight, so that his faithful staff and commanders had, metaphorically, to run ever harder to catch up with him. This system extended from the planning of air attacks to this slightly bizarre example from his own writings:

'. . . some of the men were not as steady in the face of bombing as they should have been, but the strong measures I had to adopt were soon effective, and when I moved my bed into the detonator store they decided I was crazy, and more to be feared than enemy action.'

I sometimes wondered whether this macho attitude might not be a little over the top. Nobody, I thought, could be so in love with violence and death, and still be a charming and apparently normal man. For Basil was a well-rounded character. He could charm whole flocks of birds down from the trees if necessary, and apparently without effort. He was happily married, and though he had lost an infant son in tragic circumstances he had other children coming along. He was a Catholic convert (but his wife had resisted) and though no proselytiser he had the usual strong views of the converted. He had already been awarded the DFC and three Distinguished Service Orders, and would win a fourth before the war's end. Why, I asked myself, was he so excessively fierce?

Basil's assessment of servicemen was simple. Those he approved of 'had fire in their belly'. Those he disapproved of 'had never heard a shot fired in anger'. This might produce some uncomfortable echoes of a Patton-like, pearl-handled revolver general. Such a picture could not be further from the truth, for his sense of the ridiculous, and his deep feeling for the combatants under his command, put him in a different category entirely. But what category? I never fathomed him, then or later.

Basil never allowed his personal approach to operations to degenerate into exposing his aircrews to unnecessary danger or unprofitable risks. He quoted with contempt the words of a bomber commander whom he claimed to have heard say, after one of his raids was all but wiped out, 'Send out another formation. They can't frighten me!' Basil was no expender of cannon-fodder, and he employed his usual strong-arm tactics to get himself the very best Operations and Intelligence staff officers, and to sack all those not up to the highest standard. He set up elaborate and comprehensive operations facilities and by meticulous organisation and arduous attention to detail had his sorties planned so that the maximum results could be hoped for, with the minimum losses. In doing this, he fondly imagined that all his subordinate commanders and crews were as intrepid as he was himself, and no doubts on this score ever crossed his mind. And by assuming it, he made it so.

By 1944, after 4½ years of active operations, I was trying to conceal from my Wing the growing feeling that the prospect of further excursions into curtains of flak filled me with melancholy, or perhaps one might say plain fear. Basil totally failed to sense this, which he would have found incomprehensible anyway. He would phone me at midnight to tell me that as a great treat he was allotting me a really diabolical mission. He declared that he knew how mortally offended I would be if he gave it to any other

Primus inter pares. Leonard Cheshire VC OM,
bomber leader extraordinary

Freddie de Pelleport
(*top right*) with 242,
Manston, 1941.
Bernard Duperier is
on the right (*standing*)

Rock-solid Luftwaffe
oberfeldwebel. Adolf Walter
(*far right*) with 8 Squadron
of 52 Wing at Coquelles,
near Calais, July 1940.
Günther Rall (*centre*), aged
22, was CO

Pilot officers with 66 Squadron, Cornwall, 1941. Raoul Daddo-Langlois (*right*) with the editor

Regia Aeronautica's engaging prince. Gianni Caracciolo (*left*) with Tullio Martinelli, Battle of Malta, Gela, Sicily, June 1942

South African quartet from 7 Wing, Tunisia, 1943. Jack Parsonson is on the right

'Colonel Bert', Desert leader. Bert Rademan at Alamein, 1942

Malta winner. Group Captain A. B. Woodhall, Takali, June 1942

Above: Rhodesian trinity. John Deall (*centre*), CO of 266 Squadron with engine and airframe fitters, Harry Smith and Ken Pike

Below: Californian venturer. Sid Seid with 'Mozzie', Holmsley South, Hampshire, autumn 1944

Don Jandrell (*centre*), CO of 260 Squadron in 239 Wing of Desert Air Force, during battle for Rome, summer 1944

Paragons of the U.S. 8th's 375th (P-51D) Squadron of 361st Fighter Group, Bottisham, Cambridgeshire, 1944. Ben Drew (*left*) and Bill Kemp

'I never knew another quite like Sadaaki Akamatsu.' Navy lieutenant, Pacific, 1944

Above: Target Berlin! Sir Arthur Harris – 'Bert' to the Service – C-in-C Bomber Command, High Wycombe, 1944

Right: Hugh Pughe Lloyd, a wing commander in 1940. His battle for Malta was yet to come

Above: Battle of Britain and Mediterranean master, New Zealander Keith Park with ground crews, Malta, spring 1943

'The ovation was overwhelming, almost more tham I have ever witnessed.' Cheshire on Ralph Cochrane, brilliant leader of 5 Group, Bomber Command

Below: At the Channel coast. Hermann Göring with Luftwaffe leaders, Werner Mölders (*left*) and Adolf Galland (*right*), summer 1940

Bottom: Supporting Rommel, Western Desert, 1942, the Luftwaffe's Hans-Joachim Marseille (*left*) with Eduard Neumann (*right*), exceptional *Kommodore* of *Jagdgeschwader* 27

North African dialogue, 1943. The widely experienced Harry Broadhurst, commander of the Desert Air Force, lending an ear to the U.S. 9th Fighter Command's General Strickland

Pressing it to the limit, 1945. Basil Embry, 2 Group AOC (*pointing*), with (*left to right*) David Atcherley, Peter Wykeham and H. P. Shallard, group intelligence officer

John Dundas, a 'First' at Oxford and later 609's conqueror of Helmut Wieck in the Battle of Britain, 1940

Left: OC 'A' Flight, 616 Squadron, Tangmere, 1941, Hugh Dundas with 'Robin'. A glittering future stretched ahead

Above: The Douglas-Hamiltons – and each, remarkably, a squadron commander. (*Left to right*) Lord David, 'Douglo', Duke of Hamilton, 'Geordie', Earl of Selkirk and Lord Malcolm, Cranwell product

All my own work! Richard (Dick or Batchy) Atcherley (*left*) walks away from his 'pranged' Auster, Bentley Priory, Stanmore, 1944

'Unexampled gallantry'. . .
Victor Beamish at North Weald,
July 1940

Close Desert shave, 1943. Marseille's unconventional
squadron commander and, later, *Kommodore* of JG 27,
Professor Ludwig Franzisket, outstanding post-war scientist

Talented maestro who led the Norwegians' North Weald wing.
Kaj Birksted (*right*), the Dane, with Rolf ('Ice') Berg, a
natural successor

Leader of the South African Air Force's Victory Parade,
London, 1945, Hannes Faure with 'Bomb' Finney (*left*)
and 'Lippy' Lipawsky (*right*)

Above left: Gus Walker, Rugby international and Bomber Command star,
he captured the high ground
Right: 'Ho-hum, m'dear boy, I've disposed of your belongings. . .'
The irrepressible Brian Kingcome, Cranwell-trained
'character'

Left: '. . . It's the size of the fight in the dog. New Zealand's Al Deere, leader of the Bigg wing, 1943

Below: Tiny Nel, No 40 Squadron's Tac-R specialist of Abyssinia, the Desert, Sicily and Italy

Below left: A Home Secretary's choice. Dun Smith, winner of two DSO's and three DF(eleven insatiable years

Below right: From Blenheims to jets, four operational tours in as many theatres. . . De Walker, intrepid wing commander

Lou Greenburgh, Canadian bomber captain. Success despite abject family cruelty. Here in his B-24, 1945

Bader. 'I've got £4000 put away. It's yours if you need it.'

Right: Scourge of Bomber Command. Three top Luftwaffe night fighters, 1944. (*left to right*) Helmut Lent, Heinz Wolfgang Schnaufer and Hans-Joachim Jabs.

Below: Fleet Air Arm marvels in the Desert, 1942. Bobby Bradshaw (*extreme right*), 'Lucky' Sutton is next to him

Above right: Prison liberator. Charles Pickard – 'Pick' to one and all – Sculthorpe, Norfolk, July 1943

Right: Thoroughgoing countryman with 'Sally' in line abreast. Johnnie Johnson, top scorer in the West with 38 destroyed

Don Blakeslee briefing the U.S. 8th's 4th Fighter Group, Debden, 1944. Front row (*left to right*) Jim Clark, Bernard McGrattan and James Goodson

Above left: Dambusters all, with the Chief Buster present. Guy Gibson VC with some of his 617 clutch, June 1943.
Right: He wrote his own contract. Adrian Warburton, Mediterranean history maker, 1942

Australia's Hughie Edwards. 'He did [uniquely] as many operations after his VC as before it.'

Below: Leonard Henry Trent, soon to win the VC. No 79 in the draw, he missed the prison break – and lived

Below right: Lord of the Manor, Biggin Hill, 1943. The Royal Air Force's great South African leader, 'Sailor' Malan

Right: Roman Czerniawski – 'Armand' alias 'Brutus'

Below: Fleet Air Arm immortal. David Foster at Dekheila, Egypt, 1941

Bottom: Masters of the Intruder art, No 141 Squadron's Bob Braham (*right*), unlikely vicar's son, and W. J. (Sticks) Gregory, navigating genius

Married in 1923 in Royal Air Force uniform, it was the
greatest compliment the future Monarch could pay the Service

formation in his Group. 'I know that you would never forgive me if I let someone else have it,' he would say genially. This may have been a profound error, but it was the inspired touch of the born leader. As I put down the phone I felt as if I'd just been given a bicycle for my birthday. I could reflect that like the odds in roulette, the chances were not cumulative, but the same for every throw.

When I got to the operations room to start the planning I would find that a certain Wing Commander Smith was already written into the attacking formation, somewhere near the back, where the flak and fighters were worst. This of course was Basil, who was obliged to wear a false uniform and carry false papers with a not very original alias, since Intelligence had long since informed him that he was at the top of the German list of airmen to be shot if captured. In due course he would appear in this rig for the briefing, bringing as his navigator Flight Lieutenant Peter Clapham, an operations room radar supervisor, unfit to fly, and in any case reputed to be a peace-time executive of British Intelligence. A more unsuitable navigator it would be hard to find, but there was no doubt about the fire in Peter Clapham's belly, or his ability as an amateur navigator, so he was just right for Basil. In fact Peter must have been a very brave man indeed.

In this shaky disguise Basil enthusiastically joined in with our star operations at that time, which were attacks on Gestapo headquarters in various countries. He was sailing terribly close to the wind. May 1945 came just in time for him, and before he could get himself into Tiger Force Japan surrendered.

So he survived the war, much against the odds, to become Chief of Flying Training, Commander-in-Chief of Fighter Command, and Commander-in-Chief of Allied Air Forces Central Europe. In all of these appointments I had the honour (and better still, the pleasure) of serving under him. He should have been Chief of Air Staff, and if he had the Service would have gained much in spirit and efficiency, and lost a lot of stuffiness. But he had a healthy detestation of almost all Civil Servants ('never heard a shot fired in anger') and though I often warned him not to take them head-on, because they always won in the end, in this he paid me little heed.

He had a straightforward and unsubtle mind. At Fontainebleau he came back from a conference with his immediate superior in Europe, Marshal Juin, and thrusting his face into mine greeted me with the words, 'Peter, Marshal Juin and I trust each other implicitly!' I opened my mouth to remind him that he, Basil, spoke no French, and that the wily Marshal had also been a trusted friend of Darlan, Göring, Pétain, and other questionable characters, but seeing him so happy at this diplomatic coup I held my tongue. We, the Staff, gathered round him to protect him, as we had done in action.

When he left the Service he left England, and he and his family settled in

Australia and carved new farms from the outback. Australia now has many young Embrys, and this is Australia's gain and our most grievous loss.

Peter Wykeham,
Stockbridge,
Hampshire

2
The Families

Memorable families, and their representatives, were a feature of the Royal Air Force at war . . . The Douglas-Hamiltons, the Beamishes, the Donaldsons, the MacRoberts, the Atcherleys, the Dundases, the Cheshires, the Smiths (Roderick and Jerrold) from Canada . . . Between them, and others, they typified much of the spirit and personality of the Service and left behind a catalogue of oft-repeated stories – and imperishable deeds.

In the small yet select gallery which follows, sons of four of the families are portrayed.

The Douglas-Hamiltons
'HE CAN WAIT UNTIL THE MORNING'

There were four Douglas-Hamilton brothers in the Air Force and, remarkably, all became, in their time, squadron commanders – a record which is unlikely ever to be matched. Here, the second of the quartet, and its only survivor, the wartime Group Captain Lord George Douglas-Hamilton, later the 10th Earl of Selkirk – Geordie to the Royal Air Force – offers a rare insight into the family, its upbringing and the background against which the brothers grew up to fly.

But let us deal, first, with the author's own contribution to the family's extraordinary record.

After Eton and Balliol, the Sorbonne in Paris and the universities of Bonn, Vienna and Edinburgh, Geordie Selkirk joined No. 603 (City of Edinburgh) Squadron in the Auxiliary Air Force. He had first soloed an aeroplane in 1926 – at Manston, in Kent, during the Oxford University Air Squadron's summer camp. His subsequent four-year command of 603, which ended in 1938, coincided with Hitler's frenzied arming of Nazi Germany.

Having been accepted into the Faculty of Advocates in Edinburgh (and having, on the way, been cross-examined in Latin in public!), 603's former CO reported to Fighter Command headquarters at Stanmore in the fateful summer of 1939. He asked the Group Captain, Operations, on arrival, what he was to do.

'He looked up a book,' he recalls, 'and told me I was to be Chief Intelligence Officer (CIO). And what, I asked, did that mean? "I don't know," he replied, "go to your Section and find out." And so, in 1939, we went to war.'

Once installed, a strange truth struck the newly appointed CIO.

'It occurred to me immediately that the Air Ministry had not recognised the difficulty and importance of aircraft recognition. I at once wrote to all the Service Commands and requested from each five photographs from different angles of all operational aircraft in the Command.

'Perhaps even more important was the success of Sir Patrick Hastings, sometime Attorney General [and arguably the outstanding advocate of his day – Ed.], who was in my Section. He persuaded the Air Ministry to produce models of all aircraft our fighters were likely to encounter.'

After the CIO had served Air Chief Marshal Sir Hugh Dowding, the C-in-C, throughout the Battle of Britain, there followed spells, first, in the Directorate of Training at the Air Ministry and then, in 1942, in command of the Royal Air Force station at Andover, in Hampshire, which, at the time, was devoted to Army Co-operation training.

But in September 1943 there came a day when the future Chancellor of the Duchy of Lancaster and (later) First Lord of the Admiralty must have wondered whether there would be any further advance.

Geordie Selkirk was flying a Wellington bomber out to the Middle East *en route* to take up a senior appointment with the Service's East Africa Command, whose prime task then was to destroy German and Japanese submarines operating in the Indian Ocean. Low down over the Bay of Biscay, his aircraft was attacked unexpectedly by five German Junkers 88s, operating from south-west France against the anti-U-boat patrols which Coastal Command were habitually flying in the area.

Assailed from front and rear, the Group Captain drew on all the arts that Fighter Command had instilled, turning, first, into one attack and then into another while his gunner kept up an unyielding defensive barrage. Cloud cover eventually provided blessed sanctuary, but not before one of the pursuers had been left belching ignominious smoke.

During the onslaught, a cannon shell had shattered the Wellington's windscreen and taken a nick out of the sleeve of the pilot's tunic as it passed. It was a close call – but risk-taking and near-shaves are a currency with which the Douglas-Hamiltons have long been familiar.

What, then, of the other three brothers in this unconventional family which was to provide the wartime Royal Air Force with three Group Captains and one Wing Commander – without any of them being a regular officer when war began? What was it about military aviation which possessed for each a seemingly irresistible attraction? Geordie Selkirk is himself in no doubt.

'I can only answer that it was the lure of flying in the 1920s and 1930s at a time when flying control did not exist and when the radio telephone was still unknown. The freedom and the beauty of flying was then a unique incentive . . .'

Maybe heredity also had something to do with it.

'Our mother and father were both born from strong Naval traditions; indeed, it was said on the authority of Lord Mountbatten that our great grandfather was one of Nelson's captains. Our grandfather is believed to have narrowly missed the Charge of the Light Brigade, while our father,* trained in *Britannia*, was a brilliant gymnast, known as "Pocket Hercules", and had performed some astonishing swimming achievements.'

The early life may also have contributed to the later pattern.

'One singular event should perhaps be recorded. When Admiral Lord Fisher resigned in 1915, he came to Scotland to stay with my father who was an old shipmate. Suddenly he decided he wanted to talk to Jellicoe. Accordingly, my mother, my brother, Douglo,† and myself motored to Thurso and thence to Scapa in a destroyer. We had lunch on board the *Iron Duke* and spent the afternoon learning about the mysteries of a 12.5 in. turret . . . For a boy aged nine, it was a great adventure – even if it was totally irregular.'

The individual idiosyncrasies were soon apparent, as Selkirk makes clear.

'The family has been described as a "job lot". [The brothers] were certainly very different from each other in ability and achievements . . .
'The eldest of us, Douglo, evolved slowly. He was never much addicted to book learning, but very early he showed a determination which could easily be mistaken for obstinacy. His introduction to the noble art of self-defence started at school, his enthusiasm for it continuing for ten years. He became captain of boxing at Oxford – an appointment which his son, James,* held years later. He only lost the middleweight championship of England in the final fight; he became a close friend of Johnny Brown, Scotland's very successful professional middleweight.
'But gradually aviation took over to become an absorbing interest.
'Douglo learnt to fly privately, joined No. 602 (City of Glasgow) Squadron in the Auxiliary Air Force and thereafter commanded the Squadron for ten years.

* The 13th Duke of Hamilton – Ed.
† The Marquis of Clydesdale: he became the 14th Duke of Hamilton in 1940 – Ed.
* Lord James Douglas-Hamilton, a minister at the Scottish Office in Mrs Thatcher's third administration – Ed.

'In the early 1930s, high-altitude flying became a possibility and thoughts naturally turned to the great mountains of the Himalayas and particularly to Everest, whose summit had so far defied human endeavour. A committee was formed under the chairmanship of Lord Tweedsmuir to examine the possibilities. Douglo immediately applied for the post of pilot to the expedition and was, in fact, appointed chief pilot with David MacIntyre, another member of 602 Squadron, offering invaluable support.

'At that stage in the evolution of flying, the expedition, which was wholly successful, was only just possible.* Within a couple of years, the added power of aero engines made such flying expeditions no longer an adventure.

'When war broke out, Douglo became an operations controller at 11 Group in Fighter Command. On one occasion, in May 1940, the C-in-C asked him to fly over to France in a small training aircraft to make certain enquiries.† The following year, still with Fighter Command, he took over the Turnhouse (Edinburgh) sector of 13 Group . . .'

It was while Hamilton was commanding the Turnhouse sector that one of the war's most bizarre events occurred. On 10 May, 1941, Rudolf Hess, Hitler's deputy, made his dramatic flight from Augsburg, in Germany, to Scotland and baled out. Dressed in the uniform of an oberleutnant in the Luftwaffe, he asked to be taken to the Duke, for whom he had 'a secret and vital message'. The fascinating story has been well and authoritatively told by the Duke's son, James Douglas-Hamilton,* but here Geordie Selkirk adds a postscript to this extraordinary happening.

'Douglo had met Albrecht Haushover, a fairly highly placed civil servant in the German Foreign Office, before the war . . . The exact story will never be known, but it is virtually certain that Haushover gave Hess Douglo's name and address. Hess correctly saw the need for Germany to bring peace in the West before attacking Russia. He also wished, no doubt, to do something to restore his own sagging prestige . . .'

Hitler's deputy, with a remarkably astute piece of solo navigation,

---

* Clydesdale's achievement in being the first man to fly over the summit of Everest was acclaimed worldwide – Ed.

† It was, in fact, an historic mission which took place on 17–20 May 1940, when, with the German panzers rolling forward, the Battle of France was at its critical stage. Wing Commander (later Group Captain) The Duke of Hamilton flew over to Arras, Béthune, Merville and Abbeville in a tiny, 85-miles-an-hour Miles Magister to bring back to Air Chief Marshal Dowding an up-to-the-minute report on the state of the land and air battle. On the strength of Hamilton's witness and other intelligence, Dowding took his decision to advise Churchill and the War Cabinet, in the face of opposition, not to send any more fighter squadrons to shore up the collapsing French forces, but to hold them in 11 Group for the Battle of Britain, which must follow. The decision was crucial to Fighter Command's subsequent, narrow victory – Ed.

* *Motive for a Mission*, James Douglas-Hamilton, Mainstream Publishing, 1979.

overflew Dungavel House, Hamilton's residence in Lanarkshire, and after some toing and froing, rolled his long-range Messerschmitt 110 on to its back and, with difficulty, baled out. Selkirk recalls the aftermath.

'It was a remarkable chance that Douglo was commanding the sector where the house was situated. He heard that an aeroplane had crashed and assumed that one of his night fighters had made a successful interception. As he went to bed that night he got the message that the prisoner wished to see him. "He can wait," he said, "until the morning." '

And so to the third in this line of exceptional brothers. What of Lord Malcolm Douglas-Hamilton, who, as the commanding officer of No. 540 (Photographic Reconnaissance) Squadron, based at Benson in Oxfordshire, flew, in 1943 and 1944 (tricky years in the aerial offensive), one of the most highly regarded operational tours in the picture-taking business?

He gave the lead to his Squadron by invariably picking for himself and his navigator the nasty, deep-penetration missions right into the heart of Nazi Germany – a fact that the citation accompanying the award of the Distinguished Flying Cross was quick to expose. There were easier ways of passing the time than flying, in broad daylight, an unarmed Mosquito, loaded up with cameras and extra fuel, to the nerve-centres of the Fatherland, confronted by perhaps the most lethal defensive fighter force ever marshalled in modern war.

Geordie Selkirk recaptures his younger brother's complex character.

'Malcolm had a range of personal gifts. Untrained in music, he taught himself to play the accordion, the bagpipes and that strange instrument, the ocharina. He had a wonderful voice for speaking and a special faculty for recalling apposite quotations or the words of a song. He was most welcome at a ceilidh in many parts of the Highlands. Even to this day, the people who were young at the time remember vividly his music and the charm of his humour – qualities which were by no means ignored by the ladies! Perhaps his most notable defect was his difficulty in deciding what to do! His emotions and passions varied greatly from year to year, but it was aviation which eventually won the day and, after school, he entered the Royal Air Force College at Cranwell. In the event, he became a brilliant pilot.

'Shortly after leaving Cranwell, he was posted to a squadron equipped with the Bristol Bulldog, one of the leading fighter aircraft of the day. A mid-air collision qualified him for membership of the Caterpillar Club. He was a strong and competent boxer and, during his time in the Service, won its light heavyweight championship. But he was never completely dedicated to the art.

'Soon after his marriage and after only a few years' service, he resigned his commission and became chief civil flying instructor in Hong Kong. When war came he was immediately called up. "I had only just got off on a Hurricane," he complained, "when they discovered I was a fully qualified instructor and immediately sent me off to Rhodesia." '

It was two years before he could return to the United Kingdom and longer still before he could begin his operational stint with PRU.*

In the peace that followed Malcolm Douglas-Hamilton became a Member of Parliament, winning Inverness for the Tories. He championed the cause of the Highlands in the House of Commons. As his elder brother recalls, 'he was the first to grasp the significance of the Cairngorms for winter fun – for mountaineering and skiing. That was the beginning of a place called Aviemore . . . His easy manner and speech were well suited to Parliamentary life.'

Things seldom remained the same for long with the third of the brothers. In less than four years after entering the House of Commons, he had married again and his constituents promptly called for his resignation. A by-election followed and thereafter he went to live in New York . . .

After all that had gone before, there was a tragic poignancy about the end when it came. As Selkirk confirms: 'Malcolm continued his interest in aviation and flew aircraft to the warring states of Africa. It was on one of these trips that, flying at night in a thunderstorm, he hit a mountain near Douala, in the Cameroons . . .

'A superb pilot, with many gifts in middle age, he wandered off the pathway where he belonged.'

Lord David Douglas-Hamilton may have been the youngest of the four brothers, but he surrendered nothing to the other three in independence of mind and character. In his relatively short yet distinguished lifetime, he was always 'his own man' and this is indeed the governing impression to be gained from Lord Selkirk's portrayal of his youngest brother.

'From the start he formed his own views and attitudes – sometimes with emotional determination, but always uninfluenced by other members of the family.

'Early on, he was fascinated with the remains of World War I in France

* Photographic Reconnaissance Unit.

and, even as a child, he was constantly wanting to visit the areas where the fighting had taken place. It became an absorbing interest. On one occasion he returned to this country with a live Mills bomb in his pocket!

'This early interest was later extended to the evolution of political and national movements in Europe and particularly in Germany. David got himself enrolled in a German *Arbeit Dienstlage*, which he recognised to be an instrument for Nazi propaganda. He made a variety of contacts in pre-war Germany, including that of Albrecht Haushover. He also visited Russia and climbed Mount Elbruz.

'He had a great enthusiasm for playing the bagpipes and for the music composed for them. He was another in the family who was devoted to boxing and had competed at his weight in the British Commonwealth amateur boxing championships, losing in the final bout by the narrowest of margins. His training as a pilot had begun when he joined the University Air Squadron at Oxford. On the outbreak of war, he was given a full course at the Central Flying School and, to his dismay, became a flying instructor. This meant that all four brothers were qualified instructors [a highly unusual accomplishment, which bore testimony to their collective flying ability – Ed.].

'After a year or so of instructing, David was posted to command No. 603 (City of Edinburgh) Squadron and, in April, 1942, took the Squadron out to Malta as the battle for the island built up to its climax. To reach the island, the pilots had to fly their Spitfires off the US Navy's aircraft carrier *Wasp*, from a point some 700 miles west of Malta.

'The defence of Malta was a turning point of the war. It could well be argued that when the whole force of the Luftwaffe in Sicily and Italy failed to subdue Malta the ultimate fate of Germany was sealed. 603 fought hard against greatly superior numbers and suffered many casualties.* Had David been more polite to his Air Officer Commanding (Air Vice-Marshal Sir Keith Park), he would certainly have been decorated.

'Not surprisingly, his experience in Malta profoundly affected his psychology. No life seemed to him so worthwhile as that of a fighter pilot . . .'

As things turned out, David Douglas-Hamilton, after a rest, settled for a transfer to Coastal Command and to the work of a photographic reconnaissance pilot flying a Mosquito. In this, he joined his brother, Malcolm, at Benson and at once began to fly testing sorties to pinpoint targets in enemy-occupied Europe and Germany. Place names like Peenemunde, Swinemunde and Schweinfurt started to appear in his log book. Then on 2 August, 1944, David, by now a flight commander

---

* David Douglas-Hamilton's leadership of 603 during the intense fighting was marked by the openings he created for his pilots. He gave them the chances to score instead of exploiting them himself. He was one of the Royal Air Force's most unselfish leaders in World War II – Ed.

in 544 Squadron, and his navigator, Philip Gatehouse, were briefed to cover a sequence of targets in southern, south-eastern and central France. It was their 31st trip.

Selkirk closes the chapter.

'The crew encountered heavy flak on the long mission. The aircraft was damaged and David was trying to regain his base on one engine. As he was joining the circuit at Benson, and preparing to land, the remaining engine failed. The Mosquito crashed and pilot and observer were both killed.'

The loss hit very hard. Gatehouse, an only child, who wore the ribbon of the Distinguished Flying Medal, was a highly experienced navigator, while his pilot, having survived the cataclysmic Malta battle, was now nearing the end of the second of two rigorous operational tours. The future, as his brother concludes, seemed to offer so much.

'Many people who knew David felt there was an important role for him to play after the war.'

Lord Selkirk,
Wimborne,
Dorset

The Dundases
John Dundas
THE LESSONS OF MADAME LA ZONGA

Johnnie Johnson (Air Vice-Marshal J. E. Johnson) and John Bisdee (Group Captain J. D. Bisdee) have each got between them good reasons for selecting one of the two Dundas brothers for portrayal.

Bisdee served with John Dundas, the elder of the two, in 609 Squadron throughout the Battle of Britain in 1940 and brings formidable credentials to bear upon a study of his lost friend and room-mate. A scholar of Marlborough and an exhibitioner of Corpus Christi, Cambridge, he led 601 (County of London) Squadron, with its Spitfires, off the United States Navy's aircraft carrier *Wasp* into Malta in April 1942, as the battle for the Mediterranean island rose to its peak. Two months later, he took the Squadron on to the Middle East to join the Desert fighting at the crucial pre-Alamein stage.

Staff appointments followed and so, too, did command (as a Group Captain) of 323 Wing at Foggia during the advance northwards up the Italian mainland. By then, his own tally of enemy aircraft destroyed had reached double figures.

Eschewing the offer of a permanent commission in the Royal Air Force, Bisdee rejoined Unilever, the industrial conglomerate, post-war and rose to be executive chairman of the Group's toiletries company, Elida-Gibbs ... A decorated wartime career was thus complemented by a successful commercial run in peace ...

Writing a memorial to a friend who was killed 48 years ago might seem a difficult task – but it is not. John Dundas was a quite exceptional person, as I will try to explain.

Born in August 1915 into a well-known Yorkshire family, he went from Stowe to Christ Church, Oxford, where he not only got First Class Honours in History, but was good at games, and won a half 'Blue' for squash. He also won an award which enabled him to study at the Sorbonne and Heidelberg. This undoubtedly fired his interest in European affairs.

He joined the *Yorkshire Post*, where the editor, Arthur Mann, recognised his talents, and despite his youth sent him on many assignments throughout

238

Central Europe. John was in Prague when Hitler sent his troops in. One of his colleagues on the *YP* at that time, Bill Curling, remembers him as 'an outstandingly good journalist with a great political sense' – and feels had he lived he might have become editor of *The Times*.

With all this activity and foreign travel, it must have been hard to find time for flying – but John's experiences in Central Europe convinced him that war was inevitable, and he was determined to be prepared. He joined 609 in 1938, and trained with the Squadron on Avros and Hawker Hinds. At this time, too, a regular Sergeant (later Flight Sergeant), 'Tich' Cloves, joined 609, and left a fascinating and witty diary of the Squadron as seen from the ground. He stayed with us till April 1941 – and we were lucky to have him. He describes 609's very first squadron take-off at Yeadon, in the West Riding.

'Hind K6848 was being flown by P/O Dundas, with LAC Hunter as human ballast. Forming up took some time, and the old Kestrel V engines were just wondering whether they would be required, when bang went the throttles, and twelve aircraft became airborne. But the engine of K6848 opted to cut. Deciding he couldn't clear the houses in Victoria Avenue, Dundas put it earthwards. He touched down, braked, but the wheels skidded, and the aircraft carried on unperturbed. Chopping down a windsock that enveloped a boy on a pushbike, it finally came to rest with its nose in a back garden and its tail resting on the roof of a house. The lady was restored from her hysterics with the aid of brandy, the pilot and passenger then had a sip, and an unidentified airman finished off the bottle . . . Aircraft, a write-off.'

However, the enquiry found the accident due to mechanical failure. John was exonerated – indeed he hinted that he had performed a public service in discovering the defect without loss of life!

At the beginning of the war he had only 60 hours total flying, when, after a perfunctory circuit in a Fairey Battle, he was sent off solo in a Spitfire, thus avoiding the fate of his younger brother, Hugh, and the present writer, then a VR Sgt Pilot, who had to waste time until Christmas 1939, flying round Oxfordshire in Hawker Harts. I was lucky to be commissioned and sent to 609 Squadron, at Drem, only to find that John and all the other operational pilots were at Kinloss guarding the Home Fleet. No sooner were they back at Drem, than we 'sprogs' were passed out on Spitfires – and everyone started to practise night flying, for which the early Spitfires were not at all suitable, at least when it came to landing, as the stub exhausts sent out sheets of flame and sparks, blinding the pilot. F/Sgt Cloves had this to say of a very black and rainy night:

'F/O Dundas, in L1084, made a perfect three-point landing – on two wheels and airscrew . . . some explanation like "I was landing up hill!"

'P/O Bisdee appeared to land L1082 about twenty feet in the air . . . a distinct crunch . . .'

Enough of the preliminaries. 609 Squadron was moved down to Northolt on 19 May, 1940. John was in Yellow Section on 30 May when it was ordered to patrol Dunkirk, led by the two flight commanders, since the CO was non-operational. On its way back, Yellow Section, short of fuel, lost its way in thick haze (as yet, we had not been fitted with VHF* sets for homing). The section leader got down at Rochford. John Dundas and his great friend Joe Dawson successfully force-landed at Frinton-on-Sea. On a subsequent patrol, John and section leader Frank Howell got two Heinkels, though whether they were confirmed I cannot say – I can, however, remember the enormous boost to morale given to us by 'Boom' Trenchard before our last patrol – suddenly, we all seemed to be back in the Royal Flying Corps – and with 'Boom' behind us nothing could go wrong. But the squadron losses had been heavy. All told, we had lost nearly half our pilots, mainly Auxiliaries, and in particular John's great friend and flying partner, Joe Dawson.

On 28 June, we finally got a proper CO, a regular, S/L H. S. George Darley, who set about rebuilding the squadron, getting new pilots, and training, training, training, the CO flying as an elusive target for our attacks.

Needless to say there ensued a getting-to-know period, but to anticipate events a little, Darley saw the determination beneath John's somewhat 'Auxiliary' exterior, and, in turn, John recognised the good choice of Darley as the man for the job. Darley had been with two Auxiliary squadrons (602 and 611) before, so was used to their ways.

By this time I had taken the place of Joe Dawson as John's room-mate. I can't remember how this came about, but it was a privilege, as I soon found out.

Here was a man who, under a flippant exterior, never forgot his dedicated hatred of the Nazis, whose brutality he had seen at first hand in Czechoslovakia. However much he might enjoy flying the Spitfire he never forgot it was a weapon. During his glorious but short flying career, I am sure his Merlin engine spent more of its working life with the throttle 'through the gate' than any other in the Squadron. War was a serious business and anyone who did not match his dedication was a 'stooge' – his worst word of condemnation.

Sharing a room with him was in itself an antidote to wartime worries. Our room was full of books – many sent to him by the talented actress Margaret Rawlings, with whom he shared a deep friendship.

I have a photo of him clad in white flying overalls reading *Laughing Diplomat* by Daniele Varè – a fascinating book typical of John's interest in European politics. The Italian diplomat, amid his lighter-hearted adventures, makes the point that the provisions of the Treaty of Versailles were

---

* Very High Frequency radio sets.

like a virus injected into Europe, which ensured the inevitability of World War II. John had seen the results at first hand.

Then there was the music. We got up in the morning sometimes to the classical guitar of Andres Segovia, sometimes to jazz records sent to me by a friend in the USA. John particularly liked a rumba number by Tommy Dorsey called *Six Lessons from Madame la Zonga*. It became so associated with him, that when Captain Cuthbert Orde (ex-RFC) came to draw our portraits as an Air Ministry war artist, he dedicated 'to 609 Squadron with appropriate sentiments' a cartoon of Madame, indicating to John that her lessons were not limited to the Conga!

During that summer, an unexploded bomb appeared in the ground outside our room. I would have been quite happy to accept accommodation on the other side of the Mess, but John said he was damned if he would move, so we stayed. Unfortunately my bed was just under the window! Finally, the Army got rid of it.

We were now at Middle Wallop, having twice escorted Churchill across the Channel in search of the French Premier, Paul Reynaud, and his pro-German mistress. France had collapsed. We were on our own, and felt the better for it.

Convoy patrols, which in Scotland had with few exceptions been dull affairs, now became highly operational. On 13 July, Dundas and his No. 2, searching for a convoy which, as frequently happened, was not where the Navy told us it was, got into a gaggle of Dornier 17s and Messerschmitt 110s, claiming one of the latter destroyed, and a Dornier probable.

In the first month of the Battle of Britain, 609 had done twice the average number of sorties per squadron in Fighter Command. We had also had more than twice the casualties.

In August, ex-journalist Dundas took over the 609 Squadron War Diary – and set such a standard of comment on both aerial and off-duty operations that it was later read with interest by King George VI at Buckingham Palace. He wrote, 'so far as 609 was concerned the Nazi blitz started on 8 August – four pilots engaged and accounted for five Huns'. John's score was gradually building up – on 13 August, for instance, when the squadron got among a bunch of Stukas (Ju.87s) and shot down five of them, he got one confirmed and one damaged. The Luftwaffe lost 45 aircraft on 'Alder-tag', the RAF 13, and 609 none. S/L Darley's leadership and training were paying off.

On 14 August, a mixed bunch of Heinkels and Ju.88s got through to Middle Wallop using low cloud cover, and killed three of 609's maintenance crew – crushed by a falling hangar door. In the ensuing hide-and-seek amongst the clouds, John was in his element, though he only claimed to have 'finished off' a Heinkel.

In the early days of the Battle, Sector Control had little idea of placing fighters in a good tactical position to attack. For instance, there were several attacks on the Portland-Weymouth areas on 11 August and succeeding days. Control started with '100+ Bandits' then '200+' and finally 'Very many Bandits' – and there they were – a great beehive of 109s and 110s above and up-sun of us flying in a defensive circle. 609 was alone, outnumbered by 20 to one. The surest way to get shot down was to join the circle. Darley shouted 'Choose your targets!' and John's solution was to dive across and attack the lower and opposite side of the circle from the inside so that the 110s could not tighten up their turn to get at him. He was credited with a 110 destroyed, but was hit in the radiator. 609 was lucky to have no casualties.

Owing to the distances involved from their French bases, 609 saw very many 110s. On 7 October, 609, now under its new CO, Michael Lister Robinson, was vectored on to a formation attacking the Westland aircraft works at Yeovil. Robinson broke his 'duck' with two destroyed on his first sortie. John also got a 110, but was hit from behind by a cannon shell. He landed at Warmwell with many bits of shrapnel in his leg. But, typically, he was flying again next day, with his leg in bandages. John took over 'B' Flight, and led Blue Section with F/O Tadeusz Nowierski and F/O Noel Agazarian – a Pole and a charming half-Armenian – typical of 609's varied collection of pilots – four Poles, three Americans, a Canadian, and, later, many Belgians and a Frenchman.

The *esprit de corps* was fantastic. After flying, John would load his Lagonda – a present from Joe Dawson's parents – and take off for the Black Swan at Monxton, the Lagonda's huge headlights shining through the blackout. (The landlord of the 'Mucky Duck' never seemed to have heard of the regulations either!)

John used to exchange repartee with the actor Gordon Harker, who was running the local Spitfire Fund. On 27 November a Ju.88 was reported flying along the coast after a raid. John asked Operations for permission to chase it. Refused. Could he take up a section for practice flying? No objection. This ended with John and the 88 over the Cherbourg peninsula – and John sent it down with one engine on fire. Time for home, particularly as he was over an aerodrome 'well stocked with 109s'.

I was away for this and the following day on a 48-hour pass, so rely on the memory and diary of my good friend Canadian Keith Ogilvie. On 28 November, 609 Squadron was playing host to officers and 150 cadets from Sandhurst. There were two scrambles that day. The second turned out to be a fighter sweep of some 50 109s, which approached over the Isle of Wight making condensation trails. John did not have his experienced 'Musketeers' behind supporting him. The yellow-nosed 109s obviously belonged to some crack squadron of the Luftwaffe judging by their formation and tactics. Three came down out of the sun. Keith Ogilvie, who was the rearguard 'weaver', gave the warning, but received cannon strikes in fuselage and airscrew. In the subsequent mêlée, John was heard to shout,

'Whoopee! I've got a 109' – and that was the last anyone heard or saw of John Dundas.

There is a story that the Luftwaffe came up on the international distress wavelength to ask Air Ministry for news of one of their top fighter aces, Major Helmut Wieck, *Kommodore* of JG2 (*Richthofen Geschwader*), and it was soon clear beyond doubt that he had been John's victim, but that John and his No. 2, Peter Baillon, had fallen victims to Wieck's Nos. 2 and 3. Peter's body was washed up on the coast of France, I believe, but no trace was ever found of Dundas or Wieck.

I remember arriving back at Middle Wallop from my '48' that evening, and going straight off to the Ops Room to find out if anything had happened during my time away. The WAAFs there had a continuous tea-brew for visiting aircrew.

It was there that someone asked, 'Have you heard about John Dundas?' I couldn't really take it in. Of all the pilots in 609, I had come to look on him as almost immortal. Very soon, the Royal Navy were reporting a battle between German E-boats and naval motor gun-boats off the Isle of Wight. The Germans were clearly searching for their missing ace, but neither side found anything.

I have often wondered what the story was from the Luftwaffe point of view. Their fighters were not escorting any bombers, so the sortie was rather pointless. Was it an operation ordered by the German Air Force or an ego-trip organised by Wieck and his squadrons to feed Goebbels' propaganda machine with further tales of derring-do? The said machine by then must have been rather short of ammo.

It was only after helping to pack up his books and things – and later representing 609 at a memorial service in Doncaster – that the full impact of his loss hit me.

His final score was 13 confirmed victories, and I believe it may have been more. He often seemed to pass on claims to junior pilots, who needed a boost to their morale. His ground crew, too, loved his carefree manner. One of them did a drawing of Blue Section, led by him, diving into battle.

John died without knowing that he had a Bar to his DFC. He never had a rest from battle, or a chance to show the effect of his exceptional intelligence on the problems of the RAF in war, or those of his country in peace-time.

I firmly believe that the early death of John Dundas was a loss to our whole nation.

John Bisdee,
Harting Combe,
Rake,
Hampshire

243

The Dundases
Sir Hugh Dundas
SCARLET-LINED AUXILIARY

Johnnie Johnson (see pages 354–8) knew Cocky Dundas (Group Captain Sir Hugh Dundas), John's younger brother, as well as anyone in the Royal Air Force. Brought up in widely differing circumstances, they made a pair, flying together in the Tangmere Wing, behind Bader's leadership, in the spring and summer offensive of 1941. A lifetime's friendship was moulded in the Tangmere fire.

In the second half of the European war, Johnson, at the head of his Canadian followers, stamped his mark upon the art of aggressive wing leadership and, with a score of 38 enemy aircraft destroyed on the Western Front, finished at the summit of Britain's top-scoring league.

9 August, 1941 – Douglas Bader is leading the Tangmere Wing consisting of 610 (County of Cheshire) Squadron and 616 (South Yorkshire) Squadron on a bomber support sweep over France. The leading finger-four of the Wing consists of two pairs – Bader and his wingman Jeff West, from New Zealand, and 'Cocky' Dundas and me. Two other finger-fours fly either side of Bader half a mile away and slightly astern, whilst the utterly dependable Ken Holden positions 610 Squadron down-sun and about 3000 feet higher. We are flying at about 24,000 feet above a thick layer of cloud and the visibility is good. Back at Tangmere, the controller, Woodhall, speaks in clear and measured tones:*

'Dogsbody from Beetle. The beehive† is on time and is engaged.'

'OK,' from Bader.

'Dogsbody from Beetle. There are twenty plus five miles to the east of you.'

'OK,' from Bader.

---

* These are the actual radio transmissions logged at the Beachy Head Forward Relay Station.
† The bombers and their escorting fighters.

244

Woodhall advises that more bandits are nearby. Roy Marples* is the first to see them:

'Three bandits coming down astern of us. I'm keeping an eye on them. Now there's six.'

'OK,' from Bader.

'Douglas, another twelve plus, ahead. Slightly higher,' from Woodhall.

'Eleven of them now,' Roy advises.

'OK Roy,' replies Bader. 'Let me know exactly where they are.'

'About one mile astern. And slightly higher.'

Woodhall continues to paint the broader canvas: 'Douglas, there is another forty plus fifteen miles to the north-east of you.'

Someone reports: '109s at nine o'clock. Above.'

'Dogsbody from Roy: Keep turning left and you'll see 109s at nine o'clock.'

'Ken, can you see them?' from Bader.

'Douglas,' says Ken, '109s below. Climbing up.'

Bader dips first one wing and then the other to look below. Our formations waver as we try to spot the lower Messerschmitts. I think about those above, take my eyes off Cocky, and search above. I see 109s a thousand feet higher, waiting for the ideal attacking position. I check my own gun switch is on 'fire'.

Bader says to Ken: 'I can't see them. Will you tell me where to look?'

'Underneath Billy's section, now. Shall I come down?'

'No, I have them. Get into formation. Going down. Ken, are you with us?'

We fan out alongside Bader. For the first time I see the lower Messerschmitts. We are overtaking four 109s with others on either side. Cocky is taking the extreme starboard 109, so I skid under Cocky, Bader and West to get at a 109 on the port side. I am rapidly overtaking my opponent, but before opening fire I have a swift glance to either side. For the last time I see Bader in the air, firing at a 109.

'Blue two here. Some bugger's coming down behind. Astern. Break left.'

I recognise Whaley's voice. My 109 pulls into a steep climb. I hang on and knock a few pieces from his starboard wing.

Ken watches the fight below and sees two bunches of 109s below his own position but above us. He decides it is time to lend a hand:

'Crow from Ken. I'm taking my section down. Stay here and cover us.'

'OK Ken,' from Crow.

'109s coming down behind. Keep turning.'

'They're 109s all right.'

'Line astern. Keep turning.'

'109s coming down again,' from Roy.

---

* Cousin of the Rt Hon Ernest Marples (later Lord Marples of Wallasey), one-time Minister of Transport – Ed.

'Keep turning,' from Billy.

'Break. For Christ's sake break!'

No call sign. I break hard. We all break hard. I tear through a twisting, tumbling mass of Spitfires and Messerschmitts. I look behind. I have three 109s astern. The nearest is about one hundred yards behind. I hold my steep turn, losing height as I spiral down towards the safety of the cloud. I see his cannon ports flicker as he tries to get me in his sights. Tracer bullets flash over my canopy, and then I am in the concealing white vapour.

I spin out of the cloud, recover, attack a solitary 109, and come out of France, low and fast, sometimes below the tree tops, hugging the contours of the ground, weaving to cover the blind spot behind. Streaking over the sand dunes, across the Channel and when I see the white cliffs I climb to 2000 feet and hear Woodhall: 'Douglas, are you receiving?'

There is no reply so I call the Group Captain: 'Johnnie here, sir, we have had a stiff fight. I last saw the Wing Commander on the tail of a 109.'

'Thank you, Johnnie,' courteously replies the Group Captain, 'I will meet you at dispersal.'

Back at Westhampnett, Cocky, Nip, Alan Smith and I study the large map and believe that if they were not too badly hit both Douglas and Buck Casson, who is also missing, would make for the coast and Douglas especially would bail out over the sea to try to save his legs. Cocky obtains permission from the controller and we are soon heading for the French coast again, but this time we are never more than a few feet above the Channel; it is a quietly lifting sea and we watch our height very carefully.

We patrol between Cap Gris Nez and Calais. Nip sees a submarine and attacks it and gets a slight reprimand from Cocky, who mutters something about not going after submarines on this trip. Jeff sights a dinghy bobbing up and down which is empty.

We see a large enemy rescue float, but it too is deserted and we turn to the north again. We stay on patrol until our petrol is getting very low and we barely have enough to trickle back to Hawkinge at low revs.

Whilst our Spitfires are being refuelled, Cocky is plotting his new search lines, but immediately we are airborne, Woodhall calls from Tangmere and cancels our trip. We are to return to Westhampnett and other squadrons will take up the search.

We fly home as the shadows lengthen, each of us busy with his own private thoughts. We know Douglas Bader will not be coming home and the Tangmere Wing will never be quite the same.

It was time for Cocky to go. He was tired from a long tour of operational flying during which he had suffered two shattering experiences. He was shot down in the Battle of Britain and again early in 1941, when he crash-landed his crippled Spitfire at Hawkinge. He was the last of the original Auxiliaries and loath to leave the splendid Yorkshire ground crews.

So one Sunday morning in September it was time to say goodbye to Cocky Dundas. He was posted to a training unit which had a reputation for smart, unmodified uniforms, collars and ties, and that sort of thing, and he was clearly not dressed for this occasion. Two years of fighting in that tiny cockpit had not improved the appearance of his scarlet silk-lined tunic. One of the two 'As' on his lapels was missing, as was his tie, and a vivid yellow scarf added a colourful touch to this ensemble.

We poured him into the open cockpit of the Maggie, which was not intended for such a long, sparse frame. I stood on the wing, fastened the safety straps, wished him well and shouted that a few whiffs of oxygen might improve his state of health. He turned a pair of bloodshot eyes upon me and shouted something about getting back on ops before Christmas.

The powerful Auxiliary network was soon in action and after exactly four weeks he established an all-time record when he joined Ken Holden and 610 Squadron as a Flight Commander. Soon after, he received a handsome Christmas present when he was promoted to Squadron Leader and given the command of the first Typhoon Squadron.

In the summer of 1942 I had a few days to spare, being promoted to Squadron Leader and taking over 610 Squadron; and what better than to spend them at Snailwell, on the outskirts of Newmarket, where Cocky was striving to get 56 Squadron operational on Typhoons. Eventually the bugs were ironed out of this ungainly fighter-bomber, but in mid-1942 it was greatly troubled by engine and structural failures. Several test and squadron pilots had been killed when its tail broke away; the engine sometimes seized up and caught fire, there was such a smell of carbon monoxide in the cockpit that pilots wore oxygen masks at all times, and the brute vibrated so much it was said to cause sterility!

With the Typhoons' ugly reputation Cocky had a tough job, but due to his special brand of leadership, from the front, the morale and spirit of the whole Squadron, pilots and ground crews, was quite outstanding. He had dug into his Squadron's illustrious history and the combat reports of Albert Ball and James McCudden, both exceptional pilots in World War I, and holders of the Victoria Cross, were framed on the wall for all to see. Even I, who always gave the Typhoon a wide berth, was 'persuaded', after suitable liquid refreshment, to fly the monster on a practice fighter sweep over the Channel.

After the ill-fated Dieppe operation, Cocky phoned and suggested a few days' holiday in Yorkshire and the chance of a few days' grouse shooting. I did not need a second invitation, and on the following day we set course for the home of the well-established Dundas family at Crawthorne in the West Riding.

At breakfast the following morning there was much talk of someone called 'Archie', who turned out to be the Earl of Wharncliffe, a hunting, shooting and fishing Yorkshire squire, who greeted us outside his big house, Wortley. He was the father of the lovely Diana, Cocky's long-standing girlfriend, who, alas, was not at home on this occasion; I remember her arriving at Tangmere for our Summer Ball, riding her motor-cycle, dressed in her MTC uniform with a haversack on her back, holding her ball gown and toothbrush, and looking like someone's younger brother who was suddenly transformed into a beautiful young lady.

Other members of the shooting party included a judge, a titled lady from Nairobi, whose social exploits had figured in the popular press, and a self-made millionaire from nearby Sheffield in a huge Rolls-Royce, which drew some acid comments from Archie (about the Services and the profiteering civilians) when he saw it parked next to my small Morris!

There were few grouse and my diary records that we had thirteen brace at lunchtime. When we repaired to the big house, there stood the biggest bowl of punch I had ever seen. Lunch lasted for at least three hours and about tea-time we ventured out on to the moors again, where we managed to add another brace or two to the bag without harm to either beaters or guns.

We returned to Wortley where, after more refreshment, Archie changed into his Home Guard uniform and cut a formidable figure in highly polished Newmarket boots, baggy riding breeches, a battledress with World War I medal ribbons and a Life Guard's cap which looked as if he went to bed in it!

We were invited to shoot on the renowned Allenheads Moor and, *en route*, lunched with a distant cousin, the Marquis of Zetland, who had been Secretary of State for India. Cocky told me that at some meeting in London he had been shot at and wounded, and warned me not to mention India as it would upset the old boy. Consequently after a couple of drinks in the huge conservatory we were somewhat startled when our host turned to me and politely enquired if I had ever served in India!

Lord Allendale was an excellent host and his grouse moor was superb, and I fell in love forever with the vast rolling hills, the heather, the porridge, the peat-scented water, the ever-busy Springer spaniels, the more sedate Labradors and the splendid grouse curling on the wind.

In 1943 Cocky was posted to North Africa, and I did not see him again until early 1945, when as Group Captain Hugh Spencer Lisle Dundas, DSO and Bar, DFC, aged twenty-four, he flew from Italy to Brussels Evêre, where I had a Canadian Spitfire Wing. He had already been offered a permanent commission, but after the war preferred to enter the harsher commercial world, where, because of his outstanding qualities of leadership, he reached the top.

Johnnie Johnson,
Hargate,
Buxton,
Derbyshire

The Atcherleys
A TWIN APART

Pete Brothers (Air Commodore Peter M. Brothers) was one of those distinctive Fighter Command characters, full of bonhomie, humour and decorations, who made light of the serious things, no matter what his innermost thoughts might be saying. And in his war there was plenty to be serious about.

Having entered the Service in the mid-1930s, he was necessarily in at the start, yet he was still in operational play near the end ... The Battle of Britain, the offensive years over occupied Europe and then D-Day, and all that went with it, it was an inevitable progression which took him to several squadron and wing commands – and to a healthy bag of enemy aircraft destroyed to show for it. There was little rest.

At one point along the way, he formed – and led into battle – 457, the second Australian fighter squadron to serve in the UK. Pete Brothers was exactly the sort of Pom whom those discerning Cobbers would follow.

In March 1942, Group Captain Victor Beamish, my Commanding Officer at Kenley, was shot down while flying with the Wing. He was a fearless, tough and dedicated officer, a born leader revered and respected by us all, whose loss had a serious impact on the morale of the Wing. 'If he can be killed,' ran the thoughts of my pilots, 'what chance have I? And who can possibly replace a man like that?'

The answer to the latter question arrived shortly thereafter in a Procter aircraft, which landed on the perimeter track rather than the runway and taxied up to my office door. Out stepped a lean and smiling figure. This was 'Batchy' Atcherley,* one of the famed identical Atcherley twins, ex-Schneider Trophy Team pilot, renowned for his expert and unusual aerobatic displays, a living legend. Here was a man so different, whose light-hearted manner and friendliness concealed an insistence on the highest

* Afterwards, Air Marshal Sir Richard Atcherley.

250

standards and a restless demand for and ability to get results, the only man capable of succeeding Victor without attempting to emulate him. So started a long association with this most memorable of characters.

Shortly after assuming command 'Batchy' was shot down by Me.109s over the Channel. Wishing to hear his story at first hand, I rushed to the hospital, where I found him walking about the wards, chatting to all, with his arm in a sling. 'Whatever were you up to?' I asked. 'Well, Pete, knowing that a Spitfire was more than a match for a 109 I decided to patrol St Omer† at 20,000 feet and knock them down as they came up. Unfortunately, they seemed to take no notice of me and, getting short of fuel, I set off home. Half-way across the Channel I suddenly saw some 109s behind me. There was a loud bang, the throttle lever and a finger left my hand, the cockpit filled with smoke and the aircraft went out of control. I baled out and floated down into the sea.

'Getting rid of my parachute, I tried to inflate my dinghy. The trouble with being a Station Commander is that you make everyone else do dinghy drill, but don't do it yourself. The pack was floating upside down, so I had some difficulty in reading the instructions on it. Eventually I opened it and dragged myself in.' 'Did you put up the flag so you could be seen?' 'No, from where I was sitting all I could see was a seagull, and you feel a bit of an idiot waving a flag at a seagull. Then a fishing boat appeared with chaps leaning over the side spitting into the sea and I thought they weren't going to bother, but having got upwind of me, they fished me out.'

Returning to the Mess, I was astonished to see him walk in and be greeted and fawned over by 'Crash', his Alsatian. We joined in, but there was something not quite right. Then I noticed he was wearing a DSO, not an OBE. This was brother, David,‡ calling in on his way to the hospital! Years later, when they rode in the back of my car, their conversation sounded like Batchy talking to himself, the same phrases, inflection on words and tones of voice, so identical were they.

A while later he and I celebrated in London, after which he insisted on lying flat on his back, in the 'black-out', in the middle of the road near Hyde Park Corner, with his 'scrambled egg' hat on his chest. Cars and buses with their feeble half-moon lights swerved to avoid us, until my fears for his safety were resolved by a policeman, who, shining his torch on the recumbent figure, suggested, 'Do you mind just getting up and going home, Sir?', which brought the reply, 'Can't you see I am King George V lying in state?'

Came the day the Commander-in-Chief, Fighter Command, Air Marshal Sir Trafford Leigh-Mallory, called a conference. I was bidden to accompany Batchy. Inevitably, with such a large gathering, progress was

† A large Luftwaffe fighter base.
‡ Later, Air Vice-Marshal David F. Atcherley.

slow and Batchy's interest flagged. Quickly drawing four lines on his conference pad he inserted a cross, pushed it to me and the game was on. Time passed, the pad grew thinner as sheets were used, and honours were about even when we heard the C-in-C say, 'What do you think, Batchy?' 'I'm sorry, Sir, I did not hear the question as I was playing noughts and crosses with Pete.' Whilst I flushed with embarrassment and expectation of trouble, Batchy's amiable honesty and charm won the day and no more was said.

Stories of Batchy are legion and invariably depict his high-spirited, amusing and irreverent outlook. Whilst they illustrate his humane and captivating character they overlook the serious ideas he generated, one such being the need to keep updating the aircraft industry on current requirements. He suggested that a unit be formed embracing fighter aircraft development and leadership training with chosen leading pilots liaising directly with the industry and so shortening the existing lengthy procedures through Ministries and Commands. Thus the Central Fighter Establishment came into being with Batchy as Commandant.

By now an Air Commodore, I congratulated him on his promotion. 'It is a grave disadvantage, Pete. Whenever I see my sleeve with a broad band on it I automatically jump to attention and say, "It wasn't me, Sir".'

As Commandant, he took a keen interest in the programme to replace war-damaged buildings, and, with me and the Station Warrant Officer, he visited the new Airmen's Mess. 'Pete, we must not allow the Works people to lay their usual concrete paths which the airmen never follow. We will see where they pound a path – they always take the shortest cut – and then concrete it. This will suit them and save both concrete and cost.' Turning to the Station Warrant Officer, 'Now, Mr Wickerstaffe, as the concrete is laid I want flower beds dug along each side, bulbs planted and, as the path is ready, so will be the flowers.' The SWO considered for a moment. 'You can't force nature, Sir.' I saw the charming smile, which I knew could also be dangerous, appear on Batchy's face. 'No, Mr Wickerstaffe, but you can have a bloody good try.' If that was what he wanted, nothing less would do, so already flowering plants were installed!

Other sage advice, more related to runways than paths, came from this remarkable, inventive and amusing man when Geoffrey de Havilland visited Tangmere to demonstrate the first Vampire in front of a large crowd and had the misfortune to retract the wheels instead of the flaps after landing. Drowning his sorrows in the bar, later, he was told by Batchy, 'If you can do it as Chief Test Pilot, anyone can. Don't take it to heart, but go back and redesign the cockpit layout to make it less possible.'

After the war I happened to meet Batchy in the RAF Club, when he was on a visit from Washington, where he was the Head of Airforce Staff. 'Come to my room, I have some photos to show you.' The first was of him standing beside an American jet fighter. 'This is the aircraft I borrowed.'

The next was of tyre marks zigzagging down the runway. 'This was the landing.' The third was the aircraft lying on its belly with a collapsed undercarriage, with Batchy standing beside it with a hand on top of the fuselage, for all the world like that of a big-game hunter with his prize. The fourth was of a sour-faced unsmiling US Air Force General also beside the aircraft. With some glee, Batchy triumphantly said, 'And this is the chap who lent it to me.' His many escapes from bending aircraft were always treated with light-hearted contempt for the risks he had run.

He and his twin brother, David, had a telepathic closeness. Meeting Batchy in Karachi when he commanded the Pakistan Air Force, he jested to me 'If only David had the Indian Air Force we could have a splendid set-to.'

When David later was lost on a flight post-war, Batchy sought solace in the air and flew and flew until ordered to stop, so distraught was he. While dedicated to the RAF and to flying, and remaining a bachelor, 'married' to both, he possessed the rare ability and humanity to treat all alike, whether high or low, and gained the adoration of my four-year-old daughter. He would go to endless trouble and inconvenience to assist those in difficulty.

These personal recollections, no more than vignettes, are a small tribute to a courteous and charming personality, an aviator *par excellence*, and a true 'character' in every sense of that word.

Pete Brothers,
Cullompton,
Devon

The Beamishes

THE CARING LEADER

It is both fortuitous and fortunate that Air Chief Marshal Sir Theodore McEvoy (see page 159) and Air Commodore Alan Deere (see
pages 311–14) should both have elected to provide a study of the
best known of the Royal Air Force's illustrious Beamish brothers.
Each sees Victor Beamish from a different and important viewpoint.

The one sees him through the eyes of a Headquarters staff officer
of special worth, the other from the standpoint of a squadron and
wing leader of confirmed merit.

First, McEvoy . . .

The eldest of the four distinguished brothers, Victor Beamish passed out
of Cranwell in 1923. Invalided out of the Service in 1933, he made an
almost miraculous recovery and returned to the active list in 1937. He had
already won an AFC and had, when I first met him, come from North
Weald, where he not only commanded the Sector but took part in operations and settled industrial unrest on the Station by knocking workers
into the trench they had ceased to dig on hearing an air-raid warning.

He had come as Group Captain Ops to HQ 11 Group, where he was
responsible, in 1941, for writing the orders for the daily operations in
which our fighters fulfilled Sholto Douglas's policy of 'leaning out over
France'. These operations were not universally popular among our pilots,
who found Hurricanes and Spitfire Vs not quite up to the latest Me.109s
and Focke-Wulf 190s that opposed them. Victor made a point of flying on
these operations himself and of going round dispersals finding out at first
hand what pilots were thinking. Nothing could have done more to raise
morale and reconcile the chaps to 'the stuff coming down from Group'.

Early in 1942, Victor was posted to command the Kenley Sector. It
would have been perfectly acceptable for a group captain nearly forty years
old who had shown his grasp of recent active fighting to limit his activities
to the command and administration of his Sector, but that was not Victor's
style. He flew at every opportunity, often leading the Wing. Al Deere, then
commanding 602 Squadron, wrote, 'Victor Beamish was undoubtedly the

most outstanding personality of my time at Kenley.' But on 28 March, 1942, the Kenley history records: 'A blow fell that shook the very foundations of life at Kenley. Victor Beamish was out on a sweep over the French coast with No. 485 Squadron when he was attacked by two Fw.190s. He was last seen heading out to sea trailing smoke.' Diligent searches found no trace of him.

On the road named after him at Kenley, the memorial reads:

IN MEMORY OF
GROUP CAPTAIN
FRANCIS VICTOR BEAMISH
DSO DFC AFC
KENLEY SECTOR COMMANDER
WHO AFTER YEARS
OF UNEXAMPLED GALLANTRY
BEYOND THE CALL OF DUTY
FELL IN ACTION
OVER THE ENGLISH CHANNEL
28th MARCH 1942

'If I take the wings of the morning and dwell in the uttermost parts of the sea: even there shall thy hand lead me and thy right hand shall hold me'*

Theodore McEvoy,
Bognor Regis,
Sussex

Al Deere, echoing the sentiments of Mac's lovely epitaph on the Kenley memorial, still has a clear-cut memory of the character he came to know and greatly admire. It was 1941, Al was then commanding 602 Squadron and Victor Beamish was soon to become his Station Commander – and friend. Daylight operations over northern France were in full swing.

I was looking forward to meeting Victor not only as the officer who planned our operations at 11 Group Headquarters but as one of the four famous Beamish brothers serving in the Royal Air Force. I knew the other three – George, in his pre-war capacity as Chairman, Royal Air Force, Rugby; Charles, as a fellow pilot; and Cecil, a dentist, with whom I had played rugby for the RAF in 1938.

---

* The wording of the memorial was the work of Sir Theodore McEvoy. The quotation is from the 139th Psalm, verses 9 and 10 – Ed.

When Victor stepped out of his aircraft on arrival at our squadron dispersal, I found a man of average build – not cast in the mould of an Irish rugby forward like his three brothers, as I had expected. He seemed an altogether quieter man, but there was in his face a certain resolution of purpose, a trait which was to manifest itself later on.

To my surprise, he stepped out of his Spitfire wearing grubby blue overalls without any badges of rank. As he was to fly with my squadron that day I suggested that he should put his helmet in the Spitfire assigned to him for the operation. As we walked over to the aircraft, he noticed it carried the letter 'B' and, turning to me, said with a wry smile, 'Is it "B" for Beer or Beamish?' At that moment, the mantle of a Group Captain, Operations, seemed to fall away, and there emerged a friendly, likeable officer whom I was later able to count as a good friend, despite the difference in our ranks.

Having put his helmet in the cockpit, he placed his overalls on the nearby starter trolley. When we returned from briefing, the overalls were missing. I asked the Flight Sergeant present if he knew what had happened to them, and a somewhat embarrassed NCO answered, much to the Group Captain's amusement, 'I'm sorry, sir, I thought they belonged to one of the armourers and I told the aircraft fitter to get rid of them before you arrived!'

Before the briefing for the operation, the Group Captain made it clear to me that he wanted no preferential treatment; he was, he said, 'just coming along for the ride'. Naturally, I was concerned for his safety, particularly as at the time we were having a rough ride, with the Me.109G outflying the Spitfire VB with which we were then equipped. As things turned out, the operation was uneventful and we returned to base without having sighted the enemy.

When, some few months later, Victor Beamish was appointed to command Kenley, much to the delight of all of us, I had, as one of his squadron commanders, quite a lot of contact with him both administratively and operationally. During this time, I came more and more to appreciate his qualities of leadership.

He rarely missed an operational briefing and he frequently flew with the Wing, sometimes leading a squadron and at other times the Wing itself. His quiet, unassuming presence at squadron dispersals was a necessary morale booster at a time when our losses exceeded our kills. The formidable Fw.190 (the outstanding German fighter of World War II) was then appearing on the scene and we were still in the process of re-equipping with the Spitfire IXA.

That Victor Beamish was a caring man, I can testify from personal experience. One evening when we were playing snooker in the Mess, he said to me, 'Al, you seem a bit jumpy, what you need is something to take your mind off things and relax.' This observation was made while he puffed contentedly at his smelly pipe.

The next day there appeared on my desk a packet with a note from Victor which read, 'Try this, I find it soothes the nerves.' Inside was a new pipe and a packet of tobacco. From that time on I became an inveterate pipe-smoker, and in the later war years, when sucking my, by then, smelly pipe, I was poignantly reminded of the modest, steadfast man who had shown such concern for a young officer.

I had left Kenley for a rest, after my second tour of operations, when I learnt that Victor had been lost over the Channel. Somehow, it was bound to be. Despite the pressure which I am sure was coming from above for him to reduce his operational flying, he continued to participate with the Wing. It was just not possible, nor, I suggest, was it reasonable to expect a man so imbued with the will to win to temper his natural desire to engage the enemy. It was in the air that he felt he was best able to express his fervent patriotism, taking on the enemy wherever and whenever he could.

It was one of the great privileges of my wartime service that I was allowed to enjoy Victor Beamish's support and friendship. I shall always remember him with respect and affection.

Alan Deere,
Wendover,
Buckinghamshire

PART FOUR

1 *Undefeated at the Close*
2 *Far Beyond the Normal Call*

1

Undefeated at the Close

There was one material difference between the Allies' attitude to operational aircrew and that of the Germans. We allowed ours periodical rests from the daily grind, whereas the Luftwaffe did not. Only exceptionally could German aircrew expect a breather from battle and combat. Apart from the obvious needs of staff or instruction, only wounds, illness or some other physical or psychological derangement provided justifiable grounds for a break from flying. It was a tough regimen.

The Allies, on the other hand, were much more sympathetic, adhering to the principle that an operational tour of stated or reasonable length should be followed by six months' rest and quiet. All were expected to fly one tour and, given a normal run, many would probably do two. But that was about it. Only the incorrigible enthusiasts, the pathological cases and the inveterate gamblers defied convention and extended their output for King and Country to three or even four tours . . . if their luck held.

Stripped of detail and niceties, there were broadly two categories of operators among the Allies – those who played it according to expectation and the book and the others who went on and on and on employing every subterfuge, argument and artifice to convince the authorities that somehow they were unbeatable and perpetually in the pink. They were the addicts and, for them, operations represented the 'hard stuff'. The secret agents, dropped and working in enemy territory for long stretches at a time, fell into a similar class. How they stuck the tensions only they could know.

The fact was that these marathon patriots stood out by miles. They finished up totally drained – more so than ever they were able to realise. Yet they carried their bat through the innings and, marvellously and miraculously, they remained undefeated at the close.

Ludwig Franzisket
ACADEMIC IN THE DESERT

Gustav Rödel's portrayal of Eduard Neumann (Oberst a.D. Eduard Neumann) on pages 216–9 makes it easy to appreciate the authority with which the former *Jagdgeschwader* 27 (JG 27) commander selects Ludwig Franzisket, who died in 1988 aged 71, to be the subject of the study which follows.

Fifty-four years ago, Neumann was specially placed to make the choice which secured for Franzisket command of 3 *Staffel* in I *Gruppe* of JG 27 in the Western Desert – the Messerschmitt 109 unit in which the legendary Hans-Joachim Marseille rose to be the Luftwaffe's 'Star of Africa'.

Neumann had good reason to pick the Munster academic as Marseille's leader. Now, more than half a century later, and seven years after the eminent Professor's death, he is still adamant about singling him out as one of the exceptional Desert commanders. Read on and you will discover why...

Professor Dr Ludwig Franzisket, whose brilliant and resourceful mind enabled him to rise in his career to become a highly successful biologist in his scientific field, was a respected and yet most unusual figure in JG 27 in North Africa in 1941 and 1942.

He developed into a thoroughly able, all-round fighter pilot and leader with a compelling personality, yet he was totally without ambition in the Service. He did not hesitate, therefore, to speak his mind and act independently; indeed, he had no fear at all about standing up to those in authority, whether it was in a military or political context. He had the moral courage always to say what was in his mind.

If Franzisket believed an operation to be wrongly conceived, he would say so straightly. Yet he said it in such a plausible and persuasive way that he avoided giving offence. There were many who served with him in the German Air Force who had reason to thank him for his independence in criticising and then thwarting an ill-judged plan; he may well have saved their lives thereby.

There was a good example of this near the end of the war, when Franzisket was himself the Kommodore commanding JG 27. A decision had been taken by higher authority to remove his air reconnaissance units attached to the squadrons and provide them for the Army for ground attack – a role for which they were untrained and for which they were manifestly unfitted.

Franzisket wouldn't have any part of it, although he knew quite well that his refusal could have serious repercussions for him – and he said so . . . Those whom he saved from this absurd fate are still grateful to him to this day.

As an embryo scientist in those days (he was fascinated by the creatures he found in the Desert and could often be discovered dissecting them), he had a restless, creative mind; he was forever thinking up fresh approaches to old problems. Something was always happening when Ludwig was around. With him, things were seldom dull. Moreover, his philosophy was to take things as they came; success was all the same to him whether it be achieved in the air or on the ground. It was success that mattered, not where it was gained.

His independent mind owed something to his parentage. Ludwig's father, although a strong patriot, was vehemently anti-Nazi. He opposed the government of the day. One of the reasons why his son entered the Service was because the offspring recognised that, once there, he would be shielded from political interference and well able to anticipate such problems if they looked like arising.

I had come to know Ludwig Franzisket very well when he was serving as my wing adjutant in 1940 and part of 1941. Then, we were operating together in France, close to the Channel coast. Later, in North Africa, he acted for me for some while in the same capacity.

Because he was an able leader and adept at human relations, I put him in charge of 3 *Staffel* in I *Gruppe* of JG 27 when its commander, Gerhard Homuth, fell sick. I wanted him particularly to take our 'star' and problem child, Jochen Marseille, under his wing. Marseille had never hit it off with Homuth; in fact, they did not much care for one another.

As it turned out, this was just the break that Marseille needed. Franzisket understood Jochen and knew how to handle and humour him. This remarkable airman prospered under the guidance which Ludwig provided and quickly became the Luftwaffe's 'pin-up' fighter pilot of the Western Desert. But it was the squadron commander who enabled the best to be drawn out of this unconventional young officer.

Indeed, Franzisket never ceased to admire Jochen's genius and flair for combat. 'It separated him from the rest,' he once said. 'We would always recognise his style when once the *staffel* got into a fight. We felt we

263

had to stop fighting just to watch him go to work. His brilliance was exceptional.'*

Franzisket had his own problems to contend with in North Africa. He was shot down at Alamein, badly damaging a leg on the controls of his 109 as he baled out. He left hospital before he was properly recovered so that he might rejoin his squadron. Later, he was wounded again and once more he returned to the fray before he was ready. Perhaps he had an incentive for this. He knew that his father was being maltreated by the Nazis and the Gestapo because of his political views. It certainly wasn't his love of Party or Führer that drove him on! However, as a *Ritterkreutztraeger* (a holder of the Knight's Cross), he was able to save his parents.

There was one incident, I remember, which might have ended his career in the German Air Force much earlier. He was going home on leave to Germany in 1941 and had been flown by transport aircraft from North Africa to southern Italy. There, he picked up a Messerschmitt 108, a passenger aircraft, and, piloting it himself, headed north for Germany. The met forecast predicted heavy cloud up to the Po Valley, after that the weather would clear. In fact, it didn't turn out like that and the thick cloud persisted far beyond. By that time, it wasn't possible for Franzisket to turn back; the point of no return had been reached.

Just then, by a heaven-sent chance, he spotted a three-engined Ju.52 in a break in the dense clouds flying close to him. He immediately fastened on to it, formating tight up against it despite threatening signals from the pilot and crew in the cabin. He wasn't going to let such a providential stroke slip. Eventually the two aircraft landed together in Germany.

Immediately, a thoroughly irate lieutenant-colonel emerged from the Ju.52 demanding to know what the — — Franzisket thought he had been doing. Looking the lieutenant-colonel in the eye, Ludwig put on his most plaintive, pleading look. 'Herr Oberstleutnant,' he said, 'I had no desire to die so soon.'

The lieutenant-colonel made off, lost for words!

By his progress up the ladder, Ludwig Franzisket eventually rose to command JG 27 for five months, from 30 December, 1944, until the end of the war. By that time he had been scarred mentally and physically by endless combat; the ravages of war had left their mark. But it did not stop this courageous man from returning to his studies after the war and taking a Doctorate of Biology at Munster University with high honours – the first academic to achieve the status, *summa cum laude*, since 1920.

His participation in scientific experiments, principally to study coral life, took him frequently to Hawaii. His reputation and influence in the international academic world mounted. He became Director of the old Munster Natural History Museum, professor at the University and, later,

* See postscript at the end of this portrayal – Ed.

head of the new Museum which was built and established to his pattern. It is a model of its kind and much admired, worldwide. It stands as a symbol of the Professor's work in the international field.

Eduard Neumann,
Munich,
Germany

Postscript: Eduard Neumann is, of course, in a rare position (and so, too, for that matter was Ludwig Franzisket in his lifetime) to assess the brilliant Hans Joachim Marseille's true worth; his recent comments, written specially to be read in conjunction with the foregoing portrayal, are important for the purposes of the record.

Jochen Marseille was outstanding because he possessed *all* the qualities and attributes needed in an exceptional fighter pilot. He had these to an unusually high degree.

Some pilots would have some of his advantages to a marked extent, but they did not have them all. The point about Marseille was that he was as near the perfect composite fighter pilot as one was ever likely to see. The features were all there – acute eyesight, instantaneous reflexes, a very quick perception of an opportunity, an innate 'feel' for an aeroplane and, in addition to all this, plenty of panache. He had style, dash and courage. He was a deadly marksman.

I am, of course, very well aware of the doubts that have been expressed about Jochen's total of victories [151 in the Desert and 158 in aggregate before he was killed near Alamein on 30 September, 1942 – Ed.]. There are, however, two points which may not be appreciated.

First, Marseille's keenest critics were the pilots in his own squadron. They saw what he was doing and would have been the first to know – and criticise – if they thought that his claims were not soundly based. I never heard a doubt cast on Jochen's successes in the Desert.

Second, it should be remembered that the Desert is an open and very exposed place. Nowhere was it so easy to confirm the destruction of an aircraft. There was no better place to check a victory.

Werner Schröer, a very successful pilot and leader in the Desert, who knew Marseille's flying and style intimately, will have given you his impressions on Jochen's performance and his belief in the honesty of his claims.

Schröer, before his death a few years ago, did indeed confirm Neumann's contentions. A man of transparent honesty and integrity himself, with an individual Desert total of 61 victories and 114 overall, he expressed no doubts about the validity of Marseille's reporting.

As to Jochen's qualities as a leader, he had led a squadron before he was killed and he would certainly have become a wing leader had he lived. How good he would have been is difficult to say. The problem was that, by comparison with the rest of his comrades, he was too good and too quick. He was so exceptional that it could be argued that his pilots were not of a sufficiently high standard themselves to be able to learn from him and follow him easily.

In fact, he was always glad if his squadron had a success. But it didn't often happen. He was the star. In contrast, Werner Schröer so managed things that he deliberately engineered opportunities for his pilots to shine. His whole squadron got good results. Which approach was the most important? Certainly, Schröer's way was the most correct and conventional. But, on the other hand, to have a leader of Marseille's individual ability and success helped to raise the standard, spirit and aspirations of others in combat, as well as stimulating morale at home.

Eduard Neumann's forthright and authoritative defence of Hans Joachim Marseille finds support in an important piece of research emanating from South Africa. Carel Birkby, a distinguished foreign correspondent, editor, and author of a dozen books, recurred to this topic of Marseille's claims in his *Dancing The Skies*.*

'A particularly thorough researcher, Patrick Eriksson, has checked [Marseille's] claims against British and German records. Eriksson's conclusions: of Marseille's 151 claims in the Desert, 81 are confirmed, 24 can be rejected and 46 are "possibles". A total of 69 Allied losses is available to cover these 46 "possibles", but there are also 82 other German claims for these same losses.

'It thus appears that Marseille scored at least 81 victories and, in all likelihood, about 100 to 110 in total. He apparently overclaimed by about a third, and this compares very well with British and German overclaiming . . .'

It is right here to say that Neumann utterly rejects Birkby's thesis. 'Marseille's claims were valid,' he said, 'his Staffel knew it. And they would know.'

* *Dancing The Skies*, Howard Timmins, Cape Town, 1982.

Leslie (Chalky) McQueen White
FINGERS SCREAMING FOR MERCY

Desmond Scott (Group Captain D. J. Scott) was brought up among horses and farm animals in the 'warm brown hills of North Canterbury in far-off New Zealand', and you could tell it at once. Here was a thorough-going countryman, a man of the rich earth and a ruggedly practical and determined character. A fruity humour was always ready to touch up a respectful disregard for authority.

Scottie's total operational stint in World War II was long, arduous and complete, but his command, as a young group captain, of 123 Wing, with its four Typhoon squadrons, in 1944 and 1945 brought him lasting renown.

The performance of his rocket-firing aircraft in the great battles with von Kluge's armour at Falaise and Mortain in August 1944, at a crucial stage in the break-out from Normandy, owed much to his aggressive and unyielding leadership. His squadrons – 198, 609, 183 and 164 – fashioned a catastrophic reverse for the German commander and an Alpha Plus for the Allied ground forces.

Unusually for one with his non-academic background, Scottie can write, and his pen and his imaginative mind have recaptured in *Typhoon Pilot** and his other works the events and characters of those days ...

> Gliders, losing a wing, would spin down
> like sycamore seeds.

The lightness of the touch is often there.

While resting from operations in the winter of 1942, some of us were employed as temporary staff officers at Bentley Priory, the headquarters of Fighter Command, near Stanmore in Middlesex. During this period, our chief, Air Marshal Sir Trafford Leigh-Mallory, insisted that we visit as many stations of his Command as possible. Since this covered the whole

---

* *Typhoon Pilot*, Leo Cooper, Secker & Warburg, 1982.

267

of England, Wales and Scotland as well as Northern Ireland, we had ample scope to view the overall conduct of the air war at that time. Quite often visits to familiar squadrons had their lasting rewards.

One evening I dropped into Westhampnett, an airfield near Chichester, on the south coast, to see 485, the New Zealand Spitfire Squadron, and was invited to stay and attend a party in the sergeants' mess. I had hardly entered the building when Dumbo Grant, the Squadron CO, introduced me to a powerfully built sergeant pilot whose shoulders were so wide they appeared to be bursting out of his battledress.

Sergeant Leslie McQueen White – or Chalky as he was better known – put out a hand that resembled a smoked ham and felt like the blunt end of a stable broom. Clutching my own hand in a vice-like grip he treated my arm as if it were the village pump. While my fingers screamed for mercy, a broad smile crossed his face, pushing his eyes into two slits and reminding me of a picture I had once seen of an Eskimo chieftain. I was thankful when he released his grip and reached out across a well-stocked table for a bottle of beer.

No fancy tools were necessary. He casually pulled the cap off the bottle with his teeth, took a long swig and, after a hearty belch, handed me what was left of its contents. 'Cheers,' he said in a gravelly voice. He didn't wait for my thanks as two sergeant pilots began a heated argument on the other side of the table, and Chalky, without further ado, detached himself from Dumbo and me and moved off in their direction.

I couldn't hear what was said above the noise of the party, but the two misfits, on being spoken to by Chalky, quickly disappeared – and in different directions. With my hand still smarting, I had good reason to feel impressed, nor was there any need for Dumbo to remind me who the boss was in the sergeants' mess at Westhampnett.

Chalky looked more like a lumberjack than a Spitfire pilot, although I was not surprised when Dumbo said he came from a sheep farm in the Waikaka Valley in Southland. I could immediately picture his tousled head and long arms in the shearing shed, and the sweat, pain and blasphemy of the high country muster. He would have left school about the same time as I had – in the mid-thirties – that hungry period in our New Zealand history often referred to as the depression, or the sugar-bag years.

Some weeks later I met Chalky again. It was in King's Lynn, in Norfolk, where I had been attending an afternoon cinema show. I was without my car and had joined a long queue for the last bus of the day which would take me to the RAF Station at Sutton Bridge, where I was staying the night. One glance told me that even with a bit of luck, my chances of a bus ride were slim. The queue, made up of civilians and service personnel, was three or four persons wide and about thirty yards long.

Chalky and another sergeant pilot were several places ahead of me, and further ahead still, was a tall, thin middle-aged woman who kept complaining about the pressure being put on her from behind. This appeared to be generated by a handful of Army types who had obviously been celebrating in a local pub. The complainant, on having her hat knocked askew, threatened the British Army with a furled umbrella and attempted to elbow her way forward a place or two. This was not a popular move on her part, and caused some dissension among her fellow queue members.

Chalky, full of initiative, reached forward with a long arm and through a forest of legs and pinched the woman in the rear. She let out a scream, leapt in the air, and swung her umbrella smack across the ear of a nearby soldier. The innocent recipient and his mates had good reason to feel offended. One grabbed the umbrella and broke it across his knee, and before you could say 'Home James' the queue had forgotten the bus and had transformed itself into a round riot.

Soldiers and civilians set to in noisy haste. Not Chalky – nor his mate – nor me either. Feeling like a long-tailed cat in a roomful of rocking chairs, I quickly followed my fellow New Zealanders on to the bus and nipped upstairs to the top deck, where I was able to command a bird's eye view of the frenzied scene below. Those who were wise enough to untangle themselves followed us on to the bus and the driver, sensing a load of trouble, quickly put his vehicle into gear. As we drew away from the kerb, quite a sizeable land battle was taking shape. Some of the combatants were on the pavement, some on the roadway, while two were wrestling in the gutter alongside a telephone booth.

The cause of all this was still in the centre of the argument, but by this time she had lost her hat and glasses. Her hair, previously in a bob, had come adrift and was behaving like a grass skirt in an Hawaiian hula. Chalky, comfortably seated up front, didn't even look behind. He sat talking to his fellow sergeant as if the situation he had left behind was none of his business. He saved me a long walk and as the bus bounced along the road to Sutton Bridge, I couldn't help thinking what a fine type Chalky was to have around in times of need.

Two years were to pass before I saw Chalky again. We had just flown my four squadrons of rocket-firing Typhoons into Merville, a permanent airfield near Lille, in northern France, when one of our aircraft overshot the runway and ended upside down in the mud. All who witnessed this incident rushed over to the Typhoon in the hope of rescuing its stricken pilot.

The surrounding ground was too soft to support the mobile crane and there was little hope of lifting the seven-ton aircraft by hand – try as we did. Some Spitfire pilots from 135 Wing, which occupied the other side of the airfield from our own, joined us, but it was a forlorn effort and the unfortunate pilot was literally drowned in his cockpit. The heavy flak losses my squadrons had suffered were hard enough to bear, but to lose a boy in the Merville mud seemed totally unfair.

I was sadly surveying the scene and thinking how cruel and unforgiving a Typhoon could be, when I felt a hand on my shoulder. It was Chalky White. The same hand that had almost put me through the ceiling two years earlier at Westhampnett. He hadn't changed. A little older perhaps. All he said was, 'What a hell of a way to die.'

The boy was barely nineteen and had only recently joined my Wing. We squelched back on to the concrete perimeter track where I had left my station wagon. Chalky had a vehicle there, too. A captured Citroën. I didn't ask him how he had acquired it as most of my pilots had captured cars too, but I noticed when he proudly showed me his prize that it still had dried blood on the front seat and there were several bullet holes in a door.

After asking him about the fortunes of some of the 485 Squadron boys, I reminded him of our last meeting and our bus ride from King's Lynn to Sutton Bridge. He said he faintly recalled it. I thought, 'What a man!' Who could ever forget a scene like that?

He casually told me a lot had happened since then. He had been shot down near Le Havre in the summer of 1943 and had managed to make his way back to England via Spain and without the help of the underground movement. Even his gravelly voice couldn't disguise his pleasure at that. Without the help of the underground! It was the equivalent of climbing Mt Everest without oxygen.

I didn't tell him that I had learned from Intelligence much of his escape story and asked him if he would like to bring one of his fellow New Zealanders over to my caravan that evening for a drink. He arrived with a Taihape boy, Frank Transom, and after a whisky or two, Chalky began relating the story of his incredible escape.

After being shot down by a bunch of Fw.190s he had avoided his German pursuers by hiding in a water barrel that stood alongside a château on the outskirts of Le Havre. When darkness fell he set off on a journey that was to cover almost two thousand miles . . . Firstly, to Paris, where he found temporary refuge in a Montmartre brothel . . . Then through occupied France, where he was forced to put a revolver bullet through a German guard who was unlucky enough to question his identity . . . From there into Vichy France, and over the Pyrenees into Spain . . . Thence to Barcelona and Madrid.

It was a long and hazardous journey, yet he considered his greatest enemies had been his ingrown toenails, and the staff at the British Consulate in Barcelona! The latter had apparently regarded his escape story as too incredible, and he was suspected of being a German agent. Finally cleared of this, he was put aboard a four-engined Liberator bomber at Gibraltar, but before it started up to fly to England, he was off-loaded to make way for a senior Army officer. The aircraft lifted from the runway,

270

climbed away towards England, turned on its back and crashed into the sea. There were no survivors.

It was late by the time Chalky had finished his story, and after my guests had departed, I flopped on to my stretcher and began re-living his escape and thinking of the possible long-term effects that such an experience could have on him. How was the world going to treat men of his calibre when the war was over? By comparison with the Continent, New Zealand was an island in the sun – so far removed from Hitler's war-torn Europe that people who were not involved in it would never understand. Those pilots who survived the flak storms would be strangers in their own land . . . disillusioned . . . even bewildered. It had happened after World War I. It could happen again. I dozed off to the sound of heavy bombers – 1576 aircraft from Bomber Command – carrying a record 5453 tons of bombs. They were on their way to Duisburg . . . .

Desmond Scott,
Fendalton,
Christchurch,
New Zealand

Geoff Maddern
'CLOSER THAN BLOOD BROTHERS'

Don Charlwood, the Australian author, flew an operational tour as a navigator with 103 Squadron in Bomber Command during 1942 and 1943 – a nasty time in the night offensive against Nazi Germany. The experience cut deep in his memory.

Others trod the same path, but with Charlwood there was a difference. He picked up his pen after the war and made the experience live.

While an air traffic controller with the Department of Civil Aviation in Australia, he wrote a book with a compelling title – *No Moon Tonight*.* It is one of the truly arresting literary works to come out of the air war because it exposes, in finely turned prose, the inner feelings of 'ordinary aircrew' – in his case, an 'ordinary', mixed Australian and UK Lancaster crew.

'Ordinary?' Never!

Had we chanced our own judgement, Geoff Maddern and I might never have flown together. In that event, I doubt that I would have survived the war. As things eventuated, I remember him more warmly and gratefully than any other Bomber Command man I knew. And I remember our beginnings clearly. At No. 27 Operational Training Unit, Lichfield, eighteen Australian pilots and navigators were forming the nucleus of crews, one half strangers to the other. We were left to ourselves to initiate proposals that carried even more consequences than proposals of marriage – and most were 'till death them did part'. It was noticeable that like sought like. Natural though this was, I intuitively felt it was not necessarily the right yardstick for choosing crew members. Geoff also felt it beyond his capacity to choose aright, consequently he, as pilot, and I as navigator, fell together by a process of elimination.

We were both in our mid-twenties – he twenty-five and I twenty-six –

* Angus & Robertson, Australia 1956; Panther Books, UK 1958; Goodall Publications, London 1984.

but there our similarity ended. Geoff was gregarious, quick in reactions, indomitable by nature, peppery to the point of defiance when the need arose; I bookish, rather solitary, much too prone to accept authority. In the end, every other pilot-navigator combination formed that day was broken, one through the crew becoming prisoners of war, the other seven by death in action – one of the pilots after fifty-two operations.

From the outset, Geoff was intent upon forming an NCO crew. If we were to fly together as a close-knit unit, he wanted us to live closely in daily life. I soon became aware of the deftness with which he was moulding us – a scarcely conscious deftness, I fancy. He had natural sensitivity to the qualities of others which belied an often gruff exterior. He seldom needed to assert himself with us; we soon knew his expectations without his having to reiterate them, and we knew that they spelt the possibility of success and survival. From the outset the crew became a small democracy; quite often we were abusive of each other, though never with rancour. We were prepared to accept Geoff in an instant as temporary dictator – a position he never attempted to cling to when need for it had passed.

Five years ago he lent me his diary of our squadron days. It was then forty years since we had flown together, but as I began reading, I found myself immersed in the spirit of 1942–43 and realised afresh how much I owed – we all owed – to this untidy, pugnacious, much-loved skipper, who by sure instinct had welded a crew from our diverse personalities.

His diary sometimes expressed longings for Australia, yet also a love of England – he was eventually to marry an English girl – but the parts that swept me back were pages written after some torrid experience:

13 January 1943: Take-off at 1700 hrs, bomb load 1 x 4000 lb and ten cans of SBCs. On run-up everything was beautiful; taxied to the runway and still the gauges were normal. On take-off I noticed an unusual big swing to port; corrected it the best I could and hauled her off the deck at 120 mph. 'Shag' [rear gunner] called up to say that bags of smoke was pouring from the port inner. A moment later, the motor caught on fire. Doug [flight engineer] feathered it immediately. We weren't a hundred feet off the deck, IAS less than 120. Things looked black. I levelled out, trimmed for the swing and built the speed up for a climb. Once I had her up to 1000 ft I knew the danger was past . . . Jettisoned our cargo at sea, came back and made a perfect landing . . .

A week later:

. . . The moon was very bright – a good night for night-fighters . . . Three separate interceptions were made on us. One was down below in front. He spotted us and was about to turn to try to effect an attack from the beam. I kept on his tail and went into a steep turn with him; by doing this I got behind where he couldn't see me and then did a steep diving turn the other way, into cloud. The second one came as I was orbiting. He got on to our tail and chased me north. I turned in towards him and lost him by going into cloud again . . . The third attack was from

273

beneath. I turned in towards him and, luckily for us, another Lanc came along and nearly collided with the fighter . . . we saw no more of him.

I was amused to read his exact transcription of abuse I piled on him one night on our way home from Dusseldorf. As we neared the coast of Norfolk he persisted in reminding me of a convoy that was bound to fire on us if we got close to it. I told him I was already taking avoiding action, but still he interrupted. Finally I blew up. Having recorded my imprecations, word by word, in his diary, he remarked: 'I was dumbfounded; he is usually so quiet. Such words coming from him portend big things . . .'

This indulgent, amused reaction was typical of him. But not typical when he was dealing with our Wing Commander. As we said among ourselves, Geoff conducted the war on two fronts, one against the Axis Powers, the other against the Wing Commander. At the end of our tour we realised that our survival was attributable to the fact that he had seen the Axis and the Wing Commander as equal menaces. Like all Bomber Command Wing Commanders, ours was under great pressure to get as many aircraft as possible into the air and, like others, he had crews who, for various reasons, aborted. But too often he laid accusations against aborting crews without giving them fair hearing. This state of affairs reached its nadir for us when a crew of our close friends was harangued after failing to take off. On their next operation a faulty aircraft delayed them. Rather than again failing to take off, they left three-quarters of an hour late. Straggling far behind, they proved easy prey for night-fighters. Loss of them stiffened Geoff's resolve to trust his own and our excellent engineer's judgement and stand firm. On 21 December, 1942, we reached our aircraft for take-off and found technicians working feverishly on the blind-flying panel. When the engines were run up the panel still proved to be unserviceable. With time running out, we switched to another aircraft, only to find there were no guns in the turrets, nor had it been air-tested. Geoff recorded next day:

. . . The Wing Commander hauled me over the coals for not taking off. My blood boiled. To think anyone with an atom of sanity should condemn me for my action. . . . I looked [him] up and down and then said, 'Excuse me, sir, but are you suggesting that I and my crew are lacking in moral fibre?' He hummed and hawed and gave me no satisfaction. . . . I'm not going to let the matter drop at this. No man, no matter how many rings he may carry on his arm, is going to cast aspersions on my name and get away with it.

This was only one of a number of Wing Commander/sergeant clashes. They occurred during a dark period for the squadron: no crew had reached the required thirty operations for eight months, though four had been taken off to provide instructors when in their twenties. When we broke the hoodoo it was Geoff's nearer 'enemy' who put him up for his DFM.

The end of our tour was a joyful yet sad time; the seven of us were splitting up forever. In Geoff's words, we had become 'closer than blood brothers'. On our last day on the squadron the two inebriated gunners bumped him thirty times on the floor of our room in a gesture of gratitude and farewell. Although he was to gain a fine reputation as an instructor – he converted 108 men on to Wellingtons and was awarded an AFC – his instructional life was marked by persistent attempts to get back on to operations on his beloved Lancasters; ineffectual attempts, as it turned out. Perhaps as a grandfather living back in Perth, he reflects that this was just as well.

Don Charlwood,
Templestowe,
Victoria,
Australia

Vernon Bastable
CANADIAN PARTISAN

Lesser mortals can only marvel at the punishment which some seemed able to absorb in wartime. Pavel Svoboda, the Czech flight lieutenant and author of the piece which follows, possessed a combination of mental and physical toughness, the extent of which, in retrospect, is still hard to credit.

In November 1939, he was one of 1173 Czech students to be arrested and clapped into the Sachsenhausen Oranienburg concentration camp in Germany. Twenty-five were released under a Christmas amnesty a month later, of whom Svoboda was one. But he had been warned. Within a week of his homecoming, he had escaped through Hungary and Yugoslavia to France and thence to England, where, eventually, he joined No. 311 (Czech) Bomber Squadron based at Honington, East Wretham, in Suffolk.

On his 37th – and last – operational trip, his crew's Wellington was hit over Wilhelmshaven and forced to ditch 60 miles out to sea from the Dutch coast. Only three survived six freezing mid-winter days and nights in their dinghy – to be made prisoners of war at the end of it. After endless attempts at escaping, one final try towards the war's end succeeded, not to allow recourse to Allied lines, but to provide Svoboda with the chance to join other Czech partisans fighting the enemy in their own country. And nor was that the end of it . . .

Conniving with him during much of his tenuous, clandestine existence was a Canadian of similar resource and courage. Small wonder, then, that the former Czech flight lieutenant now makes him the subject of this study.

After my second attempt to escape at the end of September 1943, I was sent back to Stalag VIIIB, the prisoner of war camp at Lamsdorf. There I met Vernon James Bastable, Canadian bomber pilot from Winnipeg, who

276

was to make a great impression upon me. Shot down earlier with his crew near Rouen, he, too, had been returned to the camp after an unsuccessful attempt to escape. We talked a lot about our experiences with the German military police and the mistakes we had made during our attempted escapes. We finally agreed that, the next time, we would try to escape together . . .

It was now the end of August 1944, and we did not want to spend another winter in captivity. The best chance to get away, we felt, was to join a working party. There was one nearly ready to go to some quarry near Metsdorf, in Sudetenland; an armed uprising in nearby Slovakia seemed likely to help us. Vernon, who was a very good organiser, had found two soldiers who were willing to change places with us. Usually very calm, he seemed quite excited. 'This,' he said, 'is it.' Within days we were working in the quarry – Vern as 'John Crabtree' from Australia and I as 'Colin Neville' from New Zealand.

It was a great advantage that we were working alongside Czech civilians engaged in the quarry. From the first day, Vern kept up the pressure, wanting to know which of them we might approach for help. We agreed to take a chance with the explosions expert; he seemed intelligent and was the gang leader. When I spoke to him in Czech, he looked at me in disbelief. But his answer was short and positive. Yes, he would help . . .

> The first attempt to get away failed, but the failure wasn't critical. After giving time to let things settle, 'Crabtree' and 'Neville' made new plans.

The following week, I was passing our friend in the quarry and he whispered to me: 'Saturday – 7 o'clock, same place.' Rendezvous was to be in the woods above the quarry.

Soon after supper on Saturday, Vern disappeared from the camp. I followed within minutes, climbing on to the roof of the washhouse and scaling the fence. Hurrying away, I found him waiting as arranged. We hadn't been seen and now we were free! So far so good.

Our friends met us and we reached the next village in darkness where we discarded our uniforms. We were at once introduced to our escort, who took us across the border to Moravia, about six miles away. There we had to stay in hiding for three days until the search for us had been called off. After thanking our escort and the farmer who had given us shelter we were given a lift in a lorry to Hranice (a town about 12 miles south).

Our destination was now the southern part of Moravia, where I was born and had many friends. We had to walk all the way – 75 miles – in pouring rain. At about 8 o'clock the next evening, soaking wet and muddy, with blistered feet, we reached my uncle's home in Bukovany, 2 miles from where I had lived. He did not recognise me and was worried and suspicious because Vern was not able to answer any of the questions he asked. My aunt, however, took pity on us and let us stay the night.

In the morning, everything was sorted out and my family agreed that we could stay for the time being. Contact was made with the underground movement, with local partisans and also with Major F. Bogataj, Czech parachutist, operating under the code 'Carbon'. Vern was determined to reach Italy against all odds, no matter how long it might take us. True freedom was what we both wanted but could not find because our contact, who had tried to help us on our way south, could not make any headway and finally deserted us.

After several days in the wilderness we were forced to make our way back to the safe home of my uncle. We told him we were now ready to join the partisans. We both knew it was a risky undertaking – much more so for Vern, who did not know the country or the language. But there were no doubts at all in his mind; he accepted this new situation with his usual smile and from that moment he had my greatest admiration and respect. A cave, cut in a disused quarry and set deep in woods high up in the hills, became our home for the rest of the war.

We managed to survive the winter of 1944–45 and were supplied with food at night by friends who lived in the village. We slept by day; by night, we went out to get to know our surroundings. Vern was very quick to find his way about and he also made good progress with his new Czech language. There was not much we could do because of the deep snow, but we used this time to organise our group of 20 men. They worked by day and brought us all kinds of information about the German army's defences and we had detailed knowledge of all the military installations within a radius of about 7 miles.

The question of arms and explosives was debated with our men and an approach was made through our contact to Major Bogataj, who was also in hiding about 15 miles away. We were assured that our request would be transmitted by the beginning of March. Our coded message came on the Czech language transmission from London. Three days later, just before midnight, we heard an aircraft approaching our prearranged dropping area bordering the edge of the woods.

Vern switched the lights on and replied to their identification letter B with our prearranged letter D. In seconds we saw 23 parachutes coming down with their precious loads. Vern, with ten men, was guarding the dropping zone while the rest of us began to gather all the containers and parachutes. By the morning we had everything partially concealed in the woods.

With horses and a wagon we moved our arsenal further into the woods, to another disused quarry, and concealed everything there. It was now up to Vern and myself to look after our arms dump. Next day with a number of helpers we opened most of the containers and armed our men with Sten guns, rifles and grenades and two machine guns. The detonators and gelignite were stored in a small cave a good distance away. Vern instructed our group in the use of their guns and showed them how to handle the grenades and detonate explosives. I was concerned with the operations and safety of our 20 comrades. We knew that sooner or later we were bound to clash with the German military police.

When Vern was confident that the basic training was good enough to start the sabotage of the German lines of communication everybody was pleased and excited. We started by destroying telephone and telegraph lines, small unguarded bridges and railway lines, but always a few miles from our base. Vern was a born leader. Everyone liked him for his calmness, efficiency and daring. He was always first in any action and the last to leave, to make sure that all were safe and accounted for.

About a week before Easter, we decided to attack a military train carrying tanks and armoured transporters. We put two lots of explosives under the rail about 50 yards apart and waited till we could identify the train. When two of our scouts down the line flashed their light we lit the fuses and moved away. Sudenly there was a flash and a terrific bang and we could see wagons on their sides and some derailed.

Our jubilation, however, was short-lived. The train had a military escort and we could see soldiers running along the carriages, firing their rifles in our direction. We were not ready or prepared for a confrontation, but we managed to vanish into the woods without casualties. This railway ran from central Slovakia to Brno, and further west, and was a vital link for supplies. It took 36 hours for the damage to be repaired.

When Vern and I parted, he to guard our munitions and I to take, with another, promised arms to our comrades, neither of us knew that it would be the last time we would see each other. About 500 yards from the hut where we were to meet our friends, we hid our weapons and went to the meeting unarmed. Minutes after our arrival we were surrounded by 18 men of the German Sicherheits Polizei and I was eventually taken to the Gestapo Headquarters in Brno.

After my capture Vern tried to liberate me from the German police, but without success. It was a hazardous and desperate attempt and it showed again his total loyalty – risking his life to save me. His courage and bravery will always be remembered, not only by me but by all those who knew him and fought with him for the liberation of Czechoslovakia. He was one of very few Canadians to be decorated with a Czechoslovakian Military Cross.

For my part, I was able to escape again during the German evacuation and join another group of partisans, with whom I operated until the end of the war. I was then flown to London, where I heard from Vern again. It was May 1945, and he was safely on his way home, but he could only stay for 48 hours and there was no chance to meet. In Canada, he rejoined the Canadian Pacific Railroad.

We kept in touch regularly until his tragic death in March 1949.

Pavel Svoboda,
Wandsworth,
London

Kaj Birksted
DANISH INVADER

The Royal Norwegian Air Force's contribution to the air victory in the West was out of all proportion to the size of its force. The Norges who operated with the Royal Air Force were a close-knit, intensely loyal and patriotic bunch. They were tough, courageous and practical and were possessed of an unexpected facility for the English language. Their temperament made them, from a Service standpoint, the easiest of the Allies to handle. They were, in fact, remarkably 'English' in their approach and outlook.

Collectively, they had amazing stories to tell of their escapes from the German occupation of their country. Their personal discipline and resourcefulness were reflected in the way they flew aeroplanes and nowhere was this more apparent than in the two Norge fighter squadrons, Nos. 331 and 332, which, together, formed the North Weald Wing in Fighter Command, led, for a period in 1943, by an exceptional Dane, Colonel Kaj Birksted.

Ragnar Dogger, ultimately a decorated major in the Norwegian Air Force, flew with Birksted in 331 Squadron and saw his leadership at first hand.

The first time I set eyes upon our Wing Commander Flying was when Kaj Birksted took over the North Weald Wing in the spring of 1943. We heard he had arrived on the station and thought he would take a day or two to settle in. But who should jump on to the platform for briefing at 1200 hours that day but Birksted!

Tall, fair-haired and speaking English fluently, he was dressed informally in his flying boots and white, turtleneck sweater. Within a few minutes even the greenest of young pilots in the Norwegian Wing knew exactly what his leader's intentions were. He made these clear in short, precise and decisive sentences, rounding them off with an equally plain message. 'Press tits,'* he said, 'at 1300 hours,' and then added a rider. 'By the way, any section of two can go down – just give me a word.'

You could have heard a needle drop. It was not at all the kind of briefing we had become accustomed to!

Wherever we flew and whatever the situation, Birksted had complete control and nothing seemed to surprise or disturb him. He always seemed to place the Squadron or Wing in the right tactical position. He was calm, completely unselfish and seemed very pleased to let his young pilots get the kills. I am sure that, had he wanted, he could have added a dozen more enemy aircraft to his own score. But that wasn't his way. He created opportunities for others to exploit.

However muddled the fighting might be, you could hear his short and steady commands from up above. And when, in a flash, it was all over, with aircraft scattered all over the sky, you would hear his unruffled voice on the RT. 'OK – re-form, angels 20,000, Amiens.'* Within moments, the Wing would have regathered and be after the Hun again.

If visibility wasn't too good, he would be carrying a Very pistol in his cockpit. 'In 30 seconds [or whatever the time factor might be] watch for my signal' he would say, and then you would see a red, yellow or whatever the correct coloured star was go up and there would be the marker around which the Wing would regroup. His concern was always for the inexperienced pilots just as much as for those who might score the victories.

On the ground, he was the complete gentleman; he would not be seen pulling rank, but rather sitting in the dispersal hut with the newer pilots around him, discussing their problems with them and listening to what they might have to say. Or it might be in the bar – or in our hangout in London, the Wellington Club – and then there would be a half-pint in his right hand.

It was due to Kaj Birksted's rare leadership that, during the time that he was flying at its head in 1943, the North Weald Wing shot down more enemy aircraft for fewer losses than any other wing in Fighter Command; and in the same period, 331 Squadron had the highest score for the fewest losses of any Allied unit in 11 Group. In Birksted's eyes, it was the bottom line that counted in the profit and loss account – the total that accrued when the debits had been set off against the credits. To him, the debits *mattered*.

So there was our Wing Leader. He knew the business from A to Z, the

---

* Start up engines.
* Re-form at 20,000 feet over the top of Amiens – Ed.

perfect gentleman on the ground and the outstanding commander in the air. He flew like an angel. And he shot like Wilhelm Tell.

Ragnar Dogger,
Trondheim,
Norway

Sir Augustus Walker

GUS

Those who had exceptional wartime records and who, thereafter, made the Royal Air Force their chosen career could be divided, broadly, into two categories. There were the few who were able to build on the operational base and progress to the top of the Service, or to a point pretty close to it, and there were the others who, for one reason or another, did not, in the event, realise the potential which, at the war's end, seemed to be there.

There was no doubt about the category into which Air Chief Marshal Sir Augustus Walker – Gus Walker, they called him – lifted his small yet resilient and athletic frame. Sir Theodore McEvoy (see page 159) recalls, in a brief note, the character who is as well remembered as any of his noted contemporaries.

I had heard of Gus but had not met him until I went on a BABS* course at Melbourne, in Yorkshire, after World War II. As SASO† 4 Group he visited the station and left me in no doubt that here was a character. His gallantry on operations had been recognised by the award of the DSO and DFC. That his right arm had been blown off while he was dealing with a crashed bomber seemed to have been an encouragement to him, though for a rugby international to lose an arm must have been the sort of blow Douglas Bader had in losing his legs.

In command of the RAF Flying College at Manby he took part in all the most exacting flying tasks, which included flying as pilot over the North Pole. When he was recommended for an AFC it was said that air officers were not eligible for the AFC. It had to be firmly represented that this air officer was. He had an unusual gift for remembering everyone he met, which endeared him to all. When I went up to Manby to renew my instrument rating I stayed with Gus and Brenda, his wife. Before I went I had spiked one eye on a twig while pruning a tree and on arrival went

* Beam Approach and Beacon System.
† Senior Air Staff Officer.

to the MO and had it dressed. After dinner their little daughter came down to greet the guests. She gazed at my bandage and asked how I had hurt myself. 'Climbing a tree,' I said. 'How old were you then?' she asked. 'Fifty-one,' I answered. 'Oh!' she said, 'I didn't know grown-ups climbed trees.'

With his one arm Gus managed to play an accurate game of golf and later he was kind enough to partner me, a 22-handicap rabbit, in a series of Admirals/Generals/Air Marshals matches at the Berkshire, where his inspiring enthusiasm ensured that, though we didn't always win, we never lost. In the changing-room it was a revelation to see Gus tying his tie and shoe-laces with his one hand.

We used to play golf sometimes with Douglas Bader and Arthur Donaldson. The games occasioned some surprise at strange but hospitable clubs, with Douglas having no legs, Gus only one arm, Arthur with fingers shot away and me bent with spondylitis, but we had a lot of laughter.

After he retired, among other jobs he took on the Chairmanship of the Royal Air Forces Association and seldom rested. His too early death left a gap that could never be filled. I am grateful to have known him.

Theodore McEvoy,
Bognor Regis,
Sussex

Michael Crossley
ETONIAN DIPLOMAT

Karol Ranoszek, who became a decorated Wing Commander and the CO of 307, the Polish night fighter squadron in the Royal Air Force, got his 'wings' serving with the Polish Air Force in 1931. When World War II was over and he later settled in South Africa, he kept up his flying in the Republic with his own aeroplane. To be an active pilot over some six decades, in war and in peace, is quite a record.

In wartime, Ranoszek had the rare distinction of serving with four Air Forces – the Polish, the French, the British and, after secondment during the second half of World War II, with the United States Army Air Force, with whom he flew another operational tour.

He regarded it as one of the special privileges of his life that he should be sent to a British squadron – and to serve under British command – on his arrival in England via Poland and France. When he arrived here all he had to his name was a toothbrush, a razor and just the clothes that he was wearing. He could not speak a word of English.

Karol Ranoszek, like others of his resolute and spirited country-men, learnt fast. He had the special advantage of getting a good start.

Michael Crossley was the CO of 32 Squadron, with its Hurricanes, when I was posted to it in 1940 after my rather miserable experiences in Poland and France. He was therefore the first CO I served under after reaching England. You could tell at once that he was a first-class officer and an excellent squadron commander, but he was also an exceptional character.

He didn't have an easy job as 32 Squadron had become a very mixed lot. Apart from the unit's basic English core, which had been knocked about a bit in the fighting over France and Belgium in support of the withdrawing forces, there were seven Poles, two Czechs and a Belgian in it. Yet Michael had the personality and the leadership to blend us all together.

Everyone liked him both on and off duty and his good sense of humour proved a particular asset. On social occasions he was, in his quiet way, 'the life of the party', and one of his favourite sayings was, 'I don't believe in interfering with bad habits.'

When I joined the Squadron, it was based at Middle Wallop, a grass airfield some 10 miles north-east of Salisbury. In addition to 32, there was a night-fighter squadron on the station equipped with Beaufighters. They had quite a few mishaps and on several occasions when we came down to dispersal for dawn readiness we would find a crashed Beaufighter on the grass field.

On most RAF stations in those days there would be a collection box in the Mess marked 'Spitfire Fund'. Crossley had connived to change this to 'Beaufighter Fund – and do we need it!'

He also used to drive an old Bentley and often when we were off duty he would bundle a load of pilots into the car and off we would go to see a film in nearby Andover. Not once that I can remember did we ever reach the cinema – there were too many pubs to call at along the way.

When, eventually, Michael was promoted and had to leave us (we were then at Ibsley, another airfield in the same sector) the house where we had our Mess was renamed Crossley Towers in his honour. It was still called that years after World War II.

Our Polish and Czech names presented quite a mouthful for the average Britisher, so Michael saw to it that each of us was given a nickname. Mine was 'Johns'. As my English happened to be a little better than the rest of my countrymen's by then I occasionally had to act as interpreter. When Michael was leading the whole squadron in the air he would give his instructions over the RT in English. Then he would call me and say 'Johnsy, tell them', and I'd translate . . .

> As Karol Ranoszek makes clear, Crossley, who was a product of Eton and the peacetime Royal Air Force, had the background and the manner to mould a cosmopolitan squadron like 32 easily together. He could humour the 'foreigners', as Karol calls them, and keep up their spirits just as easily as he did the English. The Poles worked comfortably with him and, at the same time, kept up a spirited relationship among themselves with plenty of good-natured ribbing. Nearly fifty years on, Ranoszek remembers two incidents.

A few of us flew the Hurricane at night. During a patrol over the Channel our colleague, Flying Officer Falkowski, shot down a Heinkel 111, but was himself damaged during the attack. In baling out over land, he broke a leg and was nearly pitchforked by local farmers, who took him for a Hun before he managed to explain that he was 'one of ours'. He was taken to Havant Hospital near Southampton.

Michael Crossley at once dispatched our Squadron Intelligence Officer to obtain a combat report from Falkowski, who was, incidentally, one of the very few Polish officers who had contrived to get his wife to England.

Our Intelligence Officer was a hotelier in civilian life and some gossip had it that he had been his own best bar customer. As I was to act as interpreter, we set out together in his car the next morning and made our way through the Hampshire countryside without missing a single pub on the way. We staggered into the hospital at dusk in a very jolly mood to be faced with a dismal scene.

There was old Falkowski with one leg strung up and his wife sitting beside the bed with eyes rather swollen and generally seeming somewhat tearful. When he said he had a broken leg I replied cheerfully, 'Why worry, you still have a spare one.' This wasn't appreciated by Mrs Falkowski, who at once sailed into me in Polish. I wasn't very popular. However, Falkowski recovered well and in due course ended up as CO of the Northolt Fighter Wing.

Then we had the strange saga of the cigarette case. One of the flight commanders whom Michael Crossley had appointed was getting married, so the seven Polish pilots decided to give him a wedding present, a silver cigarette case with our names inscribed on it in the order of our Polish seniority.

My name was on top, followed by Falkowski's and the remaining five pilot officers. Then there was an extraordinary development. Steadily, each of the five Polish officers perished in succession in *exactly* the order in which their names appeared on the cigarette case, reading from the bottom upwards. Towards the end of the war only Falkowski and I were left.

By then I had become CO of 307, the Polish night-fighter squadron and, on a trip to Northolt to see my friends, I called in on the Falkowskis in Ruislip. When I greeted my old colleague with a twinkle and said 'Now it's your turn,' his wife sailed into me again. I wasn't at all popular.

As things turned out, Falkowski was shot down very soon afterwards while leading a fighter sweep over the Continent, but he only spent a short time in captivity, so I could breathe freely again. He now lives in Canada. And so, by the end of the war, out of Michael Crossley's seven Poles in 32 Squadron, only two survived – more or less average for a front-line fighter squadron. I may say that my wife, who knew the whole story, took a particularly keen interest in Falkowski's fate on the basis that if he was all right then so should I be!

After he left 32, I lost touch with Michael temporarily, but, fortuitously, some years later, we met again here in South Africa. By then, he had a timber farm near White River in the Eastern Transvaal and visited us in Johannesburg. I also flew down to see him at Nelspruit in my Piper twin Comanche and took him flying with me.

He had finished the war with 22 enemy aircraft confirmed destroyed and the DSO and the DFC to show for it. There was always a lot of reminiscing about old chums and old times. It was nice to feel that my first Royal Air Force CO wasn't so far away.

Sadly, his wife, Moira, herself a former WAAF in Fighter Command operations rooms, had to tell us in December 1987 that Michael had died peacefully on his farm.

Another great character – and gentleman – had gone!

Karol Ranoszek,
Kensington,
Johannesburg,
Republic of South Africa

Hannes Faure
'HE LED FROM THE FRONT'

Charles Barry (Captain C. H. H. Barry) flew two exacting operational tours on photographic reconnaissance with 60 Squadron of the South African Air Force and was decorated for it. The latter part of the second tour in 1944 and 1945, flown high up in the specially prepared Mosquito XVIs from San Severo, in Italy, coincided with the introduction into limited service of Germany's twin-jet Messerschmitt 262 which, in a relative sense, was well ahead of its time.

Barry and his navigator, Lieutenant G. R. Jeffreys, were able to testify at first hand to the astonishing performance of this advanced aircraft. It changed the outlook overnight for photographic reconnaissance over southern German and Austrian air space. It was a tricky time for the crews of 60 Squadron.

Post-war, Barry made his mark in South African journalism, becoming a widely regarded figure with the Republic's Argus Press. Now, in his so-called 'retirement', he is still at work within the Group.

Hannes Faure is a World War II name you don't hear much about outside South African Air Force circles ... Not as Sailor Malan and Piet Hugo are known. Their names are part of history. Faure's should be there too.

He is a born leader. All who served with him know that. 'Brave as a lion and calm as a bull terrier under pressure, Hannes was quite splendid on and off duty. He was a great disciplinarian and led from the front,' says Group Captain Duncan Smith, DSO (Bar), DFC (2 Bars), CO of 324 Wing, who personally asked the Air Officer Commanding, Italy, to let him have Hannes as his Wing Leader.

'The best guy I have ever had the privilege to call my friend.' Thus says Captain Tony Biden, DFC, a former flight commander of 1 Squadron, SAAF, which Faure served and commanded with such distinction. 'He has a strong personality, is modest and never lost his temper. In any group he was the obvious leader.'

Born in 1917 and christened Johannes Philibert Morkel, he comes from a distinguished line of five generations of wine farmers, of which he was one until his recent retirement. The family emigrated to the Cape of Good Hope in 1688 with the Huguenots and Faure, where they farmed on the flats near Cape Town, is named after them. Hannes' father was a Member of Parliament and a Senator. He is related, through his mother, to the famous Springbok (rugby) Morkels.

Early in World War II Hannes applied for a pilot's course, then joined the Artillery because there were no vacancies. Two months later he was transferred to the SAAF. Within five years he was to rise to the rank of lieutenant-colonel and be decorated three times. The 'Average Plus' assessment in his logbook when he got his wings gave no hint of this, but his qualities of leadership did. After OTU on Hurricanes in the Middle East he was posted to 1 Squadron, SAAF, the crack fighter squadron that was to become synonymous with his name.

I never had the privilege of serving with him on operations. Our paths diverged when he went to fighters and I went to high-level reconnaissance. But we kept in touch and I soon learnt that the qualities I knew in him when we were in training were confirmed over and over again by those who were with him.

'In May, 1942,' says Tony Biden, 'we were based at El Gamil airfield, Port Said. Very high-flying recces were coming over photographing shipping in the area. Two of our Hurricanes were stripped of all extra weight, leaving two guns. Hannes and I were scrambled one day to intercept. We got above 30,000 ft and were hanging on our props when the Jerry passed about 5,000 ft above us. Hannes, who was leading, pulled up the nose of his aircraft, fired and spun off. I did the same.

'We both came out at about 25,000 ft, disappointed and frustrated. To cheer us up I suggested that we should do a loop together. 'No Tony,' said Hannes, 'let's climb a bit first!' He could defuse a situation with an off-beat remark. It was a habit which endeared him to his colleagues.

It happened to me. As a baby-faced young recruit I was standing in a queue for my first Service meal. With me were other pupil pilots, older, gungho chaps who looked like Springbok rugby forwards. How could I ever be one of them? I thought nervously.

Suddenly one of them leant forward and whispered in my ear, 'Does your mother know you are here?'

Immediately I relaxed. We both laughed. The well-built young man with the twinkling eyes was Pupil Pilot Johannes Faure. It was the beginning of a lifelong friendship.

In more dramatic circumstances, Duncan Smith recalls a similar situation over Sicily when Hannes was leading 1 Squadron on a wing strafing mission behind him.

'The 40 mm flak was thick and cracking too damned close for comfort. I was searching the undulating mass of rock and scrub for a convoy of German trucks and didn't realise the flak was so accurate since, in the lead, most of it was under and behind me, making life rather hot for the others.

'Clear as a bell, I heard Hannes' voice as he led Blue Section. "Hotspur Leader" – it was my call sign – "there are sparks chasing you, red hot. Have you any final message before you leave us?"'

It was typical of the man . . . the twinkle and the quick quip to ease the tension.

But there was another side of Hannes. Major Bushy Langerman, DFC, another leader of distinction, recalls it:

'We were at Lentini, in Sicily, on 10 August, 1943, enjoying a Mess party. Suddenly the whole place began to erupt as Jerry bombers came over. Heavy explosives and canisters of butterfly bombs were falling everywhere under the brilliant flares.

'Hannes was into his jeep immediately driving here, there, everywhere about the airfield to see how his men were faring and giving a word of encouragement to any who were wavering under the awful pounding, heedless of the dangers of the flying shrapnel. What an inspiration to all of us!'

Tony Biden remembers being involved in an accident about this time.

'I recall pranging my Spit into another Spit while taxiing after an "op", when my windscreen was covered with oil. Hannes was OC at the time and I was found guilty of gross carelessness and my logbook was endorsed in red ink:

Lieutenant Biden, through gross carelessness at Lentini on 31/8/43, on taxying, caused damage to His Majesty's aircraft, Spitfire JK393, by colliding with another aircraft.
Authority AHQDA3/GT1/Aug/48 dated 3/9/43.

Signed J. Faure
CO No. 1 Squadron SAAF.

'Next to it, Hannes wrote in blue ink, just two words: "Sorry Tony".

'I do not think I could add to this.'

Another pilot who served on two tours of operations with Hannes is Major Don Brebnor, DFC, who went on to command 7 Squadron SAAF.

'There were many times when I admired Hannes' skill, courage and leadership,' he recalls. 'But what impressed me most was not his 5½ kills: it was the effect he had on morale.

'For example, we would be in a sandstorm in the Western Desert . . .

an awful and awesome experience . . . tents would be damaged, some even blown away . . . and everything you possessed filled with the filthy grit . . . You would be utterly miserable.

'And there, sitting in the middle of the shambles would be Hannes Faure saying, with that affected Oxford accent he used to put on for one of his favourite jokes about a colonel at a dinner party, "I say, you chaps. I've got a tin of sardines. You bring some 'ish' (issue brandy) and let's have a frightfully jolly party, what?"

'The effect was magical. Everybody would be laughing and suddenly that sandstorm didn't seem so bad after all.

'Yes, his humour was as endearing as it was effective.'

It was a favourite expression of Hannes' – 'You Billy' – that gave 1 Squadron its proud nickname of The Billy Boys. He says it came from Waltzing Matilda ('And he sat and watched and waited while his *Billy boiled*').

He had a very different experience of the Western Desert. He was shot-up one time on a strafing mission and crash-landed about 30 miles behind the enemy lines.

'I was standing on the wing with the aircraft on its belly', he recalled to me, 'when a truck appeared over the horizon. An officer shouted "Come on!". I thought he was an Itie so I stood still. He then shouted, "Hurry up or do you want to be captured?" I shouted, "Are you British?" and when he said "Yes" I ran to the car, where they gave me a stiff rum.'

Hannes had fallen into the hands of the Royal Dragoon Guards, operating behind the lines. He was with them for two days while they shot up enemy transport and took a German officer prisoner. He drove one of the captured trucks and acted as aircraft spotter before rejoining the squadron.

After two tours of operations with 1 Squadron and part of a third tour as CO of 4 Squadron SAAF, Faure went to 324 Wing as sweep leader to confirm that he was one of the most outstanding pilots in Italy.

'He not only led the Wing from the front,' recalls Duncan Smith, 'but it was largely through his skill, drive and enterprise that we finished our conversion to a fighter-bomber role so successfully.

'He was a stickler for discipline and I believe his successes as a leader lay in the confidence he generated among those whom he led, because he mirrored his leadership qualities in a way that his pilots would copy whenever they had the chance. Nothing upset him, and the tougher the situation the better he liked it. An ideal type in a tight corner, he reminded me very much of Pieter Hugo.'

When the war ended, Lieutenant Colonel Hannes Faure, DSO, DFC (Bar) led the SAAF contingent in the Victory Parade in London. It was a proud moment for him, and an equally proud moment for those who served with him.

Now, as he settles with his wife, Rita, into retirement in beautiful Somerset West, near Cape Town, he has much to remember besides their children and 11 grandchildren. He can look back upon an exemplary wartime career. He served his country well and with great distinction. And he is one of the most modest men I have ever known.

Charles Barry,
Johannesburg,
Republic of South Africa

Brian Kingcome
PLAYING IT TOGETHER

Close friends made pairs in the Royal Air Force in wartime. Duncan Smith (see pages 322–6) and Brian Kingcome, two highly decorated officers (three DSOs and five DFCs between them) offer a good example. They played things their way in the air and, off duty, on the ground. The one complemented the other.

After customary operational contacts in Fighter Command between 1940 and 1942, it was the Desert Air Force and the Sicilian and Italian campaigns which cemented the relationship. Duncan Smith's portrayal of Kingcome which follows exposes it.

Their humour blended nicely – and so did their courage and operational endurance. While the professionalism was obvious, nothing was allowed to become too serious. Pomposity was out. A predilection for 'pressing on' (after due, but well disguised, calculation) was common to both. For Kingcome, the time spent as a cadet at Cranwell, and the training it bestowed, laid the base for a wartime run of unusual quality.

As a pair working in double harness – or something near it – the two could extricate themselves from improbable predicaments. There was the time when, as Group Captains with a mass of fighting experience behind them, they were together in London in the summer of 1944 on a mission devised for them by Sir John Slessor, their C-in-C in Italy. Harry Broadhurst, whom they were to visit, was then in Normandy with his 83 Group HQ.

The pair were enjoying the comforts of the old Berkeley Hotel and the capital's social scene when an apparently innocuous paragraph appeared in the Diary of the London *Evening Standard* drawing attention to their colourful presence in the Big City. The next morning they were called to the Air Ministry by the Provost Marshal's office and confronted by a pompous and operationally inactive fellow Group Captain, who demanded to know what they were doing in the UK anyway.

As their explanation did not convince, Duncan Smith picked up the telephone and asked the operator to put him through to the Allied Air Commander, Air Chief Marshal Sir Trafford Leigh-Mallory, who was already fully aware of the visit and its purpose. After a few animated exchanges, Leigh-Mallory asked to be passed over to the Group Captain, sitting at his desk.

A succession of suitably contrite 'yes, sirs' and 'no, sirs' followed and the receiver was lightly replaced. Duncan Smith and Kingcome withdrew from the room with aristocratic disdain, courteously acknowledging the apologies as the Group Captain held the door open. . . It was then nearly midday. The Savoy's American bar was only a few paces round the corner.

Duncan Smith reflects:

Brian Kingcome's career in the Royal Air Force might have been cut short right at the start but for his resilient mental and physical strength. While still a junior cadet at Cranwell, he was involved in an appalling motor car accident, crashing into a stone wall and causing very severe damage to face, body and legs.

He was in hospital for a long time bringing his parents and himself great anxiety since it became doubtful whether he would be able to complete his cadetship. Indeed, the medical board told him he would never fly again since he was bound to experience double vision permanently. Luckily for the Service, he recovered completely, but it took a very expensive private operation to put things right. After a break of nine months, he finished his term, passing out of Cranwell with distinction – and followed it with a remarkable war record.

Brian was (and is) a born leader and his determination and spirit in the air helped many a young fighter pilot to survive the battle. Gaining some of his expertise by his example, the new boys, most of whom were with the Volunteer Reserve, were able to settle quickly into squadron life and make a worthwhile contribution to the unit's success.

One old friend of mine, Wing Commander Don Kingaby, who served with Brian in 92 Squadron during the Battle of Britain, is a splendid example. As a sergeant pilot in the RAFVR, Don shot down 23 enemy aircraft, winning the DFM and two bars! Later, after being commissioned, he went on to be decorated with the DSO and AFC. While I was commanding 64 Squadron at Hornchurch in 1942, Don was my 'A' Flight Commander and he told me how much the pilots of 92 Squadron looked up to Brian for his fighting and leadership qualities.

It was while Brian was in temporary command of 92 that the Squadron intercepted a large enemy bombing raid on London at the height of these attacks. He shot down one of the bombers, but, following the engagement, got separated from the rest of his formation. Looking round, he saw three aircraft behind his Spitfire and then at once felt the shock and tumult of

296

bullets striking his aircraft accompanied by the sharp, painful agony of a bullet boring through his right leg.

He told me he was sure the aircraft which had opened fire on him was friendly and had not verified his identity. Severely damaged and unable to keep control of his Spitfire any longer, Brian baled out, but kept his head and did not open his parachute immediately as he was still between 18,000 to 20,000 feet and, regrettably, the enemy at that time was not averse to gunning down fighter pilots as they descended earthwards. He was in hospital for the next six weeks.

Between the ending of the Battle of Britain and the time of his arrival in the Mediterranean, Kingcome progressed in sequence through the various stages of fighter leadership, culminating in his command of the Kenley Wing in 1942. During part of a short-lived rest from battle, he placed his stamp on Fighter Command's recently formed Fighter Leaders' School, a responsibility for which he had Duncan Smith to thank, as his friend was then on the Command's air staff and in a position to exert influence. Thereafter, as Duncan Smith, who had himself been posted overseas to lead the Luqa Wing in Malta, relates Destiny took a hand.

With Brian's own posting overseas, it transpired that the ship in which he sailed, though destined for India and the Burma war, suddenly got orders to proceed through the Red Sea to Egypt while it was taking on stores at Cape Town. Once there, Brian flew on to Malta and, much to my delight, joined me at Luqa.

His greeting was typical. 'Me dear old lad, we must stop meeting furtively in these frightful foreign places ... !'

The high intensity of operations meant that we had little time for sport, but I suggested to him that we should hire a sailing dinghy. There was a boatyard at St Paul's Bay and the owner agreed to let us have a small dinghy, which we called HMS *Buttercup*. It made excellent fun.

However, one afternoon a couple of Me.109s, looking for trouble, appeared flying low towards us. They looked particularly sinister. Accepting that discretion was the better part of valour, we abandoned ship while still under sail. This was foolish and hasty, but, luckily for us, the slipstream of the 109s, being so low, 'stalled' the sail, thus swinging *Buttercup* round dead into wind and allowing us to cling to her side and pull ourselves aboard – otherwise I do believe we might never have seen Malta again.

Brian's comment sticks in my mind. 'I'm 'fraid our enemies aren't gentlemen, old lad. Pity!'

During the 'softening up' process before the Sicilian invasion in July 1943, Kingcome and Duncan Smith, and the Luqa Wing, had several

297

field days at the enemy's expense before Air Vice-Marshal Harry
Broadhurst, Air Officer Commanding, Desert Air Force, gave Kingcome (a very young Group Captain at 24) command of 244 Wing
with its Desert-hardened Squadrons – 92, 145, 601, the Canadian
417 and the South African 1 Squadron – all now equipped with
Spitfire VIIIs and IXs.

Much to his delight, Duncan Smith, recently recovered from a
virulent bout of tonsillitis and fever, was appointed 244's Wing Commander Flying. With the first stages of the Sicilian invasion now
behind, he took the opportunity to slip across the Straits to Pessaro
to see the newly created Group Captain and bring him the news. He
remembers it well.

A pissy evening followed and as I was about to take off on my return to
Malta, with my tail wagging, Brian handed me two letters. 'Be a good
chap,' he said, 'and post these for me when you get back to civilisation . . .
As you see, my hands are full here disposing of enemy resistance. On your
return, make sure you are dressed properly and are sure you know how to
salute a senior officer!'

Once again, they made a pair. But it wasn't all free-wheeling as the
Wing Commander Flying recalls.

Based at Lentini, in the central plain of Sicily, 244 Wing, along with
322 and 324 (Spitfires) and 239 (Kittyhawk fighter-bombers), were
pounded one night by a strong force of enemy bombers which wrecked a
large number of aircraft and killed or wounded over 50 Wing personnel
at Lentini alone. The Operations caravan received a direct hit, killing both
operations officers and the wretched orderly manning the switchboard.
From the enemy's standpoint, it was a highly successful operation.

Brian and his senior administrative officer, Squadron Leader Disney,
were quite splendid getting the chaos under control and repairing the
bomb damage by dawn so that the Wing could meet its operational commit-
ments. The Germans never repeated a similar attack – I wonder why?

With the winding up of the Sicilian fighting in less than six weeks,
Duncan Smith was reconnoitring airfields along the 'foot' of the
Calabrian mainland when his Spitfire suffered a technical failure and
he had to bale out over the sea. Separated from his dinghy, he spent
six tortuous, sun-baked hours swimming in his Mae West, trying
desperately to make the shore. Only by courtesy of the Almighty was
he ultimately picked up by an ageing Walrus amphibian. The outcome
is still clear in his mind.

Imagine my surprise, arriving back at Lentini, burnt like a piece of toast, tired and fed up, to find all my belongings missing from my tent, right down to my toothbrush. Suddenly Brian appeared. 'What's happened to all my kit,' I asked him.

'Ho-hum, m'dear boy,' he retorted, 'none of us thought you were going to make it. Now you've put me in a difficult spot. I've disposed of your belongings to your keen admirers!' Then I heard Brian's laugh. His well-conceived leg-pull was, of course, brilliant and exactly what was wanted to make me feel at home again.

> Italy had to be fought for all the way. Again, the two had their successes with the Wing, but the problems, as the Wing Leader recalls, were never far away.

From Sicily, 244 Wing moved to Grottaglie to support the Salerno landings and then to Gioia, near Brindisi, and Bari, where the Royal Engineers had to clear some 3000 land mines from the airfield. Nevertheless Brian and I always got sweat in the palms of our hands when landing just in case the Engineers might have missed one or two!

I remember Brian went off with Dudley Honor to visit the Desert Air Force's mobile Operations Room unit. Dudley suddenly turned down a side road going like the clappers and pitched Brian out on to the stony road, which he hit with his already scarred face, arms and legs. Bandaged from head to foot when next I saw him, only his eyes were visible. Nor was that all. I discovered afterwards that after hitting the road he had bounced off into a German minefield and dared not move until the Engineers had arrived on the scene and cleared an exit! . . . What a performance, as the actress said to the bishop!

> Then came Duncan Smith's departure from 244 Wing to take over 324 as a Group Captain. Even so, the two Wings and their commanders remained very much in touch in support of the British and American forces in the drive for Rome, the assault on Cassino and the Anzio operations. But Kingcome was due for a rest and after 15 relentless months in command of 244 he was dispatched to the Staff College at Haifa, returning in six months as SASO of 205 Bomber Group with which he was to fly missions 'just to get', as he put it, 'the feel of these monsters'.
>
> Five years after the war's end, Duncan Smith had returned to England from operations over the jungles of Malaya to take part in an Army/Air Force exercise in Germany. To his intense distress he found his old mate of many battles sick in King Edward VII Hospital at Midhurst suffering from TB – an illness which was to prompt

Kingcome's premature retirement from the Service. The shock is retained to this day.

All Brian's close friends were shattered, for but for this unfortunate happening he would undoubtedly have reached the highest ranks of the Royal Air Force. Always popular with pilots, officers and other ranks, he had that great gift of being able to make an order sound like asking a favour – true leadership in its most demanding sense.*

Duncan Smith,
Honiton,
Devon

* Brian Kingcome recovered to build and manage, with his wife, one of the most successful furnishing businesses in London – Ed.

Piet Hugo
SOUTH AFRICAN TRIUMPH – AND TRAGEDY

Among the wartime volunteers for aircrew duties in the Royal Air Force were a few who could be identified at once as 'special material'. These were the starred 'amateurs' who had already begun to make a mark in civilian life and were plainly going to resume some civilian occupation when peace returned – if they survived.

Sandwiched in between were half a dozen highly successful Service years bringing advance, achievement and distinction.

These figures were clearly labelled 'likely to go far' or, as the cliché perhaps prefers it 'destined to lead'. Robin Johnston (Wing Commander G. R. A. M. Johnston) was one of them. After Cambridge and a promising start in the Colonial Service came a war of predictable success – command of 73 Squadron in the Western Desert, a rest at the Air Ministry, then command again, this time of 65 Squadron, and, eventually, leadership of 122 Wing, with its P-51Ds, flying support for the United States' Eighth Air Force's daylight offensive against the Fatherland.

With peace, it was then back to Africa, initially in the public service, but then progressively in the commercial and industrial sector, with Unilever, Mowlem Construction, Whitbread and Anglo-American, culminating in the establishment of Robin Johnston Associates, the management selection company, in Johannesburg.

It was quite a ride.

Although we were both fighter pilots in the Royal Air Force, I did not meet Piet Hugo until just after the European war was over; the Japanese conflict was still then in progress.

Dick Atcherley (Air Marshal Sir Richard Atcherley), one half of the ebullient and famous Service twins, had formed the Central Fighter Establishment ('CFE') and based it at Tangmere on the Sussex coast. Its purpose was to study and collate fighter tactics and the capabilities of all fighter aircraft, including those of the Luftwaffe. I was a founder member in charge of the collation and took a party to Burma to discover what tactical lessons could be learnt from the fighting in South-East Asia. Another part of CFE was to be a squadron commanders' training school and this came under the famous New Zealand leader, 'Hawkeye' Wells. There were some ten top fighter pilots selected for the staff and all were wing commanders of various nationalities. It was decided that a group captain should be put in overall charge of the day-to-day work and Piet Hugo, a South African, a much-decorated fighter leader, who had fought in the Battles of France and Britain, before serving in North Africa and southern Europe, was chosen. His ability and experience fully justified his selection.

Piet was the sort of man you felt immediately you could rely on, someone to trust, a good man to have with you in a tight corner; and yet you soon realised that there was a sense of depth about him too. He was a man who would take a calculated chance, but only after all the risks had been weighed. Courteous and indomitable, he also had a nice sense of humour. It was particularly noticeable to me at CFE how all the distinguished fighter pilots from various parts of the world at once related well with him and liked him.

Standing six feet in his socks, he was athletically built, with broad shoulders, fine bone features and clear, very steady blue eyes. He had a slight, but attractive Afrikaans accent – like Field Marshal Jan Smuts, the South African prime minister, who was a godfather to his eldest daughter. It was a rather clipped accent with a distinct rolling of the r's. Much to Piet's distaste, it had on occasion during air combat caused consternation in Fighter Command's 11 Group control room when the WAAF operators mistook him for a Luftwaffe pilot speaking English!

Piet's ancestors had been Huguenot refugees and had landed at the Cape of Good Hope in 1687. Industrious agriculturalists and stockmen, they soon established themselves in their new land and, by the time Piet was born in 1917, his immediate family were sheep farming in the Karoo in the northern Cape – a vast area of low scrub where the winters are icy and the summers stifling hot, but where the conditions are good for sheep. Piet was one of 13 children, most of whom, in time, inherited their own farms.

Even as a young man, Piet had taken an intelligent interest in world affairs. As he grew older, he developed a feel for the meaning of trends in international events. Much later on, well after the war, I was often amazed at the breadth of his general knowledge. He was in his second year at Witwatersrand University in the Transvaal, studying for an Aeronautical Degree, when he had the prescience to realise that, with the way events were hotting up in Europe, there was every chance that Britain would be drawn into a war with Nazi Germany. He wanted to be in the fray.

He therefore abandoned his studies, went to England in 1938, well before the war, and joined the Royal Air Force. For an Afrikaner to join one of the British armed forces in anticipation of a war was yet another indication of Piet's independence of mind, for, even to this day, there are some Afrikaners who are still 'fighting' the Anglo-Boer War. However, at that time, Jan Smuts, himself an Afrikaner, was very pro-British and was to become one of Britain's staunchest allies. South Africa was still in the Commonwealth and both English and Afrikaans speakers volunteered when war was declared and proved to be truly formidable fighters in the Allied cause. In June 1942 they suffered grave casualties at Sidi Rezegh, some 20 miles south-east of Tobruk, in the Western Desert – just as they had done at Delville Wood in World War I – and they produced exceptional pilots like 'Sailor' Malan, who, when I met him, seemed to me rather like Piet Hugo in his great physical endurance.

Piet flew with courage and panache in the Battle of Britain in 1940, made his mark and earned himself the first of his three DFCs. His Squadron – No. 615 (County of Surrey) Squadron in the Auxiliary Air Force – had, however, suffered very severe casualties during its time at Kenley. Fighter Command, therefore, withdrew it from the line and sent it north to the Turnhouse sector, near Edinburgh, to rest and regroup. Understandably outraged by this posting to Scotland, not least because he felt that the CO, an Englishman, was being rather wet about doing anything to resist it, Piet committed himself totally to extricating 615 from its dilemma.

Realising that Winston Churchill was the Squadron's Honorary Air Commodore,* and believing in the maxim that when you have a problem you should go to the top, Piet and a fellow flight lieutenant, a New Zealander, decided to take the matter into their own hands. They caught a train to London, took a taxi to 10 Downing Street and asked to see the Prime Minister.

Busy though he was, it must have intrigued Churchill to hear that two of his squadron's fighter pilots wanted to see him. He at once agreed to have them sent in.

'Now what can I do for you two gentlemen?' growled the Prime Minister, ensuring, first, that each had a whisky in his hand.

'Well, sir,' said Piet, imperturbably, 'we are extremely disconcerted to have been pulled out of the line and transferred to Scotland. We thought, sir, that as our Honorary Air Commodore you might consider having the order rescinded. We want to get back into the fight, sir, not sit on our arses in Scotland.'

That sort of fighting talk must have appealed to Churchill, but he gave nothing away. 'Far be it from me,' he retorted 'to interfere with the orders of my senior commanders. I will, however, mention it to the Chief of the

* The establishment of each Auxiliary Air Force squadron included a titular head called the Honorary Air Commodore. 615's invitation to Churchill came from Vere Harvey, later Air Commodore A. V. Harvey, the member of parliament for Macclesfield, and later still Lord Harvey of Prestbury – Ed.

Air Staff, but I counsel you: do not raise your hopes unnecessarily. And now, gentlemen, as you may observe, I am rather preoccupied.'

It wasn't long before 615 were packing to return south, to 11 Group.

From 1941 onwards, after the Battle of Britain was over, Fighter Command's squadrons in 10, 11 and 12 Groups went over to the offensive with sweeps over enemy-occupied territory in Europe. I remember very clearly Piet giving me a vivid account of having to bale out into the English Channel one boisterous spring afternoon in April 1942 soon after he had been promoted to lead the Tangmere wing.

There had been an engagement with the enemy over Gravelines and Dunkirk. The Wing Leader had already clobbered a Fw.190 and was after another, for which he thought he would just have time, despite identifying a third which appeared to be manoeuvring for an attack. It still seemed a long way off.

The German, however, took a long, accurate – or very lucky – shot which set Piet's Spitfire alight. Calmly transmitting three Mayday calls, the Tangmere Wing Leader rolled his aircraft over on to its back and parachuted out. As he hit the sea, he realised some shrapnel must have severed the lanyard holding his inflatable dinghy to his parachute pack as it began to drift away in the half-gale which was blowing.

Deflating his Mae West, he struck out for the dinghy in the heavy sea, grabbed it and as he clambered in he noticed the water around him was tinged with red. Numbed by the cold and shivering, it was only then that he realised he had been wounded by shell splinters across the shoulder and in the upper arm.

The light was beginning to fade and the two Wing aircraft which had been circling their stricken leader had now left. The chances of surviving the night in the heavy seas which were running were slim. Just then, in one of those million to one shots which kept hope alive in wartime, a naval gunboat, returning from a patrol off the Dutch islands, spotted Piet's dinghy in the half-light as it was being tossed up and down on the waves.

The crew hauled him aboard and handed him a bottle of whisky. Not normally much of a drinker, Piet said he must eventually have drunk half the bottle – but he was able to walk up the gangway at Dover and on to dry land unaided.

Years afterwards, when we were farming neighbours in East Africa, Piet would sometimes complain of irritation around his shoulders. With a bit of help, and some probing about, tiny fragments of shrapnel would be dug out from his skin and once, I recall, a thin blue thread from his RAF battledress.

Within three months, Hugo was back in the line taking over the Hornchurch wing in 11 Group before moving on to North Africa and thence across the Mediterranean for the Italian campaign of 1943

304

and 1944. As a group captain in command of 322 Wing in the Desert Air Force, his special qualities of leadership shone forth. Towards the end of 1944, the four times decorated South African (he had, by now, added the DSO to his three DFCs) was seconded for liaison duties to Marshal Tolbukin's 2nd Ukrainian Army with the Soviet forces, and as the war in Europe closed he was posted back to the UK to take up his appointment at CFE.

With a glittering Service career behind him (22 enemy aircraft stood to his credit with others probably destroyed), Hugo resigned his commission and retired from the Royal Air Force in 1950 and resolved to farm in Africa.

By this time, Jan Smut's United Party had been defeated in the 1948 South African elections by the Afrikaner-dominated Nationalist Party, whose policies of racial discrimination, as Robin Johnston makes clear, were unacceptable to Hugo's liberal-minded European ideals. Instead, therefore, of returning to the Karoo, in the northern Cape, where he had inherited a farm, he elected to settle with his English wife and daughter (he was later to have two more daughters) at Ol Molog, in breathtakingly beautiful country on the northern slopes of Mount Kilimanjaro in what is now Tanzania. There, on virgin land and with characteristic resource, concentration and energy, he established a successful and profitable farm from scratch. Johnston, his close friend, became a next-door farming neighbour.

When Hugo applied for Tanzanian citizenship in 1969, the authorities prevaricated, withheld a decision and actually kept his passport for two years. In 1971 – and despite his wish to become a citizen, and his total commitment to the country – he was arrested out of the blue by the police and his farm immediately confiscated, with no appeal being allowed. Repeated representations by his friends to the British Foreign Office fell on deaf ears. And so, with virtually all his resources being seized save his Cessna aircraft, which was out of the authorities' reach, Hugo returned to the northern Cape.

But nothing so became the man who, in wartime, had given so much to the Allied cause as his conduct in the face of provocation and personal hurt. Robin Johnston, who was privy to every detail of this searing, poignant tragedy, and who had done more than anyone to try to secure some redress for this exceptional South African, closes the story.

It is easy to estimate in material terms what the seizure of his Ol Molog farm without compensation cost Piet. But only a man who has a gut feeling about land can understand what the loss truly meant. For nearly twenty years he had lived daily with the rhythms of ploughing, planting and watching the wheat turn from green to gold, with the ears filling out with seed as they ripened in the sun before harvesting. Added to this was the beguiling scenery in which the farm lay . . . all that he had built up over the years, his home, his possessions, his livelihood – all had been stolen from him. . . .

In 1976, I saw him for the last time. I had returned to live in South Africa and, with my wife and youngest daughter, made a special trip to see him in the Karoo. We did not want to impose ourselves upon his domestic arrangements and so stayed in a nearby hotel. He was his usual charming, courteous self. His old world manners, strength and dignity captivated my teenage daughter and, like anyone who met Piet, she was immediately impressed by him. He was deeply tanned, barrel-chested and his blue eyes were as steady as ever. We talked of many things and we laughed a lot; but there was one subject which he would not discuss.

I was greatly saddened to hear of his death a few years ago, but was relieved that it was quick – a massive heart attack. Piet was a giant in a generation of giants, and I am proud to have counted myself among his friends.

Robin Johnston,
Parkmore,
Johannesburg,
Republic of South Africa

James Alexander Williams
GENTLEMAN JIM

It is probably surprising to some that so many past and present members of the Judiciary in the UK flew operationally as aircrew with the Royal Air Force in World War II. The South African Air Force can also claim its representation on the Bench in the Republic.

Cecil Margo – The Hon. Mr Justice Cecil Margo, to accord him the necessary trappings – commanded the SAAF's famous 24 (light bomber) Squadron in the Western Desert and enjoyed a record in the North African fighting which entitled him to add the suffix 'DSO, DFC' after his respected name.

Sitting now as a judge of the South African Supreme Court, and performing numerous other public functions besides, Margo left his mark, 47 years ago, upon the rough and tumble of the Desert. Peter Atkins, former journalist with the Argus Press, flew for a time as his navigator in 24. No one is better placed, therefore, to pass reflective wartime judgement upon the future Judge.

'I'm not at all sure he wasn't the bravest pilot I flew with. I knew damned well he was scared stiff most of the time, but nothing would stop him trying to do more than his fair share of operations – and that takes real guts . . .'

As a wartime commander of a South African Air Force light bomber squadron and later of a heavy bomber wing, Jim Williams typified in character the breed of men who, in those embattled years, rose to be inspiring leaders in the Commonwealth Air Forces. A broad-shouldered giant of imposing appearance, courteous to a degree towards everyone, even the most junior 'erk, he came to be known throughout the SAAF as 'Gentleman Jim' and affectionately as 'Colonel Jim'.

His grandfather, a mining engineer, was brought to South Africa by Cecil John Rhodes. Jim's father in turn became the general manager of the famous De Beers Diamond Mines at Kimberley, in which city Jim was born. He went to that renowned school, Christian Brothers College in Kimberley, and then up to Caius College, Cambridge, where he obtained

307

a degree in engineering and a blue for rugby (not necessarily in that order of importance in those days).

Back home in 1931 he captained the Griqualand West rugby fifteen in the Currie Cup inter-provincial championships and in one great season led his side to victory against both the powerful Transvaal team and the equally formidable Western Province side. He and his brothers entered the successful family engineering group of Alpheus Williams & Dowse in Johannesburg, and he learnt to fly at the Johannesburg Light Plane Club.

When World War II broke out, he was already a senior, highly paid executive in the group, which urgently needed his services for the manufacture of wartime equipment and weapons, but he lost no time in joining the SAAF and qualifying for his wings.

As Second-Lieutenant Williams, he was some ten or more years older than the average pilot commissioned at that time, but he thrust his way firmly and irresistibly into an operational posting with 24 Bomber Squadron, one of the first South African units in the Western Desert, then flying the Glen Martin Maryland light bomber.

Somehow he managed to work his way into almost every major operation, among them the aerial battles over Crete. The Maryland was no match for the enemy's fighters, but was nevertheless used, or rather misused, as long-range fighter cover for the ships of the Royal Navy endeavouring to stem the flow of enemy troops and supplies into Crete. This was a theatre in which the enemy then enjoyed complete air superiority.

In May 1941 Jim, in his ponderous Maryland, was among the first to out-manoeuvre and shoot down a Me.110.

In July 1941, returning on a moonless night with damaged instruments after a dusk escort operation over HM ships, he was badly injured in a crash-landing. He was hospitalised with multiple injuries, including fractured vertebrae, but was back in action before he was fit.

Now the CO of 24 Squadron, he insisted on leading all the tough missions. His judgement, his technical knowledge, his battle successes, achieved with minimum casualties in the raids he led, his modesty and his concern for his crews, both air and ground, evoked complete faith in him and a sublime fighting spirit in his men.

A striking figure of a man, he reflected refinement in all his day-to-day activities. To women (a rare commodity in the Desert), he was irresistible and often had to defend himself from WAAF, Nursing Sisters and ENSA personnel, some of whose sorties were as purposeful, if not quite as dangerous, as those of the Luftwaffe.

Unlike another celebrated SAAF squadron commander, who one day in the Desert heat had stripped off all his clothes and was sprawled in an Ops Room chair when the AOC arrived unexpectedly, and who then hurriedly donned the most extraordinarily inadequate trousers to cover his shame, or rather his pride, Jim was always impeccably dressed in the light summer uniform appropriate to the Desert. Though quietly spoken, he left no doubt whatever that he was in command. He generated the impression that his main concern was the welfare of his men, each of whom felt that the CO was his special friend. His demeanour was suave and polished. There was no swearing or cursing, no raising of the voice in anger, no blustering, no swagger and no rebukes. When he briefed his crews for a raid, the atmosphere about him was one of calm discussion. He was a fearless operational leader who pressed his attacks to the hilt, but his image was not that of the tiger. It resembled rather that of the bowler-hatted, brief-case and brolly-bearing chairman, directing the affairs of a huge corporate group with cool efficiency. He invariably inspired great confidence.

The catalogue of Jim's operational career is too long to be detailed here. Perhaps a brief reference to two or three episodes will give some indication of what he regarded as 'routine'. In the Desert war, in 1942, 24 Squadron was flying Bostons. Jim's was one of a box of six aircraft in the 'Boston Tea Party', when the unescorted formation was jumped by enemy fighters over Sidi Rezegh and all six aircraft were shot down. Jim's gunners baled out while he battled to hold control of his damaged aircraft. His navigator, alone in the nose section, failed to respond, and Jim got out at the very last moment.

In a night raid over Sicily, with full bomb load still on board, he successfully evaded the searchlights which had coned his aircraft and engaged in what his navigator later described as the complete repertoire of aerobatics, including a loop (which admittedly might not have satisfied all the exacting requirements of the Empire CFS for that type of manoeuvre). In a daylight raid over Italy, in which he was leading 18 aircraft, one of the 500 lb bombs from the aircraft next to his lost its tail and its aerodynamic symmetry, so that it began to spin and was caught up and struck by another bomb released one second later. The aircraft from which it had come was blown out of the sky, and Jim's aircraft and crew were lucky to survive.

The real story of Jim, however, is not that of lucky escapes from great danger, but of the large number of successful attacks he led in more than a century of sorties, and of his benign influence as a leader. More than one young officer, who at a bad time had given up through what in those days was dubbed LMF (lack of moral fibre), was persuaded by Jim to come back and complete his tour of duty.

Jim also served for a time as SASO* of 3 SAAF Light Bomber Wing. In 1944 he became CO of 2 SAAF Heavy Bomber Wing, operating from the Tortorella group of airfields in southern Italy, and which, under his direction, attacked the Ploesti oil fields, mined the Danube and, despite

* Senior Air Staff Officer.

the severe losses sustained night after night, dropped supplies and equipment to support the Polish Uprising against the enemy in Warsaw. The Warsaw operations of the RAF and SAAF Squadrons in the group are to this day commemorated annually by the Polish people, and on that day each year the Polish community in South Africa holds a memorial service for the men of 2 Wing who fell in those missions.

There are many fine leaders and great gentlemen in the history of the RAF and its offspring, the Commonwealth Air Forces. Gentleman Jim Williams is one of that illustrious company.

Cecil Margo,
Lower Houghton,
Johannesburg,
South Africa

Al Deere
THE HARD OPTION?

Only exceptionally should officers over twenty-six years of age be posted to command fighter squadrons.

Air Chief Marshal Sir Hugh Dowding in his Battle of Britain
Despatch dated 21 April 1941

Johnny Checketts was 29 when, in 1941, he joined 485, the New Zealand Spitfire Squadron, at Kenley, in Surrey. 'Past it,' they said. Yet by the war's end, not only had he commanded 485 and, later, 1 Squadron, he had also become a front-rank wing leader – and all after 30.

Beyond that, Checketts had, among his other crises during this progression to the operational heights, been shot down by a Focke-Wulf 190 over northern France. With the help of the Resistance, he evaded capture and within a couple of months was on his way across the English Channel in a French 10-metre lobster boat, the *Suzette*, bound for Penzance, in Cornwall, having used the cover of darkness to slip away from the rest of the fishing fleet lying off the Brittany coast. It wasn't long before he was operating again over France.

When, eventually, he hung up his leader's helmet, this highly-respected New Zealander's score-line read: enemy aircraft destroyed 14 (with one shared); probables 3; and damaged 11. Nice opportunism for an embryo pensioner.

Checketts gave the Royal New Zealand Air Force another ten years of his time, post-war, before retiring in 1955 to form his own aerial top-dressing company on New Zealand's South Island. His had been a 5-star Service career.

When I think of Al Deere, who isn't a big man, the words of Alfred Price, a distinguished aviation historian, always come to mind: 'It isn't the size of the dog in the fight that counts, it's the size of the fight in the dog.'

Al had plenty of fight in him, both on the sports field and in aerial combat. He was a fine rugby footballer, able to play well in any position among the backs. He was brave and strong, but just as important was his ability to choose the right option – whether to pass or kick or run – and do so quickly. Al has always loved sport of all kinds and showed the same courage, determination and sound judgement in the boxing ring as he used to on the rugby field.

By the end of his Royal Air Force career, he had, in fact, given much of his time to the organisation and encouragement of games and physical training in the Service. He was a gifted participant and a natural captain, with a shrewd grasp of strategy and tactics. In war, he was an ideal leader of the great team we used to play for in some pretty serious 'test matches' over the Channel and northern France.

I had the privilege of serving with many excellent 'players' who had some of Al's qualities. But few possessed them collectively and to the same extent as he did. Maybe the most telling of all his special attributes was the way he dealt with people. It was so refreshingly straightforward. He listened carefully and then answered directly, whether he was speaking to Air Marshals or airmen. Al made sure he got sixty minutes out of every hour, putting the same enthusiasm and imagination into organising a weekend at the Kimul Club in London as he did into planning a sweep over Luftwaffe airfields in France. Although his ability to organise his life efficiently impressed me deeply, I do recall one occasion that had him flustered.

It began when he was allowed to drive a rather special staff car from Kenley to London for an important meeting at the Air Ministry. After the meeting, Al went to a restaurant, met some of his friends and passed a cheerful evening before catching the last train back to Kenley to re-join the war the next morning.

He was high over northern France before he suddenly remembered the car. Signed out in his name, this expensive piece of machinery had been left by him in some London street, at the mercy of every passing vandal. I do not recall an operation when Al was so keen to avoid combat, race back to base and catch a train to London. But Lady Luck smiled on him, as she so often has done. He found the car where he had left it, untouched, and returned in it to Kenley, adroitly fending off questions about its adventures.

Looking back, I now realise that Al must have heard every possible joke about his rather unusual name by the time he left Primary School, but we still trotted them out, especially when the beer encouraged us. One day, when we were flying home from France after a sweep, the voice of 'Mitzi' Darling, who was flying close to Al, sounded in our earphones: 'Are you all right, Deere?' Al didn't hesitate. 'Yes, Darling.' I suppose it was a release of tension after yet another hour of fright and sweat over enemy territory, but everyone listening laughed fit to bust.

However, for all his friendliness, Al knew how to command – and did so without either blustering or pulling rank to get his way. At briefings, he spoke forcefully and clearly, making sure that everyone knew exactly what he was supposed to do and why. Afterwards, if there had been a muddle or any disobedience, he could make us go so quiet you could *hear* the ears burning!

Nevertheless, we liked him to fly with us because he had the knack of making even the hairiest operations sound safe, sensible and survivable. He had drummed into our heads the fact that at any given moment, from take-off to touch-down, we had been carefully trained at great expense to handle any problem that arose. Usually, there weren't many options available and we only had to choose one. 'Don't dither!' was always Al's advice. 'Dithering is the worst thing that either a sportsman or a fighter-pilot can do. Even choosing the wrong option might turn out brilliantly as long as you make your decision promptly and carry it out with conviction.'

By the time I met Al Deere at Kenley in November 1941, he should already have been dead for at least a year, as anyone who has read his absorbing autobiography, *Nine Lives*,* will readily agree. Luckily for me he was very much alive. Having been taught to fly Hurricanes, I found myself posted to a Spitfire squadron and spent a trying first flight failing to master that thoroughbred. That evening, I was sitting alone in the Mess, feeling tired and useless, when this highly decorated Squadron Leader marched confidently up to me. In a few minutes' genuinely interested conversation over a beer he dispelled all my gloom.

Afterwards, I often saw Al give other sprog pilots the same treatment. He would tell them that he himself had been just as bewildered as they were when he first joined an operational squadron, that he was delighted to welcome such promising new blood into the team and that they'd soon be a match for the best the Luftwaffe could offer. There was no hint of condescension or flattery in this speech. We soon learned that 'condescension' and 'flattery' weren't part of Al's vocabulary. He had no patience with either and both his praise and his criticism came straight from the shoulder – like his punching in the boxing ring! Al always said exactly what he meant and everyone respected him for it.

I decided that his amazing survival must owe more to skill than luck and so I listened to him attentively on the ground and watched him closely in the air. Returning from a sweep to Le Havre early in 1942, we ran into a flock of Me.109s. The Germans had many experienced pilots on the Western Front at that time who kept a sharp lookout for greenhorns. Two of them singled me out straightaway.

I called for help to my sub-section leader, but he had his nose down and kept on going. Somehow, I managed to evade the initial attack and thought: 'If I can't get help from my own leader, I'd better head for the most

* *Nine Lives*, Hodder & Stoughton, London, 1959.

313

accomplished man I know.' Although Al was leading another squadron, I flew as fast as I could in his direction and tucked myself directly underneath his Spitfire. I felt like a frightened little chick, anxiously nestling up to mother hen, but I wasn't ashamed of myself.

I learned quickly from Al and we enjoyed (in retrospect!) many successful forays together into enemy territory. The fact that we also became close friends as well was merely a bonus, but what a bonus!

Looking back now, I always thought he would make his mark in some walk of life. Had he been born a generation later, that mark might have been as an international sportsman in one of the games he played so well. From his point of view, I daresay he sometimes wishes he *had* been born later, to miss the fearful experiences he somehow lived through and the injuries which have left their mark upon him.

However, he certainly chose the right option when, as a 20-year-old from New Zealand, he joined the Royal Air Force in the winter of 1937. Perhaps, then, I can leave the last word on this memorable character to Lord Dowding, head of Fighter Command during the Battle of Britain and one of Britain's greatest airmen:

'Alan Deere will always stand to me as an example of the best type of fighter pilot, whose endurance and determination brought this country through the greatest immediate danger which has threatened it since Napoleon's armies stood along the Channel shore. May Britain and the Commonwealth never lack such sons.'

Johnny Checketts,
Christchurch,
New Zealand

Wilfred Arthur
THE COBBER FROM OZ

Roy Riddel was a sergeant pilot in the Royal Australian Air Force when he joined 66 (Spitfire) Squadron at Perranporth, in Cornwall, in the summer of 1941. He brought with him a smile, a bronzed, round face and a crunchy Australian accent which flavoured a nice sense of humour. He acquired a bicycle, but soon moved up to an MG sports car. After a week with the Squadron, he might have been there for months. Australians quickly make themselves at home.

Nothing much bothered Roy until, one day, he was returning from a long shipping patrol off the Scilly Isles, some 20 miles from Land's End. With tanks getting low, it suddenly struck him that at nought feet, he hadn't heard the ground station in his earphones for some time. A glance at his compass – and, sure enough, he was heading west for New York, not east for base, and had lost contact. Even an Aussie could put 'red on black'! He made it back – just – but the engine, starved of fuel, died as he was taxiing in after landing.

Still, Cornwall and the Atlantic were good practice for New Guinea and the Pacific which followed. Eventual command of the RAAF's 84 Squadron was probably predictable. P-51D Mustangs towards the end of the war against Japan were certainly preferable to 66 Squadron's 'long-range' Spitfire IIs with their 30-gallon 'blister' tank fixed under the starboard wing – a dreadful excrescence.

Thirty-two years of dentistry, post-war, fixing molars, first in Sydney and then in Coffs Harbour, was, on the whole, much safer . . .

I suppose Wilf Arthur joined the Royal Australian Air Force with great patriotic fervour, being called up the day after war was declared in 1939 for a five-year commission – the last of the Service's permanent intake. Or was it just to get enough money together to do engineering at the University after the five-year stint? Whatever it was, it was certainly a terrific thing for the RAAF.

It's an extraordinary thing about Australia. When England gets into a bit of a stouch,* the Aussies go over in great numbers to help out. I imagine it's because quite a number of their forebears had a free passage out – even if it was in chains. In Wilf's case, it could have been patriotism, as I understand the first Arthur to come out did so first class as the not-too-prone-to-flogging Governor of Tasmania.

I first heard of Wilf Arthur when I was called up into the Air Force in Brisbane in about June 1940, and was posted to the Initial Training School at Bradfield Park in Sydney. Some friends who lived nearby, in Killara (it was a lovely big house with an acre of land and Killara golf course on three sides), arranged a tennis party at which I met Joyce and Margaret Knox. They talked of their cousin, Wilf Arthur, who had just left for the Middle East with 3 Squadron.

Wilf's exploits with the Squadron have been well recorded, even to his shooting down four enemy aircraft during one sortie and, of course, on one occasion being shot down himself . . . Unfortunately, the baddies could also shoot.

That day in the Western Desert at the end of 1941, when he got his four 'kills',† Wilf led his flight of Kittyhawks into a big mixed formation of German and Italian bombers and fighters. Having collected two Stuka dive bombers, he was then attacked by the escort. He sent one Macchi 200 spinning down, but was then himself hit. As he disengaged, another Macchi attacked, only to receive the same treatment.

However, Wilf really did manage to get himself thoroughly shot down in Egypt by one very pretty and vivacious Armenian girl, and this was where the Arthur expertise was well exhibited. When posted back to Australia after his tour in the Desert, he managed to take Lucille with him by obtaining the Movement Order. With the same typewriter, and no doubt a bit of collusion, he added the words: 'and Mrs Arthur' after Flight Lieutenant W. S. Arthur.

Back in the Pacific Area, he became CO of 75 Squadron and soon distinguished himself in New Guinea by leading the Squadron into 100-plus Japanese Zeros (fighters), Bettys (bombers) and Vals (dive bombers) after his own guns had jammed. What frustration! He spent some time at wavetop height trying to force a Val into the sea by threatening to chop off its rudder with his prop.

In all his exploits, he had a '*we* did this' or '*we* did that' attitude which endeared him to pilots and ground staff alike. And he always treated officers and sergeant pilots just the same – they were all 'mister'. I feel, taking all aspects into account, he must have been the No. 1 fighter pilot in the RAAF . . . His flying ability, his knack of sizing up a situation and

---

* Oz for a fight.
† Four aircraft was quite a bag for one sortie, but no one ever thought to query Arthur's claims. Nine months later, the brilliant Hans-Joachim Marseille got seven in one mission. Impossible, they said. But was it? – Ed.

his administrative qualities – the sum of it all must have left him at the top.

It was all evidenced later, in 1945, when he produced the Group Captain Arthur balance sheet. This was after the famous time when Wilf and the other wing leaders – Clive Caldwell, Bobby Gibbes and John Waddy – protested by threatening 'resignation' at the way the RAAF was being left behind by MacArthur and the Americans in the drive for the Philippines and the Japanese mainland. Our squadrons were being left 'to mop up' behind.

Frustrated like the rest, Wilf put it straight to the Chief of the Air Staff (Air Marshal Sir George Jones): 'You are Chief of the Air Staff,' he said, 'why don't you go and see MacArthur and thump the table and demand that we be taken on to the Philippines?'

It was his custom to say what he thought – directly. There was also that time in 1943 when an American pilot of a DC-3 transport was on the receiving end of one of Wilf's stormier outbursts. The pilot had landed at Vivagani airstrip against all the control tower's warnings while a fighter scramble was in the process of taking off. It was dangerous and irresponsible.

When Wilf returned from the scramble, he sought out the USAAF pilot and asked him why he had disregarded the warning instructions not to land. Unwisely, the American said he was the captain of his aircraft and he would decide when and where he should land.

Wilf then pointed to three Kittyhawks parked nearby. 'If you take off now without permission,' he said, 'I will also take off with those three aircraft and shoot you down.' (He would have done.)

When the pilot did take off after clearance from control, he found that Wilf had also taken off and was now tucking the wing of his Kittyhawk tight inside the wing of the transport and right up against the fuselage. There he stayed without moving until the American pilot was well on his way to Dobodura. The fellow hardly dared to look out of the window!

In 1944, Wilf Arthur, a 24-year-old group captain by now, was posted as CO of the fighter OTU* at Mildura in south-western New South Wales, where I was a staff instructor. I had by then become very interested in his cousin, Joyce Knox, and the following incident did nothing to quell my feelings.

He called me into his office one morning and said did I know there was another fellow nosing about in Sydney, and if I was keen on the girl I had better take one of the aircraft and belt off to Sydney and do something about it.

That, I thought, was a terrific order from a CO and the hell of a good way to run a war. Joyce and I were married later. It was even more

* Operational training unit.

surprising because only a month or so before, I'd busted his nose playing squash. But you'd think that by the time someone had got to be a grouper he'd have enough sense to keep his face out of the way of an opponent's backswing . . .

Decorated with the DSO and the DFC, Wilf must have been one of the original, quiet achievers and even today, in Darwin, where he lives, very few know of his wartime career and what a record he had. And this despite the fact that there is a wartime painting of him in Government House.

Adventure was still part of his life after the war. As the Australian adviser to the dairy farming industry in Vietnam, he was captured by the Vietcong and held to ransom. I'm sure it must have appealed to his great sense of humour when he was released in exchange for some bandages or penicillin – or was it both?

Perhaps he was that valuable!

Roy Riddel,
Korora,
Coffs Harbour,
New South Wales,
Australia

Tiny Nel
NO HOLDING THE WARRIOR

Christopher Shores, the accomplished air historian, once wrote of operations in the Middle East, North Africa, Sicily and Italy: 'It should be realised, though it is a little-known fact, that far and away the largest contribution in this theatre was made by the South African Air Force ... [thus] freeing British units for other zones.'*

Few typified that contribution so patently – or for as long – as South Africa's Peter Daphne (Major P. P. Daphne). He began the war flying Fairey Battles in Abyssinia, kept the ball in play for the next four years and finally saw things out commanding the SAAF's famous 60 (PR) Squadron's Mosquitoes at San Severo in Italy. In an exceptional wartime run of four operational tours, Daphne had earned the recognition which both the British and the United States air forces rightly accorded him.

It is understandable that an operator with such a pedigree should pick as his subject a dedicated combatant of comparable strain. The portrayal which follows represents as well as anything else could do the spirit which the South African Air Force brought to bear as it battled for victory alongside the Royal Air Force and the other Commonwealth squadrons.

No harm now, at this juncture in international affairs, in recalling how the land lay nearly half a century ago.

Six foot three (or more) of leathery Afrikaner, son of the Orange Free State, product of Stellenbosch University and now a schoolmaster, watched the gathering storm in Europe with the blood pounding through his veins. War – and excitement – beckoned. Exit the classroom and enter the South African Air Force. . . .

In training, he excelled; *ab initio* flying on the Tiger Moth soon found him bombing us with toilet rolls while the less adept still struggled to go solo. And so onto Hawker Harts and Hinds. Here, indeed, was 'a natural'.

* *Fighters Over the Desert*, Christopher Shores and Hans Ring, Neville Spearman, London, 1969.

319

The Kimberley skies echoed to the 'blue note' and the pupil pilots' Mess rang to wild shouts of 'Bok, Bok, staan styf'.† Tiny was at the centre, partying and cavorting with all the exuberance of Zorba, the Greek. . . .

After we had got our 'wings' and were flying light aircraft as we waited 'to go North', Tiny (together with other 'split-ass' types) was taken to see one of our number lying in the mortuary after under-flying telephone wires. But the object lesson was soon forgotten as the strains of

> Hold him down, you Zulu warrior
> Hold him down, you Zulu chief

echoed round the bar and Tiny stamped his feet on the floor until the beer glasses rattled on the tables. . . .

'Good news,' we cried, 'Abyssinia here we come.' And there was 2nd Lieutenant W. A. Nel, in the forefront, scrambling into the Junkers 52 taking us North, to begin a long and distinguished career as an operational pilot in 40 (Army Co-op) Squadron of the South African Air Force. He was to complete four tours with this squadron, becoming a Lieut-Colonel and earning the Distinguished Service Order and the Distinguished Flying Cross (and bar) in the process.

From Abyssinia and Hartebeest aircraft, it was on to North Africa and Hurricanes, and great work spotting for the 8th Army. Tiny once .flew down a wadi at Medenine at nought feet to draw the enemy's fire and so disclose the positions of the guns. In spotting tanks and troop positions, he flew like an inspired madman with the eyes of a hawk.

Away from the desert sands of North Africa, it was Malta and Sicily and thence onto the Italian mainland. There, leading 40 Squadron's Tac-R* Spitfires, Tiny enjoyed a particularly good shoot with the Royal Navy's HMS *Warspite* after *Nelson* and *Rodney* had pounded the coastal defences between Pellaro and Melito. Shot down near the Sangro river, with shell splinters in his leg, he was soon back with the Squadron, quite unconcerned and celebrating and frying eggs like a Druid priest.

Then with throttle wide open and finger well out, there was strafing near the Anzio beach-head. King George VI landed at 40 Squadron's airstrip with Tiny claiming his boys looked 'very smart', despite an unusual variety of head-dress. The King's thoughts were not, unfortunately, recorded in the Squadron's log!

Came VE Day, and renewed excitement at the prospect of war in the Far East. But two big atomic bangs put paid to that. And so it was back to Pretoria and the dull, daily round in charge of a group of cadets on an exercise in the veld where he soon found the way to a happily-situated hotel.

---

† A traditional South African game. A form of chain leapfrog played with gusto in SAAF messes. Ed.
* Tactical Reconnaissance.

Major Peter Daphne

Hi Zicki Zumba, Zumba, Zumba
Hi Zicki Zumba, Zumba, Zee
Hold him down you Zulu . . .

When next I heard of Tiny Nel, he was in the Royal Air Force. He had been in Singapore as a Group Captain or maybe an Air Commodore. Whatever it was, my informant was greatly surprised to see a lanky and distinguished-looking RAF officer of very senior rank detach himself from a group and come bounding over with the jubilant cry of 'Vrystaat!'

Retiring as a Wing Commander in 1962, Tiny and his wife made their way down Africa in a Jeep, lured back by the blood in his veins, to the open veld, the clear skies and the beautiful sunsets of the land of his birth.

My last meeting with him was at Carletonville, in the Transvaal, in 1965. Early one morning, I found a car parked outside the house. There, asleep inside, was Tiny and, next to him, a large Alsatian. He had rebelled at his 'civvy' job. 'I'm just a lackey,' he mused, and once again he was off in orbit. He had come to bid adieu. He drove away without looking back for a final wave . . .

Where are you now, Tiny? I don't know. But, as I write this, the disjointed pictures come crowding back. Tangling with thorn trees while trout fishing together at Lydenburg . . . that fireworks display at Bizerta, in Tunisia, as we sat watching the ack ack in the distance . . . 'Pinkie' Cormack* singing 'South of the Border' in the Mess – and you and Cormack playing darts with your fingers outstretched on the board in a sort of Russian Roulette . . . the record of 'Deep Purple' playing endlessly in the Mess at Addis Ababa, and the swollen bodies of flies in the wine at the Albergo Imperiale . . . your impolite interjection of 'Kak!' as we listened one day to a particularly pompous talk from a very pompous person . . .

Wherever you may be, Tiny, I know one thing. When the final curtain falls, and I push open the golden doors, I shall expect to hear your familiar and uninhibited shouts as you act as anchor man and organise yet another game of Bok-Bok (High Cockalorum), scrummaging down with the Angels . . .

Willem Andries Nel, I salute you!

Peter Daphne,
Bonza Bay,
East London,
Republic of South Africa

---

* Lieut.-Colonel C. Cormack, CO of 15 Squadron (Baltimores) and then 25 Squadron (Marauders) of the SAAF.

Duncan Smith
A HOME SECRETARY REMEMBERS

They called him 'Dagwood' in 324 Wing of the Desert Air Force during the Sicilian and Italian campaigns. It's a fair bet that no one in the Wing's four squadrons, Nos. 72, 43, 111 and 93, guessed that, 30 years or so on, their popular and able Operations Officer would become, first, Northern Ireland Secretary and then Home Secretary and a Privy Councillor in successive Labour governments in the 1970s.

Merlyn Rees, who had entered the Royal Air Force as a 21-year-old administrative and special duties flying officer after his time with one of the university air squadrons, had been through the fire of mobile Operations Rooms, and what he calls 'this closed world of army/air support', by the time the Sicilian campaign was over. Then came the move into mainland Italy in September 1943 . . .

I drove up the east coast [of Sicily] past Etna and the destroyed villages, over the moutains and [along] the route of the 78th Division to a new dirt strip at Falcone, close to Milazzo, from where our advance party was to set off for Salerno to operate under United States' command . . .

Shortly afterwards we moved up behind the army to Naples and 'liberated' Capodichino airfield, overlooking the city from where we operated for some months while the front was up on the Volturno.

It was the wrong place for us to be; a mobile wing does not need a city teeming with too many people, with cholera rampant and the nearby harbour constantly under night attack. It was not an easy time for a commanding officer . . .

That was the background against which Group Captain Duncan Smith took over command of 324 Wing in November 1943. The impression the new CO made upon the Operations Officer is still sharp in his mind . . .

From the first time we met, Duncan Smith epitomised the Royal Air Force

322

and, in particular, Fighter Command. He started as a weekend flier and found himself in the Battle of Britain; his individual successes mounted as he went to Squadron Commander and then Wingco Flying. He carried on his successes in Malta and then became Wing Commander Flying of 244 Wing, also of Desert Air Force. He had gone in advance with the 1st Airborne Division to Brindisi to locate airfields for DAF.

My regard for him grew stronger as I worked closely with him on operational matters. He knew what he wanted and this made it easy for the Intelligence Officer, the Army Liaison Officer and I to brief the various missions – the bomb line, the flak, the German units in the line, the daily intentions of the Army, etc.

Duncan Smith led the Wing in its wider sense of the term as we moved up to Anzio, through Rome to Tarquinia, across to the South of France via Corsica, back to Florence and up to the Riccione – Rimini area in that bloody awful winter of 1944.

He provoked great loyalty from the ground officers – Tiny Le Petit (Senior Admin Officer), Jim Davies (Engineering), Doc Russell, 'Akkers' Moore, Lewis Evans (Signals) and, last but not least, Donald ('Jasper' to we young whippersnappers) Menzies, the Transport Officer.

We were truly mobile – after the Desert and North Africa, and beyond, we needed no paper instruction on how to gear ourselves to our nomadic existence. Everybody knew their job, there were no rules and regulations. In true British style 'like Topsy, it all growed.'

Duncan Smith could govern with a light rein and he allowed us to amuse ourselves with the odd drink and a party, in the same mood as after Anzio he allowed us to defy the US Army and move quickly and individually into Rome.

The Wing Commanders Flying, from Cocky Dundas, Dan du Vivier, Johnny Loudon through to Barrie Heath, were well-experienced men, and Duncan did not fuss or interfere. This and his own long-term experience approach made it easier for him to fly from time to time with the squadrons on the various daily operations – fighter cover for the tactical bomber or close support for the Army. I have kept all my log books of 324's operations and Duncan kept his hand in.

One incident I recall at Lago, at a time when we had a forward unit at the Anzio beach-head. Aircraft taking off and landing had to avoid shell-holes; smoke from a cigarette, it seemed, was enough to bring the odd blast from the hills. It was 'sitting duck' country and particularly for the Army fighting in almost World War I conditions.

I had returned to Lago when the problem arose of Spitfire IXs with new Merlin engines at Anzio being unable to take off because, it was said, of 'sand in the petrol'.

In the 111 Squadron mess tent at Lago one night 'Spanner' Farrish, the engineer officer, took more than his fair share of ribbing about this from the lads. The day after I was in the Ops truck by the PSP* runway when a Spit IX taxied up to take off.

What was all this? No one had asked me. As it raced up the runway, LAC Cliff Shasby and I thought the pilot was a midget. In fact it was Spanner without a parachute under him. I knew it; off to Anzio!†

I wound the telephone to inform the Group Captain. ' "Spanner" Farrish is airborne,' I told him nonchalantly. I left out my guess as to his destination. On went Spanner to Anzio (Nettuno) vectoring 270° and the 090° straight in to make a perfect three-pointer during shell-fire as a squadron commander from another Wing crashed in a shell-hole. Duncan Smith had chased up to Anzio and observed all this.

Spanner's court martial was a success – for him. Duncan Smith was suitably hard with words but, like the rest of us, secretly admired him.

And so to the South of France and then over to the Rhône valley and up to Lyons. I led a small convoy and one night we slept under our trucks in the town of Montelimar.

At early light an 'old' English lady came asking for the officer in charge. I emerged, unshaven and unwashed, to hear her disbelieving exclamation: 'You do not look like the English officers I knew.' She was right!

At Lyons (Bron), on the bomb-splattered airfield, we had to stop to await news of our future. While we waited we experienced shades of things to come. General de Gaulle landed in his Hudson and Duncan Smith and I were in attendance – to be utterly ignored. At night the various wings of the French resistance fought each other.

In the streets of Lyons, on another aspect, I came across a hastily earth-covered bomb hole with the limbs of children poking through the earth – shot by the Germans for cheering our low-flying bombers! Nearby there were the bodies of workmen also shot for crossing with the occupying forces.

On a different note Duncan Smith allowed us to enjoy ourselves. There was a rugby match, with our team led by the former Springbok, Dendy Lawton . . . Civilisation, indeed, even though we lost. In a 'pub' one night we sang emotionally the 'Marsellaise', 'J'attendrai', etc., and spent the 'spare' money of the SAS, who were generous while also waiting for orders.

The 'champagne' campaign was over quickly and despite one of our Desert-camouflaged trucks which reached Paris 'prospecting' for 'leave' facilities, and Wing Commander Heath who slipped home for the weekend, we were facing the wrong way. Then it was back to Italy by way of a stop at a bleak, mistral-swept airfield, La Jasse, near Marseilles.

There, we learned our destination was to be Florence, where a real war

---

* Pierced Steel Plates hinged together made fine landing strips – Ed.
† Farrish wasn't a pilot and had never soloed an aircraft before! – Ed.

was still going on, bogged down in rain and snow in the mountains. It was there I had occasion to see another aspect of Duncan Smith's character.

Our travels and equipment had gone on ahead by sea. An advance party was to fly east in a DC3 down to Florence. The Spitfires were to refuel in Corsica. On 2 October 1944 it all went wrong.

To put it briefly, Florence (Peretola) 'airfield' with its gutted buildings and bomb pock-marked surrounds was smack alongside a mountain. There was nothing there but a recently constructed wooden flying control 'tower'.

The refuelling all took too long and while 111, 93 and 72 landed with no problem, 43 squadron arrived in the circuit in darkness.

On the ground I stumbled in search of flares and we erected a makeshift flare path from the lights of a truck and jeeps. A Spitfire crashed into these and the pilot was killed, as also was 'Shad' Ainsley of 111 Squadron standing by with us (how that Aussie could sing 'The Miner's Dream of Home') and the driver of the truck.

Then the Americans diverted the rest to Pisa, where there were facilities. They should have acted earlier.

So to Duncan Smith. As the CO of the wing he accepted full responsibility and at the Court of Enquiry was found to be at fault.

That is the sort of man he was. Accept the praise when all goes well and when there is blame, accept that too.*

We moved on to Riccione under DAF once more and here we were to carry out a new role – fighter-bombing in the cross-river campaign with the Army.

The armament ground crews, led by Flight Lieutenant Perry, had a difficult technical job. We had casualties as the aircrews learned a new technique, not only of flying near to the ground but of large-scale map-reading led by 'cab-rank', dawn-to-dusk patrols. If I knew the air map of Italy like the back of my hand before, I also knew every stream and village in the north-east.

This was real Army/Air co-operation and the credit for our transition must go to Duncan Smith. It was good for us all after the setback in Florence.

It was a fitting conclusion to his association with 324 Wing for, in the February, he was posted back to Naples, *en route* for the Staff College at Bracknell.

> Within three months of Duncan Smith's departure from the Wing, the war against Germany was over . . . After the advance into northern Italy and thence over the mountains to Klagenfurt, in Austria, the

* The author is right to deal with this sad episode for it exposes the character of the subject. Duncan Smith led 72 Squadron in for a safe landing and at once hurried off to oversee the quarters for his crews. The responsibility for controlling the subsequent landings lay in other hands, but it would not have been in the nature of this officer to shuffle off any blame – Ed.

future Home Secretary was eventually demobilised from Zeltweg, a former Hungarian airfield. There, he reflected upon 'my experiences and personal good fortune at having served with 324 Wing . . . It had been a long way from Africa, where it had all begun . . . In Italy many rivers had been crossed . . . So much for the Lady Astor jibe of "D-Day Dodgers". Politicians often say foolish things . . . '

More than 40 years on, Merlyn Rees, with a lifetime's experience of public affairs to draw on, sets the story of this remarkable Group Captain in the context of latter-day defence needs . . .

'[All these] years later, I trust the defence experts will not bury themselves too much in politics/economic strategic planning while forgetting the value of men and their personal bravery.

'It is on this basis that I recall Group Captain Duncan Smith, DSO and bar, DFC and two bars.'*

Merlyn Rees,
House of Commons,
Westminster

* Duncan Smith's third DFC came as a result of his part in the operations in Malaya in 1952, 11 years after his first award and seven after his second DSO: quite a stretch! – Ed.

Derek Walker
AN AURA OF LAUGHTER . . . AND SURENESS

The men and women of the Air Transport Auxiliary . . . performed . . . a task of supreme importance to the RAF. They brought the airplanes to the squadrons. In fair weather and foul . . . they kept the ferry moving . . .

The first Lord Beaverbrook, Minister of Aircraft Production in the Battle of Britain.

Diana Barnato was one of the ATA's intrepid and most decorative girls. She flew aeroplanes with the dexterity of a squadron pilot. Her father, Captain Woolf Barnato – 'Babe', we all called him – had won Le Mans three years running between the wars in the old 4½- and 6-litre Bentleys. The spirit ran strongly in the family.

Diana married Derek Walker, a Wing Commander of rare and extensive operational experience, at Englefield Green, in Surrey, on a sunny spring day in May 1944, just a month before D-Day.

Eighteen months later, and six after the war's end, Derek was killed when his P-51D Mustang crashed as he prepared to land at Hendon in North London. After some five years' rigorous fighting, it was a distressing way for a leader to go . . .

It's all such a long time ago . . . Can't remember – oh yes, I can – it's just that I don't want to go back. It hurts too much.

I want to sit by the grave . . . I can think of all sorts of little things about you while I am there. As soon as I leave, I switch off and come back into the present. That's the only way I can survive these heavy feelings in my guts and the breathlessness that would precede my tears.

But I owe it to you, Derek, I do, I do. To write about you, to tell all those people who may not have had the luck even to meet you, nor to know you as I, who was so fortunate, did . . .

That blue-eyed, twinkling gaze, then that habit of throwing your head back with a proud commanding stance, then dropping your eyelids to hide the eyes that were forever scanning the skies for enemy aircraft. You were

327

ever alert – I suppose that is how you survived four operational tours. You walked with those jaunty, swashbuckling, springy steps with a drop of each shoulder . . . Jutting chin, curly brown hair, lean figure and beautiful, sensitive hands . . .

Brave as they made 'em, a leader of men. What a loss – not only for me, but for everyone who didn't even know you, and of course for those of us who did.

You were commissioned in the Royal Air Force in 1937 and war caught you in Habbaniya, near Baghdad. Then there was all that operational flying – in Palestine, Greece, Crete and the Desert with Blenheims and Hurricanes, and then back to England with Spitfires, followed by a Wing of Typhoons (and, post-war, a Meteor jet squadron) . . . Oh yes! You were brave all right . . . No one could have done four tours of Ops on various types of aircraft in all those different theatres without guts and flair and nerve . . . You had the lot.

You could raise a laugh and pull people up and out of any desperate situation or mood. You lifted the morale and spirit – call it what you will – and you imparted the ability to continue difficult tasks to all who crossed your path and you were a good mixer and everyone liked you.

When you were in Greece, you helped to evacuate troops and the Greek Royal Family. You showed me some photographs of yourself with some of the Royal Guards dressed in their national costume. It was bad enough for them to climb into your Blenheim wearing their short, frilly skirts, but even more undignified having to put on a flying helmet over their red felt long-tasselled caps.

You said, 'I don't doubt these are tough chaps, but I'm glad the RAF doesn't dress us up in ballet skirts with pompoms on our shoes.'

When you were in Shaiba, in Iraq, the Mess wanted some fresh eggs so you flew off and 'acquired' some chickens and put them in a basket behind the pilot's seat in the navigator's compartment above the bomb bay; but they got loose in flight and fluttered and squawked around the cockpit. Things were becoming a bit dicey as you couldn't ward them off or catch them – and fly at the same time. So you put the Blenheim into a steep dive and, as you pulled out, the chickens all finished up in the back of the aircraft again.

You were a competent and sure pilot and fought with dash and courage. You sank a destroyer from your Blenheim for which you were awarded the DFC. You wouldn't tell me about it, but then, late one night, when you were slightly high, you finally said 'Ha! Bloody lucky pot shot. Straight down the jacksie.' This, I took to mean that one of your two small bombs had targeted right down the ship's funnel. Knowing you, Derek, you would have flown skilfully at a desperately low height . . . It's a terrible thing to say, with all that loss of life, but it must have been an impressive blow-up as seen from the air.

328

But do you remember our first meeting? You were the Wing Commander of your Typhoons at Tangmere, on the Sussex coast, and I brought you a squadron replacement. You happened to be in the Watch Office when I checked in to get my delivery chit signed. You thanked me for bringing the Typhoon in one piece, and said, 'They get broken later on, anyway' . . . I didn't work out how to take that.

You and I sometimes stayed at my father's house near Windsor if our leave days coincided. One day you were as jumpy as hell, and I didn't know why . . . The Invasion was imminent.

There was a gale blowing and you never slept a wink, and kept getting up and going to the window to check the storm-force winds. All night, heavy aircraft and towed gliders were droning southwards overhead – and then they all came back again . . . As we know now, the Invasion was delayed a little because of the weather . . .

You left at the crack of dawn to go back on duty and I went to my Ferry Pool. On D-Day, when it finally started, my only job, of all things on that most exciting and historic day, was to dodder along the coast with a boring little Auster, an Army spotter aircraft, from Hamble to Gosport. But I could see the great concourse of ships and all the activity at sea and in the air.

You rang me later that night and although I didn't say over the phone what I had flown (especially as it was only an Auster!), but said vaguely that I had been flying along the south coast and what I'd seen . . . 'I suppose you got in the way,' you said.

Soon the Germans were being pushed back eastwards in Normandy by our liberating forces and when your Typhoon tour ended you were given a liaison job. You worked sometimes at Uxbridge and used to fly over to France in a Spitfire to see the squadrons, which, by now, had the easily identifiable black and white stripes painted on its wings.

The little aerodrome at Hamble was designated as a 'prang patch' for any RAF or Fleet Air Arm aircraft coming back in trouble from the wars, 80 miles to the south across the English Channel. There was great faith in the ability of the crash crew and the 'blood tub' to lever anyone out of some problem should it ever happen.

Late one afternoon, the alarm bells sounded and the ATA women pilots from No. 15 Ferry Pool hurried out to see an Invasion-striped Spitfire in the circuit. It wasn't one of our deliveries. The crash men and the ambulance orderlies threw down their playing cards and rushed out to start up their wagons expecting an imminent disaster. But the aircraft made a beautiful landing and taxied up to the Mess – and out you got, Derek.

You said, I remember, 'Don't go anywhere near. I'm afraid there's a terrible smell in the cockpit.' (We thought, 'Oh dear, something awful's happened! Something dead, perhaps?')

The war had been going a long time and food rationing was drastic . . .

329

You went back to your Spit and fished out a large, circular parcel which you brought into the Mess. You had just flown back from Caen, in Normandy, and this was a huge Camembert cheese. No such cheese had been seen in England since France fell in 1940. We all fell upon it and, as we munched, you said: 'Diana, darling, this is something I liberated specially for you!'

You were unique ... You had something of everything in you ... Humour, yet wistfulness; a zest for living, yet calculated care and thoughts for others ...

It has made me unhappy to write about you, even after so long ... It isn't that you aren't here any more, but that your aura of laughter, sureness and strength has gone ... Oh, yes! you would have gone far in whatever you chose for your post-war commitment. Pity that Mustang blew up on you. Pity you died so young ...

Of course you are THE most memorable character I ever knew in the Air Force in World War II, but then I'm biased. You were my husband.

Diana Barnato Walker,
Horne,
Surrey

2

'Far Beyond the Normal Call . . .'

There were some who just had it in them to endure in war more than others, no matter what their operational role might be. There was no doubt about it. Maybe it was because their nerves could absorb the prospect of danger more readily than their contemporaries'. Or maybe, again, it was that the manifest perils of some operation did not register so acutely in their mind – or that they possessed some insulation system which automatically dampened the anticipation of fear. Or maybe, indeed, it was because the human dynamo within them – the 'press-on' mechanism designed to propel a man beyond the usual expectation of effort – just pumped out greater force . . .

Whatever it was, there were some whose achievements, no matter what the field of operation, seemed to have taken them far beyond the normal call of duty.

The dividing line between what could rightly and reasonably be expected of a man dedicated to discharging his tasks, and what the human frame could actually achieve when put to the ultimate touch, was a very fine one. It is one reason why there so often appeared to be noticeable discrepancies in the award of decorations for gallantry. Judgements tended to vary with theatres. Comparisons were sometimes odious.

Louis Greenburgh
THE WAY OF AN EAGLE

How much did Jack Dixon's rare start in the Royal Air Force contribute to the distinguished academic career that was to follow? More, possibly, than may seem likely.

Born at Broadstairs, in East Kent, Dixon had as a teenager a grandstand view of the fighting in the Battle of Britain. His first-hand witness of the aerial battles being waged overhead gave him the urge to join the Service as quickly as he could. This he achieved by enlisting towards the end of the summer of 1940 as an Aircraft Apprentice at Halton, where many a fine life was to find its impulse.

Two years at Halton led to a year as an armourer at the Operational Training Unit at Upper Heyford, in Oxfordshire; and then in August 1943, came the chance to re-muster for the longed-for aircrew duties. Delays, however, impeded the forward march and it wasn't until a month after the ending of the war in Europe that he received his 'wings' at the Service Flying Training School at Vareeniging, in South Africa.

Undergraduate years at Merton, Oxford, flying with the University Air Squadron, presaged an invitation to convert on to jets. But Final Examinations had to come first. Emigration to Canada was the next step after the University and, with it, service with the RCAF; but not as aircrew. Too old, they said, at 28! So, with talent and good degrees behind him, Jack Dixon succumbed to the academic life. Winnipeg University, where he taught French Literature from 1959, until retirement became a home from home.

Perhaps the only inevitable thing about Louis Greenburgh is that he should be called Lou. For the rest, what seemed inevitable when this story begins, in 1931, was that Lou would end up dead or in prison before he was 20. But Lou is a good example of outward appearances belying the inner man.*

---

* Even his name is wrong. He was born Greenberg. His birth certificate made it Greenburg. The RAF added an 'h'.

Lou was born in Winnipeg in 1916, but soon moved to Rosthern, Saskatchewan. When he was three his father walked out (he later committed suicide). Two years later his mother took up with, then married, another man. They began to have their own family. From that moment Lou was an outsider, and unwanted. He was made to know it in many ways.

His half-brothers were taught to hate him. He was refused the *bar mitzvah*, which they received, the refusal being tantamount to ostracism. One day, when he was eight, he found 50 cents and bought himself a Wolf Cub neckerchief and leather toggle. His step-father accused him of stealing them, and told his cousin. The cousin, to make the boy confess, tied his hands behind his back and beat him savagely about the head and face, while his step-father looked on and his mother screamed: 'Kill him! Look what his father did to me!' Concussed and terrified, Lou lay for 3 days in a field, then got further hell for missing school.

On another occasion his mother hit him in the face with a poker. Lou ran away. A farmer found him half-frozen in a cabbage-patch, fed him and took him back home. In despair Lou turned to an uncle he thought he could trust. The uncle told him he would never be accepted by his family: 'No one wants you. You'd better realise you're alone in the world.' 'Then what should I do?' 'The best thing you can do is to get a rope and hang yourself.'

When he was 15 he was kicked out, and left relieved he would no longer be a punching bag. He met up with a pal and together they 'rode the rods' for a time, travelling west. It was at the height of the Great Depression in the Prairies. Lou turned on two occasions to other family members, both well off, and was rebuffed. But strangers helped him. One night, in Vancouver, gawking at evening-dressed 'toffs' leaving a charity ball to raise money for the poor, one man came up to Lou, who was dressed in rags and hadn't eaten for two days, and gave him a meal and five dollars. Several weeks later he met that man on a construction job in the interior of British Columbia and learnt that it had been his last five dollars.

Frequently Lou came close to starvation. He was in Regina in 1935 and was caught up in the famous Communist-instigated riots of the unemployed. Coshed on the head, he was thrown into gaol. On his release from prison four months later a guard suggested that Lou should go to England and join the Army or Air Force. From a tiny seed grows the mighty oak, and from a casual word flow great consequences. So Lou rode the rods to Halifax, got taken on a cattle-boat, and landed at Liverpool.

He applied to join the Royal Air Force, but was turned down as unfit and uneducated. He wandered, slept in parks, scrounged food, again nearly starved. He wrote to the Regina prison guard, who sent him a letter of reference. On 21 July, 1937, at Kingsway Recruiting Office, with his letter, the OC took pity on him and fiddled him into the Service as Aircraftman 2nd Class, General Duties Branch.

Lou cleaned latrines and washed greasy dishes. Having mastered those skills he thought he could learn something else, preferably having to do with aeroplanes. He applied, and was accepted, for training as airframe mechanic. His first posting was to Manston in 1938.* During the first year of the war he was at Bassingbourn. There, when on guard duty outside the bomb dump, he was bombed by one of our own aircraft, which should have been bombing Germany.†

Lou applied several times to be an air-gunner – he liked the idea of being a sergeant: he was actually dating the mess-hall sergeant WAAF at the time! – but was turned down. One day his corporal told him there was a shortage of pilots. With this idea he applied – and mighty was his surprise when he was accepted! When at pre-EFTS Lou was classified for pilot training he could only marvel at the tolerance or desperation or blindness of the Royal Air Force that it take such a risk on a 'Colonial' country boy without much education. The choice, or faith, or judgement, was to be well placed.

Lou was sent to the United States for training. He went to No. 6 BFTS, Ponca City, Oklahoma. There he did both EFTS, on Stearmans, and SFTS, first on Vultee BT-14s, then on Yales. Lou was shocked to find that his instructor was a German-American, named Hans Myer. On his first night solo on Stearmans a storm came up and Lou crashed in a field and was pinned upside down in the cockpit. Mr Myer pulled out all the stops to help Lou; and Lou credits his later successes to his instructor's faith in him. But Lou's lack of schooling was a handicap; he had difficulties with some of the ground instruction, and cheated on the final examinations. But he passed them; and he excelled in the flying tests.

After the 'Wings' parade Lou was sent to Toronto to get kitted out in the coveted brevet and chevrons. There, while in the office of the Sergeants' Mess, a telephone call came through from Admin. Wing. Lou feared greatly that his examination had been twigged and the game was up and he'd be sent back to the latrines. Nothing of the sort: he had been commissioned.

Lou was now, in September 1942, 26 years of age. It was 11 years since he had left home. He had been down to 140 lb when the RAF gave him asylum; he now weighed in at 185 lb. He was 5ft 10in., had brown wavy hair, hazel eyes, and was a good-looking young man. He did not betray any obvious external signs of his boyhood experiences; but the scars ran deep, deep.

From Canada Lou was sent back to England, and training on twins. (His instructor was Alex Strell of Winnipeg. They are still the best of

---

* Could we have met? Manston is 3 miles from the author's home town of Broadstairs.
† This story has been told in Laddie Lucas's book *Out Of The Blue* (Hutchinson, London, 1985), pp. 54–7. See also Max Hastings', *Bomber Command* (The Dial Press, New York), pp. 86–9, for a slightly different version of the same event.

---

friends.) Then to Waterbeach for conversion to Stirlings. Says Lou: 'Unbelievably I topped my class, and for the first time I felt like somebody.'

After a few operations and mine-laying trips Lou was posted to 514 Squadron, flying Lancasters. On the night of 31 December 1942, target Berlin, they were badly shot up. There was little hope of their getting back to England, but Lou, with a name like Greenburgh, had no desire to fall into German hands, and pressed on. During their agonised descent the rear gunner kept reporting an aircraft shadowing them; it was, he said, a B-17 and had a 'beard' and 'whiskers'. Lou knew there were no B-17s on this raid, and he certainly knew of no B-17s with a beard! He feared the worst about his gunner's mental state. Lou ditched the heavy unmanageable bomber in the North Sea – by what miracle he never knew, for it was pitch dark and he could see nothing. He was knocked out on impact. And the next thing he knew he was up to his chin in icy water and hands were trying to pull him out of his seat. The whole crew got out and into the inflated dinghy, already half full of water. After 30 hours of extreme cold, wet and misery in high seas they were rescued. The rear gunner was taken off aircrew. Many years later Lou met by chance the pilot of a secret, experimental B-17, bristling with radar antennae, which had seen him go down and radioed his position.*

After a brief lecture tour it was back to his squadron and ops. On the night of 24-25 March, 1944, his aircraft was subjected to repeated attacks by Ju.88s until Lou could no longer control it. He ordered his crew to bale out. He was preparing to go himself when his navigator screamed that his parachute had fallen out of the hatch and begged him not to leave him. He bowed to the inevitable: he went back. Somehow he managed to right the aircraft, just 2000 feet over Berlin. The worst of it was that both starboard engines had been knocked out; Lou had a herculean task keeping the aircraft on a relatively even keel and course. After seven hours of strain and effort he actually succeeded in crash-landing it at his base. When the CO saw it he could not believe that it had been flying. Lou could not get his supper down. And to this day he has not been able to eat a full meal.†

On D-Day Lou and his crew were detailed to bomb enemy rail yards in France. He was shot down. He parachuted safely and landed in the Huns' nest. After hiding out in haystacks, ditches and caves, a man found him and hid him in his home. An informer gave him away. Lou escaped; but his benefactor, a M. Reant, was taken and executed. During the following weeks Lou was passed down the line, with false papers, and even worked for a time for the Jerries at Châteaudun. In August he found himself in the Forest of Fréterval, near Blois, with about 50 other Allied

* Lou himself published an account of this extraordinary episode in *Maclean's* magazine (Montreal, 8 September 1962), which he entitled, 'An Eerie Postscript to the Bombing of Berlin.'
† The wireless operator, who was the third crew member to remain in the aircraft, said that the pilot should have been awarded the Victoria Cross for his action.

airmen. A Frenchman betrayed them and they were surrounded by German troops. Expecting to be massacred at any time, they awoke one morning to the sound of gunfire – and to find themselves rescued by the Americans.

Back in England – and to the V-1s – Lou was posted to Transport Command, and immediately found himself dropping supplies to the beleaguered paratroopers at Arnhem. It was at this time that he received a letter from Air Chief Marshal Sir Arthur Harris congratulating him on the award of a bar to his DFC. The investiture by King George VI took place at Buckingham Palace in June 1945.

> As the author describes, there was extended service and transport flying for Greenburgh after the ending of the war in Europe. Then, after a final return to Canada, where stable employment proved elusive (his English wife had earlier left him), this indomitable character was guided, as if by the hand of Destiny, to the probation service in Manitoba. There, he worked with special understanding for 19 testing but successful years before retiring and receiving from the Mayor of Winnipeg the city's highest service award.
>
> Now 74, Greenburgh still works for the probation service – unpaid. The author concludes this incredible narrative with a final experience.

Several years ago Lou was sail-planing in the Interlake region of Manitoba, where he had been senior probation officer. He was soaring at 6000 feet when he noticed another flyer some distance away. They turned towards each other, came close, and formated for a fleeting moment. It was a golden eagle. In that split second they looked into each other's eyes. 'I was moved,' said Lou, 'as I have seldom been. I felt a oneness with Nature, and knew what it was like to be a bird, and free.'

Jack Dixon,
Winnipeg,
Manitoba,
Canada

Sir Douglas Bader
THE LOST LEADER

There are three good reasons why Sir Hugh Dundas should write this study of Douglas Bader.

First, he knew him – and understood him – as well as anyone. There are few better ways of getting to know a man as he truly is than by flying alongside him over a protracted period in wartime when the going is rough. You see him under the whip with his qualities and his defects.

Second, Dundas possessed the experience to judge. He got to know the operational game from A to Z, as a junior officer, as a squadron and wing leader and, finally, as a group captain with a couple of DSOs and a DFC commanding a wing in the Desert Air Force. Few could match, let alone exceed, his stretch on operations in World War II. He was probably allowed to go on too long.

Lastly, he could write. A spell in Fleet Street and a natural facility with a pen made a formidable combination. The pace and style of his wartime autobiography, *Flying Start*,* confirmed the point.

Douglas Bader was a leader among leaders, a leader of leaders. He possessed, in greater degree than any other officer known to me personally, the characteristics which can raise the courage and performance of followers far above their natural level.

In a few lines, written soon after the war, I described my own first impression of Bader. The place was Fowlmere, a satellite airfield in the Duxford sector. The occasion was a day in mid-September 1940, when the Spitfire squadron in which I was serving as a young pilot officer had

---

* *Flying Start, A Fighter Pilot's War Years*, Hugh Dundas, Stanley Paul, 1988.

flown south to join Bader's 'Big Wing'. It was my first day back on operations after being shot down over Dover, and I was frightened. This is what I wrote:

'After we had landed at Fowlmere we went into a hut and settled down to wait for developments. Quite soon the door was flung open and an extraordinary figure in squadron leader's uniform stomped vigorously into the hut. Instantly the subdued and somewhat queasy atmosphere was dispelled, driven away by the hard, robust character of Douglas Bader.

Much has been written of Bader. My personal debt to him is incalculable. He showed me quite clearly by his example the way in which a man should behave in time of war and his spirit buoyed me up through many dark days long after he himself had become a prisoner of war.'

Douglas Bader's whole life was a triumph. It was not only young wartime fighter pilots whom he inspired with his brave spirit; he never stopped helping and encouraging others, in all parts of the world, to cope with crippling misadventure. But I think that it was in 1940 and 1941, during those two wartime summers of violent air fighting, that he truly fulfilled his destiny. For there can be no doubt that his first and greatest aspiration was to serve and excel as an officer in the Royal Air Force; and it is for his performance and achievements in that role that he will be remembered, above all else. And yet, because of the terrible accident in which he lost both his legs only 16 months after leaving Cranwell, that performance and those achievements were compressed into less than two years of his life.

It says quite a lot for the vision of the men at the top of Fighter Command in 1940 that, in June of that year, they should have promoted a man with two tin legs, a man who had been grounded and out of the Service for eight years before the war, a man with a notably rebellious character, to command a Canadian squadron which was clearly suffering from lack of morale, lack of discipline and lack of leadership. Bader's success in quickly restoring the squadron's pride and enthusiasm for battle was notable but not, of course, unique. The history of British arms is richly illuminated by examples of how a ship, or a battalion, or an air squadron, seemingly sunk to a level beyond redemption, had been lifted up by the leadership qualities of a new commander. But in Bader's case that precious quality was backed up by a constantly and clearly demonstrated determination to engage the enemy whenever, wherever and however he could do so. And in pursuing that objective he was seen by all who served with him to be the bravest of the brave. But he was seen also as a leader with a constant and intelligent interest in providing those who followed him with the best possible chance of coming out on top in the deadly business of air fighting. And although he no doubt carefully cultivated the impression of his own fearlessness and showed that he expected others to overcome their fears and to do their duty, he knew and well understood what the weaker spirits among us were suffering. Somehow he conveyed to us and lent us a measure of his own robustness.

I had a close-up view of the Bader leadership magic during the spring and summer of 1941, when he was leading the Tangmere Wing. He liked to have the same people with him, in the air and on the ground, and whenever he flew I flew at his side. More than 60 times that summer we crossed the Channel together into the hostile skies of northern France, usually at the head of the three-squadron Wing; and as often as not there was fighting along the way. Bader's leadership of that Wing was inspirational. The going was tough and losses quite severe. Between 20 June and 10 August our squadron lost 12 pilots – more than half its establishment. Everyone knew when he woke up in the morning that there was a strong possibility that he might go down over France that day. Yet morale was sky-high. Bader somehow showed every man in each of the three squadrons what he had to do and made him want to do it. We knew that he was a man to trust, a man to follow.

His loss, when he fell from a fight near Lille on 9 August and was taken prisoner, was a terrible blow. But it was not altogether devastating, for his spirit and his example lived on, as exemplified by a splendid picture of Johnnie Johnson taken a few days later. Johnnie, who also had flown regularly as one of Bader's section that summer, had embellished his Spitfire with the message: BADER'S BUS COMPANY, STILL RUNNING. Johnnie was just one – although perhaps the most distinguished – of several young officers who flew with Bader in 1940 or 1941 and went on to be outstanding fighter leaders in their own right. I know how strongly some of them always felt the depth of their debt to Bader.

In a different but important way his influence continued to affect many of us throughout the remainder of his life, in the years of peace. His mews house in London, where he lived with his wife, Thelma – almost as important a part of our lives as he was – was a focal point for those of us who had been with him during the war. He never let a friendship dry up. He was always there, always interested, always involved.

In 1960 I lost my job. I was 40 years old, with three small children and my wife and I had recently acquired a family house in the country outside London – rather more extensive than we could easily afford and financed by a large mortgage. I received from my friends many messages of sympathy and expressions of a desire to be helpful in a general sort of way. One morning the telephone rang. It was Douglas Bader. 'Just heard the news, old boy. I'm bloody sorry. Expect you're a bit pushed. I've got about £4000 put away. It's yours if and when you need it. Sorry there isn't more.'

And that was the difference between Douglas Bader and his fellow men. He knew what he thought was the right thing to do and he did it without hesitation. His extraordinary and undoubted courage was matched only by his total loyalty to his friends.

Hugh Dundas,
Kensington,
London

Helmut Lent
A FIGHTER'S CHRISTIAN FAITH

C. G. Grey, debatably the outstanding aviation journalist of the century, wrote of Wolfgang Falck in *The Aeroplane* of 1 March 1940 – mark the date, we were at war with Germany:

'He speaks excellent English and is a charming companion . . . He reminds me much of our great air fighter of the last war, Jimmy McCudden, VC, DSO, MC, etc . . . The day the great von Richthofen was killed, McCudden . . . really moved, said to me mournfully, "I did so want to talk it all over with him after the war." I can only hope that Falck's English friends will be more fortunate.'

We were.

Falck joined the German Army on 1 April 1931, and, in clandestine circumstances, learnt to fly 'as a civilian' because the country wasn't then allowed an air force. As a starred and professionally trained officer, he rose, in the classical mould, to the heights of the Luftwaffe in World War II – accomplished pilot, squadron and wing leader and group commander, all in the West and then the Balkans; eventually he acceded to the General Staff.

In peace, his upbringing, acute mind and easy charm brought him a comparably successful career in the aircraft industry. Over some 30 years, Wolf Falck became a noted figure in Germany in two US-owned companies, first, North American Aviation of Los Angeles and then, for 20 years, the McDonnell Douglas Corporation of St Louis. His broad experience and range of contacts enabled him to open the doors that mattered.

'Sir, I wish to apply for a posting to a day fighter unit.'

There, standing in front of me was Oberleutnant Helmut Lent, commanding officer of 6 Squadron in Group 1. I was then commanding II Wing in the Group, which had been formed following the expansion of the German Air Force's night fighter organisation. The new unit had been created out of the original I Wing of *Zerstörer* Group 76.

What, then, had happened? Why was Helmut Lent asking for a posting back to a day fighter unit? The background is important to the story of this remarkable character.

I came to know the newly promoted Leutnant Lent at Fürstenwalde in the spring of 1938, when we were forming I Wing of *Zerstörer* Group 76 (ZG 76). As we were then converting from the Messerschmitt 109 to the 110, it had been renamed I. ZG 76 instead of the former III Wing of the Richthofen Group. I was commanding 2 Squadron in the Wing.

Helmut Lent made an immediate impact upon me among the other leutnants who had been posted to us. He was a sporting, agile, slim and good-looking officer, self-assured, smart and thoroughly intelligent. His sense of humour and disarming, boyish smile won over his superiors even when he was making one of his criticisms or suggestions. It was all done so naturally.

He was an individual of high ethical standards, manifestly professional and an excellent pilot, brave and daring, within the limits of his own self-discipline. It was quickly obvious that he would be one of the three leutnants whom I would invite to help me when I was establishing an NCO training course.

Lent was one of the first Me.110 pilots (we were intended to be 'heavy fighters', that is to say equipped with twin-engined aircraft) to shoot down an enemy aircraft following the outbreak of war. On the second day of the Polish campaign – 2 September, 1939 – he had scored his first victory. Three weeks later, on 21 September, he was awarded the Iron Cross, 2nd Class. And then, later still, on 18 December, he took part in an air battle over the German Bay* and shot down two Wellington bombers.

Having been promoted to lead his squadron, Lent took part in the occupation of Denmark and Norway in April 1940. There, he caught the eye with his common-sense approach and his preparedness to accept responsibility and take decisions, particularly when occupying the Fornebue airfield at Oslo. He also scored further victories and, on 11 May 1940, he was awarded the Iron Cross, 1st Class, and, shortly after that, the Narvik medal for his conduct during the fighting for this keenly contested port. He was by then at the head of the top-scoring Me.109 and Me.110 pilots, having shot down eight enemy aircraft, and already very well known.

In August 1940, 1 Wing of ZG 76 was withdrawn from the line to enable the unit to be converted to night fighters and to be trained in the night role in Germany. This did not please Lent at all. He wrote on 30 August: 'We are now changing over to night fighter operations and we are not very enthusiastic about it.'

It was understandable because, like all Me.109 and 110 pilots, who had been palpably successful in one form of aerial fighting, he did not want to

---

* The bay off the north German coast, north-east of Lübeck and south-east of Kiel – Ed.

be confronted with a completely new type of combat which, at the time, was, literally 'in the dark'.

It had been no more than a couple of months (it was on 26 June 1940, in fact) since, as the Kommandeur of I Wing of NJG 1, I was instructed by Feldmarschall Göring to form the night-fighter Group 1, and so set up, organise and develop the German night-fighter force as the newest operational arm of the Service. This order had followed the first attacks by the Royal Air Force on German territory. Moreover, it was only on 20 July that Oberleutnant Werner Streib had brought down the first enemy aircraft at night – and so broken the barren spell. Streib had shown that it was not only possible in theory, but also in practice, to attack successfully a bomber force at night.

For Lent, who had been leading 6 Squadron of NJG 1 since January 1940, the fight now began not only against attacking bombers at night, but also against the weather and over modern technology. There was, at that time, virtually no radar control and guidance from the ground, let alone any airborne equipment. The RT* was subject to interference which, with the problems of icing, the technicalities of instrument flying and other hazards of operating by night, presented formidable obstacles which had to be overcome . . . This, and the luck which, in these circumstances, was needed to spot an aircraft in the dark!

Strangely, the good fortune which one tended to associate with a pilot who had already had so much success in daytime was, at first, missing at night. A number of crews in Lent's Squadron had already shot down enemy aircraft, but the squadron commander hadn't even seen one! This made him think he was not suited to night operations and this belief, in turn, had made him come to me and ask for a posting.

We had a long talk about it because I had come to know Helmut so well after all the flying we had done together. I made it quite clear that I fully understood his request and the reasons behind it and, indeed, respected it. But I urged him to give himself, Fate and me, as a young officer commanding a recently formed Group, one more chance. I promised him that if his luck did not change, and he failed to shoot down an enemy aircraft at night during the next month, I would support his posting.

Lent was able to report his first victory at night on 12 May, 1941. The ice had been broken. Success now followed success. By 30 August, he had been awarded the Knight's Cross to the Iron Cross after achieving 8 victories by day and 14 by night. On 6 June, 1942, with a total now of 35 aircraft to his name, he received the Oak Leaves to the Knight's Cross, and then on 2 August, 1943, as a Major, with a further 66 victories to his credit, he was awarded the Sword to the Oak Leaves, only the 32nd member of the German armed forces to receive it.

* Radio Telephone.

Because of his continuing success, and taking account also of his character and personality, Lent had already been appointed, on 1 November, 1942, to command IV Wing of NJG 1; less than a year later, on 1 August, 1943, he was promoted to be Kommodore of NJG 3. However, this further advancement did not stop him from continuing to operate at night or from maintaining his run of successes. By the night of 15-16 June, 1944, Lent had taken his total of victories as a night-fighter pilot to 100 by shooting down three four-engine Lancasters. Promoted to the rank of oberstleutnant, he had the Diamonds to the Sword conferred upon him and so became only the 15th officer of the armed forces to receive the accolade.

It was both tragic and incomprehensible that, on 5 October, 1944, this exceptionally experienced and able pilot, who had survived all the dangers of night fighting in the most appalling weather, should lose his life attempting a daytime landing at Paderborn. One of the two engines of the aircraft he was piloting apparently cut while he was preparing to land and he hit a high-tension cable. Terribly injured, he died in hospital two days later, on 7 October. The poignancy of this awful accident was compounded by the earlier loss of the members of his proven and exceptional crew.

At the time of his death, Helmut Lent had an aggregate total of 110 enemy aircraft destroyed standing to his credit, 102 of which had been shot down at night – the result of some 300 combat sorties. Here was the most successful night-fighter pilot in the German Air Force in World War II. What, then, was the background to this remarkable character? What kind of an individual was he at heart?

Lent was born at Pyrehne, a small village in Neumark Province which is now in Poland, on 13 June, 1918. His father, a fervent Protestant, was the 'pastor' of the local parish and his two brothers also took holy orders. His family, who never possessed material wealth, held to a fundamental faith and all were characterised by unmistakable qualities – iron discipline, self-education, thrift, loyalty and total integrity.

Helmut's father was a devout Christian who, during the rise of National Socialism, became a dedicated fighter for those of his followers who opposed and fought the new ideology in its different forms. Because of their resolute stand, the militant Protestants were subjected to harassment and persecution.

Helmut never hesitated to avow openly his own adherence to the Christian faith. It is said that whenever he received from Hitler's hand his high – and highest – decorations, he pledged himself unreservedly to support the cause of the church active and 'militant here on Earth', and to redouble his efforts to secure for its devoted adherents some alleviation of their suffering.

His deeply held belief in the Christian ideal was expressed in almost every letter he wrote to his parents. It was this faith that gave him the strength, aided by his own disciplined mind, to meet the internal and external pressures of his wartime service and to provide the example for his subordinates to follow. His bearing and conduct offered the model from which others might learn.

Lent was obviously ambitious – but not at someone else's expense. He was ambitious in what he demanded of himself. As a strong leader, he never kept his experiences to himself, but always endeavoured to communicate them to his crews both verbally and in writing. He had two aims in this – to avoid unnecessary losses and to give his crews the best chance of success at the minimum risk.

He was an intensely creative individual, cultured and well read. History fascinated his receptive mind. He found relaxation in music, particularly classical music. At Easter 1944, six months before he died, he listened to the St Matthew Passion, conducted by Jochum, in St Michael's Church in Hamburg, which had suffered heavily from bombing. Obviously deeply moved, he confided in Major Hans-Joachim Jabs, one of the most successful of his comrades and a close personal friend: 'This was one of my greatest experiences.'

Despite his certain puritanism, strict discipline and loyalty to his principles, this rare personality was the complete human being with his comrades, jolly, spirited and entering into the fun of things – as far as operations, the enemy and the weather allowed. But he would not tolerate obscenities or jokes at others' expense. These were 'out' with him.

As one who was lucky enough to survive, it is easy to fall into the trap of overplaying – overglorifying, if you like – the memory of a person like Helmut Lent. Every one of us has his shortcomings and his weaknesses so one must be careful not to see just 'the hero' in this unique personality. But fighter pilots were always realists who gave expression to the saying: 'Warm heart, but cool mind.'

For my part, then, I shall ever be grateful for the chance I was given to serve for those few years with such a character and to have claimed him as a friend. There is only one Helmut Lent!

Wolfgang Falck,
St Ulrich,
Tyrol,
Austria

Charles Pickard

GAOLBREAKER

Dick Sugden, who has lived in Zimbabwe for nearly 35 years (his wife, Betty, is one of the country's top veterinary surgeons), is one of those select adventurers who, pre-war, eschewed a conventional, civilian career to take a short-service commission in the Royal Air Force. All his working life, until his retirement, William Richard Craig Sugden lived close to aeroplanes, either flying or controlling them.

By the time he came to be associated with Group Captain Charles Pickard, and flew with him on operations, he had a wealth of flying experience behind him . . . Malta, in the early days of the battle, and then some equally rugged stuff, first, with Venturas and then with Mosquitos of 2 Group, initially with Bomber Command but running, later, into the 2nd Tactical Air Force.

When eventually he was himself shot down over Holland in 1944 during a low-level daylight operation against the Hazmeyer electrical factory at Hengelo, he had had, as they used to say in those days, 'his lot'.

With a games player's eye for an opening and, with it, an instinct for judgement, Dick Sugden has the background to assess a man of the exceptional capability of Charles Pickard. This portrayal shows it.

Anyone meeting Charles Pickard for the first time, as I did in July 1943, could hardly fail to be impressed – very tall, 6ft 3in., blond, debonair, with an easy-going casual manner – plus 3 DSOs, a DFC, etc, a distinctive loping walk, and invariably accompanied by his Old English sheepdog, 'Ming'.

I was a Flight Commander in 464 (RAAF) squadron at that time, stationed at Sculthorpe. We had heard rumours that, at last, our Venturas ('Flying Pigs') were to be replaced, together with the Station Commander. Our AOC, Basil Embry insisted that we should now have Mosquito VIs (fighter bombers), and when Embry insisted then things started to happen

346

– fast! And so Mossies started to arrive; plus a new Station Commander – Group Captain Pickard.

Most of us knew him by name since he had starred in the film *Target for Tonight*, flying a Wellington, 'F' for Freddie. We had heard about some of his 'cloak and dagger' operations, flown to the Continent from Tempsford – dropping and picking up agents by moonlight in Lysanders, and the longer-range missions in Hudsons; we were familiar, too, with his ditching in the North Sea and the dropping of paratroops at Bruneval. We knew he would not be a chairborne CO – not many were in 2 Group as Embry insisted on almost everyone seeing a bit of the war – even the doctors and padres were encouraged to have a go! Pickard would certainly need no encouragement on that score.

Our immediate role, once we had mastered the Mossie, was low-level daylight raids. Pick and his navigator, Bill Broadley joined in our practices with enthusiasm – almost too much enthusiasm, Pick's language over the RT becoming more and more lurid. Afterwards, however, there would be light-hearted discussion and criticism, when even the lowliest could have his say.

Inevitably there was the occasional accident, usually on take-offs or landings, as the Mossie tended to swing a bit, and it was with some trepidation that we viewed a banner Pick had hung in the briefing room – in large letters: 'The next clot to prang a Mosquito through finger trouble will be posted to the bloodiest job in the Air Force.' The very next day a Mossie swerved off the runway and broke its tailwheel. Out of it stepped Pickard, smiling and as always fumbling for his pipe and matches, saying airily: 'There's always bloody something' – his favourite expression. After that we all felt better.

Our Wing's first raid was on a power station in the Cherbourg area – three squadrons, led by Jack Meakin, and essentially a try-out. Pick, of course, was participating, but as I was climbing aboard I was rather surprised to see Basil Embry and his SASO,* David Atcherley, one of the famous twins, also boarding an adjacent aircraft – with some difficulty as Atcherley's arm was encased in plaster, the result of a recent Mess party. It was these very senior officers' idea of a pleasant afternoon's outing!

The raid was quite successful, no losses, but plenty of flak damage to Pick and others, so much so that he had to feather an engine and make an emergency landing at Predannock in Cornwall. However, he turned up at Sculthorpe a bit later, full of smiles. Everything had been under control; he said that if the other engine had failed he had earmarked a French trawler to ditch beside, then order the skipper at gunpoint to set course for England. Meanwhile Embry and Atcherley had returned safely, their

* Senior Air Staff Officer.

only snag being that they had been unable to bomb as Atcherley's plaster had got in the way of the correct switches; otherwise most enjoyable.

In January 1944, our 140 Wing moved to Hunsdon – much more pleasant and closer to London. The Officers' Mess was a large mansion where Pick installed himself on the top floor, leaving a few other bedrooms for some of the rest of us; all very cosy. The weather was often too bad for any serious flying so we had some good parties. After one particularly good one Pick was still fast asleep in his attic late next morning so we carried him and his bed down two flights of stairs and into the bar, where he finally awoke, calling loudly for healing draughts.

He was essentially an outdoor man, his love of horseriding dating back to his Kenya days, and he was able to get in some rough shooting locally. At one of his previous stations he was nearly nabbed redhanded by a game-keeper, but managed to stuff the loot into the boot of his car, telling his wife, Dorothy, to lean on it and give one of her sweetest smiles.

We guessed that something special was now coming up. On 18 February, a vile, icy cold day with snow falling, we were called to an early briefing. Embry and Pickard were studying the model of a building which was apparently Amiens Gaol, and which we were to break open at 12.30 p.m. The Free French were anxious to get some of their key men out before they were executed the next day. Briefing was meticulous – 487 Squadron to breach the walls, 464 to destroy the guards' quarters, and 21 to stand off close by. Pick would be circling around assessing results and would call in 21 to flatten the whole place if the raid, so far, had been unsuccessful. Embry had been forbidden to take part, to his great fury.

It was still snowing thickly as we climbed aboard, but then came a slight lull. It still looked impossible to take off, but we saw Pick loping towards his 'F' for Freddie, stuffing out his pipe, and giving Ming a final pat. With his engines starting, we realised the game was on. Within minutes we were all airborne, visibility nil. I was flying No. 2 to Bob Iredale, but never saw him or anybody else; it was like flying in a blancmange. Suddenly, when we were (we hoped) over Littlehampton, the snow and murk cleared and there ahead was the sea, in bright sunlight, with another Mosquito in front swerving right across us. I yelled 'Get out of it you bastard,' which he obligingly did, and I saw to my horror it was 'F' for Freddie. I said to my navigator, Bunny Bridger, 'God, we'll be for it when we get home' – Pick had stressed complete radio silence at briefing, let alone being addressed like this. But at least we hadn't collided . . .

The gaol stood out like a sore thumb against the snowy ground. We collected a lot of flak over Glisy airfield, dropped our bombs on target, and beat it for home. It was then that I heard Pick's voice on RT shouting 'Red, Daddy, Red', which meant raid successful, and so 'Daddy' Dale, leading 21, had to take the squadron all the way back again. And that was the last we heard of poor Pick . . . apparently he was then bounced by Fw.190s, who shot his tailplane off . . .

After the war I heard that several Frenchmen saw Pick's aircraft shot down, and they gave him and Bill Broadley a heroes' grave close by the gaol. On the simple cross they erected on Pick's grave, they added VC to his other insignia. They, like many others, thought he deserved it. The cross has now been replaced by a permanent headstone in the war cemetery, where he and Bill lie side by side. My wife and I had the pleasure of meeting some of these Frenchmen a few years ago at Amiens, together with the girl Giselle Souhait, who had cut Pick's medal ribbons off his battledress, kept them safely and returned them to Pick's widow, Dorothy.

In the few months that I came under Group Captain Pickard's command – and in retrospect – it became obvious that I was privileged to be associated with him. His fighting spirit and powers of real leadership made him one of the most outstanding airmen of the war – a really memorable character.

Dick Sugden,
Ruwa,
Zimbabwe

R. E. (Bobby) Bradshaw *FAA*
FLEET OF ARM – AND EYE

We all know the chairman of the meeting who introduces the visiting speaker with the words: 'I'm sure, ladies and gentlemen, that Mr X needs no introduction from me' – and then spends the next 10 minutes reading out his *curriculum vitae*. Not so your editor with author David Foster.

Read Vice-Admiral Sir Roy Halliday on him on page 398 and there you have it all – or some of it. It's fair, however, to add a point. Gus Halliday picked Foster. Foster, for his choice, has 'done' Bobby Bradshaw. The interesting thing is that Bradshaw and Foster made a pair in the Fleet Air Arm. Birds of a feather . . . and all that.

Each was a stand-out in his time in the Service.

Each armed service in each theatre of World War II had its heroes. Men whose fame arose not only from their operations against the common enemy, but from their bearing . . . attitudes . . . courage, and the inspiration that they gave to less talented comrades engaged in similar endeavours.

Bobby Bradshaw was such a person. His spirit and character inspired all of us flying night sorties against Rommel's Afrika Korps in the Western Desert in 1941 and 1942. Sometimes the future looked bleak, particularly when the 8th Army was in retreat in June 1942 and had to take up defensive positions at El Alamein, less than 60 miles from Alexandria and even closer to Dekheila, our base airfield west of the city. Not since Generals Wavell and O'Connor had routed Graziani's vastly larger forces in 1940 had the enemy been so near to capturing Alexandria and Cairo. And most people thought Rommel was capable of anything.

That month, 826 Squadron (Albacores), of which Bobby Bradshaw was a member, and 821 Squadron (Albacores), to which I was attached, were often flying two sorties a night, taking off from one desert landing ground and touching down after the night's operation at another further to the east. Unbeknown to us, and his CO, Bobby was not content with two sorties; he had his aircraft refuelled, and his flares and bomb loads replenished, to make a third sortie, bombing Rommel's advancing tanks and thin-

350

skinned transports. When we finally arrived back at Dekheila with rumours circulating that we were to be evacuated to Cyprus or Palestine, Bradshaw scoffed at them. He cheerfully predicted that we would be operating at night from Dekheila and could then enjoy a good breakfast in the Mess, sleeping in real beds in cabins instead of camp beds in tents in the desert. We could then enjoy the luxuries of Alexandria when not on flying duty! His prophecy was correct, and from then until November, when Rommel turned tail and retreated from his defeat at El Alamein, we did just as Bobby had predicted.

Richard Edward Bradshaw – no one seemed to know where the 'Bobby' came from – enlisted in the Royal Navy on 21 January 1939, a week before his eighteenth birthday. Granted the rank of Midshipman (A), he qualified as a pilot and in October 1940 joined HMS *Formidable*, one of the new class of fleet aircraft carriers, operating in the eastern Mediterranean under Admiral Andrew Cunningham. It did not take long for Bradshaw, now an Acting Sub-Lieutenant (A), to make his mark, for in the London Gazette of 1 January 1941, he was mentioned in despatches for 'outstanding zeal, patience, cheerfulness and whole-hearted devotion to duty'. These attributes, aptly chosen, epitomised the manner in which he was to conduct himself for the duration of the war.

Victory in the Battle of Matapan, when what remained of the Italian Fleet after Taranto was put to flight with further heavy loss, was due in no small measure to torpedo attacks by Albacores of 826 Squadron. For his part in the battle, Bradshaw was awarded a second mention in despatches which the *London Gazette* of 29 July 1941 recorded as being for 'bravery and enterprise'.

In May 1941, 826 Squadron had become land-based in Egypt when its carrier, HMS *Formidable*, was put out of action by Stuka bombers during the German invasion of Crete. For the next two years the squadron operated in the Western Desert, bombing enemy installations and 'pathfinding' at night for the RAF's Wellington bombers. The Fleet Air Arm's slow biplanes would find the selected targets, illuminate them by dropping flares which drifted over and covered them, thus allowing the RAF bombers to attack.

In some ways this life in the Desert suited Bobby. It had an informality not appreciated in the confines of a man-of-war largely staffed with older Royal Naval regular officers. The night operations afforded scope for ingenuity which satisfied Bradshaw's avowed intention of harming the enemy in any way that he could. Having illuminated the selected targets for the RAF to attack, he would then himself dive-bomb the aiming point with extreme accuracy, continuing his dive to a lower level so that he could strafe any available enemy with his forward-firing guns. He could make the Albacore do anything he wanted and several times his observer, subjected to some hectic manoeuvres, commented with feeling that Bobby should have been a fighter pilot. In fact, when supposed to be on leave, he visited an RAF fighter squadron, and after only a cursory cockpit check, flew a Hurricane on a two-plane sortie. During the patrol, he helped to destroy an enemy aircraft, but declined to accept his share of the kill as he was 'not supposed to be there!'

In March 1941 he received his third mention in despatches for 'bravery, skill and daring in air attacks against the enemy'. The ink was hardly dry when, on 28 April, the *London Gazette* announced the award of the Distinguished Service Cross to Richard Edward Bradshaw for 'sustained courage, skill and enterprise in many air operations by night and day against the enemy in the Mediterranean'. On 11 September 1942, the *Gazette* announced that Bradshaw had been awarded a Bar to the DSC for 'bravery and devotion to duty in air operations in the Western Desert'.

After the Battle of Alamein, 826 Squadron followed General Montgomery's pursuit of Rommel westwards and continued to bomb enemy targets by day and night. Based then in Tunisia, Bradshaw took over command of the squadron early in 1943. Although he was content to stay with it after the invasion of Sicily, the Lords of the Admiralty had other ideas for Acting Lieutenant-Commander Bradshaw. First, there was a period of non-flying duty as no pilot was supposed to operate continually against the enemy for 2½ years without a break – as Bobby had done. Then came a posting to the US to form a new squadron, No. 852, equipped with Grumman TBF Avengers.

852 Squadron became the anti-submarine and bomber/reconnaissance squadron on HMCS *Nabob*, attached to the Home Fleet. The unit operated in northern waters, escorting convoys destined for Murmansk. Its aircraft laid mines in Norwegian ports being used by the Germans, bombed dock installations and attacked enemy shipping. Legend has it that in one sortie against an enemy airfield, Bradshaw flew so low over the road leading from it that for good measure he lowered his arrester hook and ripped out telephone wires attached to the poles at the roadside.

One of Bobby Bradshaw's most famous exploits occurred when the carrier *Nabob* was torpedoed shortly after its aircraft had returned from an attack on the German battleship *Tirpitz*. The ship began to settle by the stern, and with the flight deck canting at an alarming angle, the Captain realised any further flying was out of the question. The flying personnel were transferred to a waiting destroyer, but Bradshaw decided to remain with the ship, his navigator and air gunner volunteering to stay behind with him.

The *Nabob*, listing badly but afloat, started to crawl towards a home port. During the night, however, the U-boat was detected following its victim under cover of darkness and thick fog. Bradshaw offered to attempt to attack the U-boat, and without knowing whether or not it would work, he let the accelerator catapult the Avenger into the air. For the next few hours.

the aircraft flew low over the water trying to locate the submarine. By dawn, the fog was thicker, but the search went on. Then, when the Avenger's endurance was almost reached, Bradshaw flew back to the carrier and neatly crash-landed his aircraft on the sloping deck. It skidded up the deck, crashing into some other parked aircraft, but the crew were unhurt. The Avenger, a 'write-off', was pushed over the side. An officer who saw the approach and landing described it as 'a magnificent piece of flying'. In the report to the Commander-in-Chief, it was stated:

'The catapulting of an aircraft from this steeply sloping deck and heavily damaged ship in the early hours of the morning to attack or keep down an enemy submarine which appeared to be trailing the ship with the object of finishing her off was a very fine action, and we consider all concerned deserve credit.'

In December 1944 Bradshaw received a second Bar to his DSC for 'courage, resolution and skill in northern waters'.

His last wartime appointment was to command No. 828 Squadron (Avengers), in HMS *Implacable*, which joined the British Pacific Fleet at Manus on 1 June 1945, and continued operations against the Japanese until the Armistice was signed in Tokyo Bay. Bradshaw still had additional time to serve under his short service commission and was not released from the Royal Navy until February 1947.

No one who knew Bobby Bradshaw, and who met him again after the war, was surprised that he was the same happy-go-lucky fellow one had known in those early days in Egypt. He was approaching civilian life with the same resolve with which he once attacked the enemy and very soon his advance brought him a directorship of the brewer Taylor Walker. Married, he was looking forward to life, and his humour, attitude and bearing were as infectious as ever. It gave one a 'lift' just to be in his presence, and I was fortunate to have been with him on several occasions.

After what he had been through in eight years of flying duties, six of which were almost entirely involved with operations against the enemy, we all imagined that Bobby Bradshaw was indestructible. It therefore came as a cruel shock when we learnt that on 29 December 1958, Bobby, not yet 38 years old, and his wife had both been killed when their car, taking a sharp turn at night, went off the road and struck a tree.

It was a dreadful end and a terrible waste of a wonderful, talented human being.

David Foster,
Rancho Mirage,
California,
USA

J. E. (Johnnie) Johnson
'FOLLOW ME'

'As an American citizen I watched World War II build up and felt the awful menace of the Nazi war machine. In 1940, I travelled north to Montreal and joined the Royal Canadian Air Force as a member of the Free World . . .'

Thus did Dan Browne (Squadron Leader J. Danforth Browne) see his duty over half a century ago and so joined that select band of Americans who threw themselves into the fight against Hitler long before Pearl Harbor and the United States' entry into the war.

Once in Europe, the volunteer succeeded hugely, leading Canadian squadrons in Wings commanded by Johnnie Johnson until the war's end.

Success spilled over into peace and before long Dan Browne was on his way to heading up the biggest US law firm in the South. Now, he turns his attorney's mind to a study of his wartime wing leader.

```
B/CAST    V    XQF    XQE    139/149
ALL       T    SELF

FROM      83 GROUP MAIN HQ 041930B
TO        121  122  124  125  127  143  39  12'  83 GROUP REAR
          HQ TO PASS TO ADMINISTRATIVE UNITS' 83 GCC
QQY       Z    SECRET    BT

AO32 MAY 4TH PERSONAL FOR COMMANDERS FROM A.O.C.
A L L HOSTILITIES ON SECOND ARMY FRONT CEASE AT 0800 HOURS
TOMORROW MAY 5TH. WORK WILL CONTINUE AS USUAL UNTIL ORDERS ARE
ISSUED TO THE CONTRARY AND OPERATIONAL UNITS ARE TO OBSERVE
STRICTLY THE STATES OF AVAILABILITY ORDERED BY (G.C.C.)
BT        041930B

AR    K
QA    R . . . . . . 042101B
```

James Edgar Johnson, universally known as 'Johnnie' Johnson, began his combat experience at the tail-end of the Battle of Britain. It was then autumn 1940 which, on timing, was entirely fitting, for that was the end of the beginning and Johnnie belongs to the next phase of the air war.

He finished his combat experience in World War II under the terms of the 83 Group 'cease-fire' order reproduced above. I know that he was himself on active 'ops' on the second or third day preceding the order of 4 May, 1945, flying missions over enemy-occupied territory. He was then a highly decorated Group Captain and the leading fighter ace in the European theatre. He and his distinguished Wing Leader of 125 Wing, 2nd Tactical Air Force, George Keefer, were setting the example, with George leading the wing operations and Johnnie in the van for the Berlin missions.

Neither had given the slightest thought to playing it safe in those final days when only remnants of the Luftwaffe were still active. But there was the fighter-bomber and ground-strafing work to do, a most vicious and deadly form of combat which had become the lot of 2nd TAF, forged as the cutting edge of the armies which made the Wehrmacht 'kaput'.

Johnnie flew nearly 700 missions in combat from autumn 1940 until the cease-fire on 4 May, with one short period of rest. Few other Allied pilots could match that span and particularly without let-up at the very end. He flew Spitfires exclusively in combat.

This is the greatness of Johnnie Johnson as he became the Wing Leader *exemplar*. He was to symbolise, until the war's end, the endeavours of the British and Commonwealth air forces in Europe which, with those of the US Army Air Force and the Allies, were to achieve air superiority and bring telling by-products in their train . . . The paralysing of enemy armour and troop movements in the breakout from Normandy . . . The cutting of the bridges across the Seine and the Loire and, literally, destroying the Seventh [German] Army at Falaise . . .

It was the fighter-bomber – not the four-engine heavies of Bomber Command – that swept ahead of our ground forces from Normandy to the Elbe, savagely mauling the enemy in its rout.

Johnnie would, I feel sure, think it only right also to name Don Blakeslee of the US Army Air Force's 4th Fighter Group [see pages 365–71], whose exceptional leadership with the P-51D Mustangs paralleled in the West that of his British counterpart. But Don's leadership, after his two years' flying under the control of the Royal Air Force, extended from 1943 until the end of the war, whereas Johnnie's had begun in the previous two years with his command of a flight in 616 Squadron in 1941 and his leadership of 610 a year later.

There was still a lot of war left in Johnnie after the armistice. Like Blakeslee, he flew jets with the US Air Force over Korea and he was the only outsider to be briefed by the Israelis when they flew an 86 to 0 contest over the Syrians, during the fighting in the Bekaa Valley in 1982, being privileged to be shown the video and ciné film of their victories.

I first joined Johnnie at Kenley in May 1943. On my first combat sortie across the Channel I flew with him as his wingman. I was so frightened I wouldn't have known my name had I been asked. That day a 109 appeared in front of us, diving and turning as it headed for the Somme estuary. We dived and turned with it. I saw Johnnie open fire and little white puffs appeared all over the wings and fuselage of the enemy. It took me a split second to realise that I had seen my first aircraft shot down as the 109 began smouldering and we saw it crash in the delta thousands of feet below.

Shakespeare, in Richard II, had gauged the English quite well in his famous lines

> This royal throne of kings, this scepter'd isle,
> This earth of majesty, *this seat of Mars*,
> This other Eden, demi-paradise . . .

Johnnie must have sprung from that 'seat of Mars'. He is a true warrior.

What kind of a guy is he? He was, and is, an extraordinarily alert, vital and aggressive man. He perceives fact without distortion. Yet he is sensitive to every implication in any scenario and can record events with easy eloquence and poetic expression – as he has done in the three books which he has personally written. Most of all, he is his own man, which probably accounts for his voluntary resignation from the Royal Air Force at the age of 48. The Service lost a great leader.

A spectator, whimsically signing himself 'Friar Tuck', once penned the following lines

THE FIGHTER PILOT

Say what you will about him; arrogant, cocky, boisterous and a funloving fool to boot. He has earned his place in the sun. Across the span of fifty years he has given this country some of its proudest moments and most cherished military traditions. But fame is short-lived and little the world remembers . . .

That fits most fighter pilots and, generally, we were a light-hearted bunch. We had little use for King's Rules and Regulations, which we reasoned were OK for the Army and Navy but marginally restrictive for fighter pilots. Johnnie had his own brand of leadership. This included strict discipline in the air but avoided on the ground the more rigid authoritarianism which seemed to characterise the other British services. Johnnie's form of leadership could be encompassed with the only one command worth making – 'Follow me'. The Canadians did just that, motivated to fulfil their duty with great élan and pride in their role.

356

The worst discipline that could be inflicted upon anyone in our fighter Wing was, we felt, to suffer the indignity of being posted away from the unit and out of 11 Group in Fighter Command. That was the measure of the pride we felt in belonging to a crack fighter squadron in one of the most élite combat units of all time. It was an unmatchable experience.

Much has been made of the great disparity between the scores achieved by the German aces of World War II (352 in one case, over 200 in several others and numerous instances of over 100, many of the victories being gained, of course, on the Eastern Front, where conditions were different) and Johnnie's score of 38 confirmed destroyed over enemy-occupied territory in the West.

I flew with Johnnie on more than 100 sorties and I know of no one who was keener to engage the enemy. Time after time we would receive radar plots of enemy aircraft and go flat out to intercept. When we got there the cupboard would be bare.

In talking recently with the Luftwaffe's General Gunther Rall in Washington, DC (his own total was 275), I quizzed him closely on the information his squadrons received from ground control about the movements of Allied formations. Gunther held that all our radio transmissions were relayed to them as were the exact positions of our aircraft. I felt it difficult to credit his assertion that the Luftwaffe even knew when our sections and squadrons were taxiing out for take-off because of the strict radio silence we always observed.

However, there is little doubt in my mind that, in the West, the Germans saw no profit whatever in engaging our Spitfire IXBs or the US P-51D Mustangs. They saw a broader percentage in reserving their maximum efforts for the big, four-engined bomber game.

The great disadvantage which Johnnie and the other British leaders suffered in this 'numbers game' lay in the limited range of the Royal Air Force's fighters in providing cover for the bombers. Even with its ungainly 90-gallon belly tank, the Spitfire could only reach the Rhine from our bases in south-east England, and 90-gallon drop tanks were in very short supply.

When the US Eighth Air Force's daylight offensive got under way, their generals were quite justified in criticising the lack of practical support offered by the British and Commonwealth squadrons for the B-17 Fortresses on their planned destruction of enemy targets deep in the Fatherland. Greater radius of action was demanded of the fighters. The Americans even took several Spitfires back to the States for modification and then flew them across the Atlantic to England non-stop!

However, the RAF's then Chief of the Air Staff, Sir Charles Portal, took a calculated view obstinately to oppose the introduction of the necessary modifications, thereby effectively emasculating the offensive potential of his own Fighter Command.

Had it not been for the short-range shackle imposed by Portal and the British Air Staff, Johnnie and the leaders of other British and Commonwealth squadrons and wings would have come closer to achieving the totals attained by the German aces, admittedly in different circumstances. Much more important, longer-endurance fighters in British hands could, arguably, have shortened the war.

The happy marriage in 1942 of the P-51 airframe, manufactured by North American Aviation in California, and the magnificent Rolls-Royce Merlin engine, which produced the brilliant P-51D Mustang, provides the conclusive answer to the controversy.

PER ARDUA AD ASTRA is a thrilling statement of an ideal. Johnnie's leadership typified the concept, thereby providing his country with 'some of its proudest moments and most cherished military traditions'.

There is a human postscript to Johnnie's World War II achievements which is worth adding, showing, as it does, that there are forces from which even heroes will turn away.

After the war I settled in Florida, which has a larger physical area than all of England and which, at the time, had a population of only 4 million. It was truly a hunter's and a fisherman's paradise. One time when Johnnie was visiting us we hunted quail on one of the vast ranches in the centre of the State. The pointing dogs locate the coveys and the guns follow in a vehicle to flush the game. We cautioned Johnnie about rattlesnakes in the grass, but he didn't express concern. Then, just as the dogs were pointing, I noticed that one of them was leaping sideways. We walked over and there it was – a 6-ft rattlesnake with a body larger than your forearm, its head as big as a fist, fully erect and coiled back, poised for a strike. The rattles on its tail were giving furious notice to stay away.

Johnnie studied the creature for a moment or two and then turned back to the vehicle. He broke down his Purdey, cleaned the barrels and put the gun away in its case. He stated that he was through with quail shooting.

Dan Browne,
Tampa,
Florida,
USA

Guy Gibson
THE LEGEND WHO LIT THE WAY

Most of the outstanding operators in wartime could attribute their own success in part to the lessons learnt early on at the hands of some illustrious mentor. The examples are there to be cited, for usually 'the pupils' were generous in giving credit where it was due.

Such a one was the exceptional Australian David Shannon, from Adelaide, whose name is inseparable from the attack on the Ruhr dams in May 1943. What he survived during his extensive operational stretch with 106 and 617 Squadrons of Bomber Command suggests that, apart from the inevitable smile or two from Fortune, his initial grounding in the bombing arts helped to provide him with a safe passage through the conflict.

Probe Shannon's record further and you will find that during his time as a raw, but acutely perceptive, 20-year-old pilot officer of 106 Squadron, his ever-present model was a wing commander whose C-in-C once called him 'as great a warrior as these Islands ever bred'.

Hardly surprising, then, that David Shannon should have targeted this study on the mentor who gave him his operational start.

Some 46 years on, I can close my eyes, think back and there before me is a compact, nuggety figure of medium height. The stance is aggressive – legs apart, knees and calves well braced, hands in trouser pockets or folded across the chest. The facial expression appears mildly pugnacious, with the lower jaw pushed forward and teeth clamped; but the clear eyes are a give away, ever ready to break into a grin.

The figure is prepared for anything, no matter what – conduct a briefing for some squadron operation, jump into an aeroplane and go to war, or join in some uproarious party. But always there is the genuine enthusiasm, verve and vigour to be injected into the action of the moment.

This, for me, is the most memorable character of the war. He was my first squadron commander, a warrior, a comrade-in-arms, and, above all, a man who became a very close and true friend during our time together.

His luck ran out on the night of 19 September, 1944, but the fates decreed that mine was to last.

I have no difficulty in visualising Guy Gibson. What is difficult is to describe and do justice to a man who became a legend and was as great a warrior as any produced by World War II . . . Never flinch, always lead from the front and set an example: that was Guy.

It was my lucky day when in June 1942, I was posted from No. 19 OTU* at Kinloss in Scotland to No. 106 Squadron based at Coningsby in Lincolnshire, a 5 Group Unit in Bomber Command of the Royal Air Force. Guy had only recently taken over command of the squadron. He was by no means universally popular.

By some he was revered – but from a distance; some were obviously and openly jealous of him; some disliked and were scared of him; others were ignorantly scornful. But, to the majority, Guy was their leader. From them, he had one hundred per cent support and loyalty. Putting personal feelings aside, all had to listen to a man of his wartime record and experience and acknowledge his exploits and understanding of the enemy. Openly or grudgingly, they had to admire the man for his courage and his capable leadership.

In that mid-summer, the squadron was in the process of re-equipping with heavy bombers and changing over from Hampdens to Manchesters and Lancasters. Conversion flying was being done at nearby Wigsley as well as at Coningsby.

Fortunately the output of Lancasters from the factories was increasing at such a rate that the somewhat unreliable Manchesters did not come seriously into the picture, although we did fly them for a short time. Flight engineers were also only just starting to filter through, most of them having re-mustered as aircrew from their ground mechanic and fitter duties. Because of this, the Lancasters carried a second pilot, who, for several months, acted not only as co-pilot, but also as flight engineer.

I had already done a couple of operations in this capacity with my flight commander, Squadron Leader J. DeLacy Woolridge, known affectionately as Dim. Both raids had been to the port of Bremen. One day, a little later on, Guy barged into Dim's office and accused him of giving him untrained idiots to fly with him as co-pilot and flight engineer. He asked Dim who was flying with him? 'Shannon,' replied Dim. 'Right,' said Guy, 'get Shannon to report to me at once.'

I was shot over to the squadron commander's office for a first meeting that was to prove to be the start of a close flying relationship. This developed into a personal friendship which strengthened as time went on.

Guy initiated me into operations over enemy territory. When I was flying with him, I seemed to be able to read his mind and anticipate every move

* Operational training unit.

he expected of me as his co-pilot and flight engineer. Such unison was extraordinary, and Guy seemed to be able to relax when I was with him in the cockpit. I don't know what it was. I was young and had only reached my twentieth birthday a month before joining the Squadron. Guy was four years older than me.

I was a bit of a loner and certainly had never had any time for fools. Joe Palmer, my initial flying training instructor in Cunderdin, Western Australia, who was 20 years my senior, once said of me, 'Young Shannon is the wildest student pilot I have ever had on the ground but the best I have ever had in the air.' Perhaps this was the chemistry which made Guy and me click.

Guy also did not suffer fools gladly. He was selective and had a close-knit circle of friends. Apart from the common cause of hating and fighting 'the Hun', they had to be good at whatever they were doing, and when off duty had to be party enthusiasts. Heel tappers were not acceptable. Guy also had an eye and a great penchant for the opposite sex.

When he was on duty, he was as strict a disciplinarian on the ground as he was in the air. When he was off duty and relaxing, he could be one of the boys and a tremendous friend. I was lucky to join his circle in that mid-summer of 1942.

Guy and I did five operational trips together during July, before I was allocated my own aircraft. Wilhelmshaven was the first, a night trip of about 5 hours, followed by a daylight raid to Danzig, an operation lasting over ten hours. Then came Essen, Hamburg and Dusseldorf. I couldn't have been luckier to be flying with such a man and those trips all took place while I was supposed to be converting on to Manchesters and Lancasters . . . Happy days. After a month together, Guy sent me off on my first trip as captain. This was a mine-laying sortie flown in moonlight to waters off the Danish coast.

It was not until I was a fully fledged operational pilot that I was let into Guy's inner circle. This consisted of chaps like Dim Woolridge, John (Hoppy) Hopgood, Bill Whammond, a Rhodesian, Brian Oliver, our Gunnery Leader, Don Curtain, from New York, who had joined the RCAF, and Dickie Dickinson, a wild-cat rear gunner. Dickie was a pilot officer whose captain was a sergeant pilot. There were others whose names have faded with the years.

During off-duty spells and stand-downs the parties were hectic and hilarious, with Guy always at the centre. I vividly recall the local GP in Horncastle who had a soft spot for aircrew. Guy often led us to his home after a session in the Mess or the local pub. The larder was always well provisioned and booze flowed freely. Not much doctoring of the locals appeared necessary in those days. Our GP friend was usually fairly tight.

On 1 October, 1942, the squadron was moved from Coningsby to Syerston in Nottinghamshire. Syerston already had concrete runways and

Wimpeys, the construction engineers, with their Irish labour force, were about to lay the concrete runways at Coningsby. This was now an operational need.

On the second or third night in our new home, Guy said: 'Let's explore Nottingham.' So several of us piled into a flight van and headed for the city. We soon found the Black Boy Hotel. All downstairs bars were crowded with NCOs and ground crews so Guy led the way upstairs to the cocktail bar. Here, with an eye on the barmaid, and a grin for the rest of us, Guy said: 'We'll have 106 specials all round.'

'What the hell's a 106 special,' asked the lass behind the bar. 'Well,' said Guy, with another wink at us, 'it's our squadron starter. A touch out of some of those bottles on the top shelf, a dash of Angostura Bitters, some soda water and all well stirred with some ice. We'll have one now before getting down to the serious drinking.'

Polly, as she later became known to us, took Guy at his word and mixed a fearsome cocktail, the like of which could never be repeated. This, we all knocked back; but, thereafter, whenever we returned to the Black Boy, Polly would say 'A 106 special coming up,' but it had become a smoother and more palatable drink because of her knowledge of the contents of the bottles.

Our operational life on the squadron went on and, with Guy as leader, a keen competitive spirit developed between the crews to see who could be first back and have the best aiming point photograph of the target. With Dim and Bill now away on a rest and Don missing on the last operation of his first tour, the competition between Hoppy and myself grew intense until we, too, were told we could not stay on operations any longer. Guy was posted to 5 Group HQ around the end of February 1943, and Hoppy and I were also sent our different ways.

However, we met again at Scampton only days later. We were the first Guy had called upon to serve him as founder-members of his new Squadron to be based at Scampton. Others quickly appeared and soon it was like old times with intensive flying and wild parties, and with Guy always to the fore.

The task for the CO was formidable. To assemble a complete squadron of 21 crews, each of 7 men, collect some 500 ground staff, order all the equipment and bits and pieces required to operate the new unit, and then to organise the training, liaise with the Ministry of Defence, Bomber Command, 5 Group Headquarters as well as the boffins was a massive assignment. To do all this and then carry the responsibility for leading a successful attack on the Ruhr dams was as memorable a challenge as any one man could face, especially when the time span allotted for the whole undertaking was only some 6 weeks.

My wife, Ann, who, at the time, was Section Officer Fowler, a WAAF officer in the station, recalls the impression which this remarkable character left with her.

'I was an Intelligence Officer at Scampton. One of my first recollections of Guy was to be asked to fly with him. It was before the Dams raid and the Squadron was practising low-level cross countries of five hours' duration. This was roughly the time the real operation would take to the Ruhr dams and back. Guy had just got the blue glass in his cockpit and been issued with the yellow goggles designed to give the impression of flying by moonlight. He felt that we WAAF officers couldn't do our job properly unless we were given some experience of flying, and so we set off up to Yorkshire and across the moors, running up the east coast of Scotland to the Caledonian canal, and then keeping low down over the water as we headed for the west coast . . . Thence over to the Isle of Man and back to Lincolnshire and home. What struck me most was the strictness of the discipline maintained in the air. It was a very different Guy from the cheerful, friendly soul I had come to know in the Mess.

'There was one incident which lightened the atmosphere during the flight. I was standing beside Guy in the flight engineer's position when suddenly he looked at me and burst out laughing. He called to his crew to come and have a look at me. My face! My expensive Elizabeth Arden make-up gave it the effect of a clown's mask in the weird blue light of the cockpit. It certainly cheered them all, after the tremendous concentration which had been devoted to flying at such a very low level for so long.

'My other memorable recollection of Guy was when the awards came through after the Dams raid. I was asked to sew the Victoria Cross ribbon on to his battledress. It was a poignant moment for we were still all so sad about the terrible squadron losses, and Guy was facing the task of writing over fifty letters to the next-of-kin of the missing airmen.

'It seemed that after the Dams raid, the Squadron was able to relax a bit. The ceaseless and intensive training continued, but not quite so furiously. We, that is David, Guy, myself and somebody else – it could well have been Joe McCarthy – had all been to a party where everybody had got extremely merry. We were driving back to camp along the narrow Lincolnshire lanes with David at the wheel. He was going at breakneck speed and I was quite terrified. I was sitting in the back of the car with Guy. When he realised how frightened I was, he looked at me coldly and said, "What is your puny little life worth? Why are you making such a fuss?"

'When I came to think about it, compared with what the aircrew were having to suffer over enemy territory, I felt he had a point.'

All things come to an end, and after the Dams raid, Guy went to the United States, while the other survivors stayed on the squadron.

On his return from America, Guy worked at Bomber Command HQ, but he was forever itching to get back 'on Ops'. Eventually, he persuaded Bert Harris to let him go. It came as a devastating and unexpected shock to all of us who had served with him when on 20 September, 1944, we heard that he had been shot down in a Mosquito. As Master Bomber he had successfully controlled an attack on a heavily defended target over enemy territory the night before.

What a tragic loss, not only to all his friends, but to Bomber Command and the Royal Air Force. To lose a leader of such calibre at the height of the Battle for Germany was indeed a tragedy. Guy was one of the unlucky ones. We who survived are the lucky ones. We have much to be thankful for that there were men like Guy Gibson who so generously were prepared to give of their experience that the rest of us might benefit.

David Shannon,
Dulwich,
London.

Don Blakeslee
BLAKESLEE OF THE EIGHTH

James Goodson of New York City – Colonel James A. Goodson, Presidential Citation, Distinguished Service Cross, Distinguished Flying Cross (8 times), Silver Star, Air Medal and Purple Heart – all US – to give him his full due, is one of those rare individuals who seem able to succeed at whatever they elect to set their hand.

At Toronto University, the Sorbonne in Paris and the Harvard Business School, he was ahead of the game. When World War II came and he was instantly torpedoed in the good ship, SS *Athenia*, he didn't wait for America to enter the fray. He joined the Royal Air Force, there to make his mark as an Eagle Squadron volunteer before transferring to the United States Army Air Force in September 1942. In the next three years, he became one of the most successful squadron commanders in the US Eighth Air Force's famous 4th Fighter Group, the War Department in Washington crediting him with 32 enemy aircraft destroyed at the war's end.

In the peace that followed, Jim Goodson addressed himself to business and the rigours of corporate life. With a rare facility for languages to help him (he speaks four fluently and is 'conversational' in others, including Russian), he rose to head up Goodyear and then Hoover in Europe before signing on as Vice President and Group Executive of ITT (International Telephone and Telecommunications), worldwide.

Retirement didn't appeal, so he tried his hand at authorship and published *Tumult in the Clouds*,* a highly readable account of the US Eighth's day offensive in Europe and the part he played in it. It sold out.

To add more variety, Goodson lived for a while in England, at Sandwich, in East Kent, hard by the airfields where he used to land his Spitfire, P-47 Thunderbolt and P-51D Mustang some 54 years ago.

---

* *Tumult in the Clouds*, William Kimber, London and St Martin's Press, New York, 1983.

Whilst awaiting trial at Nuremberg, Hermann Göring was asked at what point he had realised that Germany had lost the war. He didn't hesitate: 'When I saw single-engined fighters from England escorting the US bombers over Berlin.'

Those fighters were the red-nosed Mustangs of the 4th Fighter Group of the US Eighth Air Force, led by a 26-year-old handsome six-footer with steel-blue eyes, a strong pugnacious chin and a character to match, Colonel Donald Blakeslee.

Blakeslee was more than the Commanding Officer. He WAS the Group. He had helped to create it. He had flown more than 1000 combat hours with it. He had imbued every pilot in it with some of his indomitable independent spirit. Indeed, had it not been for that spirit, neither Blakeslee nor the Group would have been over Berlin on the first daylight raid, nor would the Group have become the leading Allied Fighter Group of the war, officially credited with 1016 enemy aircraft destroyed.

For the 4th had not always been 'the First', as its motto now proudly proclaims. It was formed from the three Eagle Squadrons of the Royal Air Force; squadrons which had been formed of American volunteers before the United States entered the war. After Pearl Harbor, it was decided that these RAF squadrons should be transferred to the US Air Force to form the 4th Fighter Group as the nucleus of the Fighter Command of the Eighth Air Force.

It was an excellent plan, but immediate results left something to be desired. The three squadrons had never flown together as one unit and the most experienced pilots had been in combat long enough to be due for a rest period. There was also a desperate need in the US Air Force for pilots with combat experience to help build up the enormous training organisations now required. In particular, the Ninth Tactical Air Force was being formed under General Pete Quesada, who was persuading his friends, Tooey Spaatz and Monk Hunter, to let him have some of the Eagle Squadron pilots.

The worst blow came just before the Eagle Squadrons were transferred to the US Air Force. 133 Eagle Squadron, newly equipped with the latest Spitfire IXs, took off on an escort mission to Morlaix on the Brest peninsula, from which not one plane returned.

Morale was not improved by the news that the Group was to have its beloved Spitfires taken away, to be replaced by the much larger and heavier P-47. Every pilot that ever flew the Spitfire had a love-affair with that beautiful, sensitive, manoeuvrable aircraft; when the first P-47 arrived at Debden, the pilots looked at its enormous bulk with horror.

Only an exceptional leader could rebuild and inspire that rather demoralised, ill-assorted collection of tough individualists which was the 4th Fighter Group at the time of transfer.

This task was first entrusted to one of the RAF's most capable officers,

Wing Commander Duke Woolley. He had just begun to mould the squadrons into a well-disciplined Group when, after a few weeks, he was recalled to greater responsibilities in the RAF. He was succeeded by Chesley Peterson, one of the first Eagles, who was liked and respected by all, but his talents and experience were also needed back in the States, where he went on to become a Major General. The next commander of the 4th was a USAAF regular officer, Colonel Anderson, who amazed the Group by flying combat missions at the advanced age, for a fighter pilot, of 39; but he was acutely aware of the fact that the 4th needed a commander who had more rather than less experience than any other pilot, and someone they knew would not leave them.

Now was the moment of truth for the generals. They knew that Blakeslee had joined the Eagles to avoid being taken off combat duty for a rest after completing a tour of duty with the RCAF; this meant that he had far more experience than any pilot in the Group. They knew he was the pilots' choice, and that morale slumped every time he was passed over for the job. They knew that he would lead the Group with aggression and brilliance in the air. But they must have had grave doubts as to whether this dashing young hell-raiser, who only two years before had been a mere lad working for the Diamond Alkali Co. in Fairport Harbor, Ohio, could carry with dignity the responsibility of a full colonel. They must have known he would be his own man and would fight to the bitter end for what he believed to be right. But the Eighth Air Force generals, like Jimmy Doolittle and Tooey Spaatz, had been fighter pilots themselves. They picked him anyway. We were lucky with our generals.

I've heard many speeches from great men when they took over their new commands. Some were amusing, some were corny, some were pathetic, some were maudlin, some were patriotic, some were magnificent; but Blakeslee's was the most eloquent – and typical. He simply climbed on to the bar, drew himself up to his full height of 6ft 3in. and bellowed, 'Tonight the drinks are on me!'

But Blakeslee was imbued with the basic discipline of the RAF. His final speech at about 1 a.m. was also typical: 'All pilots will report for briefing at 6 a.m.'

Almost immediately, Blakeslee confirmed to the generals that he was no 'yes man'. He began a determined, non-stop campaign to get the P-51 Mustang for his Group.

Considering its weight and size, the P-47 was a remarkable plane. It could hold its own with the German fighters and, what was more important, it could out-dive them, thus taking away one of their most effective evasive tactics. With its droppable wing-tanks it could escort the bombers well within the borders of the German Reich.

After our first flight in the Thunderbolt, I said to Don, 'It sure can dive!'

'It damn well ought to!' he said. 'It sure can't climb!'

On one of the first missions, Don spotted some Fw.190s below us, immediately rolled over and went down in a vertical dive. The 190s saw him coming and dived away, but with Don's speed, he easily caught up with the last of them, closed as he usually did until he was almost ramming, blasted the German plane and zoomed back up again.

His comment on landing was, 'Yeah, it can dive!'

On a later mission to attack Le Bourget airfield near Paris, the bombers had enough Spitfire escort to allow the 4th to range more freely. Over St Omer, Blakeslee spotted what were probably two or three *staffeln* of *Jagdgeschwader* 26. He immediately flipped on to his back and started down. By the time his laconic 'Horseback leader – going down' came over the radio, he was already in a vertical dive, and soon left his flight behind. I was leading the flight next to him and, because I had seen him roll over, I was able to follow him, with my wingman. The rest of the Squadron was left behind. Even I couldn't quite keep up, even though the airspeed was past the danger-mark, where pulling out of the dive can become impossible.

'Horseback here. Get down here! There's millions of them!'

'Horseback Blue One. Bandits coming in on you from 5 o'clock high. I'm behind you.'

'O. K. Goody, I see them. But I'm going to get these two first!'

In the general mêlée, I saw Don shoot down two, but by that time we were in the hornet's nest. Each time we lined up on one of them, we had to break to turn into one of them attacking us. I saw Blakeslee shoot another one down, but I also saw more 190s coming in on him.

'Horseback Leader, break right! I'm coming!'

He turned into them, but before I could get close to him, I saw flashes on his plane.

'Keep turning, Don. I'll get him!'

'He's getting me! Where the hell are you?'

It was only seconds. It seemed like an hour. Finally, I was able to close and shoot the 190 off his tail. Blakeslee's plane was hit badly, but he kept attacking. He shot at another 190, but was hit again by another before I could shoot it down. I zoomed past the stricken 190 and finally caught up with Blakeslee. His plane was covered in oil. He couldn't see through the windscreen, so he had opened his canopy.

'I can't see, Goody. I'll have to fly on your wing. Let's head for Manston.'

I pointed him in the right direction, but then I had to leave him to break into more attacking German planes. When I was out of ammunition, I turned into them and drove them off by bluff.

When we finally crossed the Channel and I had guided Don on to the long runway at Manston, I ran over to his plane to find that both it and Blakeslee were covered in black oil (we later counted 64 20 mm cannon shots in the plane).

'I'm sorry, Don,' I said.

'Yeah! Where the hell were you?'

'Well, at least you made it!'

Then I realised that throughout the whole engagement, there was only one thing uppermost in my mind; not my own safety, not the destruction of the enemy, but giving cover to Blakeslee and not letting him down.

He didn't say much at the time, but he recommended me for one of the highest decorations. In that area, I have been fortunate, but the greatest honour for me will always be Blakeslee's, 'Thanks, Goody, you saved my ass!'

Anyone who served under him would have felt the same.

In spite of its many good qualities, the pilots continued to refer to the P-47 as the 'Thunderjug' and Blakeslee continued to plead with the generals to give us the Rolls-Royce Merlin-engined P-51 Mustang, which had both manoeuvrability and a range of nearly 800 miles.

On the day that Mustangs with Packard-built Merlin engines began to arrive in England, they were destined not for the 4th but for the recently arrived 354th Fighter Group. To add insult to injury, it was Don Blakeslee who was loaned to that Group to check them out on it, probably because General Bill Kepner wanted Blakeslee's opinion of the plane.

If Kepner thought that first-hand experience would dampen Don's enthusiasm, he was wrong. Don was more than ever convinced that 'this is the ship'. Every night, he flew back to Debden to show 'the ship' to the 4th pilots, who were soon as eager as their leader to get the plane. But Kepner was adamant.

'The 4th has the key role on every escort mission. With the losses the bombers are taking, we just can't afford to take the 4th out of combat at this time to check out a new plane. That would take weeks!'

Finally, Blakeslee asked a question. 'How long COULD you take us out of combat?'

'No more than 24 hours.'

'That's all we need!' said Blakeslee.

Kepner looked incredulous, but Don was serious.

'Most of our boys have combat experience on Spitfires. This plane's not much different. I can have them checked out in a day!'

They were, and the 4th climbed from their base at Debden in their P-51s to give cover on hundreds of missions over Europe. For the first time, the carnage over the target area was over and the bomber crews had some hope of completing their tour of duty.

On almost every mission, the 4th was involved in combat. At the height of the so-called 'Battle of Berlin', we were flying missions almost every other day and each mission lasted about eight hours, but no one's enthusiasm ever waned. Pilots fought to get on each operation.

The reason was simple; Blakeslee was on almost every mission. Every pilot had only one thought in mind – not to let down Don Blakeslee. Blakeslee's approval was all-important and superseded all thoughts of fear. The new pilots put their faith in him; old hands like those of us who commanded the squadrons, and often led the Group, knew instinctively what he wanted; we were always where he wanted us and he was always where we knew he would be.

When Blakeslee said, 'Horseback here – I'm going in,' he knew he would be covered. When any of us took our squadron into the attack, we knew we were covered. The disciplines of the RAF were ingrained in Blakeslee. He always saw to it that we were covered when we went into the attack.

But he had no time for what he called the 'prima-donnas', who he felt were only interested in building up their personal score, and hated the Press attention they received. There were no black crosses or swastikas on his plane to proclaim his 15 victories, nor was there even a name. The big squadron letters, WD-C, were all that was needed.

When Don Gentile returned from his final mission before being sent back to the States, he did a special low pass over the airfield so that the cameramen could get a good shot of his plane. Unfortunately, he came in a little too low, hit the ground with his propeller and crashed in front of the assembled crowd.

Blakeslee was furious and immediately grounded him. The PR men were horrified at this, explaining that everything was set up for Gentile to be given a hero's welcome – Fiorello La Guardia, the mayor of New York, possibly even President Roosevelt himself, would honour the young Italian-American. Blakeslee was unimpressed and expedited Gentile's departure.

I never heard him preach, argue or elaborate on 'tactics' or 'strategy'. He once said, 'They're always asking about tactics. What the hell are our tactics?'

'Well,' I said, 'in World War I von Richthofen said "Our tactics are to seek out and destroy the enemy: Anything else is nonsense." I guess that's still true today.'

Don liked that.

Captain Nolan, whose impatience with the slowness of his superiors had such tragic results in the Charge of the Light Brigade, wrote: 'The tactics of cavalry are not capable of being reduced to rule ... with the cavalry officer, almost everything depends on the clearness of his *coup d'oeil* and the felicity with which he seizes the happy moments of action.'

That might have been written for leaders of fighter pilots and may even explain why the first military pilots often came from the cavalry. In any case, it certainly applied to Blakeslee.

He had an innate instinct, enhanced by his vast experience, which helped him to convert a multitude of considerations into decisive action in a split second. That same gift enabled him to keep track of fifty or more aircraft milling around at 30,000 ft. It also enabled him to lead the Group some 1600 miles, much of it over Russia, where the crude maps he had were almost useless, and land at the Russian base on the exact minute of his estimated time of arrival.

From Russia, he led the Group over Budapest to Foggia in Italy and then back to England, escorting bombers all the way. Blakeslee said, 'This is just for show!' It was, but it showed the enemy that the Allies dominated the skies over Europe.

By the end of the war, Blakeslee had over 500 combat missions, well over 1000 hours of combat time and high decorations from the United States, Britain and other nations. But he still wasn't ready to quit.

He flew sixty more combat missions in the Korean War and continued to set records in his service career. One of these records was set in 1952, when he led the deployment of the 27th Fighter Wing of seventy-five F-84G's from Austin, Texas, to Misawa, Japan. This involved refuelling in California, Honolulu and Wake Island and, in order to bridge the final over-water leg of 2575 miles, letting down from 43,000 ft to 12,000 ft to rendezvous with B-29 tankers and continue on to Japan. Every landing, take-off and rendezvous was spot on. Don's comment was typical: 'I was proud of the men.'

He was also proud of his RAF wings, which those of us who transferred were authorised to wear over the right breast pocket, in addition to the USAF wings over the left. It may be that, in the post-war air force, these reminders of Blakeslee's meteoric rise from a kid who was only just out of high school and starting a job to full Colonel in three years was resented by some senior officers, who had graduated from military academy and followed a less colourful and much slower career.

Certainly, his independent attitude and blunt defence of his convictions did not endear him to many of his superiors. He retired from the Air Force in 1965, still a Colonel, but still flying at the head of his command, which is probably the way he wanted it.

Diplomacy was never part of Blakeslee's make-up. He was a wartime pilot and was ill-at-ease in the peacetime Air Force. He led by example, not by orders. He commanded obedience by the strength of his character, not by the rule book. He earned the admiration and loyalty of his men by his loyalty to them.

He had no time for those who would treat him as a hero. He didn't need them. He was the typical, ideal fighter commander, but he was, above all, every inch a man.

James A. Goodson,
Sandwich,
Kent

Adrian Warburton
MEDITERRANEAN MASTER

Tony Spooner (Squadron Leader A. Spooner) has spent a lifetime in aviation, military and civil, in war and in peace.

Take war first. He flew two operational tours against Admiral Dönetz's U-boats during the rigours of the Battle of the Atlantic, a pastime that most of us wouldn't have picked for choice. Flying long patrols low down over the gale-lashed ocean by day and by night wasn't a Sunday picnic. In between, he commanded the Special Duties Flight in Malta, flying those clandestine, under-the-counter operations in Wellingtons and B-24 Liberators that they still don't say too much about.

Such endeavours earned him the right to have the distinguishing ribbons of a successful operational pilot sewn on his tunic.

In peace, Spooner joined the then British Overseas Airways Corporation as a widely experienced aircraft captain helping to pioneer the establishment of the transatlantic route. His mates in the airline companies elected him chairman of the British Airline Pilots' Association, the pilots' trade union.

Add to this his activities as an author (he has served military history signally with his recent, deeply researched biography of the astonishing Adrian Warburton* of whom more below), and his ability as a National Master bridge player, and there you have our next contributor.

There was a uniqueness about Adrian Warburton which separated him from others. As Air Vice-Marshal Hugh Pughe Lloyd, AOC Malta, said of him: 'There was something about his fair-haired good looks that reminded you of Lawrence of Arabia. Like Lawrence, he was completely unorthodox and individualistic. You had to let him do things his own way.'

The uniqueness began almost at birth. His father, an eccentric submarine commander of World War I, had his only son, Adrian, christened

---

* *Warburton's War*, William Kimber, London, 1987

inside one of HM submarines. If, as most believe, the submarine was alongside in Malta, it makes a remarkable coincidence, because it was from Malta, from the airfield of Luqa, that 'Warby', as all called him, gained both of his DSOs, his three DFCs and his American DFC. Surely a unique record?

All called him 'Warby' because that is what he liked to be called and because he treated all persons alike. He was 'Warby' to the airmen with whom he played cards on the hangar floor. He was also 'Warby' to his AOC who added: 'He used to breeze into my office and tell me what we ought to do . . . nearly always casually dressed . . . but he had a magic all his own – plus flair and courage.'

Malta made Warby and, in a way, Warby saved Malta. Before his arrival in September 1940, his career in the Royal Air Force had been little short of a disaster. His pre-war training had finished on the very day that Hitler had marched his armies into Poland to start World War II.

Pilot Officer A. Warburton, with a 'Below Average' assessment as a pilot, was sent to the Torpedo Training Unit at Gosport. There he managed to cope with the single-engine biplane, the Vickers Vildebeeste. This type of obsolete aircraft was still being operated by 22 Squadron, to which he was soon posted. Warburton's only distinction at Gosport was to marry a barmaid whom he scarcely knew and whom he promptly deserted.

The next year, 1940, when Britain stood alone and in desperate need of trained pilots, Warby's career as a pilot was reduced almost to oblivion. With 22 Squadron, he failed to convert to the Beauforts which replaced the Vildebeestes and he was relegated to flying a Hawker Audax on air gunnery, drogue-towing exercises. He was also sent on a long, general reconnaissance course, where he was taught to navigate. By then he was being chased by divorce lawyers hired by the abandoned barmaid. He was also deeply in debt with Mess bills unpaid.

As his CO, Squadron Leader F. St J. Braithwaite, put it: 'It killed several birds with one stone to get Warburton out of the UK before either the law or his wife caught up with him. A navigator was needed to get a Maryland (one of three) to Malta. Warburton filled that bill.'

Fate then took a kindly hand. The leader of the three Marylands was a remarkable man of outstanding talents. Squadron Leader E. A. 'Tich' Whiteley, an Australian, had been impressed by the navigational plan that Warby had prepared for the non-stop overland journey to Malta. Consequently, when two of his three pilots went sick on the island, he allowed Warby to attempt to fly the Marylands. The results were hair-raising: a broken undercarriage, zigzag take-offs, boundary fence removed, ground loops and huge bounces; but Warby's determination shone through. As his remarkable air-gunner, Paddy Moren, remarked: 'Warby had unlimited guts. I stuck with him. I sensed that, in the end, he would prove to be the best of all.'

Occasional sorties in command were, for a time, interspersed with his navigational trips, but Warby soon established a reputation for being a daring and exact photo-reconnaissance pilot. He seemed to have a flair for it. The pictures which he and Whiteley brought back of the Italian battle-fleet in Taranto had much to do with the success of the Fleet Air Arm's famous strike with Swordfish as the ships lay at rest in the harbour. That was in November 1940, and Warburton was on his way . . .

Photo reconnaissance (PR) was the principal task for Whiteley's small Maryland Flight, No. 431. With the enemy placed perilously close in Sicily only 60 miles away, Malta needed almost daily photographs of the Axis forces' dispositions. Only from such updated pictures of the airfields and harbours in Sicily could the island's defenders read the enemy's intentions. With her inadequate resources, it was essential for Malta to be kept informed.

Warby soon established a reputation similar to that of the Royal Canadian Mounted Police. He *always* got his pictures – regardless of weather, service-ability of his aircraft or the enemy's guns or fighter aircraft.

Nor was this all. Soon, with Paddy Moren's assistance, Warby began to pile up a score of enemy aircraft destroyed on his PR missions. While never a neat pilot near the ground, he rapidly demonstrated that, once aloft, he had few equals. While never neglecting their primary PR task, he and Paddy could truly claim to have shot down more enemy aircraft than any of the fighter pilots in Malta at that time. Warby also shot up enemy airfields at zero feet and destroyed other aircraft on the ground. 'The Germans would wonder what type of Italian aircraft I was flying, and the Italians would be doing vice versa. Then I let them have it.'

As his reputation grew, and having, by then, won the devotion of the 'erks' of all categories, Warby also took, quite unofficially, to carrying a few 25 lb bombs on PR sorties. The aircraft had no bomb racks or sight, but Paddy Moren would kick the bombs out via an open hatch. With Malta being raided up to eight times a day (3340 times by war's end), the knowledge that someone was hitting back lifted the morale of the besieged and battered island.

That was the start of the legend, the rise of the way-out character with whom Tony Spooner enjoyed so close and, as his only biographer, so important a relationship. The years have not clouded the recollection.

Warby was also unique in his attire. He was apt to fly in an Army battle blouse with Royal Air Force shoulder tabs, Oxford bags and either Desert boots or slippers. He invariably wore a cravat. He carried with him, when he flew, a throwing knife and at least one revolver. 'They will never take me alive,' he would say . . .

374

The rest of the story, covering much of the next three years, was to become a catalogue of astonishing exploits. Mainly the operations were flown from Malta and aimed at the sources and lines of supply of Rommel's Afrika Korps; others were flown in a Spitfire from Heliopolis, in Egypt, whither Warburton had been sent on his phantom 'rests'. At No. 2 PRU* he knew an aircraft was assured!

But always in the Malta background was the demonstrably attractive Christina, an English cabaret dancer, who was caught on the island when war·broke out and who, as a civilian, worked in the Operations Room underneath Valletta, for which service she won, deservedly, the British Empire Medal. With her, Adrian found sanctuary and comfort much preferable to the more spartan quarters of the officers' mess at nearby Luqa, where his aircraft was kept.

There was no stopping Warburton in what he wanted to do. He would play things his way – and to hell with them. He could write his own ticket in Malta. Witness his personal decision to acquire, for his crew, two 'ground-borne' personnel, Corporal Norman Shirley and Leading Aircraftman Ron Hadden, photo mechanics, to alternate on his operational flights. Each was to win the DFM at around the time that Paddy Moren was gaining his and Warburton himself was gathering the first of his two DSOs and the first two of his three DFCs.

But as Spooner makes clear, it wasn't all uninterrupted success. With the Allies pressing on in North Africa in the autumn of 1942, Warburton was on a photographic mission to Bizerta when his Spitfire was attacked by a section of aggressive Messerschmitt 109s and, for once, he was shot down.

However, after a series of bizarre incidents, he was soon back in Malta, where they had presumed him to be dead.

'He simply walked in to his open-mouthed, but delighted, photo developers,' says Spooner, 'tossed them the film magazine he had salvaged from his aircraft and said: "Sorry, chaps, I'm a bit late." '

'The island rejoiced and Christina wept for joy. His unexpected return quashed the rumours that he was about to be awarded a posthumous Victoria Cross.'

Appointed successively to command 69 and then 683 (PR) Squadrons and, later still, 336 (PR) Wing, things seemed once again to have moved back into the customary groove. The reconnaissance work he had been doing with the US and South African Air Forces had brought him new friends and authority. Then, on 17 November, 1943, his luck changed again, never, apparently, to return. He was

* Photographic Reconnaissance Unit.

involved in a late night road accident in North Africa from which he suffered crippling injury, as Spooner recalls.

'He was badly smashed up – a broken pelvis among other injuries. He lingered for weeks in various North African hospitals. His command was taken from him. He eventually discharged himself via an open window and spent a period 'borrowing' aircraft from friendly Royal Air Force and US Army Air Force stations as he flew himself about the Mediterranean and the UK trying to persuade the medics that he was fit again to fly!'

Posted back to the United Kingdom in the spring of 1944, Warburton found that the plans for the invasion of Normandy were then largely laid. There was no part for him to play. Like George Beurling, the brilliant Canadian, before him, he soon discovered that the Mediterranean was one theatre, the Western Front something else again. Individual stand-outs from abroad often didn't fit and weren't wanted at home. Tony Spooner completes the poignant saga.

Benson, in Oxfordshire, was the home of photo reconnaissance in the UK. The Americans, whom Warby had come to know so well in North Africa, remained his friends and it was probably at the insistence of Elliott Roosevelt, son of the President of the US, and by then the CO of all the USAAF's PR activities in the UK, that Warby was appointed as the Royal Air Force's liaison officer at the Americans' Mount Farm Headquarters.

It was a ground job, but at least he was again among friends and admirers. Still, the yearning for a more active job kept gnawing away. It was principally to satisfy this urge that Elliott Roosevelt arranged a special photographic mission for Warby. He was detailed to fly across Europe to photograph ball-bearing factories deep inside Germany and from there to proceed directly southwards to visit his buddies at San Severo in Italy. That was where his old squadron was based and it was also there that he would find the South Africans, who had always made him so welcome.

The mystery of what happened on that last flight on 12 April, 1944 will probably never be solved. Warby, flying a P-38F5B – a special photographic version of the US Lightning – was accompanied by a P-51D Mustang flown by a pilot from the USAAF's 357th Fighter Group. The mission was successfully accomplished and Warby was last seen over Lake Constance, heading south. No trace either of him or of his aircraft was ever found . . .

There are some indications that he may have decided to fly direct to Malta instead of to San Severo . . . Malta, where he was known and revered and where he had won the true love of a girl who had proved almost as remarkable as he during the island's long siege . . . Warby and Malta were inseparable.

As was the case with Lawrence, rumours persisted (and still do) that he might be alive somewhere, but the chance was remote . . . He had flown 350 operational trips from Luqa alone and many more from Egypt and other Mediterranean bases. He was a symbol of the island's defence in its darkest hours. While his name is still venerated in Malta, it remains almost totally unknown elsewhere.

The island's National War Museum has established a special Warburton Corner in his memory . . . Not even his old school, St Edwards, Oxford, has gone out of its way to ensure that he is remembered for what he was – one of the very few really outstanding characters of the Royal Air Force in World War II.

Were it not for the fact that others such as Pat Pattle, Terry Bulloch and Bob Braham stand similarly unrecognised – apart from their decorations, so richly earned – Adrian Warburton would remain the one great unknown air ace of the war . . .

As a wise Greek once wrote nearly 2500 years ago: 'Time brings all things to pass.' Perhaps with the passage of time, Warby and his likes will receive the recognition which is their due.

Tony Spooner,
Upper Hale,
Farnham,
Surrey

Postscript: The editor is indebted to John Bisdee (see pages 238–43) for recalling that Adrian Warburton kept his Beaufighter next to 601 Squadron's Spitfires at Luqa. Warby arrived one morning to find an unexploded bomb outside his dispersal. He promptly borrowed a spanner from an aircraft fitter and proposed to defuse it. 'Mind what you do with that spanner,' said the fitter, 'it's on my charge!'

Sir Hughie Edwards VC
THE MARVEL FROM FREMANTLE, WESTERN AUSTRALIA

It takes an Australian to lay bare an Australian. And when the Australian subject happens to be Air Commodore Sir Hughie Edwards, VC, of imperishable memory, in his lifetime one of Bomber Command's and the Dominion's enduring stalwarts, it requires a fellow countryman with the experience, as well as the pen, to do it.

Peter Firkins, the Western Australian author, has both. Aged 18, he spent an operational tour sitting in the rear gun turret of a Lancaster bomber of 460 Squadron of the Royal Australian Air Force in 1944 during an exceptionally nasty time in the night offensive against Nazi Germany, when the enemy's twin weapons of '*schrage Musik*'* and SN2† were causing forbidding losses among the marauding forces.

Add to that the qualities – and the books – which have identified Firkins as a noted military historian, and there you have a combination to match the challenge which a study of Hughie Edwards poses.

On 4 July 1941, Wing Commander Hughie Edwards, then CO of No. 105 Squadron, RAF, led nine aircraft from his own squadron and six from No. 107 Squadron in a daring daylight attack on the port area of the heavily-defended city of Bremen. It was his thirty-sixth operation.

His tiny force flew across the North Sea and northern Germany at a height of 50 feet, weaving around the ships they encountered at the mouth of the Weser and, as they approached the target, the balloon and high-tension wires.

Light flak, pompoms, machine guns and heavy flak poured towards the attacking Blenheims, now reduced to twelve as they charged on like some irresistible force towards their main target, the docks.

Edwards had ordered his bombers into line abreast formation so they

---

* Literally, 'slanting Music' – a term used to denote upward-firing cannons in the Luftwaffe's night fighters.
† Advanced airborne radar-detection equipment – Ed.

would present a less concentrated target to the ground defences. As they flew into the target, the flak became so intense that every aircraft was hit, but they pressed on, unloading their bombs on warehouses, cranes, factories and wharfs, causing fires and vivid explosions below them.

Four aircraft were shot down over the target before Edwards withdrew his battered force, leaving behind the most successful raid on Bremen so far. The leader had planned and executed the attack brilliantly, and the award of the Victoria Cross was a fitting tribute to his own superb courage, leadership and determination.

After the award, he told his crews with his customary modesty, 'This is your VC, I was simply the person to be presented with it.'

At the time, I was at school in Perth, Western Australia, the state where Hughie had been born and bred. To everyone in Australia, his projection as a great war hero filled us with special pride.

It was another distinguished Australian airman, Air Chief Marshal Sir Wallace (Digger) Kyle, who had had a strong influence upon the award, who said to me years afterwards that this was one of the best VCs of the war 'because Hughie did as many operations after it as before, which no others could claim'.

Edwards had already won the DFC for a daring, anti-shipping strike the month before and, nearly eighteen months later, the DSO for his leadership of 93 aircraft in the famous raid on the Philips radio works at Eindhoven. When, a few weeks after the Eindhoven raid, King George VI was decorating Edwards at an investiture at Buckingham Palace, he commented that the Australian was the first man to win the VC, DSO and DFC in World War II.

Peter Firkins, who came to know Edwards very well after the war when 'Australia's greatest bomber pilot' was concerned, first, with the mining industry and then, as Governor-General of Western Australia, with the affairs of state, recalls the impact which he made upon the Royal Australian Air Force's 460 Squadron during his historic tenure as Station Commander at Binbrook, in Lincolnshire, during 1943 and 1944.

Edwards had just been posted to a senior appointment in Mountbatten's South-East Asia Command as Firkins joined the Squadron. But the stories they were telling about his time in command of the Royal Air Force station, his involvement with this élite unit and its crews, and his influence upon them, still stick in the mind 45 years on.

Hughie certainly had absolutely no idea of what the word 'fear' meant, and apart from his own extraordinary career, showed it by often taking a sprog crew* on their first operation, just to show them the ropes. This, and his stirring 'you must press on regardless of opposition' to the crews at briefing, always set a magnificent example.

Despite his exceptional record in the air, Edwards was generally regarded as sometimes having difficulty landing an aircraft – a trait shown by other distinguished operational pilots. Typical of this was the occasion at Binbrook when, having landed after a raid and finished off the runway, he sent out a cryptic order to Flying Control over the R/T: 'I'm down, send out the tractor!'

Again, there was the time when after landing and taxiing around to his dispersal bay, he said to the ground staff sergeant, 'There's something wrong with the brakes, sergeant, check them out.' On inspection it was found that he had somehow collected a bomb trolley around the perimeter track which was stuck under the tail wheel!

Ron Douglas, a brash and aggressive young pilot who had a very tough first tour with 460 including 14 of the 16 raids on Berlin during the terrible 1943–44 winter, recalls two encounters with Hughie.

On the night of 2-3 December, 1943, the squadron lost six crews in the Berlin attack with several accounted for over England on their return because of the appalling weather, with visibility zero. Edwards was in the Control Tower personally bringing his crews in. Douglas received his instructions as he made his approach. 'QBB (cloud base) 800 feet QBA (visibility) 1200 feet'. But he couldn't see a thing and in the tension of the moment replied, 'Poke your head out and have another fucking look.'

At interrogation afterwards, Hughie came up and said to him quietly, 'You'll have to watch your language, Douglas. Control is full of girls.'

About then, Douglas had somehow acquired a very bright red, yellow and orange scarf on which a WAAF was embroidering the names of the targets his crew attacked. At briefing one night, Ron, who was later to manage Shell in Western Australia and later still, to become Agent-General in London, laughed at something and Hughie quickly rounded on him. 'What are you laughing at Douglas, and take that fucking scarf off. This isn't a flying club.'

Away from the harsh realities of operations, Edwards had a delightfully soft side, in which he was well supported by his wife, Cherry, the widow of his best friend.

On Christmas Eve 1943, there were wild parties in both the Sergeants' and Officers' Messes. At some stage, early on Christmas morning, members of the Sergeants' Mess decided to go and sing carols to the Group Captain and Mrs Edwards.

A recently purchased baby grand piano had already had its legs cut off for firewood, but it was carried down and placed in the snow outside the

---

* New and inexperienced crew.

Edwards's house. Someone sat down cross-legged and started belting out 'Good King Wenceslas', whereupon everyone began singing.

Edwards came out in his pyjamas, had a few drinks and started joining in, singing a few of the bawdy mess songs until Mrs Edwards leaned out of a window and called: 'Hugh, do come in, it's too cold for you out there in your pyjamas.'

He loved the conviviality of the Mess, and at Mess parties he would render his favourite songs, 'With my hat on my side' or 'Paper Doll'. He was always among the last to leave and, with the die-hards, would remain long after the bar closed, topping up his and his mates' drinks from the pints left by others.

When he visited a Sergeants' Mess party he used to be met by three of the veteran ground staff sergeants, the three Ts – Tickle, Topper, and Thompson. They would escort him into the Mess, put him on a table and make him drink a 20 oz glass of beer.

At Officers' Mess parties, Squadron Leader Foggo, the Intelligence Officer, habitually performed the 'Muffin Man', balancing a jug of beer on his head, and stripping off his clothes as he went. The original act always left Foggo naked until, because of the presence of WAAF officers, Mrs Edwards demanded that decency should prevail. So she made him a pair of red and white polka dot underpants, with a black swastika on the backside.

The Station Commander's concern for his men's well-being never lessened. A good example was the advice he once gave Laurie Field, who had completed his tour of ops as a WOP.* The Wireless Leader suggested that he should apply for a commission, but Field was reluctant to do this because of his humble country background and poor education.

However, having finally agreed, he appeared before Edwards, explaining his reluctance and the reasons for it. The great man replied: 'Well, you shouldn't be reluctant. You have earned a commission by completing a good tour of operations and you deserve one. Have faith in yourself and go out into the world armed with the confidence that this experience has given you.'

Field took his advice and after the war became an academic and an author.

On another occasion, Ron Lawton, who was halfway through his second tour on the Squadron, was called to report to the Group Captain. Concerned lest he might be in trouble, he reported at once to Edwards. 'I thought you would have made yourself known to me,' said the Station Commander. 'After all we are in some way related.'

'Yes, we are sir,' replied Lawton, 'but I respected our different positions here.'

* Wireless Operator.

'Well, I suppose so,' retorted Hughie, 'but sit down, anyway, and let's have a drink.'

Edwards was particularly interested in anyone from Fremantle, his own home town. When Danny Rees went up for his commission, Hughie asked him: 'Where did you go to school?'

'Fremantle Boys' School, sir,' came the reply.

'So did I' said Edwards, folding up the official papers and switching the conversation to all his previous haunts and, in particular, the welfare of two of his old girl friends. A few weeks later he put Rees up for the Conspicuous Gallantry Medal, following the Peenumunde raid.

The ground staff were often the forgotten members of squadron life. They laboured on the Squadron's aircraft in the open and under all the most awful weather conditions that England provides.

Edwards was very impressed one night when an aircraft, coming back badly damaged, landed heavily on the runway. The fire tender went chasing hard after it. He sent for the Corporal in charge and complimented him on the speed with which he had got the tender out there, but was taken aback by the NCO's reply. 'Oh Christ, sir, if you don't get out there quickly you don't get any perspex!'

Perspex was a prized commodity for making brooches and other gifts, which was a profitable side line for the gifted artisans.

Hughie had misjudged the reason for the Corporal's zeal and, who knows, the NCO may perhaps have blown a Mention in Despatches for giving the wrong answer.

Edwards was only known to have once opposed the return of a member of 460 Squadron for a second tour of operations. A wild Queenslander, one of the Squadron's early crews, wanted to come back, but Hughie's outraged comment was conclusive. 'I wouldn't have that bastard back as a sergeant,' he said.

So this was the Edwards legend that I inherited when I joined 460 Squadron.

Australians were not always considered easy to manage in war, but Hughie knew how to handle his fellow countrymen. He maintained a very relaxed atmosphere while retaining a sensible level of discipline. He once told me long after the war: 'They had a fierce national pride. As Australians, they were very conscious of the ANZAC spirit and reputation and, for this reason, were consistently brave and afraid of being thought otherwise.

'Their main concern was to do their stuff with a minimum of interference from the powers-that-be, complete a tour and get back to Australia. I'm sure they didn't feel they were fighting for King, Country or Commonwealth or hold any high-sounding principles on the policy of war or their opponents. They were part of the struggle and they wanted . . . to survive.'

Ill health dogged Hughie Edwards towards the end of his life and for those of us who knew him in war and in peace his death in 1982 was a very sad occasion.

He was greatly loved, admired and respected by all of us. His life's achievements were all the more remarkable when one remembers his very humble beginnings as the son of a struggling Welsh migrant family in Western Australia.

Peter Firkins,
City Beach,
Western Australia

Adolf Gysbert Malan
SUPREME EXPONENT

Turn to page 311 and there will be found Wing Commander Johnny Checkett's study of Al Deere (Air Commodore Alan C. Deere), his fellow New Zealander and the author of the portrayal which now follows.

Suffice, then, here to say that Deere, one of the Royal Air Force's most effective, best-liked and luckiest wartime operators, has his own assured place among the immortals of World War II. Al knew the business of air fighting – and leading – better than most.

I first met 'Sailor' Malan (Group Captain Adolf Gysbert Malan) in 1938, when, for a period of three weeks, he was my flight commander in 74 Squadron at Hornchurch, in Essex. I was temporarily attached to the unit before joining 54 Squadron on the same base.

I well remember my first sight of Sailor as I was ushered into his presence in the flight office. As a wet-behind-the-ears Pilot Officer, I was full of trepidation. (Remember, in those days a Flight Lieutenant was big stuff to a humble Pilot Officer.) I can see him now, sitting behind his desk – a rugged, square-jawed individual with intense blue eyes, but with a quirky, welcoming smile on his face which, coupled with the words 'I understand we are fellow-colonials', made me relax immediately.

After a few exchanges, he said: 'I am authorising you to fly one of my Gauntlets (which 74 was then equipped with), enjoy yourself, but see that you don't break it.'

Being a member of a different squadron, albeit on the same station, I saw little of Sailor over the next year. But then the Dunkirk operations in late May and early June 1940 brought us together again. Often in the Mess in the evenings, after the day's operations, the pilots of the three squadrons at Hornchurch would exchange combat stories.

One topic was uppermost – the gun alignment on the Spitfires, harmonised to form a pattern of fire at 400 yards. 'Bloody useless,' said Sailor, 'it's time someone did something about it and I, for one, am going to do just that.' In fact, he had already ordered his armourers to re-sight all his eight machine guns on a point 250 yards distant or as near as they could to it, bearing in mind the limited movement of the outer wing guns in the Spitfire.

Sailor won the battle with the powers-that-be, as he was to win others as the war progressed. Thus were Sailor's early leadership qualities beginning to show. In his own squadron, he was the acknowledged boss, the CO being a man of indifferent calibre who left the leading in the air to Sailor.

The Squadron Commander did, however, go on one sortie, but, unhappily, was forced to land at Calais airfield, from which he was rescued by a Master training aircraft, flown in by my CO, James Leathart, and escorted by me and my No. 2. When, later that evening, I saw Sailor, he congratulated me on getting a Me.109 on the sortie, but followed it up by saying: 'You should have left the useless bugger there,' meaning his unfortunate CO. A few days later, Sailor was given command of the Squadron.

Between Dunkirk and the Battle of Britain, which started towards the end of the summer of 1940, I didn't see much of Sailor due to squadron moves north for rest periods. But then the fighting started again in earnest in July.

I was present at a discussion among the pilots when Sailor voiced the opinion that flying in Vic formation was outdated and that the stereotyped Fighting Area Attacks (FAA), which we had practised so assiduously, were also a non-starter in the context of heavily escorted bomber raids.

So out of the window went the FAA attacks. Who, anyway, was in a position to challenge the already-acknowledged expert at the time? The change from the Vics of three aircraft in the Squadron's formation was to come later when Sailor became leader of the Biggin Hill Wing after the Battle of Britain.

Our paths were to cross again from time to time in 1941 and 1942, particularly after Sailor had taken over the Biggin Wing. I was then commanding a Spitfire squadron at neighbouring Kenley. And the next year – 1943 – we came into close contact once more when, thanks to Sailor's intervention on my behalf, I was released from a staff job to become the Wing Leader at Biggin Hill. He was then the Station Commander at Biggin and I like to think that he felt we would make a good team and that I would carry on leading the Wing where he had left off. Since the days of his leadership, it had come to be generally regarded as the premier Wing in Fighter Command.

To begin with, things didn't go too well. For one thing, we weren't getting any Huns and, for another, I did not like the rigidity of the fours-in-line-astern which Sailor had himself introduced in place of the Vic formation. I favoured a much more flexible form of flying now that we were engaged with offensive fighter operations over enemy-held Europe. I therefore decided to adopt what was loosely called the 'finger-fours' formation,* but Sailor was not happy with the proposed change and suggested a conference of all three squadrons in the Wing.

The upshot was that my suggestion was unanimously accepted, causing Sailor to say, with that quirky smile I had come to know so well, 'OK, Al, you win, but I'm coming on the next sortie to see what it's all about.' He did and it turned out to be an historic occasion. The Wing shot down two Fw.190s to bring the total of enemy aircraft shot down by pilots operating from Biggin to 1000. Sailor's grouse on landing was that I hadn't given him the chance to make a kill.

From then on all was plain sailing and our total of enemy aircraft destroyed mounted steadily, much to the satisfaction of a greatly-relieved Wing Leader and the ungrudging delight of the Station Commander.

Sailor and I both left Biggin Hill at about the same time, he to form the first of the tactical wings in the newly created Tactical Air Force and I to command the Central Gunnery School which Sailor had himself founded in 1942. However, we were not apart for long, for early in 1944 I returned south to command the airfield in 84 Group of the Second Tactical Air Force on which Sailor's 145 Wing was based. And so it came about that the two of us, who had seen so much fighting together and had become such firm friends, found ourselves once more side by side in our Spitfires on D-Day, in June 1944, flying over the invasion beaches in Normandy.

It made a fitting end to what I like to think was a long and fruitful wartime association . . .

The saga of our friendship ends on a sad and poignant note. While I was in South Africa in 1964, I learnt that Sailor was dying of Parkinson's Disease. I managed to get a Service aircraft to fly to see him on his farm in Kimberley. As I taxied in after landing, I could see him standing on the tarmac between his wife, Linda, and son, Jonathan, waiting to welcome me.

From a distance, he looked just like the old Sailor, but when I got closer I could see that he was being supported by Linda on one side and his son on the other. It was only later that I learnt from Linda that when he heard I was flying in to see him, he demanded to be taken to the airfield, saying there was no way he would not be on his feet there to greet me.

I stayed with the family for about two hours in the most distressing circumstances, for I soon realised that Sailor still had all his faculties but could not manage to carry on a coherent conversation. Indeed, it was only through Linda being able to pass on the gist of what he was saying that I could gather his meaning. It was a sad, sad occasion seeing for the last time a much-loved old friend, critically reduced in weight to a skeletal 7 stone, propped up on a settee, striving desperately to articulate upon our many battles together.

When the time came to say the last goodbye, there were tears in our

---

* Four aircraft positioned like the tips of the fingers of an outstretched hand. – Ed.

eyes. I had never been so moved and the memory of that day still remains with me . . .

Much has been written about the air aces of the Second World War and there has been speculation about who was the so-called 'greatest'. How can such a judgement be made? Not by victories alone, of that I am certain. Sailor had more than most, but it was his other attributes which scored so heavily in his favour . . . His leadership which manifested itself so early . . . His exceptional foresight in the development of fighter operations . . . These, and other features, single him out, in my book, as the supreme among supremes.

There are few, if any, among his real contemporaries who would challenge this assessment; and I, for one, who knew him perhaps better than most, would challenge any who might gainsay this judgement.

It is right, I feel, that I should touch on Sailor's retirement from the Royal Air Force. Although he wrote to me in a letter* 'I don't think I could have faced a peacetime Service,' I believe the decision was forced on him by his treatment as the war ended. He was then still commanding 145 Wing of 2nd TAF, which he had formed for the Invasion and led up to within weeks of final victory. But then he was relieved of his command – mysteriously, as all in the Command who knew him thought at the time – and replaced by a much older officer with no operational experience.

What could have been the reason for this? Authoritative opinion had it that his wealthy and socially acceptable successor knew the right people in the right places and wanted to be seen at the sharp end when the final whistle blew. Inexplicably and coincidentally, Sailor had been treated with much the same sort of medicine as had been prescribed for his earlier Commander-in-Chief of Fighter Command, 'Stuffy' Dowding, some five years before.

Like Stuffy, he took his medicine without complaint. But what a loss a man of his calibre was to the peacetime Service!

Alan Deere,
Wendover,
Buckinghamshire

There is another first-hand impression of the great South African, seen through different eyes, which should be recorded by way of a postscript. James Leathart (Air Commodore J. A. Leathart), often called 'The Prof' by his followers in 54 Squadron on account of his

* Addressed from HMT *Carnarvon Castle*, Plymouth, and dated 25 February, 1946. Malan was about to sail for South Africa – and home – Ed.

specialist and technical knowledge, remembers Malan when they served together both before and during the early part of the war.

Sailor was already at Hornchurch with 74 Squadron when I arrived there at the end of 1937 on posting to 54. As I recall it, he was already married and lived out; certainly, he was not, then at least, a leading member of activities in the Mess or away from it in the pubs and clubs, etc.

My first close contact with him was after the Battle of Britain had started when he backed me up in a demand for a greater supply of 'de Wilde' ammunition. We demonstrated the standard and the tracer rounds firing from rifles on the range against petrol cans in the presence of armament officers from Group and Command. The 'de Wilde' won the incendiary contest 100 per cent.

Sailor was an excellent shot – as was Stanford-Tuck. I think he was the first at Hornchurch to get a camera gun. The results certainly gave truth to his claims. Many of his films were used subsequently for national publicity . . .

James A. Leathart,
Wotton-under-Edge,
Gloucestershire

Leonard Trent VC
GOLFING VC

James Sanders, the New Zealand journalist, author and artist, may not have served with Len Trent in wartime yet he is a natural to write this study of his immortal compatriot who survived the butchery of the Blenheims at Maastricht in 1940 to win the supreme award for gallantry three years after.

As an anti-shipping strike and reconnaissance captain in Western Europe, and the same again, later, in the Middle East and Mediterranean theatre, Sanders learnt at first hand all about the stresses of operational life in the face of an undeniably resolute foe.

Former feature writer of the *New Zealand Herald* and now the author of upwards of 15 published titles, he draws on the memory of his friendship with one of his country's favourite sons to secure this record of a man's selfless endeavour.

I first met Group Captain Leonard Henry Trent, VC, DFC, RAF (Rtd), in the clubhouse of the Warkworth Golf Club, North Auckland, in 1982. I was a newcomer to the district at the time, but comparatively old as a devotee of the Royal and Ancient Game; and when I signed on as a member of the club (of which Trent was the president), his reputation both as a war hero and a crackerjack golfer was not unknown to me. I found him to be a cheerful, witty and most friendly fellow.

Knowing that I was a writer, Athol Gubb, a fellow club member and one of Trent's mates since schooldays, said: 'You should write Len's story. His full history has not been told!'

That was surprisingly true. A biography was, indeed, well overdue. So, between shots in our game one day, I put the proposition to Len as Hutchinson (NZ) Ltd had agreed to publish a story that I would write. If Len agreed, he and I would share the royalties. Okay?

Len mulled over the idea for a few days and then consented. And so the project began. We found the most satisfactory method was that he should relate his reminiscences on to electronic tapes. He would feed me the instalments whenever we met at the golf club and I would transcribe the unfolding story on to paper. Of course it meant a devilish lot of typing, condensing, and checking on my part, but the job of writing was completed within a few months and the book, *Venturer Courageous*, appeared the following year.

The essential facts of Trent's winning the Victoria Cross are documented Air Force history. As a New Zealand-born squadron leader serving in 487 (NZ) Squadron, RAF, he led his force of 12 Ventura bombers in a daylight raid over occupied Holland on 3 May, 1943. The target was the Amsterdam powerhouse. Ten Venturas were shot down, Trent's being the last to fall – but not before its bombs were released over the target area. Of the total of 40 aircrew in those ten aircraft, only 13 escaped death to become prisoners of war. Len Trent was one of those prisoners.

Confined in the notorious Stalag Luft III, he became one of the prime movers in the big tunnel break of 24 March, 1944. Of the escapees who were recaptured, 50 were murdered under Hitler's personal order. Trent, the 79th and last to emerge from the 'freedom' end of the tunnel, was caught before he could get far.

He suffered great hardship in the infamous westward march when the Germans moved their prisoners away from the Russian advances, but, with the capitulation of the enemy in Europe, he was returned to England, where he elected to remain in the post-war RAF.

Notification of his winning the Victoria Cross came on 1 March, 1946 – almost three years after the Amsterdam raid.

Len Trent was born in Nelson, New Zealand, on 14 April, 1915, and became hooked on flying after his first joy-ride flight in a Gipsy Moth at the age of seven. He was employed as a clerk when, in 1937, he enlisted for a short-service commission in the RAF. After arriving in England he was posted to 15 Squadron and, with the outbreak of war, went to France with the Advanced Air Striking Force. Converted from Fairey Battles to Blenheims, his squadron made continuous strikes against the German troops that were pouring into the Low Countries. From those operations Trent became one of the war's early winners of the DFC.

So Len Trent saw a lot of combat in those early days. That he elected to remain in the service after hostilities is testimony enough of his love of Air Force life. He rose to group captain, became an Aide-de-Camp to the Queen and spent his last years with the RAF as Bomber Command Representative in the British Embassy in Washington. He retired from the service in 1965.

That he was a war hero of quiet courage and bold daring has been exemplified. But he was also a man of deep sensitivity, emotional when relating the deaths and hardships of his wartime companions and – later – stoic and dignified in the acceptance of his own sentence. Among his lesser known talents was his gift for painting in oils and watercolours.

Early in 1986 Len was hospitalised with cancer of the pancreas. He rallied sufficiently to believe that he was strong enough to attend the gathering of Commonwealth Victoria Cross Winners that year in London.

I departed for England on family business in May, quite expecting to hear of Len's arrival later that month. Alas, I heard the news of his death in a phone call from Laddie Lucas on 19 May. Len's old PoW cobber and Laddie's fellow Spitfire ace, Jack Rae, had phoned Laddie from New Zealand to tell the sad tidings.

The Royal New Zealand Air Force, under whose banner Len Trent had served in two stages of his Air Force career, gave him a military funeral with full honours. It was a fitting valediction for an outstanding officer.

James Sanders,
Browns Bay,
Auckland,
New Zealand

James MacLachlan
THE PRICE OF COURAGE

Courage on operations took on several different forms. All were demanding, but there was one brand which seemed to many to require the most. This was the kind that compelled a man to return for more after once enduring some lacerating experience. He didn't have to – indeed advisers and friends pleaded with him not to. But still he came back; talked his way back.

Geoffrey Page came into this category, and won admiration and distinction thereby. Shot down in the Battle of Britain, burned and terribly wounded, he was lucky to survive. Months in hospital and endless operations followed. But, despite it all, he forced his way back into the fight and, as a squadron commander and wing leader, achieved, against all the odds, greatness.

His philosophy and experience enable him to recognise greatness in another when he sees it . . .

So many pilots I flew with in World War II remain indelibly imprinted in my mind, despite the passing of the years. There was one, however, who was undoubtedly memorable in every sense. His name? Squadron Leader James MacLachlan, DSO, DFC and two bars . . .

'Mac', as he was affectionately known to his brother airmen, joined the Royal Air Force before England and Germany came to blows over the tragic pawn of desolated Poland. During the Battle of Britain he took to the air to defend his motherland on the battlefield above the downs and white cliffs that are so dear to English hearts. A happy, laughing boy, he threw himself into the fray with the same enthusiasm as he would have tackled a game of cricket or football. For his daring and achievement he was duly decorated and thanked by his King and Country. With the battle over, 'Mac' then looked around for the next hottest spot he could find. The selection was not difficult. The island of Malta was receiving the same treatment as that meted out to Britain just a little while before, and her defenders were being pressed by a stream of German and Italian aircraft overhead. Blond, six-foot MacLachlan was soon taking his toll of the enemy over the Mediterranean with his deadly deflection shooting, but it needed a man with a dozen pairs of eyes to cope with the odds against him. Either that or the luck of the devil himself. The curtain was nearly drawn over the career of the youthful defender one sunny afternoon as an Italian fighter settled on his tail in the heat of a whirling, crackling dogfight.

A hail of cannon shells ripped his aircraft to shreds, and 'Mac' sailed quietly down beneath the white silk canopy of a parachute towards the soft blue sea . . . But minus his left arm, which was now a mangled mess of flesh, bone, blood, and uniform material.

From this point onwards, the outstanding heroism of this lad, with the enchanting boyish smile, began to make its mark on his fellow fliers – and the enemy. Having been picked up and rushed to the hospital, he displayed the qualities which were to endear him to all who were fortunate to enjoy his friendship; Mac never made acquaintances. On being wheeled into the operating theatre to have the stump of his arm trimmed, the army surgeon placatingly remarked: 'That's the end of your flying days, my lad. Soon you'll have a nice ground job at home, flying a desk for a change, and helping to keep an eye on the girls!'

All the doctor received for his conciliatory words were an impudent grin and a seemingly rash wager.

'Fly a bloody desk!' exclaimed Mac, 'not on your life. Tell you what, Doc, I'll bet you a fiver that I'm piloting an aircraft again within two weeks.'

Soothingly the surgeon agreed and the anaesthetic was administered. Twelve days later, Mac came to claim his money from the incredulous medico. Thus was the foundation laid for the story that was to become a legend in the Royal Air Force.

From that time on, Mac's pursuit of the foe became even more relentless. On his return to England he entered the field of Night Intruding. This consisted of sitting over German airfields in occupied France and awaiting the return of the enemy bombers after their night sorties to English cities.

The job had its problems and its dangers. Complete radio silence had to be observed. Navigation had to be undertaken with the aid of a small orange cockpit light and a map gripped between the knees, as Mac did not possess the luxury of a left hand to hold it, nor were the scientific aids of radar provided in his single-engined, single-seat Hurricane. Patience and skill assisted the stout heart and soon the dividends began to show as burning Junkers 88 bombers and Messerschmitt 110s lit up the darkness of the French countryside.

German night fighters were soon set to look out for Mac and others indulging in this nocturnal sport, and extra light flak batteries lined the airfield perimeters. The boyish grin grew larger at this stepping up of German defences and he increased the number of his nightly missions accordingly.

*   *   *

Although we had both joined the Royal Air Force in pre-war days and had fought in the Battle of Britain, it was not until the summer of 1943 that we first met. We had several things in common. My hands had been badly burned in an air fight and so we both knew the difficulties of physical handicap. But now we found ourselves attached to a unit bearing the interesting title of 'Air Fighting Development Unit'. Every type of allied, and many enemy, aircraft were at the disposal of this organisation so that relative trials could be carried out and the information passed on to the combat squadrons.

Then, one day I learned, to my undying envy, that Mac had managed to obtain permission to use one of the experimental aircraft on a 'lone wolf' mission against the enemy. His plan was simple. Our unit had two Mustang P-51 fighters equipped with special engines that made them the fastest operational fighters in the world at that time. He intended to fly across France at tree-top height, through the German fighter defence belt, attack any aircraft flying in what the enemy considered to be his safe areas, and return home, all in broad daylight.

I watched his preparations from afar as he planned his trip down to the minutest detail. For hours he would fly around the English countryside at a height never exceeding fifty feet and usually lower, until he had perfected his low-level navigation. When you consider that the average motorist has difficulty finding his way around with a map and signposts, the skill of this one-armed man travelling at two hundred and fifty miles per hour (cruising speed) at zero feet has to be admired.

Special dark green paint was sprayed over the top surfaces of the aircraft to harmonise with the colour of the French landscape, so that enemy fighters would have difficulty in picking out the fast-flying raider against a similar-coloured background. His shooting, which at worst was excellent, he brushed up on the practice ranges; it would be wasted effort to find one's prey and then not be able to strike in a swift and deadly manner.

Finally all was ready, and Mac departed from our inland base for an airfield situated on the coast closer to the hostile shores across the Channel. Nothing was heard from him until a day or two later when the sinister green Mustang flashed between the hangars, and one-armed Mac had returned. Later in the Mess I attached myself to a group who were listening eagerly to the recounting of his mission. As far as he was concerned it had been a failure, and disappointment showed itself on his clean features.

After crossing the French coast he had sighted enemy fighters above and behind him, and he immediately discovered the one flaw in the carefully planned mission. The earlier model of the Mustang had a poorly designed canopy which left the pilot with a bad blind spot fifteen degrees either side of dead astern. A job of this type could not be carried out if the pilot had the constant, nagging worry of not knowing if an attack was coming from behind.

394

Reluctantly Mac had turned for home and, by giving the Mustang her head, was able to leave the Focke-Wulf fighters behind. I listened to all this with great interest, and later that evening I spoke to Mac when finally I found him on his own.

'I heard you telling the others that you are going to abandon this daylight intruding and return to night work,' I said. 'Is that true?'

'Yes, old boy,' he replied. 'I don't see much future in getting a load of cannon shells up your jacksie just because you can't see the bastard coming up behind!'

'Would you have any objection,' I asked, 'if I cribbed your idea and used the Mustang for the same game?'

In retrospect I realise that this was the height of conceit suggesting that I might succeed where this experienced pilot had failed. However, instead of treating the question with the contempt it deserved, he slapped his knee and roared with enthusiasm.

'So you think it's a good idea too, eh! Thank God someone else thinks so. Nothing but opposition from everyone ever since I started.'

The words came tumbling out like an opened sluice gate. 'Two Mustangs! That's the answer. Must get another aircraft, but come and look at the maps first.'

Resolved now to act in concert, these two highly accomplished operators then set about a vigorous schedule of preparation, flying at low level over hundreds of miles of countryside with the pair of aircraft maintaining station 400 yards apart in line abreast, simulating to the last detail the operation which was planned. Each knew the risks which an original, deep-penetration mission of this sort, flown in daylight at tree-top height, would entail.

Moreover, Page was acutely aware of the strain which would be imposed upon his mate with his physical disability.

On combat flights, Mac allowed himself the luxury of an artificial arm which was clamped to the throttle lever, and there it stayed until he unscrewed it at the end of the mission. On normal routine trips, he denied himself this scientific aid even though he might be handling a four-engined bomber, such was the man.

With all now made ready, MacLachlan and Page moved from their inland base at Duxford in Cambridgeshire, down to Lympne, a forward airfield, close to Folkestone and Dover on the south-east coast of Kent, there to await the right weather conditions over France – 10/10ths cloud with a base at 2000–3000 feet (to provide the backcloth against which hostile aircraft would be silhouetted and easily spotted – and to offer sanctuary for the P-51s in emergency).

The following day was tailor-made for the job, as Page vividly recalls.

At 0915 we took off and set course for France. The channel crossing was uneventful except for a few bewildered seagulls and a strong sinking feeling in the pit of my stomach. We slipped across the coast without a visible shot being fired at us. Mac's navigation never failed and, in a matter of minutes, we were skimming over the roof tops of Beauvais and heading south for Rambouillet. Soon the broad River Seine slipped by beneath us as our aircraft sped southward, widening the gap between ourselves and the friendly shores of distant England.

All of a sudden, there they were! Three enemy aircraft flying in close formation 1500 feet above and ten miles ahead. Apart from the initial gasp of astonishment and delight at seeing the culmination of weeks of hard work and planning, there was little time to appreciate the beauties – and the grimness of the moment.

A crackle of gunfire ripped out over the peaceful woods beneath and the port aircraft burst into flames from Mac's withering blast. Fascinated, I watched our dying enemy fly along in a flaming mass of steel, wood and fabric, and dive in a seemingly slow and dignified manner into a house on the edge of the forest.

The game of fox and geese was on with a vengeance as we endeavoured to destroy the remaining two aircraft before the enemy fighters took off to intercept our raid. Soon, we were able to send them on the same journey as their companion had taken moments previously, before continuing on our way southward and further from home.

An instant later we sighted another aircraft and Mac's unleashed Mustang leaped into the attack with its cannons and machine guns* spitting fire. Strikes appeared over the unfortunate victim and he dived steeply to earth. It was my privilege to finish him off on the way down and the wreckage was strewn over a large field.

On we flew to Bretigny, where greater satisfaction awaited our blood lust. German night fighters were carrying out their final daylight checks before preparing for their nocturnal harassing of the RAF bomber force. Two of them were preparing to land at their base as we closed from behind. Mac attacked the one furthest away from the airfield and pieces flew in all directions from the Junkers 88; once again it was my task to finish off a job that needed little completion. The aircraft disintegrated on striking the ground.

For some incredible reason the observer in the second Ju.88 had failed to notice his friend's ignominious end and his pilot continued to carry out his prearranged landing. As he held off a few feet above the runway the

* This was an experimentally-armed P-51 from the Air Fighter Development Unit – Ed.

end came swiftly and mercilessly. In a blazing sheet of flame the aircraft struck the concrete and skated drunkenly down its length. Mac had struck again.

Needless to say all the flak gunners around the airfield had witnessed the fate of their countrymen and all hell was let loose as we weaved our way across the centre of the 'drome. But it was our day and we slipped through the stream of innocent-looking orange balls that rose lazily from the ground in our direction. After that, the journey home was uneventful, a kindly rainstorm hiding us as we slipped safely over the coast for base and a large tankard of frothing ale.

Alas, on a subsequent trip our luck did not hold and Mac was forced to crash-land shortly after crossing the enemy coast. The only field available was too small in which to make a belly landing and, as a horrified witness I watched the sleek green Mustang break into pieces as it ploughed through an orchard at the end of the field.

As I circled above, I could not honestly hold out any hope for Mac, whom I had come to love as a brother . . .

It was three years before I received official notification that Squadron Leader J. A. F. MacLachlan had died of wounds three weeks after capture and that his body lies buried in the French cemetery at Pont L'Eveque, in Normandy.

Here, indeed, was a memorable character.

Geoffrey Page,
Wheatley,
Oxfordshire

David Foster

FOSTER OF PALEMBANG

Vice-Admiral Sir Roy Halliday was twenty years old when he began his operational service with the Fleet Air Arm in World War II, one in a line of resolute naval pilots whom the Royal Air Force regarded with a mixture of admiration, incredulity and respect.

The circumstances of their tasks and the equipment with which they were expected to discharge them made their lot unenviable. None coveted their hazardous operational role. Yet they tackled it with a buoyancy and spirit which set them apart.

When Gus Halliday eventually completed his service in the mid-1980s as Director-General of Intelligence at the Ministry of Defence, he could look back on a career which had embraced the gamut of responsibilities – land-based and carrier-borne operations against both Germany and Japan, peacetime test pilot and squadron commander and, via the British Naval Staff in Washington, promotion to senior appointments.

An unyielding will, confidence and a disciplined mind lay at the base of the advance in war and in peace . . .

I knew quite a lot about David Foster before I met him. Like all people who gain a reputation for outstanding ability within their profession, the message spreads ahead of them and one has a feeling of deep familiarity which is, of course, entirely based on hearsay and legend.

David, like me, was an RNVR officer serving as a Fleet Air Arm pilot. I first heard of him through a close mutual friend and colleague, Lt Donald Judd, DSC, RNVR, when we were serving together in Royal Naval Avenger Air Squadron 845, operating from HMS *Chaser* in 1943 hunting for submarines – our contribution towards the Battle of the Atlantic.

Foster and Judd had already completed an operational tour together, serving in Royal Naval Albacore Squadron 826, based ashore during 1942 in the Western Desert in support of the 8th Army. Their principal task was flare-dropping to illuminate German Army targets and enable RAF Wellingtons to carry out night-bombing attacks against Rommel's forces.

It was from this background that, during off-duty periods in the wardroom bar of our Atlantic-tossed escort carrier, Donald Judd told me about flying Albacores and various naval aviators who were to become wartime legends, among them David Foster.

My memory of David is a very clear one. Not because he indulged himself in outrageous eccentricities to attract attention to himself, but because his leadership, moral strength and personal qualities epitomised the very young leaders in World War II in all three Services who carried the burden of exceptional responsibilities way beyond their years.

These facts gradually unfolded as Judd told me about the aviators in 826 Squadron and I began to appreciate that David Foster was unusual for various reasons.

He was born of an English mother and an American father and therefore had dual nationality. He could have arranged things so that he waited in safety and eventually joined the US Forces after Pearl Harbor. Instead, while reading Economics and History at Cambridge, he volunteered at the earliest opportunity in 1940 to become what was then regarded as a quick one-way ticket to eternity – a Fleet Air Arm pilot.

There were reasons for Naval Aviation being regarded in those days as a dicey prospect. To the obvious dangers of operational flying were added the dual hazards of flying single-engine aircraft for long distances over the sea with only rudimentary navigational aids, and, on returning to the aircraft carrier, being faced with the problem of landing the aeroplane safely. About one in sixty deck landings was a major accident in which the aircraft was severely damaged, and even if the pilot did survive in one piece his nerve and confidence were disturbed.

David was rich, which certainly made him different. His father, Bob Foster, was then Managing Director of Colgate' Palmolive in the UK (David eventually became President and Chief Executive Officer of the US parent company in post-war years) and he had invested his son with many of the advantages that money could buy. However, contrary to what one might have expected given such a background, David was, as I discovered after I met him, completely unaffected.

My squadron disembarked from HMS *Chaser* and for about six months was shore-based at the Royal Naval Air Station, Hatston, in the Orkneys, where, among other things, our task was to intercept German warships attempting to break out into the Atlantic.

Subsequently, 845 Squadron, together with the greater part of the Fleet Air Arm, was transported by troopship to Ceylon (now Sri Lanka), where 845 embarked in another escort carrier, HMS *Ameer*. This massive movement of Fleet Air Arm Squadrons during 1944 was to augment the forces under the Supreme Command of Lord Louis Mountbatten, then Commander, South-East Asia. Our enemy was now Japan.

At this time, David Foster, already decorated for gallantry for his exploits in the Western Desert, had also arrived in Ceylon as CO of Royal Naval Avenger Squadron 849, preparing to embark in the Fleet Carrier HMS *Victorious*. He was concerned to acquire a new senior pilot and invited Donald Judd to join him and to bring with him two 'experienced' Avenger pilots. After a certain amount of string-pulling, I was one of the two selected.

Thus I joined 849 Squadron, led by David Foster, whom I now met for the first time, with my old friend Donald Judd as senior pilot.

Henceforth my knowledge of David was a personal one and the next year proved to be the most exciting, difficult and dangerous for quite a few young aviators. All of us in the squadron placed our trust – and our survival – in the judgement and professionalism of this one man.

It is salutary to recall that the average age of the pilots and observers was no more than 22 and that David, at the advanced age of 24, was in command of a 24-aircraft squadron of some 300 naval airmen with the responsibility for being the primary and only effective striking force of a 30,000-ton aircraft carrier. His two-years advantage in age, coupled with a wealth of operational experience, gave him a standing and authority which, in peace-time, could only have been achieved after many years of service. Additionally, every one of our aviators was, in fact, an RNVR officer (i.e. a temporary gentleman), while all the ship's senior officers were permanent career men. This was, to some extent, a reflection upon the rapid war-time growth of the Fleet Air Arm and also its high casualty rate.

David quickly made his mark. His operational briefings were clear and to the point, his manner quiet but firm; but, above all else, his leadership and airmanship, when once we were off the flight deck, were exemplary. As a result, the squadron's confidence and effectiveness steadily improved.

Our operational flying usually consisted of maximum effort from all four Fleet Carriers in company – the striking force of the Far East British Fleet. The air squadrons yielded up to a maximum of 240 aircraft, their task being to attack targets in support of the 14th (Burma) Army. This meant longish flights over the sea, followed by similarly long transits over primary jungle, to reach the target. These operations were opposed in varying degrees by Japanese fighters and the inevitable anti-aircraft fire around the target.

Initially our losses were relatively light, but there was, nevertheless, a sorting out of the men from the boys. Those few who clearly lacked the moral fibre to continue were sympathetically but swiftly dealt with by David, who clearly appreciated the dangerous effect of retaining a weak link in an otherwise sound chain.

Our first real test came with orders to attack the two largest Far Eastern oil refineries at Palembang, in Sumatra – formidable and strongly-defended targets.

We spent days studying models and photographs of our targets, as well as rehearsing the sequence of events and necessary drills under David's close tutelage. The nights before the operation were passed sleeping fitfully on the open quarterdeck to avoid the fetid and humid atmosphere of a tropically hot and non-airconditioned ship, too often imagining the consequences of being shot down or, even worse, becoming a prisoner of war. None of us had any delusions about the future, or lack of it, if we were captured by the Japanese. There was now a significantly noticeable atmosphere of apprehension and nervous tension evident in the behaviour of the aircrews – a reaction which was to prove well justified.

David sensed the tension. No doubt he was feeling the same way, but he rallied our spirits and confidence by exuding an unaccustomed aggressiveness and chatting optimistically about our chances to each of us. His task was made extremely difficult by the cancellation, due to bad weather, of the first fly-off, which was due to launch at first light on 21 January, 1945.

One always felt sick before being catapulted off for a strike; a twenty-four-hour delay did not help to settle one's stomach. Unfortunately, the next day's weather was no better and, as a result, it was with intense relief that, on the third morning, we got rid of our butterflies and David was able to stop moving among us doing his ministering-angel act. At first light, we set course for Palembang . . .

We struck the refineries on two successive days. The damage inflicted was considerable and the attacks were so successful that both the King and Winston Churchill made personal signals of congratulation.

Losses on this, the biggest single operation ever carried out by the Fleet Air Arm, were considerable. Forty-one aircraft were lost to enemy action (many by dive-bombing through balloon barrages), of which, in 849 alone, we lost ten of the 19 aircraft used. Some aircrew were killed and more injured, but most unfortunate were the eleven who were made prisoners of war by the Japanese. All were subsequently beheaded, four being from 849 Squadron.

Thus, the problem of maintaining the morale and motivation of the aircrew as we steamed to join the US Fleet in the Pacific was a major one and it fell squarely on David Foster's shoulders. Fortunately, we spent some 3 weeks *en route* in Sydney, Australia, for much needed rest and recreation, and consequently, most of us were refreshed by the bright lights, and those that weren't were replaced, as were the aircraft we had lost.

The Japanese were no longer winning the war and, by the beginning of 1945, were attempting to strengthen their air defences against the ultimate and inevitable assault on their homeland.

We sailed from Sydney with the same four fleet carriers forming the striking force of the British Pacific Fleet. Our main task was to prevent the Japanese air force from staging back to mainland Japan via the various

401

islands in the Ryukyu group, including Formosa (now Taiwan). This we did by continually bombing their airfields and intercepting their aircraft when they attempted to stage through. It was a battle of attrition, kept up relentlessly for weeks and months on end, and punctuated by Japanese kamikaze (suicide) attacks on our ships, which took their inevitable toll.

Finally, as our targets moved further north and were eventually located on the Japanese mainland, the aircraft-carrier war came to an abrupt end with the dropping of the first atomic bomb. *One remembers the enormous relief, the immediate release of tension and fear, with which this event was greeted. A very different reaction from the ethical and sometimes misguided arguments one hears on the subject today.* (Editor's italics.)

As the war in the Far East approached its dramatic climax, David and I found ourselves relieved of all naval responsibilities and travelling as passengers aboard the troopship *Rangitiki* heading for the UK via the Panama Canal.

One day when we were on the upper deck resting in lounge chairs, I remember studying his face and thinking about his war, some of which had been so much a part of mine.

He had endured the same tensions, the same fears and the constant awareness that tomorrow might never come, just as the rest of the squadron aviators had – but for far longer than most of us. The additional factor was that as well as having to be a superlative leader in the air, setting an example with sang-froid and courage, his toughest job had been back in the ship.

While the rest of us tried to relax, his concern had been to study us individually, to encourage us to continue to dedicate ourselves to our operational task, and calculate just how much longer it might be before the cracks appeared.

For these reasons, I remember David above many others. He spent most of the war flying operationally and much of it as a commanding officer. His outstanding decorations for gallantry barely do justice to what was an exceptional contribution far beyond the normal call of duty.

I will always recall him for another, rather different reason. He was my best man and picked up the tab for a remarkably fine luncheon – in October 1945 – at the Mirabelle restaurant, in Mayfair.

Roy Halliday,
Bank,
Lyndhurst,
Hampshire

'George'
JUGOSLAV HERO

If you believe, as the editor fervently does, that, in wartime, the Almighty kept certain of His servants safe in the face of mortal danger because He had work for them to do later on, then The Right Reverend Denis Bryant, formerly Bishop of Kalgoorlie, in Western Australia, is probably as good an example as any. No contributor to this collection has had a more compelling record – and that's saying something . . .

Three operational tours with the Royal Air Force, first as a navigator and, later, as a pilot – Fairey Battles in France in 1940, moving on to Blenheims in Bomber Command's 2 Group still in 1940 and 1941, just about the most hazardous start anyone could devise in World War II. Then Special Duties on B-24s (Liberators) in the Middle East, dropping secret agents by moonlight in the mountain regions of the Balkans . . . And, third and lastly, a final stint against the Japanese over jungle, swamp, waste and ocean in the Far East . . .

As a decorated wing commander with a permanent commission, post-war, the path was pointed inexorably upwards. Then came The Decision to substitute The Ministry, with all its sacrifices, for an apparently certain future in the Royal Air Force. Australia beckoned, and a dedicated and selfless theological career of exceptional distinction opened beyond.

He was 'George' to me, a hand-picked Yugoslav volunteer with an unpronouncable name (it was Jor-something-ivic) who was living in England. He had been selected in 1941 by the Special Operations Executive in London to be brought out to Egypt, briefed by the SOE in Cairo and eventually dropped in his homeland by the Special Liberator Flight, based at Fayid, in the Canal Zone. His immediate task would then be to make contact with, and assist, General Mihailovic and his Cetnik resistance movement, and maintain a radio link with Cairo.

'George' was quite a character. He would have to be to face the tough, arduous life in the mountain hide-outs with the guerillas he was to join.

From the word 'go' we hit it off and in a few, short days became close friends . . .

In the late days of 1941 and the early days of 1942, Germany, after invading Yugoslavia, bombing Belgrade, obliterating the Royalist army and advancing into the centre of the country, had run up against fierce opposition. Initially, this came from the staunch Royalist officer - General Mihailovic, who, with his Cetniks, was offering stubborn resistance to the German forces by attacking armed convoys, troop movements, railways and bridges.

The Cetniks were operating in bands of some 50 to 100 in well-executed raids in Serbia, Bosnia and Montenegro, taking advantage of their local knowledge and skill in operating from rugged bases in the wild, mountainous territory.

Word was also reaching SOE of another group of resistance fighters called Partisans – Communists under the leadership of Josip Broz (nicknamed Tito) – who were also putting up fierce resistance to the Axis forces in other regions.

Initially, air support was given exclusively to Mihailovic by the British; but then information came through that while the Cetniks were indeed strongly opposing the Germans, there were occasions (and they were becoming more frequent) when Mihailovic, expressing his violently Royalist and anti-Communist feelings, would join forces with the Axis commanders in attacking Tito's Partisans. Civil war in Yugoslavia was on!

It was all very confusing and becoming necessary for reliable officers, with wireless operators, to be sent in to assess the situation. Whom should Britain support? Which was the strongest force of resistance in Yugoslavia? 'George' was part of one mission among several, dropped into the country with supplies to try and unravel the problem. To me, it was one of the toughest and most uncomfortable of the special operations undertaken in the European theatre of war.

To allow these missions to reach their objectives, the agents were to drop out of a Liberator bomber after running the gauntlet of a long and often dangerous flight across the Mediterranean Sea from Fayid to the mountains of Montenegro.

There, pinpoint navigation (aided by Astro-navigation) would take them to a valley in the midst of the high peaks, where the sound of the aircraft's engines would become audible to those waiting on the ground. Fires would then spring to life in the shape of an 'O', a 'T' or 'X' to indicate the dropping zone. This would be followed by the firing of prearranged colour cartridges to identify the guerillas below.

Engines throttled back . . . wheels down . . . flaps down . . . and the pilot of the Liberator would feel his way down between the mountains to make the drop.

'George' would sit on the wooden 'chute' at the rear of the aircraft with his parachute clipped to his harness and also hooked on to the side of the aeroplane, his legs stretched out towards the exit through which he would slide. Two revolvers hung on his belt alongside some knives; bandoliers were slung around his shoulders under the harness, his eyes glued to the amber light up ahead of him as he waited for it to turn green.

Green it is and out he goes!

In the darkness below, he knows that if he misses the fires, it could mean landing among German troops, or a pack of wolves, or in a forest of high trees where he could become suspended. He closes his eyes as the ground approaches, puts his legs together, and waits!

He hits the ground and rolls over, gasps, gathers in his 'chute and looks around to see if he can see others of his mission. He does, and so he sets off with them in this rugged land, which is his land, to reach the fires in the distance – and be among friends. A successful 'drop' has been achieved!

It was not always that way for 'George'.

As a Royal Air Force Warrant Officer and navigator, I met 'George' as he approached our aircraft standing on the tarmac at Fayid in the evening of 23 March, 1942. He was wearing a Royal Air Force brown leather, wool-lined flying jacket, his parachute harness fitted to him. He carried his parachute pack in one hand.

We had met some days before in the briefing room, and something dynamic and magnetic about him had immediately attracted me. I took him back to the Mess for a meal and an evening which was memorable for the tales he told of Yugoslavia and how he longed to go back to his native land.

Now he, and we as a crew, were about to make a first practice 'drop' at night before allowing his dream to become a reality. He came towards me, his face grinning all over and his arms outstretched. Suddenly, I was engulfed in a great 'bear hug'. I was worried that he had no flying helmet; but he said he wasn't comfortable with it and that was that. You did not argue with 'George'.

So we put him on board, showed him the improvised 'exit chute' through which he would leave the aircraft and went through the rest of the procedure.

We took off as the sun dropped below the horizon, climbed to 2000 feet and set off into the neighbouring Desert, where a temporary dropping zone had been marked out. A few lights had been set out to identify it.

Two successful runs were made to drop 'containers' well within the dropping zone. Then came 'George's' turn. The despatcher settled him on the 'exit chute', hooked his parachute on to the aircraft, lined him up ready to leave and waited for the amber light to turn green. I gave the signal as the dropping zone came up to the aircraft's nose. The light turned green, the despatcher thumped 'George' on the back and out he went!

A few brief moments' quiet was shattered by a shout from the rear gunner in his turret. 'The parachute hasn't opened, Skipper. He's still hanging on the end of his strap. I'm looking straight into his face!'

Obviously the release pin on his parachute was faulty and hadn't pulled free to release the cover and let the parachute silk open. Probably it was badly bent. We climbed a couple of thousand feet and tried a few short dives and climbs to shake him free, but to no avail!

Once again we heard the voice of the rear gunner. 'He's still there, skipper. He's twirling round on the end of his line!'

What to do? We certainly couldn't go back to base and land; we'd kill him. There was only one thing we could do – gain a little more height, put the Liberator into a dive and then make a succession of dives and climbs more vicious and powerful than before. The voice of a very relieved rear gunner eventually came through. 'He's gone, skipper!'

When 'George' was finally brought in from the Desert and back to base he looked awful! All the twisting and turning on the end of his line had battered his face, cutting and bruising it badly. One of his ears was a sorry mess and needed stitching. There was no way that he would be able to make the forthcoming drop into Yugoslavia. He would then have to wait another month for the next moon – that is if, after his nerve-wracking experience, he would ever want to make another parachute descent!

Being 'George' he was furious about this, but, after protesting volubly and repeatedly, he accepted the inevitable decision to wait a further month.

We celebrated his survival a few days later by throwing a magnificent party for him in our Mess. There he left us, ostensibly to return to his quarters in Cairo. We later discovered that, in fact, he had gone straight along to an Army camp where he had friends, hitch-hiked his way up the Desert to the front line and got involved in the fighting with the 8th Army. 'George's' one aim in life was to 'get at' the Germans – any Germans.

He came back in time for the drop the next month.

We had confirmation that it was highly successful, that all members of the mission had landed safely in the dropping zone and that they had been able to join up with the Cetniks. All this came through to us via SOE in Cairo from the wireless operators who had dropped with them.

As we did a last circuit of the fires in Yugoslavia before setting course for home, I like to think that 'George' gave me a wave from his beloved homeland. I know I offered a little salute to a very brave man and an unforgettable character as I sat at my navigation table and drew a line in the direction of the Mediterranean and home!

I have often wondered what happened to him.

Denis Bryant,
Cottesloe,
Western Australia

M. T. St John (Pat) Pattle
NO OPTION FOR PATTLE

Air fighting in World War II had much in common with playing games. It is one reason why, for example, the adept cricketer or baseball striker, the opportunist fly-half or quarter back was so quickly into his stride at the controls of a Hurricane or Spitfire, a P-47 Thunderbolt or P-51D Mustang.

Another similarity between the two was the utter uselessness of trying to compare the outstanding performer in one theatre with the nonpareil in another. There never was a like-with-like basis upon which to pronounce judgement; circumstances were far too disparate.

It follows, therefore, that any attempt to make a comparison between the prowess of Pat Pattle, the great South African exponent of early Middle Eastern fighting, with that of his later counterparts in the West, will be fatally flawed. Operating conditions, aeroplanes, opportunities and odds were altogether too diverse.

What is undeniable, however, is that Pattle, as a professional operator, was, in his time and place, wholly exceptional, an unforgettable player in the Big League, whose contribution far transcended the normal expectation of duty.

Here, then, ready to testify to the fact, are two first-hand judges of this character – the Allies' answer to Marseille – whom relatively few had the chance to come to know. First, Air Marshal Sir Patrick Dunn – Paddy Dunn – an officer of intellect, balance and experience, who commanded 80 Squadron in the Middle East at a time when Pattle was, first, a member and then a flight commander of it. And second, the Cranwell-trained Wing Commander G. V. W. Kettlewell – Jim Kettlewell – who knew the South African as well as anyone, serving or operating with him for more than three years, and having the signal advantage of flying with him in 1941 in the rigours and inequalities of the fighting in Greece. Let us, first, set the stage for these two portrayals.

Squadron Leader Marmaduke Thomas St John Pattle (the Royal Air Force shortened it all to Pat – Pat Pattle) came from an extensive and relatively senior military background with strong British antecedents. His upbringing on his father's farm in South Africa, in wild and rugged country, encouraged a sharpness of eye and a ready instinct with a gun. Rugby football, which he played well, was an obsession.

An overwhelming desire to fly military aircraft was initially thwarted by the South African Air Force with its rejection of his services in the mid-1930s. He then looked overseas – to the Royal Air Force, which proved a more prescient judge with the grant of a short service commission.

By 1938, Pattle was a fighter pilot with 80 Squadron, based at Ismailia in the Canal Zone of Egypt, already possessed of the finest flying training in the world. To this he could add the advantage of serving with high-quality contemporaries whom Paddy Dunn saw through the acute eyes of a CO.

My impression was of a collection of tall, confident, blond, blue-eyed young men who took up a lot of room and were untroubled by any doubts. Their Squadron was one any officer would be proud to command.

Pat stood out among them being dark, middle height, spare, well built but not large. His cast of countenance was more thoughtful, perhaps because he had not had an easy run from earthling to airman: perhaps because he saw ahead as others did not. Relatively unobtrusive, he was soon to be a Flight Commander with a reputation. No other could get on his tail and stay there: few could prevent him getting on theirs: his lively handling brought suspicion that he over-strained his aircraft, but no visible confirmation was ever produced. Day by day, he methodically pieced together his science of air fighting and imparted much of it to the pilots in his Flight.

Rather a striking physical feature were his grey-green eyes: remarkable eyes, which seemed to look beyond limits and spot what was coming before others did. Remember, there was no radar in the Middle East – only sharp eyes spotted the enemy.

It was two years before Italy entered the war and the Middle East became a theatre. By then, 80 Squadron was even better trained and impatient to put its skill to the test: rather sorry for the Regia Aeronautica which at first it faced. Fortunate indeed was a Squadron Commander given charge of such a ready-made command. He should have nothing to do save contrive encounters with the enemy.

It was, therefore, a considerable shock for me to be wakened in a sticky dawn twilight in Egypt in August 1940, only a few days into the Italian war, to be told that four pilots (out of four) – Pat Pattle, Wykeham-Barnes,* Lancaster and Rew – patrolling from an advanced landing ground, were missing. A follow-up signal relieved, but did not dispel, the gloom – Lancaster back, badly wounded; Pat and Wykeham-Barnes baled out; Rew down in flames. Not an encouraging opening stand.

First aid to morale might be required, but in the event was not. The two parachutists walked homeward and were picked up by the Army.

Pat described the engagement in cool, analytical terms. He had shot down two of the enemy before being overwhelmed by numbers and forced to bale out at 400 feet, which he seemed to consider unremarkable. He described his parachute springing in the cockpit; debating whether to pick it up and throw it out and follow, or grasp it to him and go out together: neither course a problem, both coherently registered in a mind totally under control.

He described the formation aerobatics of the Italian pilots with tolerant amusement and felt as if he had been an intruder in a rehearsal for a Hendon Air Pageant. Now he looked for a return fixture to put things straight. This was managed within a few days when Pat led a Flight and scored two more.

Shortly came the saddening but understandable division of 80 into two Squadrons. One Flight was hived off to become 274, the first Hurricane squadron in the Middle East, and Pat stayed with 80 Squadron and its Gladiators.

He then went from strength to strength, first in the Western Desert, but soon in Greece, where he became a legend in command of 33 Squadron, equipped with Hurricanes. He was now playing his winning hand, but in a losing battle.

This was a dreadful campaign conducted under a variety of discomforts and privations. The weather was atrocious; accommodation makeshift and even unhygienic; food poor; movement continual as squadrons, flights and sections dispersed and were harried in retreat from landing ground to landing ground. There was no radar, poor radio, and our fighters were outclassed and outnumbered by Me.109s alone. In this desperate situation only steadfast grip and resourceful reaction could delay the slide. Nothing could stop it.

Pat proved a superlative example in command of 33 Squadron: competent on the ground, brilliant in the air, courageous wherever he was and piling up a personal score which there was neither time nor person to record, or extol, for posterity.

Whether his 41 confirmed victories is the whole or part of his total, nobody knows. His greater achievement was as multiplier for the less experienced, teacher of the less talented, and comforter of the fearful

* Later, Air Marshal Sir Peter Wykeham.

whom he fortified with his own confidence and for whom he made a bleak outlook seem hopeful.

Had he operated in Western Europe or the later African campaigns his name, score and fame would have spread into all the books. Indeed, he would not have been killed, as he was on 20 April, 1941, flying with a fever upon him. A Group Captain or doctor, or both, would have been around to ground him until fit again. In Greece, there was no such person. Pat, commander on the spot, sole judge of his condition, man in charge, holding the bridge, followed his conscience, driven by his sense of duty; he led and fought, his few outclassed Hurricanes against a host of Me.109s and was overwhelmed.

A self-reliant fighting man of unquenchable spirit and peerless perform-ance to whom fearful odds appeared no more than evens, left to himself, could do no less. For Pat, there was no option.

Patrick Dunn,
Cookham Dean,
Berkshire

> Jim Kettlewell, (Wing Commander G. V. W. Kettlewell), fellow offi-cer and intimate friend of the South African, rounds off the Pattle study.

Although much of what happened in those days is clouded with the passage of half a century, Pat left an impression which is just about indelible.

On the surface, there was nothing arrogant or aggressive about him, but, like the rest of us he did not take kindly to being worsted. One evening, when I was returning with him from Cairo to Helwan in his Auburn motor car, he underpaid the garage man, who had, he reckoned, given him short measure at the pump.

When Pat started to move off, the unfortunate man threw himself on to the bonnet and was thereupon taken protesting, and at speed, several miles from the city and then dumped unceremoniously to make his own way back . . .

When the Squadron left Egypt for Greece, Pat's score, I think, was ten and this continued to mount steadily . . . In the end, he was a double DFC, but I believe that decorations and fame were of minor concern to him. He would, for example, offer suitable targets to other members of his Flight at the expense of his personal score . . . The satisfaction of a job thoroughly well done was reward enough.

That the Squadron was so successful was due in no small part to his clear briefing before take-off, his intuition for tactical positioning and his skill in handling a formation when an attack was developing. If things went wrong, his debriefing would be constructive rather than derogatory. Aware of the importance of morale, he was quick to give praise where he thought it was due.

On one occasion I was leading a Flight as top cover to his on an eventful patrol and, by some miracle, had managed to keep him in sight. His praise for 'brilliant sub-leading' was fulsome. 'Whenever I looked up,' he said, 'there you were, ideally positioned.'

I recall, too, at the end of another particularly active patrol, led by Pat, I had to force-land in an Albanian field. When he got back to base and found I was missing, he immediately resaddled his aircraft and flew back to the combat zone to try to locate me.

He found the aircraft first and then, in due course, me; but he need not have come – or he could well have sent someone else.

He did much the same on an earlier occasion in the Western Desert. He heard that the CO of a neighbouring Blenheim squadron was reported missing. On his own initiative, he wrote out a message asking for information and then flew low over the middle of the nearest enemy camp and dropped it; such was Pat's comradeship.

He lost his life in a great air battle over Athens. It is known that, in a milling crowd of aircraft, he increased his own score and then went to the rescue of others before himself succumbing.

I firmly believe that he was a frugal claimer . . . Who knows what his total score might have been had he been credited with everything due to him? He was the complete fighter pilot and leader and, on that day over Athens, the Luftwaffe did itself a better turn than ever it knew. Pat will always be top scorer in my 'Hall of Fame'.

(It is worth recording, as a tailpiece, that at a symposium of a Greek historical society held recently in Athens to study the air war in that theatre, it became very clear that, nearly 50 years on, the name 'Pattle' is still revered in Greece. He is remembered as an outstanding defender of the country's freedom.)

Jim Kettlewell,
Virginia Water,
Surrey

Roman Czerniawski
BRAVE POLISH 'TURNCOAT'

Tadeusz Andersz, (Squadron Leader T. Andersz), vice-president of the Polish Air Force Association in Collingham Gardens in London's South West 5 district, is a patriotic figure to whom his country's former (and still fervent) air force community is easily drawn. Behind him lies a composite story of courage and endurance in war and peace which touches the extremities of human endeavour.

A young trainee officer and pilot of the Polish Air Force pre-war, Andersz fought with the French Air Force in the Battle of France until the collapse in June 1940, made his way to England in a 240-ton Dutch cargo ship and then joined his countrymen in 315 Squadron, ultimately becoming its commanding officer some four years or so later when, with its long-range P-51D Mustangs, it took its place in 133 Wing of 84 Group in the Second Tactical Air Force.

In the interim, there had been a sojurn in the Polish Wing at Northolt in Fighter Command and then, at the urging of his mate, Francis (Gabby) Gabreski, a spell with the 61st Squadron in Hub Zemke's 56 Fighter Group, during the US Eighth Air Force's relentless daylight offensive against Nazi Germany in 1943 and 1944.

Nor did the flying end with World War II. There were other missions to add to the sum of his extensive and well-decorated experience.

In a phrase, Tad Andersz has had 'quite a career'. Consider, then, the circumstances which surround his selection of a character for study.

The contribution of the Polish Air Force to the Allied air effort was a determined, ruthlessly discharged, aggressive affair. Here was a relatively small, professionally efficient force which obtained results out of all proportion to its size. Its output per man was exceptional, its dedication complete. But the losses also were great. More than 2500 of its aircrew did not survive.

And what of the outcome of such selfless endeavour? The vision of a free and independent Poland was as remote after six years of battle as ever. We, in Britain, had gone to war in the first place that Poland might be freed from the Nazi yoke. But no sooner had victory been won, and the aim achieved, than another regime, equally repressive and cruel, was clamped on her brave people.

After the conferences of Tehran, Potsdam and Yalta had redrawn the map of Europe, Poland, despite all her exertions in the Allied cause, found herself a vassal state of the Soviet Union. Her fate became a gnawing tragedy of the post-war world.

But such a depressing background cannot cloud Polish courage in the war years. Tad Andersz picks an example which, for sustained nerve and tenacity, can hardly be beaten.

Roman Czerniawski was a regular officer in the Polish Air Force. When war broke out, he held the rank of captain with a pilot's qualification. To further his career, he had obtained the diploma from the Warsaw Staff College and from the *École Supérieure de Guerre*, in Paris. He was trilingual.

When France capitulated, he stayed behind the enemy's lines in the occupied zone and, together with two other Polish officers of the Intelligence Service, organised, in Toulouse, in July 1940, the first secret cell in France. In November, he moved to Paris and under the cryptic name 'Armand' he formed an intelligence agency – *'Interallié'* – with the intention of covering the whole of occupied France.

During the next 12 months, this tightly organised espionage net sent many important messages to its sources in Britain with whom it had radio contact. Often, four messages would be sent in a single day. The information included the de-coded *Ordre de Bataille* of the German armed forces – a remarkably accurate transmission which covered de-ciphered details relating to the 22 German divisions and their locations, 120 airfields and the movements of the pride of the German navy, the battle-cruisers, *Scharnhorst* and *Gneisenau*.

After this, and a dozen crossings of the German border, plus a pick-up by a British Special Duties Lysander from the occupied zone – and a parachuted return – Roman Czerniawski reckoned he had the measure of the espionage game. But then his luck ran out.

At first light on 18 November, 1941, Roman, together with his net of 64 agents of mixed nationalities, was arrested by the German *Abwehr** and imprisoned at Fresnes, near Paris. By an unfortunate mischance, the Germans had tracked down Roman's headquarters. His secretary, who was of Swiss/French origin, did the rest. She betrayed every member of

* Germany Military Intelligence.

Interallié and, as such, became the principal character in the famous 'La Chatte' double, double-agent affair.

Some idea of the measure of co-operation which existed between *Interallié* and its London counterpart can be judged from the final radio message received by the French-based net. 'Very important, very urgent. Imperative you find new routing for your direct transmissions in the Cherbourg region.' Alas, the warning came too late . . .

As Tad Andersz recounts, the events that followed the arrest of Czerniawski and his 64 disciples were complex, nerve-wracking and, to those innocent of the ways of espionage, almost incredible. Throughout the awful hours of interrogation and haggling with his German captors, one thought remained uppermost in Roman's mind – how to introduce some subterfuge whereby his followers might be saved from the virtual certainty of death by firing squad.

On the German side, there had been astonishment at the measure of success which *Interallié* had achieved in gathering and transmitting secret information. Indeed, so impressed had Colonel Oskar Reile, the head of German counter-intelligence, been with the information gleaned from a probing of Czerniawski's headquarters that he mounted an exhibition of the findings at his own HQ in St Germain, near Paris, as a warning to others of the sinister quality of the enemy's espionage network.

For General Karl-Heinrich Stülpnagel, the Germans' Paris-based Military Governor in France, the discoveries posed a different question. Why could not similar, extensive information about the Allies' military strengths in Britain, and their plans, be obtained?

And this, in turn, provoked another thought. Could not the brilliant Czerniawski – this small, quiet, unassuming and softly spoken Pole, whose astute mind and intellect hid a will of steel, be turned to the advantage of the Fatherland? Might he not be 'persuaded' to set up a model of *Interallié* in Britain? The bargaining counter would be his own life and the lives of his 64 agents now in captivity.

When the ploy was put to him, Roman was alive to one of the prime rules of espionage – that of 'co-operation' by 'disinformation', the regular stock-in-trade of the double agent. He was also aware of the price to be paid by his betrayed adherents if he did not 'co-operate'. He placed their fate before his own . . .

In the long-drawn-out poker game that followed, Czerniawski offered 'co-operation' in exchange for three undertakings:

1   A guarantee from the German government of privileged status for Poland in the eventual peace treaty if his actions contributed to Germany's victory over communism (i.e. over Russia).

2   Prisoner-of-war status for his 64 agents, and their transfer to prison instead of the concentration camp – or death – and

3   No secret German intelligence surveillance after his release from captivity and the subsequent prosecution of his 'co-operative' plan.

After days and nights and weeks of pressure-bargaining with the Stülpnagel and Reile, Czerniawski's terms were accepted and confirmed by Admiral Canaris, the head of Central Intelligence in Berlin. The plan was to be given immediate expression. Overnight, 'Armand' of *Interallié* would become 'Brutus', 'Armand's' counterpart in Britain.

After a series of clandestine moves, the Pole crossed the Spanish frontier and made his way to the British Embassy in Madrid. There, he partially disclosed the plan, after which he was accompanied by the British Consul to Gibraltar, where an aircraft was waiting to take him to Britain.

After meetings in England with Colonel Stanislaw Gano, chief of the Polish Intelligence Service, and then with General Sikorski, the Polish Prime Minister-in-Exile and C-in-C of the Polish Armed Forces, Roman Czerniawski and his plan, code-named 'Big Game', were passed on to the British Intelligence Service. It required all Czerniawski's persuasion to convince the British authorities of the authenticity and practicality of the projected operation. He threw down his trump card on the table – the safety of his 64 collaborators remaining condemned in enemy hands.

Argument prevailed, an organisation was agreed, and 'Operation Big Game', which was later to be blended with 'Operation Fortitude' – the much larger and more comprehensive undertaking designed to convince the enemy of the Allies' intention of landing in the Pas de Calais – was to be directed initially from a house on Richmond Hill, Surrey. Tad Andersz picks up the story.

'Brutus' sent his first message to Germany at the beginning of January 1943. As British Intelligence recognised that the enemy might well evaluate the messages as false, it was decided to feed a measure of strictly correct information, often only temporary in character, but none the less important.

At first, Colonel Reile was disappointed with the meagre quality of Roman's messages; but, later, 'information' fed by the Germans' 'double-cross' network in Britain* tended to confirm the validity of 'Brutus's' transmissions, and belief in the Pole's trust was established.

It is important to mention that the knowledge of the Germans' reaction

---

* Many of the enemy's agents had been rounded up in Britain and were now working, under Allied control, in a 'double' capacity – Ed.

was obtained by de-coding messages circulating between their staffs and units. The code-busting apparatus used for this was derived from '*Bombe*', a clever modification to the Germans' cipher machine, *Enigma*, which, in a cunningly conceived reconstruction, three Poles had been able brilliantly to develop, pre-war, and make available, in great secrecy, to Britain and France. The resultant unravelling of the German codes was of incalculable value to the Allies and lay at the base of Britain's palpably successful *Ultra* intelligence net centred upon Bletchley Park in Buckinghamshire. An example of a reconstructed *Enigma* machine can be seen today, in all its historic importance, at the Polish Institute and Sikorski Museum at Prince's Gate, in London.

> With the early planning of the invasion of the Continent, 'Brutus' and his 'Big Game' operation were absorbed within 'Operation Fortitude', with its all-embracing activities, and the Richmond HQ moved forward into Kent. As D-Day approached, the aim was to confirm the enemy in his belief that, for obvious strategic reasons, the main cross-channel thrust would focus upon the Boulogne-Calais area, falsified initially by a dummy run to Normandy. The Allies' complex and elaborate plan, to which 'Brutus' was making his own significant contribution, was completed by early May 1944, perfectly timed, as Andersz now shows, to precede the opening of *Overlord*.*

A search of the German archives after the war revealed that the enemy's maps, dated 15 May, 1944, had embraced the up-to-date information transmitted by 'Brutus' and his Allied colleagues. An accompanying annotation by General Jodl, then at Hitler's Central HQ, confirmed the effectiveness of the deception. 'Seven signals from the agent,' he noted, 'enable us to reproduce the entire plan for the Allied invasion.'

After the D-Day landings on 6 June, the transmissions continued to 'substantiate' the illusion that the main assault would still be mounted across the narrow Straits to the Pas de Calais. Such was the strength of the impression created by Operation Fortitude upon the German High Command that, two days before D-Day, Field Marshal von Rundstedt, the Commander-in-Chief in the West, told his staff that he did not expect the invasion in the next few days.

At the same time Field Marshal Rommel, commanding Army Group 'B', comprising the 7th Army in Normandy and the 15th in the Pas de Calais, seized the opportunity provided by his wife's birthday to take a short leave and visit her at Ulm, their home in Germany.

On the actual day of the massive landings in Normandy, 'Brutus' had sent Colonel Reile the following message: 'Today I personally saw the

* Code name for the Invasion Plan.

King with Churchill and Eisenhower at the Headquarters of the 1st American Army Group in Dover with General Patton outlining the likely deployment of his troops.' *Ultra* was able to confirm that the information was passed at once to the German commanders and that it was on Hitler's desk some 30 minutes after its transmission from England . . .

With the advance of the Allies through France and into the Low Countries, the long-awaited news of the release of the 63 agents (one had died while in prison) by British troops came in January 1945. However, because of the operation of the Official Secrets Act and the then 50 years' rule of secrecy, they never knew to whom they owed their lives nor could they be made aware of the real extent of their leader's achievements.

'Operation Fortitude' had been proved to be an unqualified success. It had saved countless thousands of lives and casualties. Although more than 40 agents were engaged in it, none doubted the contribution which Roman Czerniawski had himself made to its success.

This courageous officer – 'Armand' alias 'Brutus' – who had been invested with the Polish Virtuti Militari and Polonia Restituta, the Cross of Valour with two bars, the British OBE and the French Croix de Guerre, died on 30 May, 1985. His ashes were laid in the Polish Air Force Cemetery at Newark, in Nottinghamshire.

At his funeral, we, his friends and comrades, paid homage to a great patriot, bowing our heads in salutation and praying for his soul and his salvation.

Tadeusz Andersz,
Kensington,
London

John MacGown
SMO EXTRAORDINARY

Alex Thorne (Squadron Leader G. Alex Thorne), for many years the distinguished editor of the Royal Air Forces Association's *Air Mail*, built a decorated war on precision.

After 18 months of instructing, he completed a course at the Royal Air Force College, Cranwell, learning about meteorology, navigation and flying twin-engined aircraft. With that behind, it was an easy step to four-engined aeroplanes, but less easy, one suspects, than to have settled, in the testing months of 1943, into the Pathfinder Force's 635 Squadron with its Lancasters, based at Downham Market in Norfolk . . . And even less easy still to have earned the right to join that élite set of captains called 'Master Bombers' – and succeeded.

'If you want to see something in the dark, don't look too hard for it.'

That advice, given to aircrew in World War II by Wing Commander John Cecil MacGown, DFC, MD, ChB, was always an effective opening to a talk on night vision training. It was, of course, subject to further elucidation to show that there was a degree of sense in it, especially in the early days of the war, when bomber aircrews were flying for hours on night raids over a blacked-out Germany. Their aircraft were equipped with little more than a compass, airspeed indicator and an altimeter, and until H2S and other radar aids became available only a small percentage of their bombs were being delivered within a radius of three miles of the targets.

At the beginning of World War I MacGown had interrupted his medical studies at Edinburgh University to join the Royal Flying Corps. He survived three years as a fighter pilot, apart from being shot down once and eventually escaping. At the end of that war he returned to Scotland and completed his medical course five years later. He had always hankered to visit the Far East, so off he went to join a doctors' practice in Hong Kong, where he learned to speak Cantonese fluently and became Commodore of the Hong Kong Flying Club. Whilst out there he met Marjorie, a newly arrived nursing sister at the General Hospital. She still speaks about the time he asked her to marry him. She said 'yes' and he replied 'Good . . . What's your name?' (If Doc had a failing it was that he could not remember names!) Then came World War II – not because he married her, of course – and back he came to join the RAFVR in the Medical Branch.

Doc was posted as ophthalmic specialist to Bomber Command, where he became increasingly concerned by the losses among aircrew on night raids. He spent a lot of time helping them to understand and apply the techniques that could be used to improve their night vision. His 'to find it don't look at it' advice, for instance, was based on the fact that in the dark one is apt to concentrate too fiercely in a direct line towards where the object of one's search may be, ignoring the fact that the range of vision encompasses a much wider area, especially in the lateral plane, if proper use is made of the parts of the eye's retina known as 'rods'.

Anyone can test this by concentrating on an object directly ahead and, without moving the eyes away from that object, make a conscious effort to look also at objects to the side. It is surprising how one can become more aware of their existence at that moment.

Through Doc other aids became available for pilots, bomb-aimers and gunners – anti-glare searchlight glasses, and special eye drops to improve night vision by dilating the pupils, were among the methods employed to reduce the strain of night operations and he never ceased in his efforts to make things easier and safer for the aircrews. Nor did he do it all in the safety and comfort of his office.

When Doc – a tall, lean, fair-haired, craggy Scot, then in his mid-forties – announced that he wanted to go with one of the crews on a night operation he was met with the reply: 'You cannot. You are a doctor and therefore a non-combatant.' He replied: 'I believe I can go as a doctor on optical research and to study at first hand the effects of combat operations among aircrews.' Soon afterwards he went on his first op – to Berlin in a Lancaster. It was the first of 52 operations he flew with different crews on most of the major enemy targets.

On 15 August 1942, a new Group was formed in Bomber Command. It was the Pathfinder Force commanded by Air Vice-Marshal Don Bennett. Its main task was to plan the bombers' routes to the targets and spearhead the attacks by marking them with coloured flares, acting as target indicators. Bennett recruited his personnel from the most experienced airmen and it was not surprising that Doc was appointed the Pathfinders' Senior Medical Officer. It was not long before he had established a reputation among the squadrons in the new Group with his concern for the well-being of all who served in them.

For example, he knew that the last two or three operations in a crew's 'tour' was a particularly nervy time for it. Its members had survived so far and, in their language, the possibility of getting the chop in the final run-up was a thought which often could not be dismissed from their minds.

The last trip was the worst – and Doc understood. On many occasions he arranged for one of his 'optical research' trips to coincide with a crew's last sortie so that he could go with it to lend, as he described it, a spot of moral support. It never failed.

When Pathfinder crews had proved their efficiency – usually when they had completed around fifteen operations – they became entitled to wear the Pathfinder badge over the left pocket of their jackets. It was in the order of things that Doc received his award, and he was as proud of it as he was of the pilot's brevet awarded to him in World War I. A couple of months later he attended one of the regular meetings of Bomber Command MOs, some of whom were taken aback when they saw the Pathfinder badge on his tunic. On his return to headquarters he was told by Don Bennett that an order had been received from the powers-that-be to the effect that Doc must take down his badge because 'as a doctor he was classed as a non-combatant in the present war'.

Doc was too big a man to argue. He unpinned the badge and handed it to Bennett, who had only five words to say – just 'Leave it to me, Doc.' It must have been nearly a year later when Doc received a letter from Air Chief Marshal Sir Arthur Harris congratulating him on the award of the Distinguished Flying Cross. Later that day Bennett handed back to Doc his Pathfinder badge and told him that his DFC was in recognition of his participation in many operations against the enemy over a long period in the war.

When the war ended Doc went into practice as an ophthalmic specialist in Wimpole Street, London. He also took a leading part in establishing the Pathfinder Association and Club in Mayfair. One of the objects of the Association was to assist ex-Pathfinders in every possible way on their return to civilian life and he was personally responsible for introducing many of them into worthwhile jobs. He was President of the Association for five years until he and Marjorie moved to the Isle of Islay, off the West Coast of Scotland, where they spent many happy years together. Sadly, Doc died in 1979. Marjorie is still there leading an active life in their house and with her many friends on that beautiful island.

Alex Thorne,
Thames Ditton,
Surrey

J. R. D. (Bob) Braham
THE NIGHT THAT 'CHIEFY' RAND WEPT

What's in a night-intruder crew? Plenty. And few could provide as much as the combination of Michael Allen (Flight Lieutenant M. S. Allen), the author of this study, and his redoubtable pilot in No. 141 Squadron, Harry White (Air Commodore H. E. White).

In terms of operational duty (and escapes) you couldn't separate them. For four years of war they shared their tenuous lives going through the gamut of night-fighter roles. They made an effective, independent pair who knew most of the questions – and the answers – and who were adept at playing down their own considerable achievements.

There weren't many crews who collected, as they did, half a dozen DFCs between them – three apiece – and were still scoring victories in the closing months of the war. Between them, during three tours, one in Fighter and two in Bomber Command, they completed 106 missions together and had 13 victories on the slate when the opposition called it a day.

It provides Michael Allen with the background to assess the qualities which made Bob Braham, one-time CO of 141, the most successful intruder of them all – the unquenchable Braham who was to die prematurely in Canada in 1974, aged 52, with his flying honours still thick upon him.

It was the autumn of 1943 ... John Randell Daniel Braham (the Royal Air Force called him Bob because in his previous Squadron, No. 29, there were already three 'Johns' and they didn't want another) was commanding 141 Squadron in 100 Group of Bomber Command. For the past three months he had been pioneering the first night-intruder sorties (code name: Serrate), planned directly in support of Bomber Command's night offensive against targets in Germany and occupied Europe.

Our task in the Squadron was to seek out and destroy German night fighters which were then reaping such a terrible harvest among the four-engined Lancasters, Halifaxes and Stirlings as they infiltrated the bomber stream, pursuing it through the target area and harrying it on the way home.

Braham, aided by his navigator, the exceptional Flight Lieutenant W. J. (Sticks) Gregory (later Wing Commander with the DSO, DFC and bar and DFM), had planned and flown the first of these high-level support operations in June of the same year. In the next three months, he and Sticks Gregory had proved the worth of these missions, shooting down seven German night fighters and damaging two more.

It was the success of these sorties, under Braham's leadership, which had resulted in 141, re-equipped with Mosquitoes in place of its Beaufighters, being transferred from Fighter to Bomber Command and 100 Group, the entity which contained the squadrons then being trained in the use of the new radar counter-measures. Indeed, so successful did these operations become that, by the war's end, they had reduced significantly the menace posed by the Luftwaffe's *Nachjagdgeschwader* (night fighter) units.

By then, Bob Braham had brought his own total for the war to 29 enemy aircraft destroyed and, as the *Guinness Book of Records* now confirms, his tally of decorations, uniquely, to three DSOs and three DFCs – a record that is likely to stand the test of time.

But now, on this autumn day of 1943, three crews of 141 Squadron were preparing to take off on another series of bomber support missions. In the twilight of a beautifully soft evening the countryside looked marvellous – particularly to those of us who were about to leave it!

There was Bob, the CO and Sticks Gregory, who had been operating together for some three years; there was Harry White and myself, who had also been around for some time without having much to show for it; and, additionally, there was a new crew – the pilot, a young flight sergeant, and his navigator, a sergeant.

I suppose, as the 'pre-match' tension built up, as we walked a few paces, yawned and walked back or as one or other of us disappeared behind the adjacent hangar for a last-minute relieving action, the new pilot felt that someone ought to say something. Turning to Bob Braham, he managed, despite his dried-up throat (which I certainly also had!), to blurt out: 'I – I suppose it's all right for you, sir . . . I don't expect you feel anything!'

Even Harry and I were taken aback by the vehemence of the CO's reply. He swung round and almost snarled out, 'Don't be such a bloody – – ' (the remaining words were new to the young flight sergeant), and then in a much warmer tone he said: ' – – of course I do, and it gets worse every time – – '

In retrospect, this exchange, first of rebuff, but then of encouragement and understanding, is interesting. It proves that that trite phrase, sometimes used to describe men like Braham with an exceptional record of front-line service, 'Of course he didn't know the meaning of the word fear . . . ', as being very far from the truth.

The CO was showing that he felt just the same as the rest of us before an 'op'. It was what he felt and did *after* take-off wherein lay the difference. Here, the words of our highly-regarded Intelligence Officer, Buster Reynolds (later Alderman Cedric Hinton Fleetwood Reynolds JP, a solicitor by profession), who knew Bob better than any of us, got to the heart of it. 'Bob Braham's 100 per cent dedication and commitment to the task, whatever it might be, set him apart from other people and lesser mortals.'

Braham's unrehearsed asides in moments of operational stress told us much about the man's personality and character. There had been a revealing moment a few weeks before, on 17 August, 1943, at the time of Bomber Command's critical attack on Peenemunde. One flight of 141 had seen the bombers out and the other saw them in. Harry White remembers it well.

'Bob, with A Flight, was back on the ground 1½ hours after take-off, well before we, in B Flight, set off. Diffidently and politely, as behoved a Flying Officer talking to a Wing Commander, but perhaps with just a tone of slight remonstration in my voice, I said, "You are back early tonight?"

'His instant reply was typical and had that ring of truth and bravado. "Anyone who gets two is entitled to be back early." We all knew the pressing feeling of wanting to set off home even after one kill, let alone two!

'However, in a curious, paradoxical way, Bob's manifest reticence could be said to have acted against the potential success of the rest of the Squadron. He never told us "how he did it". Most of us learnt a fair part of our trade exchanging stories in the bar, late into the night. Bob seldom joined those groups. He didn't share his experiences with the rest of us. We all knew how successful he was, but he seldom, if ever, explained what he did and how.

'I do not suggest that Bob should have given us a demo himself, but it could perhaps have been a help had he done more to explain his methods to the rest of us. It was all a bit like that epic Spitfire briefing we overheard at Tangmere one day in 1941 when the Wing Leader rushed out from the phone in dispersal and only had time to shout "Button B, you bastards"* before setting off with the whole wing for France.

'As to his independent mind, he was certainly "his own man". He did things his way and didn't take kindly to being told by others (Group in particular) what he ought to be doing. In the early days at Wittering, he would draw a line on a map, almost at random, and that became the route for the night. It was as good a way of doing it as any . . . '

Braham probably enjoyed being what he was – a successful and dis-

---

* Indicating the channel to use on the radio telephone in the aircraft.

tinguished Air Force officer. And that, indeed, was what he looked ...
Young (he was 22 when he was promoted to Wing Commander), clean
shaven, narrowed blue eyes, lips pursed with the hint of a mischievous grin
never far away and a noticeably square chin. With a thick crop of fair hair
brushed straight back and parted in the middle, he was of striking appearance. Added to this, he was well built and had the alert, energetic figure
of a boxer, a sport at which he was no mean hand!

Looking back now, I have the impression that, had he lived in a different
age, grown a great flaxen beard and worn a winged metal helmet, instead
of a leather one, he would have looked just like the Viking chiefs of one's
imagination. Nor is this being too fanciful, because his philosophy of life
had much in common with theirs – although you would have been treated
to some very Anglo-Saxon phrases if you had tried to tell him so!

Bob, whose father had been Vicar of Duxford, the parish which included
the well-known Cambridgeshire airfield, from 1940 to 1942, was, in fact,
one of the most outstanding fighter pilots Britain has ever produced, with
his wartime career settling into three clear-cut phases. The first was from
September 1939 until December 1942, when he was operating with 29
Squadron within Fighter Command mainly on home defence by night, but
sometimes by day, particularly in bad weather. He rose to command A
Flight with the rank of Squadron Leader.

From January to October 1943, he was commanding 141 Squadron as
a Wing Commander and then, thirdly, there was a spell on the night
operations staff at 2 Group HQ, ostensibly to give him a rest from operational flying. In fact, by an arrangement he came to with his AOC, Air
Vice-Marshal Basil Embry, one of the few senior officers whom he held
in awe and esteem, he continued to fly offensive missions, being restricted
to one every seven days. The truth was that, for Bob Braham, operational
flying acted like a drug, and the addiction was intense.

Between February and June 1944, during his time on the staff, he would
go off in a Mosquito in daylight, often taking some highly surprised,
'resting' navigator with him to scour the occupied countries and Germany
at low level. These operations were called Rangers; and Rangers, as practised by Braham, were, in fact, a blank cheque to go looking for trouble.
On 24 June, flying his 313th sortie of the war, he found it over Denmark
in the form of two Focke-Wulf 190s, which shot his aircraft down close
to the coast.

By a superhuman piece of airmanship, Bob managed to crash-land his
Mosquito, with port engine and wing ablaze, safely on a beach. He and
his navigator were then fortunately able to scramble clear of the aircraft
uninjured, to be taken prisoners-of-war. Wing Commander (Night Ops)
at 2 Group had finally met his match.

There was a revealing and intensely moving sequel to this
shattering loss.

Flight Sergeant William Rand, Bill Rand, better known to 141 as 'Chiefy' Rand, was a proud Fitter I, a pre-war Royal Air Force regular and a tough, hard-bitten senior NCO in charge of the ground crews of A Flight. He was the scourge of Fitter IIs and lesser fry and he had looked after the former CO's aircraft all the time that Braham was commanding the Squadron. The standard of maintenance demanded – and given – was implicit in the relationship.

It was July before we heard at West Raynham that Braham and his navigator were both safe and unharmed. The dramatic announcement was made at a Squadron party of pilots and navigators and their ground crews. A roar of spontaneous and prolonged cheering greeted the news.

Flight Sergeant Rand's reaction was quite different. As the others were cheering, he fell to his knees and covered his head with his hands. When, after a moment or two, he got to his feet his eyes were streaming with tears. 'Thank God!' he cried. 'Thank God he's alive.'

It was all he could say . . .

Michael Allen,
Holbeton,
Plymouth,
Devon

Postscript: It is instructive to record the entry in Braham's log-book on 24 March, 1944, shortly before he was shot down. He was flying a Mosquito VI, SY-H, borrowed from 613 Squadron; his navigator was Squadron Leader Robertson and they had moved forward to Coltishall, in Norfolk, for the operation.

Day Ranger – Grove – Aalborg (Denmark): 950 miles. Saw Ju.52 and Ju.34 four miles south of Aalborg. Came up astern of Ju.34 (which had wheels down) and shot it down in flames from 800 feet at 50–100 yards range (2 secs cannon fire). Then chased Ju.52: one attack astern at 150 yards . . . E/A crash-landed in a marsh, 10 miles south Aalborg and turned on its back. Shot it up on the ground. Landed back Swanton Morley.

The utter ruthlessness of the killer pilot.

Final Salute

HM King George VI
THE PILOT WHO WAS CROWNED KING

When Peter Townsend (Group Captain P. W. Townsend) was appointed Equerry to the late King George VI in the early spring of 1944, he was selected from a very short list of hand-picked Royal Air Force wing commanders. Then 29, public school and Cranwell-educated, able, brave and good looking, with easy winning ways, he was regarded by the P Staff officers as a natural. An innate modesty hid a wide operational experience and a total of enemy aircraft destroyed running comfortably into double figures. His decorations matched his record. With a courtier's unaffected manners, he epitomised to a point the meaning of that curious up-market phrase, *persona grata*.

When Peter retired from the Service some 12 years later as a highly publicised Group Captain, he went to live abroad and turned his hand to writing books. He could write and he was successful. Who better, then, to close this collection of remarkable World War II characters with a personal portrayal of arguably the bravest monarch in British history?

One afternoon in February, 1944 I was shown into the green-carpeted Regency Room at Buckingham Palace and into the presence of the late King George VI. Candidate for the post of equerry, yet frankly a young nobody, I had felt some trepidation at the prospect of being closeted alone with His Most Excellent Majesty . . . King of This Realm . . . Defender of the Faith . . . Emperor of India . . . However, I kept reminding myself, he and I have one precious thing in common: we are both RAF pilots. The King had won his wings sixteen years before I was awarded mine; he was the first pilot ever to be crowned King.

He stood there, a slight clean-cut figure in naval uniform – the one that became him most, for he was first and foremost a sailor. His finely chiselled features and large blue eyes, his reassuring smile and quiet, rather shy demeanour made me feel, quite simply, an immediate and natural sympathy for him – all the more so because his stammer occasionally brought his

429

conversation to an abrupt and silent standstill. Having myself a congenital if infrequent stammer, I felt all the more warmly towards him. Of the many adversities that he overcame during his all too short life, his speech defect was perhaps the one which demanded of him the greatest and most enduring courage.

Courage – of the kind that often passes unnoticed – was his supreme quality. As Prince Albert he entered the Royal Naval College, Osborne, in 1909, just after his thirteenth birthday, and was soon noticed as a friendly easy-going personality, a boy who 'shows the grit', and 'never say I'm beaten' spirit. Although almost permanently bottom of his class and sternly but kindly admonished by his father, King George V, the young Prince Albert struggled on bravely and passed into the Royal Naval College, Dartmouth. It was while a cadet there, in 1912, that he first met the man with whom he was later to work so closely in the salvation of his country – Winston Churchill, then First Lord of the Admiralty. It was at Dartmouth, too, that Prince Albert was first afflicted by the gastric trouble which was to cause him such great suffering. At this stage, characteristically he never reported sick. A naval officer who had known him at the time remarked later: 'His courage was amazing'; and another: 'He had tremendous guts. He would never let you down and never asked for a favour.'

At the time the Prince could be quite a devil. He was once punished, with eight others, for 'skylarking' and another time, with a band of friends, for letting off fireworks in the loo.

As a midshipman appointed to the battleship *Collingwood* in September 1913, he was known, for convenience, as 'Mr Johnson'. Not yet nineteen years old, he was aboard the *Collingwood* when war broke out in August 1914. But scarcely had the ship settled down to a war routine when he had to be transferred ashore to be operated on for acute appendicitis. After convalescing, he was sent to an office job in the Admiralty, a thoroughly disconsolate and frustrated young man, only too well aware that thousands of others of his age were doing their bit – and dying – at the front.

Early in 1915 the Prince, now a sub-lieutenant, returned to sea, again in HMS *Collingwood*. But only three months later he was once more suffering terribly from what he called his 'inside troubles' and, for the second time in his short career, invalided ashore for treatment. During the months that followed he wrote time and time again to his father begging to be allowed to return to sea. Finally, when *Collingwood* sailed with the Grand Fleet on 30 May, 1916, to meet the German High Seas Fleet, Prince Albert was again aboard as second in command of 'A' turret. Next day he was living – and apparently enjoying – the full fury of the Battle of Jutland. 'Well does Great Britain merit the Empire of the Seas', wrote a Spanish admiral more than a century before, 'when the humblest stations in her navy are supported by princes of the blood.'

As the summer of 1916 ended, the Prince was struck down yet again by his chronic affliction and yet again transferred to a shore job. Not until May 1917 did he manage to get appointed to the battleship HMS *Malaya*, only to fall seriously ill with the same complaint which, this time, put an end to his career at sea. Rather than lose contact with the Navy, he applied, with the warm approval of his father, to join the Royal Naval Air Service station – HMS *Daedalus* – at Cranwell. Before he could take up his appointment he was prostrated once more by his 'inside troubles'. At last they were diagnosed as a duodenal ulcer and after a successful operation Prince Albert arrived – or, shall we say, went aboard – HMS *Daedalus*, high and dry on the Lincolnshire plateau, in January 1918. For the time being he had a ground job as OC No. 4 Boy Wing.

Although he had yet some way to go before becoming an aviator, the Prince was moving inexorably in that direction. Before long he went up for his first flight – in low cloud and pouring rain. To a senior officer who tried to persuade him to wait for better weather he replied in so many words, 'While I'm not all that keen to go up at all, I shall be no keener tomorrow. So let's get it over now.' To his mother, Queen Mary, he wrote 'It was a curious sensation . . . I did enjoy it on the whole, but I don't think I should like flying as a pastime. I would much sooner be on the ground. It feels safer!'

A few weeks later, on 1 April (of all days!), 1918, the Royal Air Force came officially into existence. Prince Albert was promoted to Flight Lieutenant then, in August, to Squadron Leader, commanding No. 5 Cadet Wing at Saint Leonard's under the redoubtable Brigadier-General Critchley, the initiator, in 1926, of greyhound racing in Britain. In only three months the young squadron leader had become an inspiration to the cadets; he was then moved to the headquarters in France of General (later Marshal of the Royal Air Force) Sir Hugh Trenchard, venerated since as 'Father of the RAF'. With the Armistice in November 1918, the Prince joined General (later Marshal of the Royal Air Force) Salmond's head-quarters at Spa, in Belgium. It was here, walking in the hills with Captain Cunningham Reid, that he confided to the latter that, since he was repre-senting the Royal Family in the RAF, he felt it his duty to become a qualified pilot. Cunningham Reid reminded him that flying had its dangers; more men had been killed at training camps in Britain than on the Western Front. But the prince's mind was made up; if the first of his rare qualities was courage, another was his sense of duty.

His flying training, on an Avro 504, began in earnest in March 1919 at Waddon Lane airfield, later to become part of Croydon airport. His instruc-tor, Lieutenant (later Air Chief Marshal Sir William) Coryton, found him an intelligent and conscientious pupil. 'By instinct,' he said, 'he was able to use eyes, hand and brain in unison.' (It was no coincidence that the Prince was an accomplished, not to say daring, horseman and tennis player of championship class – he later played for the RAF.) By July he was ready for his first solo, but at this point the powers that be demurred; they insisted that Coryton should remain in the front (instructor's) cockpit during the flight. But Coryton averred, 'I never touched a thing. I had my hands on the struts (in front of his own windscreen) during the entire flight.' The Prince put his machine through the usual manoeuvres: landing on a mark from 2000 feet, spinning both ways, figures of eight and aerobatics. Next day he successfully completed the statutory 80-mile cross-country flight and after passing his ground examinations was awarded his wings on 31 July, 1919. Considering all the obstacles of health and red tape that he had to overcome his pilot's wings represented a great personal achievement, all the more so because he was not at heart enamoured of flying, as we who did it for sheer joy.

A few years later, in a speech to the Pioneers of Aviation, he confessed, 'I may say that I am a very indifferent pilot, but I know sufficient to realise what difficulties had to be overcome by them (the Pioneers) and what courage was needed to surmount those difficulties.' (Though unintentionally, he could not have said a truer word about himself.) 'I cannot deny', he went on, 'that . . . there have been occasions when I was very glad to get down on my own feet again.' (Have we not felt the same?)

During World War II it was on the ground, on the receiving end of the Luftwaffe's bombs, that the pilot-prince, now King George, kept in touch, often all too closely, with flying. His courage, and that of Queen Elizabeth, was exemplary. Both narrowly escaped death when, on 13 September, 1940, at the height of the Battle of Britain, enemy bombs hit Buckingham Palace, above which, defiantly, flew the Royal Standard – the sign that the King was in residence. 'We saw two bombs falling into the quadrangle,' said the King. 'We saw the flashes and then heard two resounding crashes as the bombs fell about thirty yards away . . . We looked at each other and wondered why we weren't dead.'

A little later the Queen remarked, 'I'm glad we've been bombed. It makes me feel I can look the East End in the face.' As the Luftwaffe reduced the East End – and other districts – to rubble the King and the Queen went out among the ruins sympathising, encouraging. Once, from a group of survivors, came a cry 'Thank God for a good King!' 'And thank God for a good people!' came the King's reply.

During those heroic days the King himself suffered tragic bereavement with the death on active service of his younger brother George, Duke of Kent. The Duke, an air vice-marshal before the war, had asked to be 'demoted' to air commodore, in which rank he was able to do sterling service for the welfare of RAF units in the field. On a visit to my own squadron at Croydon, in the thick of the Battle of Britain, we were able to appreciate his warmth and simplicity. Two years later, in August 1942, the charming, courageous Duke was killed when, on a flight to Iceland, his aircraft crashed in bad weather.

To end on a less regretful note: it was the Chief of the Air Staff, Sir Charles Portal, who informed me, early in 1944, that he was recommending me for the post of equerry to the King. Not long after that first meeting with His Majesty at Buckingham Palace he and his family left to spend Easter, the lady-in-waiting and myself in attendance, at Sandringham. At morning service that Easter Sunday we sang, among others, hymn No. 140: 'Jesus lives . . .' As we came to the end of verse 2:

> This shall calm our trembling breath
> When we pass its gloomy portal . . .

I glanced, very cautiously, towards the King, to be met with a furtive, charming smile. He had clicked (I hasten to add that Sir 'Peter' Portal was in fact anything but gloomy).

For the King's example of simplicity (in all his grandeur), for his humanity and above all for his quiet, unyielding courage, I shall remember him with lasting admiration and – let me humbly say – affection.

Peter Townsend,
Le Perray-en-Yvelines,
France

Index